W9-BYA-457

Stop Staring:
Facial Modeling and Animation Done Right™

JASON OSIPA

SAN FRANCISCO | LONDON

SYBEX®

Associate Publisher: Dan Brodnitz
Acquisitions Editor: Mariann Barsolo
Developmental Editor: Pete Gaughan
Production Editor: Liz Burke
Technical Editor: Keith Reicher
Copyeditor: Suzanne Goraj
Compositor: Maureen Forys, Happenstance Type-O-Rama
CD Coordinator: Dan Mummert
CD Technician: Kevin Ly
Proofreaders: Nancy Riddiough, Emily Hsuan, Monique van den Burg
Indexer: Ted Laux
Interior Design: Caryl Gorska
Cover Design: Caryl Gorska, Gorska Design
Cover Illustratrations: Jason Osipa

Copyright © 2003 SYBEX Inc., 1151 Marina Village Parkway, Alameda, CA 94501. World rights reserved. No part of this publication may be stored in a retrieval system, transmitted, or reproduced in any way, including but not limited to photocopy, photograph, magnetic, or other record, without the prior agreement and written permission of the publisher.

LIBRARY OF CONGRESS CARD NUMBER: 2003104322

ISBN: 0-7821-4129-3

SYBEX and the SYBEX logo are either registered trademarks or trademarks of SYBEX Inc. in the United States and/or other countries.

Mouse King images owned by, and used courtesy of, Mattel, Inc. © 2003 Mattel, Inc. All Rights Reserved.

The head provided in the accompanying Maya scene files and illustrated throughout this book is a likeness of the author and owned by him. The scenes, model, and images of this head may be used only for the reader's personal use and practice; they may not be used for any public display.

The CD interface was created using Macromedia Director, COPYRIGHT 1994, 1997–1999 Macromedia Inc. For more information on Macromedia and Macromedia Director, visit http://www.macromedia.com.

TRADEMARKS: SYBEX has attempted throughout this book to distinguish proprietary trademarks from descriptive terms by following the capitalization style used by the manufacturer.

The author and publisher have made their best efforts to prepare this book, and the content is based upon final release software whenever possible. Portions of the manuscript may be based upon pre-release versions supplied by software manufacturer(s). The author and the publisher make no representation or warranties of any kind with regard to the completeness or accuracy of the contents herein and accept no liability of any kind including but not limited to performance, merchantability, fitness for any particular purpose, or any losses or damages of any kind caused or alleged to be caused directly or indirectly from this book.

MANUFACTURED IN THE UNITED STATES OF AMERICA

10 9 8 7 6 5 4 3 2

Dear Reader,

Thank you for choosing *Stop Staring*. This book is part of a new wave of Sybex graphics books, all written by outstanding authors—artists and professional teachers who really know their stuff, and have a clear vision of the audience they're writing for.

At Sybex, we're committed to producing a full line of quality books on 3D graphics and animation. With each title, we're working hard to set a new standard for the industry. From the paper we print on, to the animators we work with, to the visual examples our authors provide, our goal is to bring you the best graphics books available.

I hope you see all that reflected in these pages. I'd be very interested in hearing your feedback on how we're doing. To let us know what you think about this, or any other Sybex book, please visit us at www.sybex.com. Once there, go to the product page, click on Submit a Review, and fill out the questionnaire. Your input is greatly appreciated.

Best regards,

Dan Brodnitz
Associate Publisher
Sybex Inc.

Software License Agreement: Terms and Conditions

The media and/or any online materials accompanying this book that are available now or in the future contain programs and/or text files (the "Software") to be used in connection with the book. SYBEX hereby grants to you a license to use the Software, subject to the terms that follow. Your purchase, acceptance, or use of the Software will constitute your acceptance of such terms. ■ The Software compilation is the property of SYBEX unless otherwise indicated and is protected by copyright to SYBEX or other copyright owner(s) as indicated in the media files (the "Owner(s)"). You are hereby granted a single-user license to use the Software for your personal, noncommercial use only. You may not reproduce, sell, distribute, publish, circulate, or commercially exploit the Software, or any portion thereof, without the written consent of SYBEX and the specific copyright owner(s) of any component software included on this media. ■ In the event that the Software or components include specific license requirements or end-user agreements, statements of condition, disclaimers, limitations or warranties ("End-User License"), those End-User Licenses supersede the terms and conditions herein as to that particular Software component. Your purchase, acceptance, or use of the Software will constitute your acceptance of such End-User Licenses. ■ By purchase, use or acceptance of the Software you further agree to comply with all export laws and regulations of the United States as such laws and regulations may exist from time to time.

Reusable Code in This Book   The author(s) created reusable code in this publication expressly for reuse by readers. Sybex grants readers limited permission to reuse the code found in this publication, its accompanying CD-ROM or available for download from our website so long as the author(s) are attributed in any application containing the reusable code and the code itself is never distributed, posted online by electronic transmission, sold, or commercially exploited as a stand-alone product.

Software Support   Components of the supplemental Software and any offers associated with them may be supported by the specific Owner(s) of that material, but they are not supported by SYBEX. Information regarding any available support may be obtained from the Owner(s) using the information provided in the appropriate read.me files or listed elsewhere on the media. ■ Should the manufacturer(s) or other Owner(s) cease to offer support or decline to honor any offer, SYBEX bears no responsibility. This notice concerning support for the Software is provided for your information only. SYBEX is not the agent or principal of the Owner(s), and SYBEX is in no way responsible for providing any support for the Software, nor is it liable or responsible for any support provided, or not provided, by the Owner(s).

Warranty   SYBEX warrants the enclosed media to be free of physical defects for a period of ninety (90) days after purchase. The Software is not available from SYBEX in any other form or media than that enclosed herein or posted to www.sybex.com. If you discover a defect in the media during this warranty period, you may obtain a replacement of identical format at no charge by sending the defective media, postage prepaid, with proof of purchase to:

Sybex Inc.
Product Support Department
1151 Marina Village Parkway
Alameda, CA 94501
Web: http://www.sybex.com

After the 90-day period, you can obtain replacement media of identical format by sending us the defective disk, proof of purchase, and a check or money order for $10, payable to SYBEX.

Disclaimer   SYBEX makes no warranty or representation, either expressed or implied, with respect to the Software or its contents, quality, performance, merchantability, or fitness for a particular purpose. In no event will SYBEX, its distributors, or dealers be liable to you or any other party for direct, indirect, special, incidental, consequential, or other damages arising out of the use of or inability to use the Software or its contents even if advised of the possibility of such damage. In the event that the Software includes an online update feature, SYBEX further disclaims any obligation to provide this feature for any specific duration other than the initial posting. ■ The exclusion of implied warranties is not permitted by some states. Therefore, the above exclusion may not apply to you. This warranty provides you with specific legal rights; there may be other rights that you may have that vary from state to state. The pricing of the book with the Software by SYBEX reflects the allocation of risk and limitations on liability contained in this agreement of Terms and Conditions.

Shareware Distribution   This Software may contain various programs that are distributed as shareware. Copyright laws apply to both shareware and ordinary commercial software, and the copyright Owner(s) retains all rights. If you try a shareware program and continue using it, you are expected to register it. Individual programs differ on details of trial periods, registration, and payment. Please observe the requirements stated in appropriate files.

Copy Protection   The Software in whole or in part may or may not be copy-protected or encrypted. However, in all cases, reselling or redistributing these files without authorization is expressly forbidden except as specifically provided for by the Owner(s) therein.

It's all for you,
Tina.

Acknowledgments

First, of course, thanks to the people at Sybex, who really wrote this book: development editor, point man, and "the guy" Pete Gaughan; Dan Brodnitz, associate publisher; Mariann Barsolo, acquisitions editor; Liz Burke, production editor; Keith Reicher, technical editor; Suzanne Goraj, copyeditor; Maureen Forys, compositor; Margaret Rowlands, cover coordinator; the CD team of Kevin Ly and Dan Mummert; and all our proofreaders. For helping with the book, and bringing to it so much more than I could alone, I thank Jason Hopkins, Chris Robinson, Kathryn Luster, Chris Baker, Imre Tüske, Craig Adams, and Robin Parks. ■ Professionally, I owe you all dearly and thank you for what I've learned and for trusting me to do things I wasn't sure I could do: Phil Mitchell, Owen Hurley, Jennifer Twiner-McCarron, Rob Hudnut, Michael Ferraro, Ian Pearson, Chris Welman, Gavin Blair, Stephen Schick, Tim Belsher, Derek Waters, Sonja Struben, Glenn Griffiths, Chuck Johnson, Casey Kwan, Herrick Chiu, Chris Roff, and James E. Taylor. ■ Friends and family—who, if I'm lucky, still remember what I look like—thanks for understanding my crazy ambitions: Mom, Dad, Veronica, Jorge, Christopher Emmet Buckley Esq., Gigi, Papi Chucho, K.C. Kane, Connie Adams, everyone in Winnipeg y todos en Acapulco, Screamin', Spiers (2), everyone at Surreal, all my great new family in Washington and Alabama, my old Richmond High friends, my VFS classmates, all of the guys and gals I mentored at VFS, Eric Hedman, all the amazing folks on the EP team, Michelle Meeker and Jenna Chalmers for working hard on getting some quotes, and Shawn Van Bemellen. ■ We love you, Gramma Babe.

Foreword

In choosing computer graphics and digital animation, you've chosen an artistic medium where you are truly limited only by your imagination. From extreme realism to total fantasy, the art of computer graphics can help you express your creative vision.

No one should tell you that this will be easy. The tools you've chosen for your craft are powerful and complex, and there is no quick and dirty way to master them. However, by focusing on the techniques and strategies that are most relevant to your goals, you are taking a step in the right direction.

Drawing out what is human and, thus, what animates a face is truly an art. But that isn't the only piece of the puzzle. You also need to master the tools of your craft to ensure you have the skill to convey your vision to the screen. Books like Stop Staring can help you do both—both creativity and technique are helped by having a good teacher.

In Stop Staring, Jason Osipa provides you with the tool you've been looking for. Osipa knows what works and what doesn't; his methods are proven, and they're taught here with the evidence and authority of how well they work. By drawing upon his own production challenges and experiences, he allows you to learn from his mistakes and his successes. So smile or grit your teeth, but look in the mirror and figure out what that looks like, then make it happen on screen!

—Danielle Lamothe
Product Manager, Books and Training
Alias|Wavefront

CONTENTS AT A GLANCE

Table of Contents

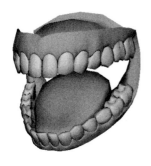

Introduction

Animation has got to be the greatest job in the world. When you get started, you just want to do everything, all at once, but can't decide on one thing to start with. You animate a walk, you animate a run, maybe even a skip or jump, and it's all gratifying in a way people outside of animation may never be lucky enough to understand. After a while, though, when the novelty aspects of animation start to wear out, you turn deeper into the characters, and find yourself wanting to learn not only how to move, but how to *act*. When you get to that place, you need the tools and ideas to fuel your explorations, and here they are.

Animation is clearly a full-body medium, and pantomime can take years to master. The face, and subtleties in acting such as the timing of a blink or where to point the eyes, can take even longer and be more difficult than conquering pantomime. Complex character, acting, and emotion are almost exclusively focused in the face and specifically in the eyes. When you look at another person, you look at their eyes; when you look at an animated character, you look at their eyes, too. That's almost always where the focus of your attention is whether you mean for it to be or not. We may remember the shots of the character singing and dancing or juggling while walking as amazing moments, but the characters we fall in love with on the screen, we fall in love with in close-ups.

Stop Staring is different than what you may be used to in a computer animation book. This is not a glorified manual for software; this is about making decisions, really learning how to evaluate contextual emotional situations and choosing the best acting approach. You're not simply told to do A, B, and C; you're told *why* you're doing them, *when* you should do them, and *how* to make it all possible.

Why This Book

There is nothing else like *Stop Staring* available to real animators with hard questions and big visions for great characters. Most references available have more to do with drawing, and musculature, and understanding the realities of what is going on in a face, than with the application of those ideas. While that information is invaluable, it is not nearly tangible and direct enough for people under a deadline who need to produce results fast. Elsewhere, you can learn about all of the visual cues that make up an expression, but then you have to take that and dissect a set of key shapes you want to build and joints you have to rig. You'll likely run into conflicting shapes, resulting in ugly faces, even though each of those shapes alone is fantastic.

Stop Staring breaks down, step-by-step, how to get any expressions you want or need for 99% of production-level work quickly and easily, and with minimum shape conflict and fantastic control. You'll learn much of what you *could* learn elsewhere while also picking up more pertinent valuable information you *couldn't* learn elsewhere. Studying a brush doesn't make you a painter, using one does; and that is what this book is all about—the doing and the learning all at once.

Who Should Read This Book

You should. If you've picked it up and you're reading this right now, then you have curiosity about facial modeling, animation, or setup, whether you have a short personal project in mind, plan to open your own studio, or already work for a big studio and just want to know more about any part of the process from construction all the way up to good acting. If you're a student trying to break into the industry, this book will show you how to add that extra something special—be the one that stands out in a pile of demo reels—by having characters that your audience can really connect with.

If you have curiosity in regard to anything facial, you're holding the answer to all of your questions on how to get this stuff done efficiently, easily, and with style.

Maya and Other 3D Apps

There are obviously some technical specifics in getting a head set up and ready for character-rich animation, so to speak to the broadest audience possible, the instruction centers primarily around Alias|Wavefront's Maya. The concepts, however, are completely program-agnostic, and I have created similar setups in several different 3D programs.

How *Stop Staring* Is Organized

While *Stop Staring* will get you from a blank screen to a talking character, it is also organized to be a reference-style book. Anything you might want to know about the underlying concepts of the how and the why of facial animation is in Part I. All animation, modeling and shape-building to do with the mouth is in Part II. Part III takes you through everything related to the brows and eyes. Part IV brings all of the pieces together, both literally and conceptually.

Part I, "Getting to Know the Face," teaches you the basic approach used throughout the book. Each chapter in this part is expanded into detailed explanation in a later part of the book: Chapter 1 in Part II, Chapter 2 in Part III, and Chapter 3 in Part IV.

Chapter 1, "Learning the Basics of Lip Sync," introduces speech cycles and visimes.

Chapter 2, "What the Eyes and Brows Tell Us," defines and outlines the effect of the top of the face on your character.

Chapter 3, "Facial Landmarking," brings in broader effects such as tilts, wrinkles, and even the back of the head!

Part II, "Animating and Modeling the Mouth," refines the visime list and sync, then shows how to build key shapes and set them up with an interface:

Chapter 4, "Visimes and Lip Sync Technique," delves deeply into how to model for effective sync, and shows that building good sync is less work than you thought but harder than it seems.

Chapter 5, "Constructing a Mouth," attacks the detailed modeling you'll need for a full range of speech shapes.

Chapter 6, "Mouth Keys," shows you a real-world system for building key sets—one that invests time in the right shapes early so you can later focus on artistry undistracted.

Part III, "Animating and Modeling the Eyes and Brows," guides you through creating a tool to put the book's concepts in practice beyond the mouth. From there you'll learn how to create focus and thought through the eyes:

Chapter 7, "Building Emotion: The Basics of the Eyes," shows you which eye movements do and don't have an emotional impact—and how years of watching cartoons have programmed us to expect certain impossible brow moves!

Chapter 8, "Constructing Eyes and Brows," builds the eyeballs first, then the lids/sockets, connects all of that to a layout for the forehead, and eventually shows you how to make a simple skull to attach everything else to.

Chapter 9, "Eye and Brow Keys," applies the key-set system from Chapter 6 to the top of the face, bringing in bump maps for texture and realism.

Part IV, "Bringing It Together," takes all the pieces you've built in Parts II and II, brings them together into one head, weights them, and rigs them for use.

Chapter 10, "Connecting the Features," teaches you to take each piece of the head—eyes, brows, and mouth, plus new features such as the side of the face and the ears—pull all of it into a scene together, and attach them to each other cleanly.

Chapter 11, "Skeletal Setup, Weighting, and Rigging," focuses on rigging your head, including creating the necessary skeleton, and weighting each of your shapes for the most flexibility in production. In this chapter you'll learn how to turn one character into another, how to re-create the shapes using joints for video games, and even how to set up to directly manipulate points on mixes of shapes.

Chapter 12, "Interfaces for Your Faces," demonstrates the benefit of arranging and automating your setup to make all your tools accessible and easy. Not only will you see how to build your own interface—and to incorporate expressions; in the process you get the ready-to-use Stop Staring interface!

Chapter 13, "A Shot in Production," presents five different scenes through the complete facial animation process, taking you inside the mind of a master animator to see how and why every pose and move was made.

The Companion CD

The CD you'll find in a sleeve at the back of this book is an integral part of the learning for *Stop Staring*. By giving example scenes, models, sound files, animations, MEL scripts, and plug-ins, you not only get tools that you can use to control any head you want, you get to see and work through the thinking process in bringing characters to life. There are several scenes in which you can see for yourself the layered approach to getting a character to jump out of the screen and connect emotionally to the viewer.

Contacting the Author

You can best reach me through my website, `www.jasonosipa.com`.

PART I

Getting to Know the Face

Before *we start animating, building, or rigging anything, let's be sure we're speaking the same language. In Chapter 1, I talk about talking, pointing out the things that are important in speech visually and showing how to ignore the things that aren't. Narrowing our focus to lip sync gives a good base from which to build the more complicated aspects of the work later. In Chapter 2, I define and outline, in the same focused way, the top half of the face. In Chapter 3, we zoom back to the entire face—the tilt of the head, wrinkles being a good thing, and even parts of the face you didn't know were important.*

Each chapter in this part is expanded into detailed explanation in a later part of the book: Chapter 1 in Part II, Chapter 2 in Part III, and Chapter 3 in Part IV.

Learning the Basics of Lip Sync

I love this stuff. When more than a few people told me I should write a book about my approach to facial animation, I started to take note. They saw how I took something so complex, so daunting, so evil, and made it so easy, simple, and—dare I say it?—*fun!* The trick is the implementation: the building techniques to make sure the mouth can get into all sorts of shapes convincingly and to have those shapes interact with each other attractively. In modeling for facial animation, mix and match is the name of the game. Instead of building individual specialized shapes for every phoneme and expression, we'll build shapes that are broader in their application and use combinations of those to create all those other specialized shapes. On the animation front, it's all about interface, and maximum control for minimum effort. You want to spend your time being creative and animating, not fighting with the complexities that can emerge from having a face with great range. It doesn't sound like there's much to these concepts for modeling and animating, and, yeah, they really are small and simple—but they're huge in their details, so let's get into them.

Before we can jump into re-creating the things we see and understand on faces, we first need to figure out what those are. Starting on the ground floor, we're going to break down the essentials of lip sync and learn the only absolutes. Next, I'll go into how basic speech can be broken into two simple and basic cycles of movement, which is what makes the sync portion of this book so simple. Finally, at the end of this chapter, I take those two things—what's essential and the two cycles—and actually build them into a technique for working.

- **The bare-bones essentials of lip sync**
- **The two speech cycles**
- **Starting with what's most important: visimes**
- **Building the simplest sync**

The Essentials of Lip Sync

People overcomplicate things. It's easy to assume that anything that looks good must also be complex. In the world of 3D animation, where programs are packed with mile after mile of options, tools, and dialog boxes, overcomplication can be an especially easy trap to fall into. Not using every feature available to you is a good start in refining any technique in 3D, and not always using the recommended tools is when you're really advancing and thinking outside the box. Many programs have controls and systems geared for facial animation, but those same programs usually have better tools in their arsenals for the job.

If you've ever tried lip sync in CGI, it has probably been frustrating, complicated, difficult, and unrewarding. By the end of it, most people are just glad to see it get done and regret deciding to involve sync in their project. Another approach currently being explored is facial motion capture or automated sync. Neither of these looks very good or has much artistic flair—yet.

Don't despair; I will get you set up for sync quickly and painlessly so you can spend your time on performance (the fun stuff!). If your bag is automation, there's still a lot of information on how to bump the quality up a couple of notches on that, too.

The lip sync portion of facial animation is the easiest to understand, because it's the simplest. You see, people's mouths don't do that much during speech. Things like smiles and frowns and all sorts of neat gooey faces are cool, and we'll get to them later, but for now we're just talking sync. Plain old speech. Deadpan and emotionless and, well, boring, is where our base will be. Now, you're thinking, "Hey! My face can do all sorts of stuff! I don't want to do boring animation!" You're right, your face *can* do all sorts of things, and who would ever want to do boring animation? For the basics, however, we're not going to complicate it yet—that'll come later. In a very short while, in Part II, we'll build a model of a mouth that can do anything your mouth can do, and more, but you need all this stuff in your head before you can get there.

When dealing with the bare-bones essentials of lip sync and studying people, we've whittled it down to two basic motions. The mouth goes closed/open, and it goes narrow/wide; all of these are illustrated in Figure 1.1.

Figure 1.1

A human mouth in the four basic poses

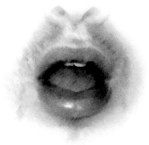

That's really, at its core, all that speech entails. If we were lip-syncing a character with a plain circle for a mouth (and we will in just a minute!), the shapes in Figure 1.2 would be all the keys we would need to create the illusion of speech.

Your reaction to this very short list might be, "What about things like F where I bite my lip, or L where I roll up my tongue?" That's just the point of these early chapters. We ignore those unique and complicated shapes, strip the process down to what is absolutely necessary to be understood visually, and then build it back up from a solid base. If these two controls—Open/Closed and Wide/Narrow—are all you have to draw on, you get creative about how to utilize them. Things like F just get pared back to "sort-of closed." If you were to animate this way and stop the animation on the frame where the "sort of closed" is standing in for an F and say "That's not an F!" you'd be right, but in motion, you hardly notice, and what we're talking about here is motion. As a standard in this book, I'm going to try *not* to concern us with the individual frames, so much as the motion and the impression it gives.

Animating lip sync is all smoke and mirrors. What is *really* happening isn't relevant; it's all about the impression. How about M? "I need to roll my lips in together to say M; I can't do that with a circle-mouth-thingamajig." Sure you can, or at least you can give that same impression—just close it all the way; that's good enough. When you get the lip sync good enough and focus on the acting, people only notice the acting. The sync becomes visual noise!

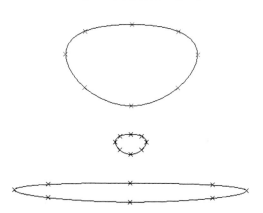

Figure 1.2

A circular spline mouth in the same four basic poses

Analyzing the Right Things

Let me take you on a little real-world tutorial of what's important, and what's not, in action. There can be a tendency—and it's not necessarily a bad one—to slow things down to the frame-by-frame level and analyze in detail what happens so that we can re-create it as animators. Here's an example:

Look in the mirror (or don't) and slowly, deliberately, and clearly enunciate the word *pebble:* PEH-BULL. We're trying to see just what exactly happens visually, on our face and lips, during that word, so we can re-create it in animation. Think about or watch what your lips are doing—all the details: The little puff in your cheek after the B. The way the pursing of your lips for P is different than for B. How your tongue starts its way to the roof of your mouth early in the B sound and stays there until after the end of the word. All these details gives you a pretty good idea of how to analyze and re-create the word *pebble* in animation, right? Wrong! That's exactly the wrong way to do it. That's how you would do it for a character who was speaking slowly and deliberately, and enunciating clearly. This is how a mirror can be dangerous if used incorrectly: over-analysis. None of these things, these details, are wrong—they're just not necessary, and I'll explain why in the next paragraph.

This time, at regular, comfortable, conversational speed, say "How far do you think this pebble would go if I threw it?" How did the word *pebble* look? Check it out a few times, resisting the urge to do it slowly. As far as the word *pebble* is concerned, the overall visual impression is merely closed, a little open, closed, a little open. That's it. In a sentence spoken regularly, the word *pebble* will most likely look the same as *mama* or *papa*. Say the phrase again with that in mind. Try not to change what your mouth does, but instead notice that the Opens and the Closeds are the most significant things happening during the word. The mouth doesn't open wide enough (in this case) to see a tongue, so why would you animate it or need to spend time thinking about it? Because it's "correct"? That would be like animating a character's innards. You can't see them, but they're there, so animating them would be the "correct" thing to do, right? Wrong. It's a silly waste of the time you could otherwise spend on the acting.

The Opens and the Closeds are the most important of any of the things a mouth does. That's why puppets work. Does it look like a puppet is really *saying* anything? Of course not, but with the flapping of the jaw happening around the same time as the sounds the actor makes, your brain fills in the connection. You want to believe that the character is talking, and that's why the only truly important action in the word *pebble* is open, closed, open, closed.

This is how you analyze the right things: search for the overall impression, not the details. It's very easy to learn how to do this, but very hard to master; luckily you have a good coach.

Speech Cycles

This approach of identifying cycles and "visimes," which you'll learn more about in just a moment, is likely very different than what you know now. If you're looking for a phoneme-to-picture comparison chart, you're not going to get it here, because in this approach there is no absolute shape for each sound, and to point you in such a direction would do more harm than good. Each sound's shape is going to be unique, and you'll learn to identify it and its components. To start, let's talk about the two speech cycles.

In its simplest form, there are two distinct and separate cycles in speech: open and closed, as in jaw movement, and narrow and wide, as in lip movement.

> When I say "cycle," I'm merely referring to how the shape will go from one to the other and then back again. There are no other stops along the way. The mouth will go open, closed, open, closed; the lips will go wide, narrow, wide, narrow.

These two cycles don't necessarily occur at the same times as each other, nor do they go all the way back and forth from one extreme to the other all the time. The open and closed motion generally lines up with the puppet motion of the jaw, or flow of air—*almost any* sound being created—while the narrow and wide motions have more to do with the *kind* of sound being created. In the phrase "Why are we watching you?" we get this sequence for the Wide/Narrow:

Word	Wide/Narrow Sequence
why	Narrow, wide
are	No change/shape
we	Narrow, wide
watching	Narrow, slightly wide
you	Narrow

Simple, right? Now let's look at the jaw or Open/Closed cycle. "Closed" refers to a position not completely closed, but closer to closed than to open.

Word	Open/Closed Sequence
why	Closed, open, closed
are	Closed, open, closed
we	Closed, slightly open
watching	Closed, open, closed, slightly open, closed
you	Closed / no change

That's it for the essentials. We're going to get into more shapes and controls and special cases, but there it is. The backbone of this book's lip sync technique has to do with simple analysis of the Wide/Narrow and Open/Closed cycles; over time, we'll add more and more levels, each one simple on its own, to create complex, believable performances.

These cycles will be the foundation on which we build everything else. Taking the lead from the human mouth, I've based all of this book on the "simpler is better" mindset. Your mouth is lazy. Go on, admit it. It hits the major sounds and fudges over the rest, like someone whose name you forgot but say hi to anyway, hoping they don't notice you garbled it. It makes good sense; it's efficient.

I've had programs and books and teachers all show me sets of shape keys for sync I had to build, that included things like G. Why would we build a shape for or pay special attention to the letter G? Whether it's hard G or soft G, you can say it with your mouth in any of the shapes shown in Figure 1.3.

Now, these are obviously all pretty different. If you were, however, to try and say a soft or hard G with your mouth held in each of these poses, you could do it without much trouble. In 95% of cases when the letter G comes up in sync, we're going to ignore it—that is to say, it will get no keys in the animation. Further to that, we will most certainly not build a shape for G; how would we pick just one?

The G sound is actually created in the throat, not by the lips nor the open/closed positions of the mouth. This whole example with G is to illustrate the criteria of visimes. What are visimes, you ask? Read on.

Starting with What's Most Important: Visimes

So, we've decided that we're going to go with a less-is-more approach. That's good. For this non-inclusive approach, however, where we're trying to exclude all the extraneous mouth positions, something you'll need to know is what *must* be included. There are certain sounds that we make with our mouths that absolutely need to be represented visually, no matter what: visimes. These are the sounds that can only be made by the mouth with specific characteristics to the mouth shape, or range—such as narrow for OO, as in *food*, or closed, for M, as in *mom*. There are more visimes to address than the Open, Closed, Wide, and Narrow can properly do, but even these must-see shapes can be "cheated" to fit into the "circle mouth" setup you've seen and we're about to build.

Figure 1.3

All varieties of G

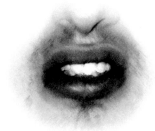

Why Phonemes Aren't Best for CGI

The most common key sets and setups out there for public consumption are based on *phonemes,* which means "the sounds your mouth makes during speech." To base sync on phonemes seemingly makes perfect sense—it's the way it's been done for years with classical animation—but for the newer world of CGI, it can be overly complicated. Phonemes worked fantastically on paper, where nothing comes for free; every frame must be drawn, and a little popping from frame to frame was just part of the style. In CGI—in anything, really—the eye is drawn to what is out of place, and generally, most computer animations don't have keys on every frame, or even every second frame. If just on the mouth there's a key on every frame of your lip sync, you had better believe that's where all eyes will be; not a good thing.

In the search for a better system for CGI sync, something became very apparent: There are three different *kinds* of sounds you can make during speech, and not all of these are very easy to see! Phonemes-based sync lumps all of these sounds together, and that is what precludes it from being the best solution for us. The important point I'm coming to here is that during speech some sounds are made primarily with your lips, some are made primarily by your tongue, and others are made in your throat and vocal cords. The only ones you absolutely have to worry about every time in animation are the sounds made primarily by the lips.

> I say "primarily" because combinations of all these ways to make sound occur all the time. Also, you could argue that your throat makes *all* sounds, but that would be a cerebral standpoint, not an artistic one, like saying we should include the lungs in sync—and believe me, we're not going to be doing that!

Phonemes are sounds, but what matters in animation is what can be seen. Instead of phonemes, of which there are about 38 in English (depending on your reference), what we're going to base our system on is "visual phonemes," or *visimes*. Visimes are the significant shapes or visuals that are made by your lips. Phonemes are sounds; visimes are shapes. They're all you really need to see to be convinced. You obviously cue these shapes based on the sounds you hear, but there aren't nearly as many to be seen as there are heard. The necessary visimes are listed in Table 1.1. Remember that these are shapes tied to sounds, not necessarily collections of letters exactly in the text.

Words are made up of these even if they aren't spelled this way; the word *you* comprises the two visimes EE and then OO, to make the EE-OO sound of the word. As we move forward you'll learn that if there is no exact visime for the sound, we'll merely use the next closest thing. For instance, the sound OH as in M-OH-N (moan) is not really shown on this chart, whereas OO is. They're not really the same, but they're close enough that you can funnel OH over to an OO-type shape.

	VISIME	EXAMPLE SOUNDS	RULE
	B,M,P / Closed	**m**urder, **p**lantation, cheru**b**	Lips closed
	EE / Wide	ch**ee**se, m**e**, charity	Wide
	F,V	**f**ire, **f**ight, **V**irginia	Lower lip rolled in
	OO / Narrow	d**u**de, **u**se, f**oo**l	Narrow
	IH	tr**i**p, sn**i**p	Taller or wider than surrounding shapes
	R	ca**r**, **r**oad	Narrower than surrounding shapes
	T,S	bea**t**, **t**raffic	Taller or wider than surrounding shapes

Table 1.1
Visimes

That's just 7 shapes to hit, and only a few of those are their own unique shape to build! Analysis and breakdown of speech has just gone from 38 sounds to account for, to 7. Some sounds can show up as the same shape, such as UH and AW, which only need to be represented by the jaw opening.

Open Mouth Sounds

So many sounds have no real shape to them, so they're out as visimes. Another group of sounds (Table 1.2) have no shape in the sense that the lips aren't doing anything in particular, but they have the common characteristic that the mouth must be open. I don't consider these visimes but instead refer to them as open or jaw sounds, even though by my own definition, they are visimes. It's a layered reason that takes layered thinking. Visimes as we identify and animate them are really aspects of lip positions, not whole mouth positions. Since the jaw, and therefore the mouth, is open in so many shapes, I've just kicked it out of the visime club because it would make things more difficult, the number of explicit combinations would explode, and you would be back out at phonemes again. Open mouth sounds should be considered separately from visimes.

For example, an OH sound (which should be read as a very short OH, not like the word OH, which is broken down to OH-OO) is just a degree of Narrow and some Open—which is

	SOUND	EXAMPLE SOUNDS
	UH	f**u**n, s**o**me, th**u**nder
	AH	bl**a**st, b**a**t, V**a**ncouver
	OH	sn**ow**, f**oe**
	AW	**o**xford, g**o**lly, l**aw**n

Table 1.2
Example Open Mouth Sounds

really the same as an OO sound, but with different amounts. Instead of referring to sounds as their phonetic spellings, such as OH or AW, I like to break them down further to their components. For me, OH simply becomes a semi-Narrow shape and some Open.

By separating out what's really happening, not just in motion but within each frame, into some basic elements, you can animate faster and better, and more precisely tailor your shape to the sound you hear. This isn't saying to break down the overall content of the sound OH and open it first, and then make it narrow, as in OH-OO, which is how you'd read OH. It's saying to look at only that first part, the OH sound, and figure out what it's made of using the ingredients of Wide, Narrow, Open, and Closed. It's like a trumpet. There are three valves and there's a mouthpiece—that's it. Combinations of these few things can produce varied sounds and beautiful complex melodies, but at its root, it's still just three valves and a mouthpiece.

When we identify visimes, we really are ignoring the open mouth portion of open mouth sounds. After we finish keying and identifying the visimes quickly, we go back to the start and add in the open mouth/jaw motions. By treating these separately, we can move through animations very quickly. If your only goal is visimes, you can burn through a long animation extremely quickly. At the end of that, it doesn't look like much but you are left with a simple version of the lip sync you can then build on, simply by going back and identifying where the jaw must be open.

This approach is much faster than meticulously trying to get every sound right as you move through your animation at one steady pace. This way, you end up with a jumping-off point for finessing. The time you spend animating sync and expression will be more heavily weighted towards the *quality*—with the quantity out of the way, you'll have more time for it. This method applies to any system, not just mine, where you have control over the building-block components of shapes, as opposed to separate and distinct whole-mouth shapes based on phonemes.

> Disclaimer: These choices of what is and is not important are based on my own experience. This is not torn from another book, university study, website, or anything else. These aren't even real phonetic representations; they're presented this way because if you're like me, those phonetic alphabet symbols with joined letters and little lines and marks all over them in dictionaries don't mean much.

Visimes Aren't Tied to *Individual* Sounds

One visime shape can represent several sounds; you might not read the AW in *spa* and *draw* with the same letters, but you can represent them with the same visual shape. This is going to give us fewer things to animate and think about as animators, leaving us more time to be performers.

Visimes are the only sounds that have an absolute criteria visually. There's a rule tied to each that we'll cover in further detail in Part II; for now, if you look at Table 1.1 again you'll see them to the right. To give clearer examples of these rules: You can't say B or M without your lips closed. You can't say OO without your mouth narrow, and so forth.

Now, this isn't to say that for *every* F sound, you'll need the biggest, gnarliest, lower-lip-chewingest, gum-baringest, spit-flyingest F shape—just that you need to make sure something, anything "F-like," happens in your animation to represent it. That's what visimes are: the representation of the sounds through visuals that match only the necessary aspects. Visimes are not entire poses. F is not a shape, it is part of a shape. The whole shape may be smiling or frowning, wide or narrow, but the lower lip is up, and the upper lip is up, giving us what we need for an F.

Representative Shapes

You may notice some disparity between the Narrow/Wide–Closed/Open distinctions and the visime set, which I summarize in Table 1.3. There is, and there isn't. As long as we represent the visime in some way, we're all right.

VISIME	DESCRIPTION	SCHEMATIC
B,M,P / Closed	Closed	
EE / Wide	Somewhat open + wide	
F, V	Somewhat open	
OO / Narrow	Somewhat narrow + somewhat open	
IH	Somewhat wide + open	
R	Narrower than the shapes around it, if they're not already narrow	
T,S	Wider than the shapes around it, if they're not already wide	

Table 1.3

The Visimes' Representation on an Open/Closed Narrow/Wide Mouth

The last two, R and T/S, take us into the next concept in a world full of exceptions to the rule: relative shapes. EEs don't need to be the widest shape ever, just wider than the shapes surrounding them. Same with OOs or OHs. They don't need to be the narrowest, just narrower than their neighbors. That's how the system works. Instead of giving ourselves 20 unique keys that contort the whole mouth into an unmistakable shape, we use fewer, simpler components that can combine in different ways with other shapes to create those big unmistakable shapes. Working this way leaves us more flexible to customize each and every shape to the vocal performance, with much less work than it would be to do it the other way.

Relative Shapes

As just mentioned, there are shapes that are relative. To make this distinction clearer, anything with an *er* on it is a relative shape. An OO sound is a narrow shape; it's absolute. An R is simply narrow*er*. Absolute shapes take precedence over relative shapes.

Here's an example of relative shapes. In the phrase "How are you?" the OO in *you* is not as narrow as the OO of *you* in "Do you chew?" In the latter, because all the sounds are OOs, there are variations in the intensity, and the OO in *you* is the strongest.

> The process of deciding which shapes take precedence in strings of similar sounds is explained later, in Chapter 4, "Visimes and Lip Sync Technique."

If that's a little confusing, that's all right; understanding comes with practice. A lot of the system involves looking at a sentence and, instead of trying to define the shapes in absolutes, seeing them in relation to the previous shapes and the shapes that follow.

"Who are you and what are you doing?": Wide/Narrow

We know how to cheat visimes using Wide/Narrow/Open/Closed, as per Table 1.2, so we need practice identifying those visimes.

I'll use the phrase, "Who are you and what are you doing?" since it has all sorts of wide/narrow travel. Let's do Wides/Narrows first; we'll do the Open/Closed pass second. I've included images with both Open/Closed and Wide/Narrow, to make it easier to follow, but focus on the width more than the height through this next passage. Much of the information and reasoning here jumps ahead to things not yet explained. This is a glimpse of the thought processes you'll learn in action.

"Rest" in the following chart refers to the *width* of the mouth as it is at rest, in the default position. In the visuals in this chapter, it's the width of the Closed shape. But though its width is that of the Closed shape, the shape is not necessarily closed. It's hard to give visuals for visimes, as they change every single time! As an example, if a shape is narrow, then goes wider, it goes wider relative to the narrow—which basically returns it to the width of the mouth at rest.

Word	Wide/Narrow Sequence
who	Rest, narrower
are	Little wider (rest)
you	Narrower
and	Wider (rest)
what	Narrower, rest
are	No change in width
you	Narrower
doing	Narrower, wider

When I talk about working in passes, I mean going through the sound, scene, or process from start to end, dealing with only one goal at a time, and then returning to the start to go through a *second* or third time with a different goal in mind. To properly grasp sync by visime, I strongly recommend that you work in the passes described.

who I started with rest, not because of some mysterious H visime that occurs, but because without rest, we wouldn't see that the narrow OO shape to follow was narrower than anything. I created something for the OO shape to be relative to.

are This will be wider. Being exclusively affected by the Open/Closed of the mouth in this case (the main sound being AW, which is an open mouth/jaw sound), this is made wider not because it needs any particular Wide/Narrow, but instead because it's sandwiched between two OOs. With something wider between them, both OOs will have more punch. If you're wondering why this has no need for a specific Wide/Narrow, take a look at the visime list: R is *relatively* narrower, not just narrow. R should be narrower than its surrounding shapes, but since both of its surrounding shapes are already narrow, it gets *cancelled out*.

you Narrower; this has an OO sound, which needs to be represented, but that's it, nothing fancy. A true visime breakdown would be from EE to OO, EEYOO, but we went slightly wider in *are* to enforce the OO in this word, so that aspect of starting wider was already taken care of—we already had that effect. "Less is more" can be tricky sometimes!

and Again, this needs no specific Wide/Narrow shape, if we're referring to our visime list looking for a match, so we widen it to make the OO sounds around it look narrower. This concept of shaping the mouth opposite to its surrounding shapes in time is called, well, opposites, and is explained in Chapter 4. Opposites is an idea not unlike anticipation.

what This has two shapes (a concept we'll move onto next). With the *w* portion of the word we need an OO shape—it's a visime. With the *ut* portion of the word, UH-T, we've hit a (sort of) special case. T is one of those relative visimes like R. We widen the mouth on this sound to show that another visime besides UH is present. Nothing specific, just wid*er* than UH.

are Like the previous *are*, this one's tricky; it's influenced by Open/Closed only. There's nothing characteristic that needs to be done with Wide/Narrow. We're going to use this sound like many of the preceding shapes, to emphasize its surrounding shapes. Since the next sound is an OO, and we're already at a somewhat wide shape, we don't want to narrow it, because that will take away from the impact, or unattractively lead into the next sound. We don't want to widen it, because that would indicate a visime we're trying to hit, which we're not. So, we effectively "hold" the shape we already have. It may not seem like it, but this reasoning is a subcategory of opposites called *stepping*, also explained in Chapter 4. Briefly described, stepping is for when you've got multiple similar shapes in a row trying to out-extreme each other. You can pause on each one briefly to give each a moment of its own, and then move on.

you As before, this sound is in the easy territory of a basic visime. OO visime = narrower key. The EE sound in the word *you* only really gets played up at the beginning of a sentence or after a long pause.

doing For the do portion, we need to consider the surroundings before we can choose what to do. At the end of the preceding word we went narrower. This sound, too, should lead us narrower, but by narrowing twice in a row, we risk not seeing the first shape, as we breeze right by it to even narrower. Remember "stepping" from *are* two words ago? That's what we'll do again here. You may need to take some strength away from the OO in *you* to leave the OO in *do* something to be narrower in relation to. The *ing* portion is wider. This is partly because IH is a visime, and also because *ing* is most definitely not an OO sound. Sometimes we need to key *away* from surrounding sounds as much as we need to key into them.

"Who are you and what are you doing?": Open/Closed

Now let's look at the Open/Closed for "Who are you and what are you doing?":

Word	Open/Closed Sequence
who	Open, semi-closed
are	Open, semi-closed
you	Open, semi-closed
and	Open, semi-closed
what	Open, semi-closed
are	Open, semi-closed
you	Open, semi-closed
doing	Open, semi-closed

Interesting. Hmm. That all looks like the same motion over and over. And the reasoning is not present; the conclusions are just laid out for you! This is a bit of an oversimplification, because of timing and strength of the motions, but in essence, the Open/Closed cycle is going to be a function of syllables. The jaw or Open/Closed should be treated like a sock puppet. If all we had as a tool to work with was Open/Closed, we should still be able to convince people that the words were coming out of the character's mouth (albeit somewhat sock-puppety!). This is the process you will learn to use.

The Simplest Lip Sync

You're ready for your first sync tutorial!

Let's put this simple stuff to the test. It's easy—trust me. We don't want to get bogged down in expressions and fancy heads and shapes just yet; there's a whole book ahead of us going into that stuff in detail, so for now we're going to do some copying of expressions and really basic point-pulling for the sake of the exercise. This may seem a little like jumping through hoops, but it gets us to a start-point really quickly.

> Every practical instruction needs a tool, but you might be using any of several good 3D animation programs. For my hands-on tutorials, I prefer to use Maya, but the principles will carry over to other software; you'll just have to do a little bit more digging, finding the specific buttons and tools. I've set up rigs in several packages and the logic does apply, and work, in all.

Creating a Sync Tool 1: Shapes

First we're going to breeze through creating our shapes. In the next steps I'll have you create a simple circle and a set of Narrow/Wide and Open/Closed keys along with an interface. This little model in hand, we can start on some of the early practical work of the book. If you would rather not build it yourself (I recommend highly that you do), you can load the finished setup from the CD; in the Chapter 1 folder, look for `SplineMouth.mb`.

Units! For the duration of the book, I speak in terms of 24 frames per second (fps) and the Y axis as the world up.

1. Create a circle. A circle of eight points will look *most* like the visuals to follow, but any circle will do. In Maya, choose Create → NURBS Primitives → Circle □.

2. In the option window, make the "normal axis" Z (this makes the circle upright as opposed to flat).

3. Name the circle Mouth.

4. In component mode, modify the shape so that it looks almost like a flat line. (It's important not to just scale the object; make sure you're manipulating CVs.) The easiest way is with all the CVs selected to scale (close to) flat in Y.

5. Duplicate Mouth two times. Make sure Copy—not Instance—is selected in your duplicate settings. Move the two duplicates away from Mouth and each other, so they are all separate.

6. Select one of the duplicates and name it OpenClosed. In component mode, reshape it to look like the example here, which will represent the open mouth. Be sure you're moving the lower and outside points, and not the three upper ones.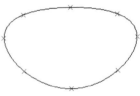

7. Select the other duplicate and name it WideNarrow. In component mode, reshape it to be wider, like the image here, which will represent the wide mouth. Be sure to include *all* the points in the widening, not just the end ones; otherwise this won't work properly.

8. Now that we have our shapes, select the two duplicates and then Shift+select Mouth. In the Animation module, press Deform → Create Blend Shape. This assigns OpenClosed and WideNarrow as shapes to be used by the object Mouth.

9. Select Mouth again, and in the Channel Box under Inputs, highlight blendshape1. Rename it MouthShapes.

If you want, you can now hide, *but don't delete,* OpenClosed and WideNarrow. We shouldn't need them later but just might.

Okay, that's it—we have the art side of things ready to go. These are the shapes we'll use in our first setup.

Creating a Sync Tool 2: Setup

Now for the expressions. If you don't know expressions or don't understand what you're doing as you go through the steps, don't worry. I'll be describing it later, specifically in Chapter 12, "Interfaces for Your Faces." All we'll be doing right now is linking the shapes we've built to one simple control mechanism, so that we can have Mouth morph into each of these shapes *and* combinations of them in a very user-friendly way.

To reiterate, we will not be using the blend shape editor to control our faces. If you're looking for the part where I explain it, where to find it, how to set driven keys, or anything like that, you won't find it. We will be using home-made interfaces, using scene objects as the controls and expressions to link those to the shapes. I'll refer to these as our sliders. The main reason for doing so is that you can tie multiple shapes onto controls to make the wrangling of many sliders much easier. Chapter 12 is dedicated entirely to the ideas used to create the sliders, and instruction on using some included MEL Scripts to set up your own character's head with ease.

> If you are a MEL guru or Expression wizard, this setup may seem sloppy or too simple; it's designed to be easy and accessible. If coding talents are at your disposal, feel free to re-create this in any manner you see fit, but do go through and first set up the described rig to get a feel for the functionality. I'll refer to using a rig like this throughout the book.

1. Create a locator and duplicate it. In the Hypergraph, Outliner, or however you prefer to do it, make locator2 the child of locator1.

2. Rotate locator2 to 45° in Z and scale it to 2,2,2. This is just to make it more selectable.

3. Rename locator2 MouthControl.

4. Open the Attribute Editor and select the MouthControl tab, then open Limit Information → Translate. (When you open the Attribute Editor, it defaults to Rotate; be sure you're doing this under Translate!)

5. Check all the boxes and fill them in as shown below, limiting the motion to horizontal and vertical as viewed from the front. We're also limiting the range of movement within that view to keep our control under control!

▼ Limit Information							
▼ Translate							
			Min		Current	Max	
Trans Limit X	☑	-1.00	<	0.00	>	1.00	☑
Trans Limit Y	☑	-1.00	<	0.00	>	0.00	☑
Trans Limit Z	☑	0.00	<	0.00	>	0.00	☑

6. Move locator1 out of the way of the mouth. MouthControl, being the child, should follow. MouthControl, as I'm sure you've guessed, will be how we manipulate the shapes on Mouth.

7. Select Mouth and then in the Channel Box under Inputs, highlight MouthShapes.

8. Go to Window → Animation Editors → Expression Editor.

> Another way to reach the Expression Editor is to right-click in the channel box over the name of an attribute and select Expressions.

9. In the Objects window on the left, highlight MouthShapes. You should see WideNarrow and OpenClosed appear in the Attributes window to the right (along with "envelope," which is generated automatically by Maya; we're going to ignore it). Highlight the WideNarrow attribute. In the Expression box near the bottom, type the following:

```
MouthShapes.WideNarrow = MouthControl.translateX
```

Maya is case sensitive, so be careful that you copy this exactly and that you've named all your objects correctly. When you have that typed, press the Create button at the bottom left. If it worked correctly, you should see the expression change to read:

```
MouthShapes.weight[#] = MouthControl.translateX
```

The number in the brackets may be [0] or [1]. It's Maya renaming the shape node to its behind-the-scenes Maya name. The number 0 or 1—even 2, 3, 4, or, in later heads, numbers up into the 20s—refers to the shape in the order it was selected for becoming a blend shape, starting at 0. When Maya changes that name after you hit the Create button, you know the connection was made.

> In the expression window, you can also use the standard Ctrl+C, Ctrl+X, and Ctrl+V to copy, cut, and paste text into the expression window. If you select an object and an attribute in the top windows of the Expression Editor, Maya fills in a box just under that labeled Selected Obj & Attr, which creates the full string of Object.Attribute for you, so you can copy and paste it! It's a fast way to ensure that your spelling and capitalization are correct.

10. Highlight the OpenClosed attribute. In the Expression box near the bottom, type:

```
MouthShapes.OpenClosed = -MouthControl.translateY
```

Be sure you include the little minus sign before MouthControl—that's very important. Again, if it worked, the expression should change subtly. The shape name should change to read "weight", and a number in brackets.

```
MouthShapes.weight[#] = -MouthControl.translateY
```

That's it. We're done finicking with yucky expressions. Now we have a *super* basic mouth to play with—but hey, it's a mouth. The 45-degree rotated locator we renamed MouthControl is now a slider for our mouth that works in two dimensions, X and Y. Translating the locator controls the mouth. We connected MouthControl and Mouth so that left and right on Mouth-Control will make Mouth go through narrow and wide, while up and down will open and close it. Kind of neat, huh? Where else have you ever seen anyone say you could control all your basic sync with one slider? Nowhere! It's not dissimilar from some painting programs in which you can select a range of colors because four extremes are laid out for you, and you just click in the area that looks like the right mix.

This mouth is pretty simplistic. Right now there is really only one shape—Wide—and we're creating the Narrow by telling Maya to do the opposite. Pulling the slider left, you'll see the "fake" Narrow shape. That plus some Open/Slider Down should create a pretty good OO shape. If it's not quite how you want it, unhide the object WideNarrow and widen it, which will in turn affect Mouth's shape. Since in Narrow, we're looking at the *opposite* of the WideNarrow (which is Wide), the wider you make Wide, the narrower "Narrow" can be. Backwards-tastic!

Using the Sync Tool

In the scene with your mouth, continue on as we use *the slider, the shapes that slider controls, and what we've learned about syncing by visime* to go for a test run. As I said before, sliding left and right will make the mouth widen and narrow whereas pulling the control up and down will open and close it. Let's do a practice word without any sound, one of the easiest for this particular rig. The word: *why?*

> If you're finding that the frame numbers aren't lining up for you, give your preferences a look and make sure they're at 24 fps; film. In Maya, you can find the option for frame rate under Windows → Settings/Preferences → Settings. Other programs will have this setting; you may have to poke around a bit to find it.

First analyze the word by sound and equate that with visimes. Sound out *why,* and you should end up with something like OO-UH-EE. OO and EE each need specific shapes, whereas UH is merely open. The way I like to do things is to first key the Narrow/Wide stuff and then go back and get the Open/Closed stuff. Since this sync is so incredibly short, we're going to put the height into the visimes as we go. After all, there are just two of them! The goal here is to get you rolling with the interface and to offer a taste of how this all works. By the end of the book, you'll have an array of sliders like this (and some others), hooked up to a myriad of shapes and a great character face to play, or even work, with.

In your scene, on frame 0, set a key with your control at 0,0 positionally; your mouth should be in its default state, closed, halfway between narrow and wide, much like in Figure 1.4. If yours doesn't match this perfectly, close enough is close enough. This is something we'll later refer to as "capping."

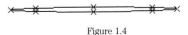

Figure 1.4

A default mouth

Now on frame 10, move the slider down and to the left, until it looks like a good OO. X,Y values of –1, –0.2 should be about right, as in Figure 1.5. Set a key! You've just set the OO part of *why*, or, OO-UH-EE.

Now go to frame 30 and move the slider all the way to the right and up a little bit. That should put it at about 1, –0.2, as in Figure 1.6. Set a key! You've just set the EE part of *why*. All that's left to do is take care of the UH part.

Moving back to frame 20, simply pull the control down so that it opens the mouth in the middle of the word, as in Figure 1.7. Try –1 in Y. Set a key! You're done.

You've keyed the visimes in the word *why:* OO-UH-EE. Play it through a couple of times— not bad for a few seconds' work. Identifying visimes all on your own steam and working through the special cases will take a little time, but not too much more than that bit right there.

Now, I recommend going back and looking at the phrases we've already dissected, using your new toy (I bet you would whether or not I told you to—it's fun!). This little rig really is how we're going to get into some very complicated performance, and it illustrates quite well the less-is-more approach I'm preaching. There will soon be a little army of sliders and controls just like this one, each custom-made for a different type of motion and shape.

The setup we just did could directly be translated to work on some beautiful shapes and characters. It's just a matter of getting those built so we can use them. We're only playing with a circle for now, but that's so we can get some practice at our basic concepts of both shapes and controls before we get too crazy; with some patience, I think you'll amaze yourself with your work in a surprisingly short time. On the CD, there's some sound for you to play with. Files for each of the examples we've already walked through are in the Chapter 1 folder, named *sentenceName*.wav. (If you need help loading sounds into your software, please see Chapter 4.) If you follow the directions in the text and try lining your mouth object up with the sound, you should have some pretty good results fairly quickly. Then turn the page—there's plenty more where this came from!

Figure 1.5

OO of OO-UH-EE

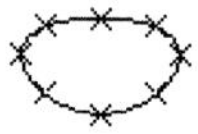

Figure 1.6

EE of OO-UH-EE

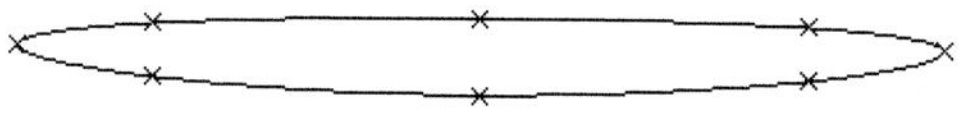

Figure 1.7

UH of OO-UH-EE

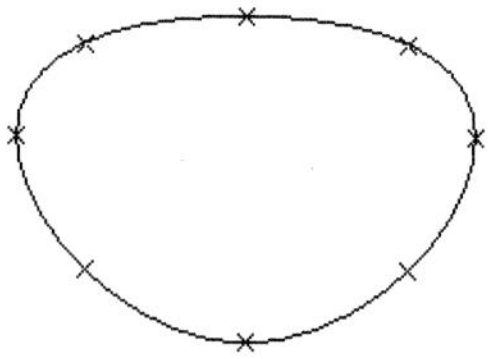

CHAPTER 2

What the Eyes and Brows Tell Us

With our feet wet in the puddle that is sync, it's time to shift our focus to another introduction. Basic sync will lend credibility and draw focus to a speaking character, but without any emotion coming through, that character isn't going to mean much to the audience. Most emotion comes across in the top half of the face, with the eyes, the brows, and the eyelids. Most commonly, the brows get the bulk of the attention from animators, when the time should really be spent on the eyes and eyelids. When you sit down and talk to someone, you look them in the eye. Your gaze may not stay there for uncomfortable lengths of time, but it surely bounces to and from eye contact; that's the go-to point. If you do this, so does the person you're talking to, and therefore, in reference to emotion, the place most commonly referred to by us humans is the eyes, not the brows.

This is the first of many situations where I'll talk about the concept of *landmarking*. In a nutshell, the stuff in the surrounding area of what you *think* you're looking at is what you actually perceive. In this instance, the eyelids tell you most of what you'd think the brows do. The brows do indeed help us to create emotion, but what exactly do they do?

- **The two major brow movements**
- **The upper and lower lids' effects on expression**
- **Perception vs. reality in eyelines**

The Major Brow Movements

Much like the mouth and its two cycles of Wide/Narrow and Open/Closed, the brows have Up/Down and Squeeze. A lot of animators focus much of their attention solely on the first. Brows Up/Down clearly have a lot to add to facial animation and expression, but not in the ways you might think. The brows Squeeze is in fact the most telling thing the brows are capable of. A degree of Squeeze is involved in most any expression.

Brows Up and Down

A common approach to brows Up/Down has them embody the alertness, or even simply sound volume, of a character. If a character is yelling, the brows are high; if the character is not, they're low. Both of these states are illustrated in Figure 2.1. Sometimes Down can be used for anger or determination. These uses of the brows aren't necessarily wrong, but they're very limited. You get into all sorts of trouble when a character yells and then, well, yells more. It's easy to blow your character's acting range on the first line of dialogue, and then have nowhere to go on the second.

Getting into the acting portion of facial animation, it's important to realize that subtlety is king. If we use the brows merely as an up/down gauge of the character speech volume, it's not going to add anything to the performance, but instead merely tag along with the sound. Not just yet, but soon (in Chapter 7 "Building Emotion: The Basics of the Eyes"), I'll build on this, but the things going on emotionally happen before the things going on visually. The emotional shifts in a character's visual performance should lead the vocal performance. If the character has a line that is sad and then it shifts to an angry one, the visual facial representation of that shift should happen before the line. We think things before we do them. To lend credibility

Figure 2.1

Brows Down and Up

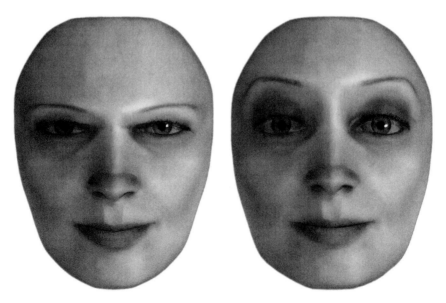

to the things we animate, we should make the emotional context of a scene slightly lead the sound. We're talking frames here, not seconds or minutes. All this is why I tend not to use the brows Up/Down in a strictly alertness- or volume-based manner, but instead as emotional keys. They work (mostly) in conjunction with the Squeeze and eyelids to create poses, not motions.

Brows Squeeze

The Squeeze is by far the more interesting of the two motions in the brows' toolbox. If, without looking in a mirror, you were to explain what a "mad" expression on the brows was, you'd likely think it's that they drop low, and arc, as in Figure 2.2.

That this is how we interpret "mad" on the brows is a feat of the conventions used in cartoons. This is indeed a shape people associate with anger, but it's not entirely accurate. If you now look in a mirror and make a mad face, you'll notice the brows only squeeze. That's it. Figure 2.3 shows some real-life angry brows.

Figure 2.2

Stylized mad brows

There's no crazy swooping shape; if you're seeing one on your face, it's because you're cheating, tilting your head, and manipulating the shape through perspective. I'll get to that in Chapter 3 "Facial Landmarking", but for now, hold your horses, straighten your head out, and let's keep going. Your brows may drop a little bit, but not enough for that downward movement to be perceived as the main motion. It's the scrunching of the skin between and just above the brow's hair that really makes someone look mad.

Now let's try "thinking." It's a little tougher to pick a pose for, but let's do it. Look in a mirror (or don't) and put on your thinking face. It's not dissimilar, is it? The brows squeeze— maybe not as much as "mad," maybe you've got one eyebrow a bit higher than the other—but mostly, it's the brows coming together. Now put on your sad face. Behold, it's similar again. The brows raise, and the brows squeeze.

The Brows Squeeze Is Every Expression

As we discussed in the previous section, just about any ol' expression is going to do the same thing: squeeze the brows. Some level of squeeze on the brows is involved in almost any emotion. To get more specific, squeeze denotes "thought." Absence of squeeze is generally absence of any wheels turning. It's the combination of the brow squeeze, the brow raise, the tilt of the head, the eyes, and the eyelids, working together, that creates an expression. That sounds like it's complicated and so much harder than just having a mad shape and a sad shape and an excited shape to use, but in fact it's so much easier, and credible; and best of all, there are only a few concepts to it. Now, you already know that squeeze is a part of almost every expression, if used with the right combination of other things, so you're already started on learning.

Figure 2.3

Real mad brows

Moving right along... Since I shied away from portraying alertness and volume in the brows' Up and Down, and they weren't anywhere to be seen in the Squeeze section, would you like to know how to do that? It's easy.

The Upper Lids' Effect on Expression

To keep in line with how I've talked about sync and the eyebrows, I'll tell you what the major motions of the upper eyelids are, even though they're much simpler in movement than the rest we've covered so far: Wide/Closed. Period. There are all sorts of specific points along the way between wide open and closed shut and each has its own meaning, but from Wide to Closed is basically it.

Start with the notion that the upper lids hold a lot of information, but it's not absolute. Just like some of the visimes in Chapter 1 "Learning the Basics of Lip Sync"—such as T and R, which are merely relatively wider or narrower than what's around them, nothing absolute—so are the upper lids. Simply put: All the information in the upper lids is relative. The iris and pupil are what the lids are relative to. If there were no eyeballs in the sockets, the upper eyelids wouldn't tell us a whole lot. That's gross and probably seems weird, but it's a point to think about. The iris and pupil serve as a reference point to tell us *how* wide or closed the eyelid is; the eyelid alone means nothing. Think of it like one of those "hit the pad with the hammer" games at carnivals. The markings on the slide tell you how hard you hit. If we can see white in the eye above the iris and pupil, the lids are wide; if the lid is low enough to cut into the pupil's silhouette, they're narrow. If we can't see the eye, the lids are closed.

The Upper Lids Show Us Alertness

All this is tied to alertness. In other words, the more alert we are, the more light our eyes let in and the wider they get. The less alert we are, the less light our eyes let in and the more closed they are. Allowing and blocking light is all the eyelid does (besides blinking, of course which is something completely unrelated to this). With no iris and pupil, we couldn't read that effect. For example, Figure 2.4 is a set of eyelids, with no iris and pupil drawn in.

Eyes, right? No big deal. Now look at an iris and pupil drawn into Figure 2.5.

Figure 2.4

Eyeless sockets

Figure 2.5

Regular eyes

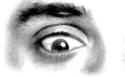

Figure 2.6

Eyes up/sleepy

Figure 2.7

Eyes down/alert

Eyes, right? Again, no big deal. Now in Figure 2.6 the same iris and pupil have been slid higher in relation to the eyelid, which hasn't changed at all.

Wait. That's different. Why is it different? It looks sleepy. Why does it look sleepy? Because the iris and pupil are partially covered; it appears as though the lids are blocking some light into the pupil, something that happens when we're sleepy, or bored, or for any number of reasons. The point is that the eyeballs moving in an unchanging lid are changing the overall facial *expression*, not just moving about positionally. In Figure 2.7, you'll see the same eyes with the iris and pupils moved down instead of up.

Hold on. This guy's excited. He's all bug-eyed. That's weird. Once again, the eyelids and brows haven't intentionally changed expression; the iris and pupil have simply moved! That doesn't make sense, does it? Well, yes, it does. This brings me back to what I touched on earlier with the brows. Using the brows to accentuate the alertness or vocal volume of a character is not as effective, since the brows usually have more to do with the type of expression, not the intensity of it. The upper eyelids are almost exclusively the visual key we as humans use to perceive someone's alertness. The way we achieve that perception is by looking at the eyelids' position relative to the eyeballs, using the pupils and irises as the measuring stick.

This is just something we have to be ever aware of—which is really the point of these first three chapters: not to teach you everything there is to know, but instead to have a base to draw upon when we make certain decisions when building our models and key shapes. (We'll go over most of this again in more detail in Chapter 7.) The eyelid's level is *always* relative to the iris and pupil, no matter where they may be looking. That's what I meant when I said the upper eyelid's information is relative. As the eyes turn here and there, the expression/level of alertness is going to change almost randomly. It just won't do if every time the eyes look up you'll have "sleepy guy," and when they look down you'll have "fraidy cat guy—look out!" We have several ways to tackle this problem automatically, through rigging simple or complex head setups that you'll read about in Chapter 11, "Sketletal Setup, Weighting, and Rigging" and in Chapter 12, "Interfaces for Your Faces," but the most important thing right now is that you're aware of it. Before we get that far into the book, though, there is an elbow-grease way to deal with this little detail, and it's what I'll describe next.

Figure 2.8

Pupil-and-iris-o-meter

Alert

Normal

Sleepy

The Upper Lids Stay Relative to the Pupil and Iris

For a simple knowledge-based fix (as opposed to a rig, for just this moment) or method to avoid unexpected expression changes, the upper eyelids should hold their relationship to the eyes. In CG terms, the *upper* lids should behave as though the eyeballs are their parent objects (vertically). To maintain expression throughout eyeball movement, the upper eyelids should seemingly close some as the eyeballs look down and widen as the eyes look up, as in Figure 2.9. If there's still some convincing needed as to the validity of this, get a friend to look up and down in front of you and watch their upper eyelids. If their lids don't behave as I've described, get them to a hospital. Quickly.

Figure 2.9

Eyes up and down, expression maintained

The Lower Lids' Effect on Expression

Now that we know enough about the upper lids to last us for a while, it's lower lid time. The "lower lids"—or "Squint," as we'll refer to them in this book—are actually the visual effect of an area of muscle called the *orbitularis oculi*. When I say "lower lids" in this book, I mean the whole area including the upper half of the cheeks, the outer edges of the brows, and even the skin between the eye and the ear! Figure 2.10 shows this area in darker gray.

> The actual orbitularis oculi muscle extends up and over the upper eyelid. The area shown refers to the area we will affect in our key shapes.

That's not really how you'd identify the lower lids if someone asked you to point at them, I know. The affected area is very broad. Referring to the cheeks as an independent area that emotes is a leading cause of badly done facial animation, so with "lower lids Squint" I picked

Figure 2.10

Lower lids Squint

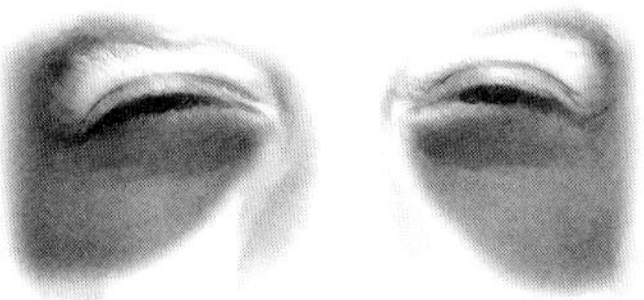

a name that was better suited—not to mention that it makes a nice pair with the upper lids.

This main muscle surrounds the eye, and its motion is like a squeeze Figure 2.11 shows the "track" all the different areas are on—the affected areas and the directions they move—as the lower lids flex.

So, in actuality, it's a squeeze and a twist, both. Everything pulls in toward the eyeball, and the outer areas have to get around some skull to do that, so they have to curve in toward the eye as they travel. This is the motion that causes "crow's feet" wrinkles on people. Even in babies, there's all this skin that's trying to move into the same spot, so it has to bunch up. The squeeze and twist of the lower lids is a major, major thing and one of our most basic and important controls.

The Value of a Good Squint

So we've got a name and a motion in lower lids Squint, but what does this shape do for us? In short, it's an emotional intensifier, and it can help create focus in a performance. It's not necessarily tied to volume or alertness, or even a specific emotion; it just intensifies all emotion.

Remember when we were saying that the squeeze in the brows all alone can mean "think"? Well, this lower lid Squint makes *that* think *more* think. I can't tell you a logical reasoning for this or give you a medical or anthropological reference—it's just the way it is. I'm talking to you as 100% artist, 0% intellectual on this point. A good visual example of the lower lids intensifying an emotion is a "mad" expression on the brows. There's Squeeze, there's a little bit of downward movement, the head is tilted forward, but there's still one thing missing. In the first image in Figure 2.12, we've got everything minus the lower lids Squint, and then in the second image, the Squint is included.

Do you *feel* the difference? It can be subtle to look at it and compare, but the squeezed lower lids adds so much determination to the mad expression. I look at those two and think the first one is mad; the second one is full of hate. Sometimes when you're animating, that's the difference in performance you need to find, and knowing how to get it helps.

Figure 2.11

Squint motion

Figure 2.12

(left) Squeezeless anger and (right) anger with squeeze

Squint Is Not Emotion-Specific

Now, obviously lower lids are not only available to us as a tool to show hatred and bad things; used properly, happiness and even sorrow or frustration are intensified, and feel more real. Often in a smile, animators will feel they need a control for the cheeks. The effect they're looking for should come from the mouth smile key spreading over a large enough area of the face combined with the effect of the lower lids. If you look in a mirror and smile trying not to include your lower lids, it can look very contrived. To do the same thing and consciously flex your lower lids or squint, you'll see the opposite, a more genuine smile. I had a friend I would joke with long before I was in CGI and I would tell her it seemed that she had to trade her eyes for her teeth whenever she smiled.

Squeeze Across Different Styles

The lower lids are also very heavily used in styles that aren't just human, even though all styles are somewhat rooted in human cues. Characters that have what I call "clamshell eyes"—an eyelid that is made of a collapsed sphere and tracks the eye's surface—also use the lower eyelid similarly. Pick your favorite CGI movie and watch how a toy, a bug, or maybe even a monster with these clamshell eyes will actually *grow* a lower eyelid for certain expressions. The lower eyelid is such a fantastic tool for expressing so many things that I can't possibly cover them all until we use it in scene context. For now, just know that you'll need it, and you'll love it.

Eyelines: Perception vs. Reality

So if the brows squeeze tells us there are thoughts trucking through the head, and if the brows up/down tell us what kinds of thoughts those are, and if the upper eyelids are a window to alertness, and if the lower lids intensify and modify emotions...does the eyeball itself have anything to do with emotion? Not really, no.

In the context of a scene, looking down while saying something may tell us there's shame or fear or bashfulness, or any number of things, but that has more to do with the overall head pose, facial expression, and dialogue than the fact that the eyes are pointed downward. Someone could be looking down for any number of reasons.

We're all done dealing with expression in the top half of the face until Chapter 7; for the rest of this chapter, I want to talk about how the eyeballs primarily tackle the hefty task of telling us where the character is looking. How strange. The eyes tell us what's being looked at. Simple, right? Let's read between the lines:

The eyes, *not the head,* tell us what's being looked at.

Headline vs. Eyelines

Something I see all the time in computer animation is eyelines—where the eyes are pointed—done improperly. A common tendency is to animate *head*lines—that is, to point the entire head at the character's focus. If my head is pointed at something, that's where I'm looking, right? Well, technically it's not wrong; it just doesn't communicate clearly with an audience. There's no reference, the iris and pupil are dead center in the eyelid, relatively, so there's a lot of interpretation that has to be done by the viewer.

Here we go with references and relative stuff again: If the white to the left and right of the iris is equal, the eyes are pointed straight forward in relation to the head. To carry that to a real-world scenario, if two actors were standing next to each other on a stage, eye contact would mean they'd be facing each other nose to nose. Yes, technically, they're looking at each other, but it's a little unnatural.

Implied Eyelines

What will better show where the eyes are looking is an *implied* eyeline, not a "geometrically correct" one. That's right, all you folks who constrain eyeballs by pointing them at a locator or null—I'm saying Don't do it. It looks bad. Sure, in 3D space it is correct. It is correct *to you*, the one person with the ability to orbit around in a scene, but our job is primarily to communicate with our audience from a chosen framing—and if it doesn't *look* right, it isn't right.

> Real-time free-camera game animation may be the exception to this rule, but splitting the difference between the eyes and the head is still something you should try and do the second that you do have control over the camera, like cut-scenes.

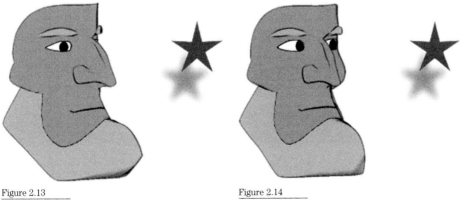

Figure 2.13 ____

Correct eyeline sans flair

Figure 2.14 ____

A more interesting eyeline

Figure 2.13 is a 3D model with the eyeballs constrained to a focus on an object in front of it, and the head pointed directly at the object.

There he is, looking at it. Yep, looking right at it. No one can argue the factuality of him looking at it. But it's pretty darn boring, don't you think? Now, let's spice it up a little tiny bit. In Figure 2.14, let's do it my way. Now we can see more of his face, which almost always looks better, and we've made it obvious beyond a shadow of a doubt that he is most definitely looking at that star, because the eyeballs are sitting to the right of the eyelid opening, not balanced in the center. The reference we have is that eye; if there's more white on our left, he's looking to our right. It's a simple perception equation.

The funny thing is that in my scene, a top-down wireframe, with lines drawn in so you can see where the head and eyes are pointed, looks like Figure 2.15.

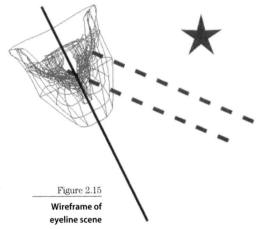

Figure 2.15

Wireframe of eyeline scene

Even with that knowledge, I still like the eyeline in Figure 2.14 better than the one in Figure 2.13. Seeing a character's face is going to go a long way toward helping their performance, and all that matters in an eyeline, like anything else, is the perception, not the fact. Figure 2.13 gives a better impression of looking to the right; our brain fills in the part about the focus being the star, as it's also to the right. Approaching eyelines this way will convince an audience ten out of ten times, where an aim constraint may not. Once we get the basics of "Which way are the eyes pointed?" sorted out in our scene, the audience is distraction-free and ready to read the lids, the brows, and anything else we want to act with.

Distraction Is the Enemy of Performance

This is to become a recurring theme. There are certain things we can do that will distract an audience, make them figure something out. Missing our sync by a couple of frames, moving the brows instead of lids when a character screams, or making the audience question where a character is looking—any of those things will break the illusion that our character lives, breathes, thinks, and exists just past their television screen.

CHAPTER 3

Facial Landmarking

Facial animation and modeling does indeed involve knowing how to lip sync and how to use the eyes, brows, and lids for expression. *Good* facial animation and modeling, however, involves knowing a whole lot more than that. Good acting and modeling means knowing about the relationships between features on the face, what the changes in those relationships will do to the model and/or expression, and how to be in total control of all those variables with the simple tilt of the head, or the addition of a crease.

- **Introduction to landmarking**
- **Landmarking mouth creases**
- **Landmarking brow creases**
- **Landmarking the tilt of the head**

Introduction to Landmarking

As I said briefly in Chapter 2 "What the Eyes and Brows Tell Us," landmarking, as I refer to it in this book, means noticing the area *surrounding* what we think we're looking at—that's where we get the real cues for the impressions we get. Landmarking is used in two ways: to analyze creases and to measure *distances* between features. By landmarking, we can study what effect those two things, creases and distances, have on perception of everything from eyelines to brow expressions to mouth expressions.

Landmarking is used to identify what overall perceived change has been created in a way that might not be obvious. That is a big mouthful and concept, to be sure, but it's one worth understanding. Landmarking is realizing that a tilt of the head may have more to do with why someone looks mad than the shape of the brows does, or that a wrinkly brow may make some-one look more excited than does raising those brows even higher. Think of it like this: When you enter your neighborhood on your way home, you know you're near home because you're surrounded by landmarks—things you recognize—that tell you so. If your neighborhood (minus your house) was demolished one day, you'd still intellectually know where you lived; your address wouldn't have changed, and all the directions, the turns, and the streets would be the same, but something about the trip home would *feel* a heck of a lot different, wouldn't it? Landmarking on the face is learning to spend most of your time looking at the neighbor-hood first, and your house second.

Landmarking by Example

For a more visual representation, take a look at Figure 3.1, a plain old mouth. Modeling a smile from this mouth, most people would concentrate solely on the lips and try not to man-gle the rest of the face too much. A basic battle plan would be to pull the corners of the mouth out to the sides and up, revealing more of the teeth. The resultant shape is wide and arced; it's everything we associate consciously with a smile. Doing it like that is not necessar-ily a wrong approach, but it would look like Figure 3.2.

I'll do some talking about "shapes," "key shapes," "blend shapes," etc. These are, well, differ-ent shapes that get assigned as target or key shapes to one master head. That head can then draw upon, or morph into, each one of those shapes. This can be done using Maya's built-in interface found under Window → Animation Editors → Blend Shape, or you can create your own interfaces to drive the values, as I do. To create blend shapes, select the target or key shapes, and then the master (default) head. In the animation module, select Deform → Create Blend Shape.

Figure 3.1

A default mouth

Figure 3.2

One unusual smile

Supervising other modelers building facial key shapes, and even doing it myself when I was newer at this, I saw this all the time as a first-pass for a smile shape. Figure 3.2 has all the pieces we consciously recognize as a smile, but it's not right—I think we can all agree on that. It doesn't *feel* like a real smile, and in a lot of ways, it doesn't feel extreme or broad enough. It looks as though it's a fake or tortured smile; it's a little creepy, actually.

A gut instinct for correcting this would be to make it bigger. Just make it bigger. To pull this mouth wider and taller and farther back would actually just make it look worse. When looking at the result of that, we'd have the same reaction, and probably try widening it again. Before long, we'd have a smile where we could see into a giant mouth, we'd have all the back teeth and gums exposed, the mouth practically peeling the face off, and it still wouldn't look genuine or extreme.

Now in Figure 3.3 is the same *mouth* again, with one big difference.

The surrounding area of the face, just outside of the mouth, up to and including the cheeks, has changed rather drastically. There's a massive crease and shift of the surrounding skin mass now. All of a sudden, the smile looks genuine, and wide. Why is that? It's because of that crease. Creases (which I'll go into more specifically in the later sections of this chapter) communicate the simple fact, whether as an illusion in CGI or the fact of real life, that skin is being displaced. It's very apparent that the same mouth shape with and without creases yields a completely different look.

Figure 3.3

A genuine smile

Fixing a Shape by Fixing Its Surroundings

The inclusion of the crease is the result of using landmarking. Specifically here, we're looking to and using the effects on the surrounding area to emphasize the *perceived* primary area. The problem we're faced with as artists, in this example, is how to make a smile that doesn't look wide or genuine, look wider and genuine. The solution is not to widen the mouth or add some genuine sauce, but instead to show that the shape is already wide, by showing that it is affecting the rest of the face, too. By adding the more natural look of skin with the creasing, it looks more genuine.

The Landmarking Process

Landmarking can be done for a complex of reasons and serve a variety of uses. The crease for the smile is something often overlooked, but now that you know to look for it in a smile, you'll never again forget it. If we were really doing a top-to-bottom landmarking of a smile, what we'd be doing is looking at a real-life smile and analyzing everything *except* the mouth in itself—we'd look to its proportions and surrounding area. We'd make a list of those things, either physically or mentally, in referential or landmarking terms, and make sure to include them in the shape we build for our character. If we were critiquing work, we'd have stuff to pull from our bag of suggestions.

Something of this nature might be as simple as looking at Figure 3.4 and making a list of five small observations:

1. The mouth is 1.3 times wider than default, 1.3 times *deeper* than default.
2. The lips move up 1 upper lip height.
3. The eyes squint.
4. The mouth pushes cheeks (effect visible almost all the way back to the jaw).
5. A crease appears, apex directly down and in line with outside edge of eyes.

Even that simple list will help us identify things we might not otherwise. We may also take the information and deconstruct it. For instance, the smile usually has an effect all the way up to the lower lids, or upper cheeks, but if we were to include that squint in a basic smile, we could run into problems with mixing our shapes together, so we'd build everything *but* that into the smile shape. A squint shape by itself mixed with a squint that's included in a smile could get ugly. By laying out all factors involved, you can identify certain reusable attributes in shapes, which becomes a very powerful tool in deciding key shapes to build in a set. That sort of information and planning, however, is best left for later. In the modeling section for shapes, Chapter 6 "Mouth Keys," it all gets explained in depth.

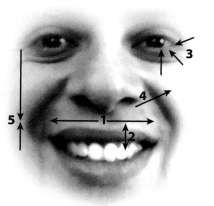

Figure 3.4

Looking for landmarks in a smile

Landmarks Are Obvious When They're Alone

Looking at the smile crease again, this time in Figure 3.5, you'll see an odd mix. The picture has the *mouth* returned to its default position, but with the crease from the smile. This is what we should be picturing mentally when we're landmarking something, truly ignoring the supposed main focal point—in this case, the mouth. Here the crease looks very dramatic, and almost silly in how pronounced it is, but, when smiling occurs, it's real. This exact shape with the mouth in default, but with the smile creasing, is something you'll never see in life, nor as a shape we'll build, but it's here to illustrate just how pronounced that crease really is. It's intense. With the smile on the lips not present we can focus better on the crease and how it looks in relation to the face. It's amazing, when you see it this way, to believe that it's such a commonly overlooked part of a smile. It is, in fact, the *most important* part of a smile.

Figure 3.5

Smile crease on a non-smiling mouth

You may be wondering whether landmarking is exclusively concerned with the areas around the mouth; they are most definitely a big part of it, but not all there is. In the next section, I'd like to focus on the creases around the mouth and then move on to sections covering creases around the brow and the tilt of the head.

Landmarking Mouth Creases

The area around the mouth, as you just saw, creases during a smile. Translating this knowledge into a key shape for a 3D model that will look right, move well, and render without shading errors is a completely different and more complicated topic.

You now know that you'll need that surrounding mouth area to crease, and how that crease will need to look, at least in the case of a smile. Knowing this, we can start to think about mapping out the points of a model to be prepared for that movement—a sort of preemptive modeling strike. This is much like deconstructing the specifics of an individual shape and seeing if it can be made up of different smaller, reusable shapes. Thinking in these terms is very efficient. It's extremely advantageous to build a model to cooperate with what it will eventually have to do, because with the wrong point layout, life can become very miserable, in a square-peg round-hole sort of way. For example, forcing a diagonal crease down a square grid can get ugly very quickly.

Landmarking to Plan a Point Layout

You should plan to look at all of the different shapes and creasing that the mouth will have to do (landmark them), comparing all of the different shapes and planning the point layout of the model in the way that best compromises for all the shapes. That sounds like a lot of brain- and legwork, so it's very lucky for us that the way we humans move our faces and the way we crease is extremely efficient. Every expression on the mouth needs pretty much the same point layout, so compromise isn't even a worry. The smile crease is the same crease we'll see in a sneer or scowl; there's just different emphasis in different places. The crease (and bumps) in a frown appear on the same area of skin as the smile, but the whole area moves down instead of up. Every expression shares the same features, just uses them in different ways.

The Main Crease of the Mouth Area

The area of skin where creases occur on most people is on a curved track between a point about a centimeter (or a little less than half an inch for all you people still using that old imperial system) off of the side of the mouth and continues up to where the top/side of the nostril meets the face, as in Figure 3.6. I've mapped out a matching grid with the shaded line illustrating where the crease skin is. I went over the top of the nostril, to put emphasis on the skin behind it, since that's what we're looking at.

If you look extremely closely in a mirror, and if you're over 15 years old or so, you should be able to make out a faint line on your face along this darkened one I've pointed out, even when you're not expressing. That's the crease, or more accurately what becomes the crease. That's the one that creases in your smile, scrunches up in a scowl, and frames the outside of a frown. It's also the very same line that will eventually frame the front of your jowls when you get older. The fact that it gets creased in every single emotion is part of the reason that happens!

The Same Crease Does Different Things

Here, I'd like to point out the different ways that one crease, the one that appears in smiles and frowns and sneers, behaves and moves in those positions.

Smile In a smile, this area pulls up and out, much like the simplistic *impression* we get from a smile, but you can see that we get that motion from the area immediately surrounding the mouth, not the lips. The mouth area *moves* into this shape like curtains drawn open on a stage, or classic drapes in a window, as illustrated in Figure 3.7.

You'll notice, too, that into and out of the crease from top and bottom, the skin bends into the apex; it's not a straight line or curve. That tightest point is approximately where the muscles that create the smile are anchored most firmly, so they get pulled the farthest and crease the most. This is how a smile looks on my face, and this is the most *common* shape type for smile creases, but it's not the rule.

Different people do crease differently, so if some of this doesn't *exactly* match your own face, or the face of the person you use as reference, don't be too distracted by that. It's a detail; for the most part, all of this still holds very close to correct. The amount of information I'm trying to communicate in this book dictates that I'm going to have to generalize here and there, so I'm going with the most common shapes and creases. In Chapter 5 "Constructing a Mouth" and in Chapter 6, where I talk more about modeling and key shapes, the necessities of a shape such as a smile separate from the specific shapes I build, leaving you to model the shapes *you* want to see.

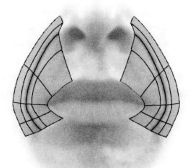

Figure 3.6

Default crease layout

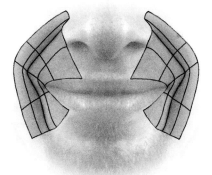

Figure 3.7

Smile crease layout

Figure 3.8

**Frown crease layout &
another view**

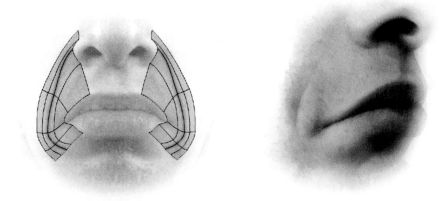

Frown In Figure 3.8, I've tracked the grid model over a picture of a frown. Of the three mouth shapes discussed here, the crease is the least apparent in the frown, so in the second image of Figure 3.8 the crease is shown from a second view. Once again, you'll notice that the row that was in the apex of the smile crease is at the base of the frown. You'll also notice that the line that is darkened, the center of creasing, travels to exactly where the crease occurs. That is always the case, and a good thing for us, too; that line goes to the crease, wherever it is, period. Knowing that makes our job building shapes less ambiguous.

Scowl/Sneer In Figure 3.9 we've got a scowl, or sneer. This one is interesting because it shares many things in common with both the smile and the frown. The look of the mouth—the lips themselves—is very much like that of the frown, only shifted vertically upward. The crease, as always, is shared; it's as deep as in the smile, but the tapers are reversed. What I mean by that is that in the smile, the crease goes from the nostril side to the area surrounding the mouth and down from there toward the chin. In that shape the focal point of the crease, the deepest part, is where the crease changes direction. In the scowl, the focal point of the crease is right next to the nose, and the crease then tapers down to where the smile crease changed direction.

The area where the crease changes direction is easiest visualized as drapery. When drapes are pulled back, they have a very distinctive shape. The point at which the drapes are tied and the curve of the hanging drapes changes abruptly is what I'm referring to as the deepest part of the crease.

Intensities of a Crease Matter

The scowl crease as compared to a smile crease opens up another whole world of detail. To simply *have* a crease is a step in the right direction. The *right* crease with the *right* focal point is another, more challenging step to take. In Figure 3.10, I've shown the mouth crease for your viewing pleasure. I've got the depth/intensity of the crease shown by width and darkness. The darker and wider, the more intense the crease. As it thins, it tapers back to a smoother, flatter face. You can see that they are very similar but completely opposite.

The smile has its main focal point out to the side of the mouth, while the sneer is most intense behind the nostril. This difference is quite important.

Even the Big Boys Sometimes Get It Wrong

I've actually seen this mouth-crease detail missed in big-budget feature films. Human characters indeed had the detail of a crease when they smiled, but the distribution of the crease was *even* all the way down from nose to mouth. The overall shape was correct, but the intensities of the creases were, as I said, even. To some animators who knew that the creases have a lot to do with expression, it seemed obvious why many expressions got a little confused. Whenever a human character smiled, it looked awkward or forced, or as if there was some undertone that wasn't supposed to be there. There was always an element of sneer in the happiness. It hurt the facial performances in a subtle but, I think, important way.

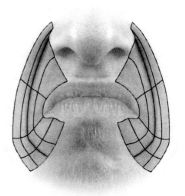

Figure 3.9

A mad layout

Figure 3.10

Smile and scowl crease intensities

Creasing Applied to Each Shape

The creasing in the mouth is absolutely full of detail and idiosyncrasy, and we can't cover it all at once and expect you to remember it. Each mouth shape we model in the book will have its own important crease information right along with other aspects that get flushed out; I just wanted to make sure you were getting a feel for how important and different the information can be.

The brows, while "creasy" in a lot of the same ways, have some of their own unique fun.

Landmarking Brow Creases

The mouth's main crease is most visible on the smile, which is very close to (and in some setups *is*) the Wide shape. That's right, the same Wide of Wide/Narrow fame. The creases on the brows are very similar, in that they occur on the Up/Down and in the Squeeze. Yes, these concepts all do relate together; you've just got to wait a little bit for all the loose ends we've frayed to tie themselves back together again.

Brows Up/Raise

The easiest, and therefore first, creasing discussion we'll have for the brows is Brows Up, or Raise. Figure 3.11 is an image of brows raised. Let's repeat my favorite phrase: It's not necessarily wrong. The problem with Figure 3.11 is that the brows are raised, yes, but they don't give the impression "I'm raised as far as I go." Just as in the case with the mouth, raising them further won't solve that problem, whereas the simple addition of creases, as in Figure 3.12, shows the brows looking more taxed, more extreme. The creases tell me that they're being pushed pretty far out of their default position.

Figure 3.11

Raised brows, no creasing

Figure 3.12

Raised brows, with creasing

The brows—specifically the eyebrow *hair*—haven't moved between Figures 3.11 and 3.12. This may seem like a rehash of the mouth concepts, and in some ways it is, but they're very different in how their details work. When dealing with the mouth, the distraction and misplaced stuff had to do with the lips, whereas on the brows it's the eyebrow hair that tries to steal your attention. This is the part of the brows that gets over-manipulated generally. What's extra unfortunate about that is that the brows occur over the border of the eye socket and the forehead. That's a bone. The problem in CG with moving brows up for extra emphasis is that typically the ridge, the front of the skull, gets melted away. In their default position, the area of mesh between the eyelids and the brow ridge are fairly well connected by the geometry, meaning that when the brows need to move up more than a little bit, the forehead gets shrunken and the eye sockets grow taller. That's not normal. As I said, that's a bone; it can't do that. In real life the skin on the brows travels over the surface of the skull, but recreating that effect with shapes can be hard (we do it in Chapter 9 "Eye and Brow Keys"). This is another great reason to put the emphasis on the creasing, rather than just making the brows go higher.

The Shape of Brow Creases

Brow creases on most people appear like waves. There are layers, not all perfectly lined up, but generally moving together with peaks just outside and over the eyes. There are usually a pair of smaller creases that don't continue all the way across the brow that live just above the arc in the brows. To show how important those are, look at the two images in Figures 3.13 and 3.14. One is simply raised brows and the other is a scared or concerned shape. The brow hair is obviously different, as the skin the hair is growing out of has moved, but look closely at those creases above the brow peaks.

In the scared one, they're not nearly as pronounced, and their emphasis is toward the center of the forehead. In the raised image, you're getting the information that the raise is happening pretty evenly, across the brow, or you could even look at it thinking that the bulk of the upward force is coming from above the brow peaks. These creases are telling you as much about the expression as the hair on the brow ridge.

Figure 3.13

Wave-like brow creases (raised)

Figure 3.14

Scared brows

Brows Down/Squeeze

With the brows' Down shape, you've really got a misnomer. We talked briefly in Chapter 2 about how trying to drop your brows doesn't really drop them. They move downward a bit, but it's more of a side effect of squeezing them. Working forward with that, there are two major kinds of creasing that occur from squeezing the brows. There's the classic vertical crease(s), as in Figure 3.15, and there's the harder "turbulence" style creasing that's more like bunching than creasing; it's more of an anti-crease, as in Figure 3.16.

 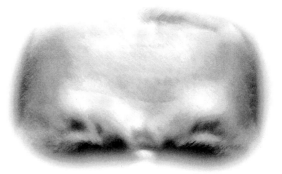

Figure 3.15

Squeezed brows, vertical creases

Figure 3.16

Squeezed brows, bunching creases

In simpler setups and characters, 10 out of 10 times I'll recommend you go with the first, the vertical lines; they communicate more clearly at a glance, and it's an easy shape to build, both in model point layout and in the key shape. If you really want to make a character realistic, the bunching, as in Figure 3.16, is going to go a long way further to impressing and convincing an audience of the character's emotions. As a shape to build, though, it's a bad one. Most people's brows are some unique combination of the two.

I'm firmly convinced you could do forehead furrow IDs just like fingerprints and retinal scans!

The bunching brow shape is convincing because it's hard to put a finger on it. It's nothing as overt as the creases in a brow raise or the fold in a smile, but just like those others, having it will sell the pose better than brows so low they cut into the eye's silhouette, which brings us ever so quickly to our next topic: cutting into the eyes' silhouette.

Landmarking the Tilt of the Head

If you look back to the two images in Figure 2.1, in the first section of Chapter 2, you should see that I cheated. Brows Up and Down, it was called. Reading the topic heading for this section and looking at those pictures, it should be pretty obvious exactly *how* I cheated, too. Do you have it? That's right: the tilt of the head, among other things, can influence how high or low the brows look. This all happens based on their perceived distance from the eyes. The closer to the eyes the brows appear, the lower they look. In this, the final section in the introduction to landmarking, I'm going to talk a lot about how a change in perspective can seemingly move features of the face. In Figure 3.17 you can see how easily this illusion was created.

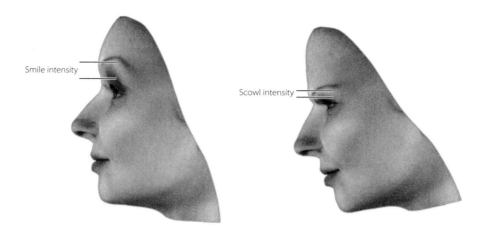

Figure 3.17

Side view of Figure 2.1

Perspective and the manipulation of perspective is something we all do with our heads for some strange reason. When you're mad, you probably express it, in one way, by tilting your head forward. This isn't because it's heavy, or you're trying to point at people with your forehead, it's just a thing we do. In fact, if you have a mirror handy, simply look into it, maintain your eye contact with yourself and tilt your head forward. You look pretty angry, don't you? No expression changed in any way you'd expect, no facial muscles were flexed, but you look angry, so your expression did indeed change.

Here's another fun one: Smile. In a regular relaxed manner, smile. Now, again, maintain your self-loving gaze and tilt your head forward. Now you look quite insane or devious. Tilt that back and forth. Happy, crazy, happy, crazy, happy, crazy! Okay, stop. The point I'm making here is that, much like creases, another set of landmarks is distances. In this case, the most important distance relationship in expression is the distance between your eyes and brows. Manipulate that distance through perspective, manipulate the expression.

Every Expression Has a Tilt

Every expression has its "home tilt." There is going to be a way to hold the head that will emphasize that particular expression. That may seem like a fun thing to know and be able to work with, but once you start thinking about it, let me tell you, it becomes an obsession. Since there's usually *a* home tilt, there's usually an infinite number of *wrong* ways to tilt the head, and it's easy to get wrapped up in that.

In the case of creasing, there could most definitely be a stylistic choice not to include creases on a model and instead emphasize the shapes themselves in a different, more cartoony way, but this concept of the tilt of the head carries through all possible styles from hyper-realistic all the way to toon shaded demon babies. If your character *is* a head—like, say, a green eyeball of a monster—the entire body tilts as though it were just the head. It really does works for any style.

The Significance of Tilts

The head tilt is also a technique I use very often, if not always, to embellish sync—it draws the eyes' attention from the mouth. I noticed the significance of the head tilt for the first time while rewinding a videocassette of a live TV show. In every close-up I was noticing that people really move their heads a lot during regular talking. Sped up, it looked like they were going to snap their necks. It was scary. Simply traveling from start to end of a sentence usually requires a nod or two. Heck, every time people are agreeing with each other, they don't make one stoic nod at the end of the sentence or during the word yes—people nod their heads before, during and after the sentence they hear and respond to positively.

The Benefits of More Animation on the Head

What's nice about tilting the head through dialogue is that it livens up other animation on the body. In pose-to-pose animation, a technique carried over from classical animation, characters hit major key poses in their performance for a scene, and basically hold them. There may be smaller motions, such as the "swimming" of hands as a character searches for a word or settles into or anticipates out of the poses, but it's basically pose, hold, pose, hold. Another advantage to animating the head through the dialogue is that people are looking to the head and eyes anyway, and if you keep that area alive, the facial poses can hold a little longer, therefore come across stronger, and for the time-conscious animator, save some of the effort. And as I pointed out, all this head movement also draws attention from the mouth, since when it's not sitting still in one spot it's not as easy to hyper-analyze. That may seem like a cop-out, but it's not. I go back to the notion that animating the characters' lungs for the sake of realism is silly. If there's anything you can do to make your life easier, while still turning out good work, you should do it. Tilting the head is one of those things you can do to help yourself.

Musical Head Tilts

The main way I like to key the head-tilting through animation is musically. To better explain: I tend to repeat the sound back to myself, mimicking the actor's vocal performance, but with my mouth closed—I basically hum the line to myself. Yes, it's something I try not to do in public, but it works. Generally, the highs and lows in the tonal quality will translate very naturally to the head-tilting. High note, tilt the head up; low tone, tilt the head down. When the actor gets sing-songy, by hitting several kinds of sounds, high and low, in a sentence, so does the character. It's surprisingly effective and easy. In the last chapter, where together we'll work through some animation, you'll see this in action.

The tilt of the head doesn't get its own section beyond this introduction, but it does get brought up extremely often in other chapters, tutorials, and topics, so you need to be aware of it as a concept. Congratulations! You are officially one leg up on people who skipped this chapter or don't have this book!

PART II

Animating and Modeling the Mouth

Now that you've been introduced to the two speech cycles, visimes, the two major brow movements, the effects of the upper and lower lids, and of course creasing and head tilting—whew!—it's time to devote closer attention to one topic at a time. With all that background, the little stuff in the rest of the book will make more sense to you.

Pushing aside all but the bits that are crucial to lip sync, I focus in this part on the mouth, in both modeling and animating technique. After we move through some animation tutorials and finesse our sync, you'll be able to go and build a mouth capable of doing all the things you understand it needs to do. Once that is done, there's nothing left to do with the mouth but build all the key shapes, preparing you for Chapter 12, "Interfaces for Your Faces," where we hook that baby up to an interface!

CHAPTER 4

Visimes and Lip Sync Technique

Here we go, the first cut into the meat of the book. The big thing for you to keep in mind, which I'll try to stress, is that while moving through this and the next few chapters, I want you to learn what is important and unimportant in sync. Pay close attention to the things I include and *don't* include, as we progress; things left unmentioned aren't priorities for now.

Beginners and pros alike will very likely have a first reaction of thinking that this approach is too simplistic. In many ways, my technique *is* very simplistic, but you'll quickly see that it's merely the first layer of many. The concepts are easy, but sometimes the sound can make the application difficult. The sync animations come in waves that all merge together to provide a solid performance. In Chapter 1, "Learning the Basics of Lip Sync," you were exposed to phonemes, visimes, and some very basic technique in Wide/Narrow cycles. Here, all we're going to do is take all of that a step further with some practical applications, instruction, and, of course, more descriptions and imagery.

- **Identifying and breaking down visimes**
- **The best order of building sync**
- **Practice, practice, practice**

Sync: Wide/Narrow Grows Up

First off, as we get more into the specifics of my techniques, I must say this: it's subjective. If the way to interpret text into visuals was a science, every piece of lip sync out there would be bang-on, and nothing would have any more or less style, it would just be "correct"; you wouldn't be reading this book, and I'd have fallen in love with some other subject, or I'd have a killer paper route. There are programs that are getting much better at using sound to generate sync, but even there, in the best setups available, there is still something missing or way too much included, as compared to what you get out of a well-trained artist. Most automatic systems make a great demo, but you would never use the output in any real production. I think it will happen one day, just not yet. What follows is the way I do it. It's a way that works, it's a way that makes sense, and, I think, a way that looks great considering how little effort you have to put in.

So the relationship of the main cycles in speech between Wide/Narrow and Open/Closed is still going to remain the same; it's just going to grow up a little bit from here on in. Wide/Narrow is by far the most important part of most visimes, but it's not the whole deal. If you refer to the visime chart in Chapter 1, you'll notice there are other things, like "taller" and "lower lip rolls in," included in visimes, and at this point, we need to start considering them. So, as we move on, understand that everything I said and you understood about Wide/Narrow and Open/Closed in Chapter 1 is still the same. It's just that the Wide/Narrow cycle has evolved and merged into the greater whole of visimes.

Remember also as you read on that although they are both important and come together to create the look of speech, Wide/Narrow (now visimes), and Open/Closed do not get thought of at the same time in animation. By breaking them apart, we can focus on each of them more intensely. The whole look of speech is the result of these two cycles intertwining, and thinking of them together makes the process much slower and more complicated than considering them separately. As separate entities, they are easier to teach, easier to understand, and speedier to work with.

Visimes vs. Sounds

So I've talked about how visimes aren't whole shapes, they are just parts of shapes. We will use a similar approach throughout the book: We will build parts of shapes to facilitate constructing more flexible and precise whole shapes, and set up interfaces that parallel the simpler thinking and analysis of visimes.

Since the visimes are components, not whole shapes, each can have multiple appearances, and that's why I shied away from showing picture-to-visime comparisons too heavily in Chapter 1—it's a little too ethereal for an introductory chapter. For all the talking I can do to describe shapes, the best thing is just to show you. Sometimes shapes have width attributes, sometimes they don't; sometimes they have Open/Closed values, sometimes they don't. When working with varying levels of rigs, all you can do is match the vital components of each shape as it comes up in the sound, as best as you can with what you have. If your face doesn't have lips-rolling-in shapes, and you want to say B, just close the mouth. If you want to say F, just bare some upper teeth, or even just open the mouth. It's the best you can do with what you have, so don't dwell on it—keep moving on to the next shape in the animation. Rarely will an audience stop believing your character over something like a fudged F; it's not important to the plot. The best thing you can do is give a good impression of the sounds.

The Visimes

The shape sets you'll have after getting through a few more chapters will include the shapes pictured in Figure 4.1.

The Smile is basically your Wide, though it obviously pulls double duty as a smile. I'll often refer to Upper Lip Down and Lower Lip Up as the "lips-rolling-in" keys, because they do that more than they move up and down.

Figure 4.1

The nine shapes we'll use to create all of the visimes

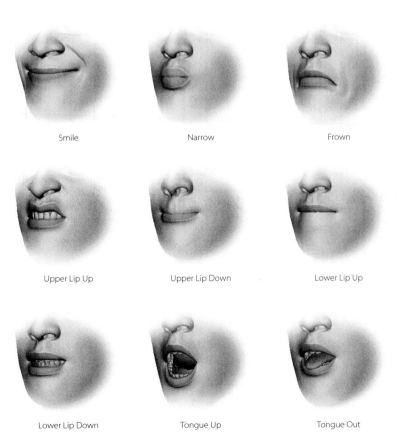

Smile	Narrow	Frown
Upper Lip Up	Upper Lip Down	Lower Lip Up
Lower Lip Down	Tongue Up	Tongue Out

Using combinations of these shapes together will create for us the visimes I've talked about.

B / M / P / Closed This shape has many, many, many forms, as you can see in Figure 4.2. It can be a Smile, as long as the lips are closed. It can also be a Narrow, or Frown, again, as long as the lips are closed. It all comes down to one simple rule: are the lips closed? In most setups there are shapes we'll use to roll the lips in, so if it's needed, the shape can be even more than just the lips meeting, it can be the lips pulling in, which is very effective for the stronger sounds linked to this visime. This sound can be keyed in either the first or the second pass, but it can't be ignored, ever.

EE / Wide The terms EE and Wide are interchangeable. By definition, this shape is really only the width, but in practice it is almost always going to be accompanied by some baring of teeth and/or Open, as shown in Figure 4.3. A closed smile, that can be defined as a Closed shape, is also a Wide. The way that visimes are just pieces of shapes should be starting to fall into place for you now. Seeing that visimes are not all exclusive, they can be paired. A closed smile is both a Wide and a Closed visime.

F / V This has varying definitions based on your key set. Look at Figure 4.4 for some examples. At the lowest end, without a full set of keys for lips, it can be represented with semi-Closed. With the simple key set, as you'll read about in Chapters 5 ("Constructing a Mouth") and 12 ("Interfaces for Your Faces"), the upper lip can be pulled up to show some upper teeth, and the jaw closed beyond Closed (using a value less than 0 for that shape, something our slider controls will accommodate). For F in the full key sets, the upper lip pulls up to show the upper teeth, and the lower lip rolls into the mouth, for the upper teeth to press against. There is no width definition for this shape whatsoever. It can be Narrow, or Wide.

Figure 4.2

The different forms of Closed

Figure 4.3

The different forms of Wide

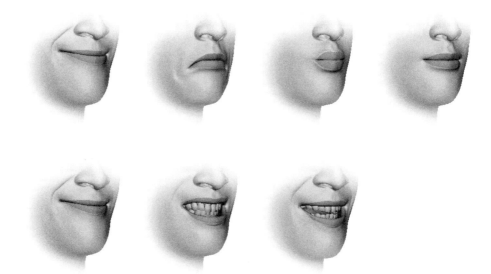

Craig P. Smith
Animator/Illustrator
560 Estudillo Ave. Apt. #1
San Leandro, CA 94577
510-332-6641
www.phoenix-studios.net

Figure 4.4

The different forms of F

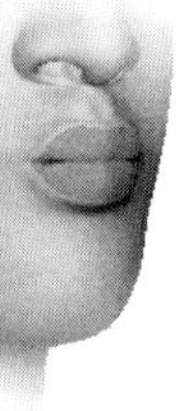

Figure 4.5

The Narrow shape

OO / Narrow OO and Narrow are interchangea[ble] … definitely tied to width; it is the Narrow half of the … don't
mix very well with a Narrow, or pucker-type, …
CGI, so this shape, although sometimes pictu…
sions, is usually pretty much just the way it i…
Narrow (Figure 4.5) is the closest thing to a…
for visimes. Sounds like OH and AW are jus…
with a little less potency and some Open/Clo…
tant to remember, though, that they are not their own shape, they a…
derivative of Narrow and Open, and in animating should be thought
of in just that way.

IH / T / S Relative shapes are fun, they make you think harder! IH and T/S are the same (after
all, by definition, they are both "wider"), but they are different enough in their sounds that I
thought it might be too confusing to put them together in any visime lists. Since the shapes
are relative, their look floats depending on their surroundings. Next to a Narrow, they move
wider, which may not even be as wide as the default shape, also referred to as "rest." So even
though they have Wider as an attribute, they can really, on a global scale, be Narrow. Figure
4.6 is two pairs of images showing IH/T/S *next to* other shapes, to help clarify this.

Figure 4.6

IH is relative, so here it is pictured next to the default shape and a Narrow shape for reference.

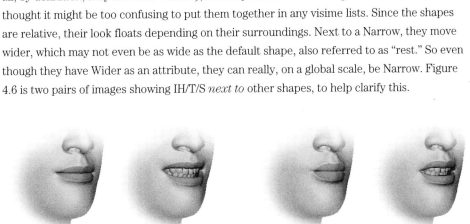

Default shape   The IH visime   A narrower shape   A narrower IH

Figure 4.7

R is also relative.

Default shape   The R visime   A wider shape   A wider R

R R, being another relative shape, is just the opposite of IH/T/S, this time narrower. In anima-tion, you can almost pretend the character can't quite pronounce their Rs, and lean on Ws, like little kids sometimes do, leading you to OOs. When I was a kid, my sister used to "listen to the wadio." Sometimes, with an R sound, I'll also add in a little bit of height to the shape. This isn't always something that is necessary, or even desirable, but it's a good thought to have if the R sound in a scene isn't reading well. Another thing about R is that it involves the tongue being raised slightly. If you have a tongue, raise it; if not, ignore it—no one in the audi-ence will even notice. An important note with R is that, really, it's wrong, and I know it's wrong. You can say R with your lips in any shape; it just usually benefits from the motions described. As with IH, I'll show the shapes in pairs (Figure 4.7), as being relative—there is no "correct" shape, only a shape correct in relation to another.

The Non-Visime Sounds

I'm not going to cover all sounds, because not all sounds are important. For anything not listed here, just slam it into the nearest-sounding thing that is identified. If there's more than one sound that it could be, just pick one; the worst thing that could happen is that you have to change it slightly as you tweak the scene. If a sound is that lost in the mix, it's probably insignificant to the visuals, anyway. Remember, the visime list was condensed down to what it is by determining which sounds had necessary visual cues, and to let all else drop by the wayside. These are some of those less cut-and-dried shapes. Something that's interesting, as you read these, is to actually try to create the sound yourself, contorting your mouth into all sorts of shapes, proving for yourself their lack of importance as specific shapes.

> The following images should *not* be used as direct reference when you lip-sync a scene. The reason that these are here is to help give you advice, and ideas, but they're not meant as a "This sound is this shape" reference, which is part of the reason that they are not visimes. I don't like the idea of tying sounds to exact shapes; it's a potentially misleading instruction. Still, these are here for some help when you might be stuck. With each, I've provided "visime cheats," shapes whose criteria you might borrow to represent these non-visimes.

L / N (Visime Cheat: IH or R) L and N are primarily a function of the tongue, which, if you haven't noticed, I do not treat as important. The tongue can add a lot to a character, but is time-consuming and frequently over-animated, which leans my tendency away from using it too often. It's one of the things that, in my professional work establishing what characters will and will not have, I leave until the end, seeing if I can convince the powers-that-be that the tongue is not even necessary. For L and N, the mouth's shape can be here or there; the only qualification is that it is open at least slightly, since L requires a flow of air (Figure 4.8). The cheat visime is really either direction, wider or narrower. It doesn't so much matter what happens, as long as something happens to widen or narrow the mouth at least a little bit. As a result, there's not much in the way of important shapes to show, just the effect of the tongue.

Figure 4.8

The tongue up for L

D / SH / TH / NG / J (Soft G) / H (Visime Cheat: IH) SH, TH, and NG can be treated almost exactly the same as IH, T, and S. The tongue gets involved in TH by setting itself between the teeth (see its separate demonstration in Figure 4.9), but that isn't necessary for the impression of a TH. The overall impression is a Wider shape, for all these cases. You'll notice that saying it aloud, NG, or ING, as in *surfing*, is exactly the same *sound* as IH, but with a little NG sound in the throat at the end, so it looks just like IH!

AW / OH / UH (Visime Cheat: Narrow + Open) These are basically combinations in varying amounts of Open and Narrow (each is depicted in Figure 4.10). Usually the way these sounds are animated is by keying the visimes around them, and then opening the jaw for the syllable. The transition of width overlaid with the opening of the mouth usually creates the shape for you automatically.

EH / AH / UH (Visime Cheat: Wide + Open) These are the siblings to the above AW, OH, and UH; they are mouth-open shapes (Figure 4.11) but with a mix of Wide instead of a mix of Narrow involved. You'll notice that UH is found in both the Narrow + Open and Wide + Open groups; it can really go either way depending on the context.

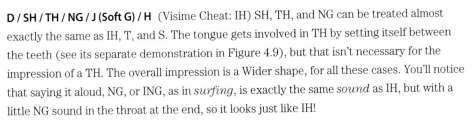

SH, NG, T, J, H   TH

Figure 4.9

These sibilants have an overall impression of "wider."

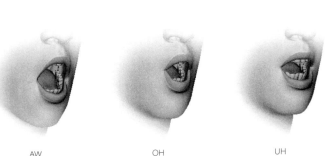

AW   OH   UH

Figure 4.10

Some narrow, open vowels

Figure 4.11

**Some wide,
open vowels**

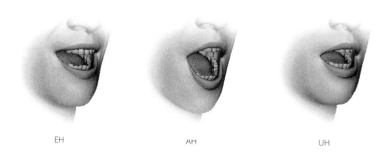

EH   AH   UH

Hard G / K There is absolutely, under no circumstance or twist of fate, any situation that calls for these sounds to have a specific shape. There may be situations where a character really hits the sound, but the mouth will do nothing except possibly flex the position it's already in, or push it a little further, be that Narrower or Wider. There's really just throat involved in these sounds.

Breaking Sounds Down

What we've just gone through are the pieces used to make up speech—visimes—and ways to think of the sounds that aren't visimes. The next thing to learn about has to be how to take the sounds you hear and turn them into those pieces.

As much as there are rules and ideas to teach about visimes and sounds, there really aren't rules you can tie to *text*, because language is fluid, and no two people say the same word the same way, and often the same person doesn't say the same word the same way twice. All we've got are guidelines. Following are the ways I would take words and break down their sounds, as if they were spoken in a fairly "normal" way. With some example sounds that I have (which we'll use later on), I intentionally had the actors speak with accents or in heavy character style, so that this process of breaking down the sounds, not the text, would be more clearly understood.

Spelling, Respelling, and S-P-EH-L-IH-NG

You could break down the word *spelling* into components as listed above—as S-P-EH-L-IH-NG, P-EH-L-IH, S-P-EH-EE... and there really are a number of other ways to do it, too. When I say breaking the word down, I'm talking about saying it aloud and respelling, or at least re-thinking, it in a way that is represented with simpler components, some of which are visimes. Simpler is better. You want to look for the minimum that will be convincing, and then work the animation up to a higher level of detail instead of including everything and weeding out unnecessary animation.

There's no advantage to respelling words sound for sound with EEs and IHs and OOs. If you remember back to Chapter 1, where we saw that the word *pebble* is visually interchangeable with *mama* or *papa*, that's what I'm talking about here. In the word *spelling*, if the sound previous to the start of the word is anything *but* Closed, we can drop the S completely. S just needs to bare a little teeth or be a little Wide—almost anything covers that *when it's next to a Closed shape.*

If the S is the start of a sentence, or happens after a long silence, it needs some height and width. Next, the P in *spelling* is a visime, so we know we have to address it and how, with the mouth closed. For the end of the word, there are a number of ways to think of it, but in all iterations, it's an EE, IH, or NG, something that boils down to Wide, or Wider. Spelling can easily become S-P-EH-EE. In motion, in a sentence, that's all you'll need, at least as far as visimes go. EH isn't a visime, it's a function of the open mouth/jaw, so you can see we're really only dealing with S, Wide/Tall; then P, Closed; and EE, Wide. In regard to the dropped L sound, it's still in my mind, it's just not important to my initial breakdown of the sounds. There is a layering approach to sync, as I teach it, and the tongue is done in later stages.

With practice, you'll see that this modified spelling will help you think less about the text and more about the sound in your specific performance, something that will loosen up your sync and provide you less-rigid guidelines to work within. It's the way that I think it and do it, and it's why I'm no fan of phoneme-based sync. This is much easier, and more attuned to the performance than to the text. S-P-EH-EE is a much easier sequence of shapes to tackle than spĕlĭŋ, I'd say.

Following are some words and a middle stage of breakdown, so you can better see how they got where they ended up.

Word	First Pass	Final Breakdown
fountain	F-AH-OO-N-T-IH-N	F-AH-OO-IH
photograph	F-OH-T-OH-R-AH-F	F-OH-T-AH-F
shepherd	SH-EH-P-R-D	SH-EH-P-R
stop staring	S-T-OH-P S-T-EH-R-NG	S-OH-P S-EH-R-IH

Funneling

Funneling is really two processes you'll use, while working as I just described in the previous section. First, you can "funnel" non-visime sounds into visimes, such as Z to S, and D to T, and second, you "funnel" when you reduce multiple visimes into one.

The reason I identify so few visimes, as I use the term in this book, is to make it so that you don't have to memorize every little specific combination of letters and sounds. You just learn, in your own work, to *funnel* the sounds you hear into their closest visime relative. By giving you only seven main visimes to look for, I'm trying to guide you into thinking about all sounds more simply and finding ways to mash other sounds into those seven.

If you write *literacy* as L-IH-T-EH-R-AH-S-EE, you're doing all right in converting regular text to pieces that look like mine, but not so great at using the process to its fullest potential. One thing to try is clumping sounds, funneling them, as I did in my previous examples. IH, T, and EH, the second through fourth sounds, are very similar, and the L is of little importance visually, so quickly, in your own mind, think about whether you can cover them in one shape—something along the lines of Wider, or Wide—and represent it that way in your spelling. That would give you IH-R-AH-S-EE or EE-R-AH-S-EE. The next thing that jumps out is at the end of the word, that the S is a Wider, and the EE is a Wide. There's a good chance we could get away with IH-R-AH-EE. Look in the mirror and make up a sentence with the word *literacy* in it. At normal conversational speed, alternate the word *literacy* and the sounds "IH-R-AH-EE" as you repeat your sentence, and see if IH-R-AH-EE holds up visually. On my end, in my mirror, it does just fine.

I recommend guessing how I'll break words down, and then comparing your guess to what I've done. Look at the reasons and descriptions for what is different to see if there's something you maybe didn't think of. The more thought you put into the process at the beginning, the faster it becomes second nature.

The Best Order of Sync Operations

You know many of the steps, but now you'll learn the order to do them in, and why. I strongly recommend the order of hitting visimes first, then the Open/Closed, and then any advanced work, which I'll describe in the next section. The reason for that order is, I like to get work done fast, or at least get very far very fast. Giving yourself a quick start, you'll have more time to spend on the finishing touches. In my experience, the last 10% usually takes 50% of the time, so I like to sprint when I start, and give myself the most time for finesse as possible. Working in this order, and only having one goal at a time, you can defeat the tendency to get too deep into the process too early. The sync you have after working visimes, then Open/Closed, will by no means be finished, but it will be at the tuning stage fast, fast, fast.

I almost force myself to rush. Did I get the shape? Not quite the way I think I should have. Did I get it well enough? Yes. Move on. No love, no finesse, no babying of the material. It's all business to start with. All that art can come after you've laid down the basics. You have to trust yourself and know that you'll get to the details at a later time; for now, "no touchy!"

So the first part of the sync process is to work quickly through visimes and through Open/Closed. Oh, yeah, there's more to do, but let me show you how this much works before we push on.

Learn-While-Doing Sync: "Hey, buddy, I don't like your face"

The best way to learn is to do. So to demonstrate how you should sync—especially the order in which you should analyze sync—I'm going to show you how I do it. Before we use some real sound, let's explore what we'd do with a phrase, and what a nice one it is: "Hey buddy, I don't like your face." It's written to be followed along with any head or mouth, so you can proceed with just the Chapter 1 spline mouth, or come back when you've got a more robust face to work with. I won't give frame numbers to work on, as this is just text-based analysis—we're not as far as animation yet, but it's worth following in a scene for practice.

Following the recommended order, we will proceed with visimes and then with Open/Closed. Usually, this would be done over the entire scene, or at least in sentence-long chunks of a scene. For this example I'm going to treat each word like its own line. By shortening the return time on each word, you'll see more clearly why we can drop certain sounds in the visime stage, as we come back to pick them up with the Open/Closed.

In the written reductions of the words, I've cut out many "open mouth" sounds that I would usually leave in, to emphasize the different attention I give the two separate cycles. These sounds would usually stay in so that the text remains legible, but for the purposes of separating visimes from the product of Open/Closed, I've removed them. In later examples, they'll be left in. Also, I've gone through and shown a progression for the stages of my "S-P-EH-L-IH-NG," which will also not be the case in future examples; I'll usually just show the end result. Think of this as the place where I'm very explicit about all the stages and thought processes.

All that said, here's the process of breaking down "Hey buddy, I don't like your face" into visimes and Open/Closed:

hey (visimes) The order of the thought processes and the end result for visimes for this is: H-EH-EE → IH-EH-EE → IH-EE. What better way to start than with a special case? H is not a visime, and in most situations, it is ignored. When it cannot be ignored—a decision made by trying, and seeing that it doesn't look good—we funnel it over to IH, Wider. To spell the word out in terms closer to visime-only would be IH-EH-EE. Since EH is mostly a function of the mouth Open, it's dropped and the visimes left are just IH-EE, almost like "hi." Since IH is relative, and EE is not, IH will be right around the default width, maybe slightly wider, and the EE will be Wide. The whole word just goes from somewhat Wide to Wider. This covers the Wide/Narrow portion of visimes, but there's also the added dimension of the lips' height. There are no lips-in sounds, like B, M, P, but there are IHs and EEs. Both can benefit from some added height, so I'll add in some height, at an even level throughout the word.

hey (Open/Closed) The sequence here is semi-Closed, Open, semi-Closed. Since there is a flow of air during the H sound, we need the mouth open slightly to begin with. The main sound comes through the middle of the word, so that's where the jaw is most Open, and then we almost close up for the end. Just as I've described, this is basically animating the Open to the syllables. Of note here is how breaking the EH out of the middle of the H-EH-EE may have seemed weird above in visimes, because it ignored the EH sound, which is important. By adding the jaw in, during where the EH occurs in the word, we've created the EH sound even though it was not explicitly considered in the visimes. EE + Open = EH. This is the way we can eliminate too much to think about during the visime pass; the pieces come together in later passes, such as the Open/Closed and finesse.

buddy (visimes) B-UH-D-EE → B-UH-T-EE → B-UH-EE → B-EE. The logic here goes through several stages. First, the D gets funneled over to a T (which itself is the same as IH), as it's the closest shape in a sound relationship. Then, since the T and EE are pretty much the same, with no really big need for distinction (an artistic call), the T goes away to leave the EE alone. From there I removed the UH, as it's more a function of the jaw. All we're left with is B and EE. The B is mainly a function of the jaw, but also, for the lips to meet, there is obviously a lip height issue, so the B stays in.

buddy (Open/Closed) Closed, Open, semi-Closed, semi-Open, semi-Closed. The starting Closed is actually the same finishing Closed from the previous word. This bounces through Open/Closed twice, because there are two syllables. The motion is more subtle for the second half, I have concluded based on what looks good in my experience. In regular form, you might start with C, O, C, O, C, and then reduce the second syllable in the finessing stage; I'm just getting a head start, knowing from experience what usually looks best.

I (visimes) This is AH-EE or UH-EE, which reduces to just EE. This brings us to something new. The last visime is Wide, and so is this one. This is a job for opposites. That's something we'd usually leave for the finessing stage, but I want to answer as many up-front questions in this example as possible. To keep the two sounds more clearly separate, I recommend having a slight movement narrower between the sounds to keep each differentiated, but that's the kind of detail I would work out later.

I (Open/Closed) Sequence: Closed, Open, Closed. As you're probably coming to expect, this is just an Open/Closed based on syllables and with the first Closed just piggybacking on the previous word's last Closed. This Open will help put back in the UH or AH we ignored in the visime stage. See how well the two steps work together?

don't (visimes) Funnel this as: D-OH-OO-N-T → D-OH-OO-T → T-OH-OO-T → T-OO-OO-T → T-OO-T → OO-T. This is the first case where we're going to bridge across visimes in two words. As you can remove or "funnel" visimes of the same type inside of a word, you can do the same across words. The divisions in the words and sounds is something that we create in our writing, but isn't really there in the sound. Since the D is moved over to a T and the T comes out of an EE (from I), we'll just drop it. Next, the OH isn't really a visime, but it is a lesser strength of OO, so we'll think of it that way. When you do that, you end up with two OOs next to each other, and can drop one. The N isn't a necessary visual, so we'll just go straight to the T. All we're keying is a Narrow and then Wider.

don't (Open/Closed) This sequence is Closed, Open, Closed. Borrowing the first Closed from the end of I, this again is just representative of the syllable, and, with the Open happening as the mouth shape moves from Narrow to Wide, gives us our OH shape in the middle.

like (visimes) L-AH-EE-K → L-AH-EE → L-EE. L is a weird sound because it can't really be ignored, but it also has no specific look, besides the tongue, which we're not thinking about at this stage. Since L is sandwiched between two Wides—the T from the previous word and the EE in this one—I'm going to knock it back to slightly narrower. The AH will get created through the opening of the mouth, so we ignore it, and the K is insignificant, so we're just left with L-EE.

like (Open/Closed) Closed, Open, Closed. At this point, there's not much more to say about it!

your (visimes) EE-OH-R → EE-R. The OH leading into the R is really leading to the same shape, so we'll drop it and let the Open/Closed pick it up. Basically, we have Wide, Narrower.

your (Open/Closed) Closed, Open, Closed. Syllable-tastic!

face (visimes) F-EH-EE-S → F-EE-S → F-EE. The F is a visime, so it's not going anywhere. The EH is composed of the motion from one visime to another plus the jaw, so we drop it here. The S is not really going to be any wider or less wide than the EE, so it can be ignored, too. We're left with F-EE.

face (Open/Closed) Closed, Open, Closed. Borrow the Closed from the last word, Open and Close over the duration of the word.

Finessing Sync

Once you've done the basic analysis of visimes and Open/Closed that I've already talked about, the following sections take you through completing lip sync as far as instruction can take you. The total process looks like this:

1. Identify visimes.
2. Identify Open/Closed.
3. Identify relative shapes between absolute ones.
4. Insert opposites and steps.

That last mile is always going to be up to you and practice!

Weighting the Rules

Everything is relative. The rules I've laid out as absolutes and relatives seem clearly defined, but even the absolutes like Wide and Narrow are relative. There really isn't a hard-and-fast guarantee of the intensity of a shape being perfect for a word. The shapes built for a character may read as wider than for another. 50% Wide on Tito may be equal to 75% Wide on Jermaine. That would mean that Jermaine would need to be animated at slider/control levels 25% more extreme than Tito.

That is one of many variables that enter into the mix; another is the location of a visime in a phrase or word. If you have 5 EEs in a row, you've got a bit of a problem, as the mouth will essentially sit in the same Wide shape while the jaw goes through its motions. In a situation like that, you may need to reduce the effects of some of the EEs so that you can "step" into and out of the more extreme EEs, even though they're all EEs.

Relatives between Absolutes

When a visime such as T, S, or R, which are all relative to their surroundings, comes up between two absolutes of the same function, there's a conflict of rules. A Wider between two Wides isn't necessarily Wider. For example, a Wider between two Narrows is easy—it's Wider. A Wider between two defaults (the width in the default pose) will be Wider, as in *Shasta*. The S and T would be wider than the As.

That same Wider between two Wides? Might not be wider. There will be situations where it will possibly even go slightly Narrower. A T/S between two EEs will either get smaller or stay the same. The word *cheesy* gives a good example: CH-EE-S-EE. The S is by definition wider, but between two EEs, it should be made narrower to make those EEs look wider. The S's relative rules can bend to make the stronger rules appear stronger.

Opposites

Once you start "weighting the rules," other new ideas become available. First, using or identifying *opposites* is when you make the decision to create a keyframe in the opposite direction to strengthen the look of those shapes around it. If you've got a long stretch of repeated Wides, opposites would be dropping in Narrower keys between those. Sometimes this happens in place of a visime; sometimes it will happen between them, and you'll need to add keys.

Take the words *sheet metal*: SH-EE-T-M-EH-T-UH-L → EE-M-EH-T-UH. The M, part of B/M/P/Closed, has no real necessity in width. It can be a Smile, a Frown, or a Narrow—it just needs to be Closed. Since, in this case, it falls between an EE and an EH, which are both Wide, I'm going to choose to strengthen these Wides by narrowing the mouth during the M. This doesn't need to be a pucker, or even close to an OO, just narrower than the shapes surrounding it. That provides both surrounding shapes more identity as Wides. It's similar to the more global animation concept of anticipation, where you move left before you move right, to communicate better with your audience what's happening.

Stepping

Stepping is a cousin of opposites. The same situations and criteria evoke both opposites and stepping; it's a judgment call which technique to use. In opposites, if you see several Wides in a row, you might start dropping in Narrower keys between them. With stepping, instead of having three Wides at 100% each and three Narrower shapes between them, you'd make the first Wide a weaker wide, the second EE/Wide more than that, and, finally, you'd make the third the most intense. All you're doing is weakening the first time a shape hits, so that the next time it can have somewhere to go.

The word *believe* is a good example of stepping being very useful: B-EE-L-EE-V →
B-EE-EE-V. If I were to knock out one of the two EEs here, the word would probably be too
"floaty" through the middle, usually the case when the same visime repeats over multiple syllables. Instead of making both EEs the same, I'd make the first maybe 40% and the second
around 75%. The significance of that is that if I was just syncing the word *bee* all by itself, I
would likely use more EE than 40%, but for *believe*, by cutting EE back for the first of two
syllables I allowed the second to have an identity as an EE as well—I left myself more EE
range to move toward.

> Use opposites and stepping only when necessary. This method of identifying and correcting
> repetition just isn't necessary all of the time. If certain words or phrases look good repeating
> away, there's no need to add more complexity; it's when they look broken or ugly that you
> can turn to this!

Sync Subtleties

This section outlines some remaining tidbits and doo-dads for sync that don't really fit nicely
into any other sections. They are their own islands unto themselves, but useful information
just the same.

Cap the Ends

At one time, this was a step I would explicitly include in the process, but I'll state it once here
and be done with it. The first thing I do when I start any sync is to set keys on each and every
control slider on the first and last frames of the scene. In very long scenes, I'll often key all
sliders at the start and end of each phrase, just to make sure the face "cleans itself up" after
each section. I recommend that step one in your sync be "capping" the ends, of the scene and
phrases. It makes no real difference to the final product, but it makes maintenance of all your
sliders less intense as you work.

Earlier Is Better

Light travels faster than sound. I don't really know if it's that, or if it's the way that human
speech works and we need to get our mouth into position before we can make certain sounds,
but visuals happening before sounds is better. If you sync, as you should, exactly to the sound
on a frame-by-frame basis, your visuals will look late when played back with the sound. The
amount to push your visuals ahead, or your sound back, can vary from one to five frames, but
it's always going to look better, once you're done, to have the visuals happening very slightly
ahead of the sound. On a decision-making level, if you have a shape you're trying to hit, and the
sound is occurring between two frames, favor the earlier one—that, too, usually looks better.

Percussive Sounds

Certain visimes, mostly the percussive ones like B, M, and P, need to be shaped and released earlier than the sound. In some cases, they even need to be held for a few frames, so that it's very obvious that there was a hold and a release. The reason is that the sound is actually made in the release of the shape, not the creation of the shape. If a B, M, or P doesn't look quite right, just shuffle it up a couple of frames earlier, and/or hold it for a few frames.

Oh Yeah, Almost Forgot the Tongue!

The mouth has a set of visimes, the tongue has its own. To include the tongue in the main visimes would push the level of complication out again, and that's not something I want to do. The tongue should be one of the last things you do in regard to sync. Its own set of visimes is more phonetic and looks like what's laid out below. Of very important note: Do not animate the tongue like a tail! Most animators given the chance to do some overlapping animation will jump all over it. If you do that with the tongue, it looks awful. Just…just don't be a statistic.

L, N, D, T, S, C, EE These will all involve the tongue moving up in the mouth.

TH This type of sound, and sometimes S and T sounds, will push the tongue forward in the mouth, sometimes even poking out between the teeth.

Wasn't that easy?

LOADING SOUND IN MAYA

Loading sound in Maya is a two-step process after you've loaded a scene with a lip-sync head. In your scene, go to File → Import. Browse to the audio file you want to use, and then hit the Import button; your sound is now in your scene environment but not yet set up to play.

To hear the sound play back, right-click over the timeline, and from the Sound submenu select the name of the sound file you just loaded.

If your playback settings are set to real time, Window → Settings/Preferences → Preferences → Timeline, play back the scene as you usually would, and you'll hear the sound. To get a good approximation of the length of the sound, you should set the end time of your scene to accommodate the sound. Just look at the waveform; where it visually ends, the sound's done!

Sync Example 1: "What am I sayin' in here?"

On the companion CD, open the file WhatAmISayingInHere.aif. (You are welcome to animate as we go, or just read through and come back to do this later.) The sound clip says, "What am I saying in here?" What we're going to do is simply listen for visimes, pick a frame for each, and move forward.

A couple of process tidbits about these examples. First, I'm working at 24 frames per second. Second, the little mouth graphics with each word are *not* what your mouth should look precisely like; they're icons, schematic representations of what the sounds would look like after completion. And third, the number of images for each word does not reflect anything except the number of images I felt I needed in order to show you the *motion*. If I were to cut out all but just the visimes, you might not get a sense of the animation, but sometimes the visimes are all that is necessary.

Identifying Visimes

On the timeline and waveform (Figure 4.12), I've shown visimes using a line with a triangular head. This will represent any visime, be it Wide, Narrow, Tall, or otherwise. (A marker for each would get a little bit kooky.) This symbol will be reused throughout the book for showing where the visimes occur in the sound.

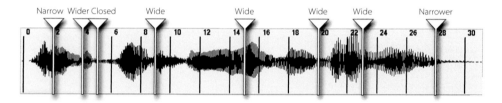

Figure 4.12

Sound waveform, with visime keys marked, for "What am I doin' in here?"

Following is my interpretation of the sounds.

If you are following along using a mouth or head setup, key no jaw motions yet. Key only Wide/Narrow and lip height shapes (lips).

what: OO-UH-T The first word, *what,* I would break down as OO-UH-T. Since UH gets nixed as a visime (it's a jaw movement), that leaves us with only two visimes to key for the word: OO and T—Narrow and Wider, respectively. Easy enough; let's go find them in the sound. After scrubbing through a few times, I've got them on frames 2 and 4.

Frame 1   Frame 2   Frame 3   Frame 4   Frame 5

"Scrubbing" refers to dragging the time slider of a program back and forth to hear the sound and watch the visuals forward or backward, fast or slow depending on how fast you move the time slider. It is another way to play back audio or video with a flexible frame rate, without hitting the Play button. It is common practice, and highly recommended, to scrub frequently while lip-syncing.

am: AH-M AH, being mostly an Open sound, gets no attention yet, so all we have is lips closed, for M on frame 5. Be sure that any height given to the lips is removed, or even rolled in, and we'll come back to key the jaw in the Open/Closed pass. There is no specific width for any of the sounds in *am*.

Frame 4   Frame 5

I: UH-EE EE is a visime (Wide) and UH is not. A Wide key on frame 9 should do it.

Frame 6   Frame 7   Frame 8   Frame 9   Frame 10

saying: S-EH-IH-N N doesn't enter into the equation, but it's there for an easier read. If we just leave visimes, all we have is S, Wider, on frame 10, and something to cover both EH and IH, Wide, on frame 15.

Frame 10   Frame 11   Frame 12   Frame 13   Frame 14   Frame 15

in: IH-N IH is Wider and Taller, but since it's next to a proper Wide, in *saying,* it shouldn't go wider, as that would diminish the previous Wide. In these situations, one option—and what we will do here—is to simply hold the shape. This is like stepping on a very small scale. On frame 20, use the same Wide value as on frame 15.

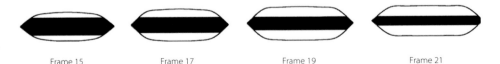

Frame 15   Frame 17   Frame 19   Frame 21

here: H-EE-R H isn't a visime, but it helps us read the word. We get an EE, Wider, on frame 23, and an R, Narrower on frame 28.

Frame 21   Frame 23   Frame 25   Frame 27   Frame 29

And there you have it—visimes, the first layer of sync in this method. If you *are* following along, you may think you've done something wrong, as this doesn't look right at all; to play it back looks quite mumbly. Yes, you are doing it right. It just takes the addition of the jaw before it looks like much. Now we're going to layer in the motion of the jaw.

Identifying Open/Closed

On the timeline and waveform (Figure 4.13), I've denoted Closed keys with a flat-headed line and Open with a circular-headed line. Later, you will see ovular heads on some lines, which means semi-Open. These, like the triangular visime symbols, will be reused throughout the book. The Open/Closed keys get more detailed representation than the visimes because there are not as many positions to describe, and they're not as obtrusive.

Open/Closed are much easier to identify and animate than visimes, and it will help to make this mumbly mess take shape as a speaking mouth. Here, listen for the syllables. Simply listen for sounds that can only be made with the mouth open. In other words, just set Opens and Closeds based on syllables. In many cases, we need not set the Closed key at the start of the word if the previous word ends with a Closed, which most do. Not doubling up keys like that makes it easier to clean all this up in the end.

> If you are following along using a mouth or head built and set up using this book, only set jaw keys in this section.

what: OO-UH-T Closed (frame 2), Open (frame 3), Closed (frame 4). Line up the Closeds with the OO and the T, and plant the Open in the middle. Remember, it's just syllables we're looking for, and each one gets an Open/Closed cycle.

Figure 4.13

Waveform with Open/Closed keys

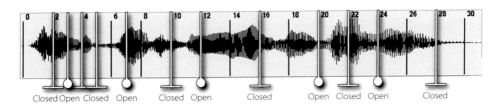

am: AH-M Open on the A, Closed on the M (frame 5) is the obvious choice, but since the A doesn't actually have a frame of its own, it shares a frame with the T. For now, I'll leave it Closed, as from the T, and come back to clean it up when I finesse the work.

I: UH-EE Following along by syllable, this one's Open on UH (frame 7) and Closed on EE (frame 10). There's nothing but basic work here.

saying: S-EH-IH-N Officially, the word *saying* has two syllables, but in this delivery (the only one that matters) the actor has said "sayin" rather quickly, in one long syllable, almost as if he had said "sain"—so it's a one-syllable word, and that's how I've broken it down. Open on frame 12, Closed on frame 16.

in: IH-N Open on the IH (frame 20), Closed on the N (frame 22); easy stuff.

here: H-EE-R Open through the EE (frame 24), Closed on the R (frame 28).

Now we're getting closer. You may have noticed that in not all cases did I put the syllable opening for a sound on the same frame as the visime for that sound. It reflects the nature of the two cycles—they are not necessarily going to be having all details occurring at the same time, and it's just another of the many reasons we attack visimes separately from Open/Closed.

Finessing

This is where we turn mostly to our function curves (otherwise known as FCurves). I like to use FCurves to see what can be done to our sync to make it better. To open the Graph Editor and see your curves, select the sliders/controls whose curves you want to see and go to the Window menu, and select Window → Animation Editors → Graph Editor.

If you look at the timeline in Figure 4.14, you can see I've added several "Narrower" marks with a V-shaped head. These marks will show shapes that are not explicitly their own visime, but are visime-like additions for any number of reasons; mostly, those marks will reflect opposites and stepping.

At this stage, the work becomes less directional. You can move through in frame order, but I find that by looking at the whole, and attacking the most offensive pieces, I can quickly narrow down what I need to make the sync look good.

Figure 4.14

Waveform with sub-visimes marked

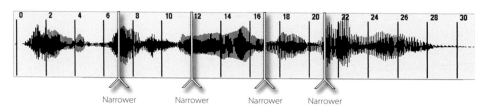

Inserting Opposites or Stepping

Looking at the animation and the Graph Editor, you may notice that after frame 2, we move wider and stay at EE/Wide all the way until the end of the sound, where we finally move narrower with the R in *here*. In animation, this means the mouth is Wide, and flapping its jaw during all of that time—not so good. As I explained with opposites, it can be as important to key *out* of shapes as it is to key into shapes themselves.

In this instance, we have five EEs or Wides in a row. To remedy this, we can just drop in opposites. In between the EEs, drop in Narrower keys, not full OOs—but you get the idea.

The frames I'll say need Narrower keys are 7, 12, 17, and 21. This I decided by picking the middle frame between the offending visimes, and if there's a decision made favoring one frame or another—if the *middle* is actually between frames—picking the earlier one.

The Tongue

Since the tongue is incredibly simplistic, we can look at the phrase as a whole and just target the sounds that should be addressed. "What am I sayin' in here?" should have the tongue up on the T in *what*, the S and N in *sayin'*, and the N in *in*. Easy as pie. If you want to get really fancy, you can push it a little bit forward for the T and the S, but do it slightly early, so that the audience can see it. If you wait for the sound, the teeth are blocking the view!

What Bothers Me

Watching the scene as it is now, a few things still bother me, and that's where I'll focus my attention. It's always good practice to decide everything you like and don't like before just steaming ahead with fixes. It keeps you more on track. Here's a short list of my concerns right now:

- The first word, *what,* seems to start late.
- I don't like the "long" or "held" Closed between the T in *what* and the M in *am*.
- The two Ns on *sayin* and *in* don't need to close all the way, as they do.

With the first issue, the *what* seeming to start late, the solution is very simple once we look at our jaw (Open/Closed) curve, which is pictured in Figure 4.15.

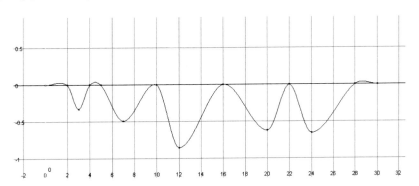

Figure 4.15

Uncleaned FCurve

The jaw is held closed up until the OO in *what*. The simplest way to get a word to seem to start earlier is to open the mouth or move into the visime shape earlier. Since the Open is quite obviously held back until frame 3, I'd try first opening that earlier. What I would do here is delete the Closed key on frame 2. Your curve should look something similar to Figure 4.16. The word now seems to come out at the right time.

The next thing I didn't like was at the end of the same word. The T, held Closed next to the M, didn't look good to me. The Open/Closed seems to be the culprit again. In Figure 4.16, you should see that the Open is held for two frames. This is for the end of the syllable in *what* and the M in *am*. If you have to choose between dropping a jaw motion (Open/Closed) and a visime, favor the visime—lose the Open/Closed. Delete the Closed key for the T, and look at your animation again. The curve should appear as it does in Figure 4.17.

The final big complaint I had with this was the closing up completely on the Ns in *sayin* and *in*. To look at the jaw curve and modify it is easy. Figure 4.18 shows the fix.

Figure 4.16

I deleted the Closed key at frame 2 to make the effect of the Open creep in sooner.

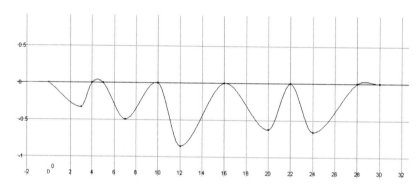

Figure 4.17

Another deleted key, at frame 4

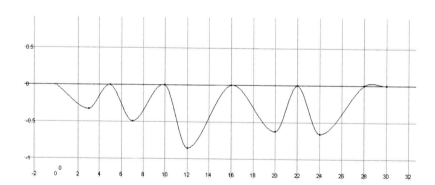

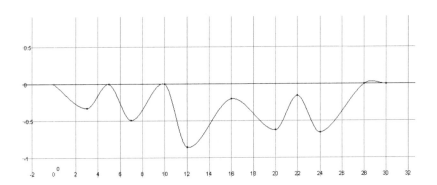

Figure 4.18

Moving the key on frame 16 down in the graph editor

This wraps up the distance I can take you with instruction as far as the basics of sync go. The rest is up to you and your own artist's eye. In Chapter 13, "A Shot in Production," I'll go through and do more of this detailed work, and discuss what I'm doing and why, but after the point we've reached here, it really is just your own flair that takes it to finished. Well, that and practice. There shouldn't be too much further to go before you're doing sync that's very impressive. Emotion comes into this, and getting all sorts of neat asymmetry and character into the work, but that gets covered in Chapter 13, where we bring all the pieces together in a scene. For now, let's keep practicing this sync thing.

Sync Example 2: "Was it boys?"

On the CD, find the sound file `WasItBoys.aif`, and I'll take you through another round of sync. Remember, we'll go through and get all the visimes, come back once for the Open/Closed, and then wrap it all up with some final touches when we finesse it.

Identifying Visimes

The entire phrase reads "Was it boys?" (Figure 4.19 presents this sentence as a keyed wave-form.) Let's get right to it!

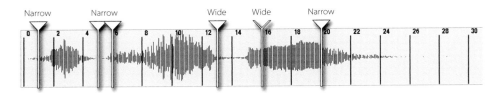

Figure 4.19

Waveform with visimes for "Was it boys?"

was: OO-UH-Z OO is a visime, so on frame 1, put a Narrow key. UH can be forgotten, as it will get attention in the next pass. Z gets "funneled" over to S, Wider, on frame 5.

it: IH-T The only visime here is the T (frame 8), which is Wider.

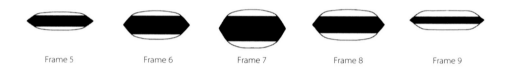

boys: B-OH-EE-Z B being a percussive sound means we'll have it happen early, and hold for a frame, too. Since the B *sound* hits on frame 15, we're going to set the lips portion of the Closed (the lip height) on 13, and hold it for 14. That's two keys. OH is just a combination of Open and OO/Narrow, so it appears as Narrow, or like a weak OO would, on frame 17. EE is a visime and gets a key on 25. Z, which is basically S, is Wider, and that falls around frame 28.

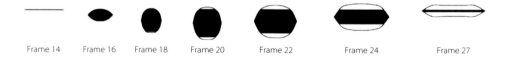

Okay, check your watch. That should have only taken a minute or two. Neat, huh?

Identifying Open/Closed

Let's quickly move on forward with the Open/Closed, plotted in Figure 4.20.

was: OO-UH-Z Closed on the OO (frame 1), Open on the UH (frame 4), Closed again on the Z (frame 5).

it: IH-T Open for the IH (frame 7), Closed for the T (frame 9). Don't bother with a Closed at the head of this syllable, as it's usually best to piggyback on the previous word's last Closed if you can.

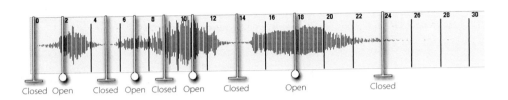

Figure 4.20

Waveform with Open/Closed for "Was it boys?"

boys: B-OH-EE-Z The B needs to be Closed (frame 14), to work in tandem with our visime pass, and the Z needs to be Closed (frame 27), as it caps the end of our word, but that's a big long space between those. We'll just drop in an Open key right in the middle (frame 20) and leave the tweaking for our next step. Gotta move!

Finessing

Before proceeding, watch your animation several times over. Look at the big picture, not the details. Find the things that bother you. If you've picked out some things you don't like, that's good; it gives you focus as you proceed. As I illustrated with *pebble* in Chapter 1, avoid frame-by-frame analysis: you'll end up fixing everything, and over-animating so that the mouth is popping into extremes too quickly. Let's continue through our process. I'll fix the things that bother me, and hopefully that will tackle most of your concerns, too.

Inserting Opposites or Stepping

Looking for ugly repeats, we'd have two in this phrase. With the two Wides on frames 5 and 8, we should drop in a Narrower key on frame 6, and between the two Wides on frames 25 and 28, we can add another Narrower key on 26 (Figure 4.21). In this case, the amount that you will want to key opposite, or Narrower, looks best when you do it very slightly—or just hold the previous key, otherwise known as stepping. That's what I meant when I said that the exact same situations can lead you to use opposites or stepping; it's always going to be an artistic decision as to which one to use.

The Tongue

In "Was it boys," the two S sounds are going to get some lift and maybe a little bit of "out" motion.

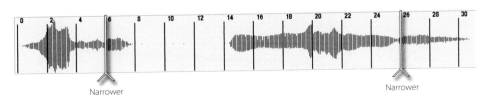

Figure 4.21

Waveform with sub-visimes for "Was it boys?"

What Bothers Me

If I were to make a list of complaints, watching the animation, they would be these:

- I don't particularly like any of the Closeds (except for the B) in the scene; they seem *too* closed.

- I really dislike the long Closed between frames 9 and 14.

- There's an odd bounce or jitter near the end between frames 25 and 30.

For the overall closed problem, there's a simple solution. Make the Closeds not quite so closed. Starting with the first instance that doesn't look good—the Closed on frame 5—the curve, shown in Figure 4.22, provides two options.

Option one is that we can simply pull the Closed to less than closed, but then we have a bit of a bounce that is unattractive. This is starting to look like a good place for some stepping again. I pulled the Open on frame 4 a little more closed and pulled the Closed key on frame 5 down toward it, to make it look like Figure 4.23.

> There is no rule that you cannot revisit previous stages of your work. If you've already gone through an initial pass of opposites and stepping but think that another round of them will help a problem you see afterward, jump back into using those techniques!

Figure 4.22

Uncleaned curve

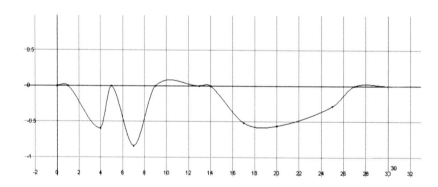

Figure 4.23

Here I stepped the curve on frames 4–5.

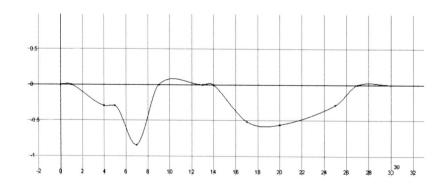

On to the second Closed, which is actually linked heavily with the second problem I listed. The long hold between 9 and 14 is ugly. The easiest way to make a hold that is held too long look better is to shorten it! I'm going to do that by moving the key on frame 9 to frame 10, as in Figure 4.24.

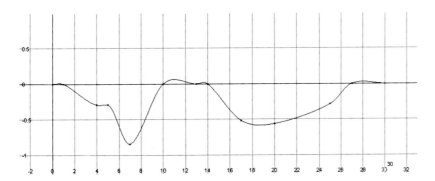

Figure 4.24

I moved the key from frame 9 to frame 10.

The initial fix we set out to do here is to reduce the amount of Closed. Next, I'd hold the mouth Open a little bit until the B in boys, as shown in Figure 4.25.

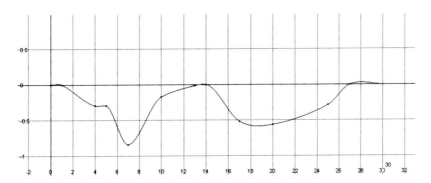

Figure 4.25

The key on frame 9 was pulled down.

Last but not least in our Closed massacre, just go ahead and delete the Closed key on frame 27 (Figure 4.26), letting the mouth taper to Closed to the end of the scene.

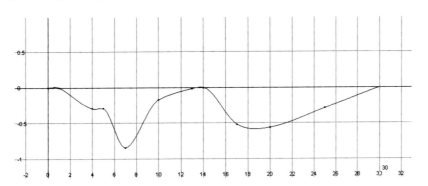

Figure 4.26

I deleted the key on frame 27.

We've addressed concerns one and two, so now we're left with the odd jitter at the end of the word *boys* (frames 25 to 30). As you've likely picked up on, my approach will be to look to the curves for the cause of the problem. In Figure 4.27, we've got both our Narrow/Wide and Open/Closed curves shown.

Looking at the curves from 25 to 30, it's obvious that it's the Wide/Narrow curve that is the delinquent. We actually inserted the key on 26 during our opposites pass, and then the mouth returns to default, as we keyed it to the end (or at least we should have as our first step—remember "Cap the ends"?). The result is a wobbly back and forth that's no good. There are two things we could do: delete some keys and smooth it, or try to step into the shape. Fewer keys is better, so my choice, and one that works, is to just delete the erroneous key and smooth what's left. Smooth curve = smooth motion. See Figure 4.28.

There you have it. We've now gone through two basic lip sync animations, which should get you off to a good start, but the expertise is going to come with practice. There will be more of the same in Chapter 13, where I take you through whole scenes—and in that case, we'll go far beyond just sync—but if you'd like more immediate practice, there are many sound files available to experiment with on the CD. In fact, at this point, almost all the CD contents involving sync and sound are fair game; go play!

Figure 4.27

Looking at the curves can help pinpoint problems in animation, like the odd movement between frames 25 and 30.

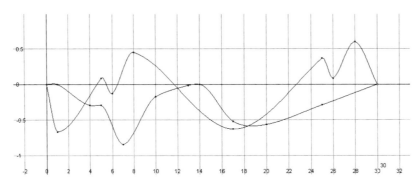

Figure 4.28

The errant key removed, making the area between 25 and 30 smoother.

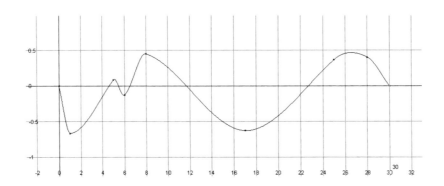

CHAPTER 5

Constructing a Mouth

Now you may be wondering why, five chapters into the book—almost halfway through—we're now taking our first look at modeling. You need to model before you can animate, right? True, but if you don't know what your model needs to do, it's likely not going to work well for that task.

With the simple spline mouth in Chapters 1 ("Learning the Basics of Lip Sync") and 4 ("Visimes and Lip Sync Technique"), there was something that worked well with little effort: the mixing of the different shapes. They cooperated. You could have both the Wide/Narrow and Closed at 100%, and the mouth didn't look too bizarre. Since we're not going to build a shape for every phoneme, but simply the elements to create the major visimes, the shapes built have to fit into some technical restrictions to make them cooperate just like the spline mouth. The shape of your character's mouth can be anything you like, but the point layout has to be capable of what you want the face to do. Having points arranged in a way that allows movement makes everything at every stage of the work easier.

- ■ **The best point layout**

- ■ **Building the lips and surrounding mouth area**

- ■ **Building the nose**

- ■ **Building the teeth and tongue**

The Best Point Layout

I can't very well just tell you to put a certain point in a certain place for all situations, because every character and every face is different. The best point layout isn't a roadmap I can draw for you, it's an idea. The best point layout is always the one that, in wireframe, looks as if you can see your character's facial muscles.

Terminology check: When I say *point layout* I am referring to the arrangement, the pattern, in which points create an object. *Points* can refer to CVs or vertices, any control point on a mesh or patch.

Do you remember in Chapter 3 ("Facial Landmarking") where I talked about how the Smile, Frown, and Scowl all need the same points? That was talking about the layout, not a specific shape. Building a model of my own face, I can just look at a picture or mirror, make a smile and frown, and easily know where I've got to have the points; I can see where the creases are. With anything that's not human, or even a human character that's not derived from photos, you're going to need a good idea of how that character will smile, frown, and scowl before you even finish building the model in its default bored pose. Luckily, as I mentioned back with the smile, frown, and scowl, the point layout needs across all characters and emotions are pretty much the same.

As we proceed through this chapter, spend your effort maintaining the point layout, not necessarily the exact shapes you see in the pictures.

Modeling in Circles

You're going to be seeing a lot of circles. Everything to do with important point layout is always going to be concentric circles—the mouth, and later the eyes, all have point layouts that circle them. Not all meshes are going to be perfect circles—in fact, most won't—but the point *layout*, the way the points all connect together, should be very close to perfect circles. Figure 5.1 is a face model with bad point layout.

The reason that Figure 5.1's layout is wrong is that, yes, the point layout is *clean*, and there are circles around the mouth, but it doesn't readily facilitate facial movement. Creasing in the right areas would be almost impossible, as those areas are vertically gridded and do not follow a layout even vaguely similar to any expression or emotion. Figure 5.2 shows what I prefer, and here's why: good point layout isn't simply to model cleanly, it is to model *for movement*.

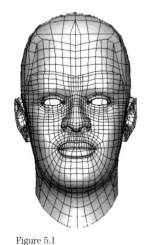

Figure 5.1

Clean, but bad, point layout for a face

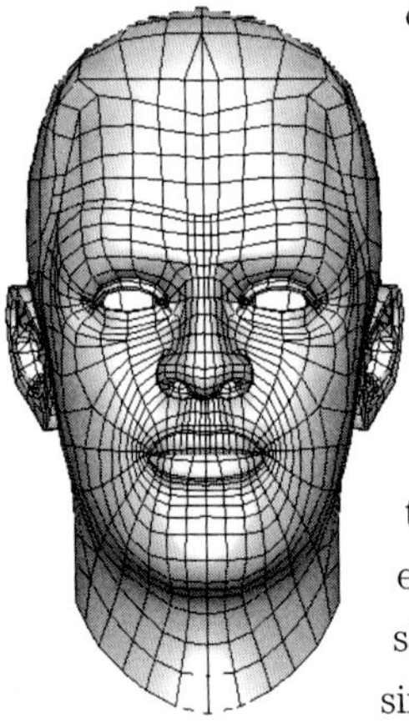

Figure 5.2

A layout that lines up with where the creases will be is a good foundation for building heads.

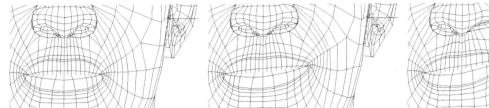

Figure 5.3

This layout provides important feedback as to what the face is doing, even in wireframe.

Modeling for Movement

For facial keys to look good in motion, they have to be modeled out of the default shape in such a manner that everything *between* the default and the extreme keys looks natural; this is why circles in the layout, properly placed, are good. Besides better matching the movement of the face, the circular point layout lets you, the creator of these shapes, keep track of where your model has stretched and what's been compressed, because you can see your points at even, regular intervals that relate to the movement. See Figure 5.3 for a default-to-smirk transition that works. Even though the face is not shaded, you can see where the creasing occurs, where there has been a stretch between rows, and where points have been forced together.

All this is to say that there really is a right and a wrong way to build your face for *your* shapes the way *you* want them to look. If the importance of this hasn't yet made an impression, gimbal lock provides a CG-centric example. Sometimes, when you're animating near "gimbal lock," you set two keys on a character's arm and the in-between motion turns out as some strange wiggle and flip movement. That's because visually the two keys looked to make sense from one to the next, but mathematically they're very different. Facial keys can work the same way. It's not just the key that makes it look good—it's how you got there and where you came from.

Gimbal lock is the name for when two of your three rotation axes—X, Y, and Z—are in very similar planes. The effect is that two of your rotations produce the same movement, and one of your rotations seems to be missing (as it's lined up with another!)

EASIER IS BETTER

Something you never want to do is fight your layout in the key shape stage (Chapter 6, "Mouth Keys"). If building a particular key shape, such as a smile or frown, proves too difficult and seems as if it will just not work, the layout is likely not right. This is a theory of mine: If it's too hard, you're doing it the wrong way. You can always grunt your way through issues, willpower always prevails, but if you can make your life easier, it's best to. There's nothing wrong with backing up a few steps and fixing an underlying problem; in the long run, it'll save you time.

By keeping close track of what we're doing and how, we can minimize the work that is involved in fixing problems related to awkward layout.

If I were to give you explicit tutorials on every kind of different character, this book would be a lot more expensive, weigh a ton, and take eons to read. What I'll do instead is frame everything, as I have thus far, on concepts, and lean heavily on reality for the reasoning behind them. The rules for layout, however, are very global and do apply to all styles.

Building the Lips

Lips for a human character should be arranged approximately the same way whether you're working in Maya, Softimage, 3ds max, or Hash, with polys, subDs, NURBS, or Hash splines. Artistically, it's the same whether you're working from rotoscopes or design drawings, or just winging it. We'll start on this lip model with just a circle. In most 3D instruction, you'd start the entire head with a sphere or a cube, or any other number of things, but not here—we're doing it with a circle. We'll build the important parts, mainly the eyes and the mouth, that need to be built a certain way, and then connect the *bridge* areas to fit. The reasoning is simple: Whatever you start with finds its characteristics in the final model, and a circle is more forgiving than a sphere when it comes to the mouth.

We're going to build the mouth open, model the hard stuff while it's easy to get at, and then compress it down. After the lips are finished we'll move on to the surrounding mouth area, to include the tip of the nose and the area on the face that creases.

Getting Started

Start with an 18-point circle. The circle can be linear or smooth, it doesn't matter—remember, point layout is all that matters. You'll be able to easily turn this into polys or subD surfaces afterward. Create the circle so that it faces the front view (flat from the side and top views).

Figure 5.4

Pull back the points that are near to the Y-axis (a), then pull back the adjacent points as well (b).

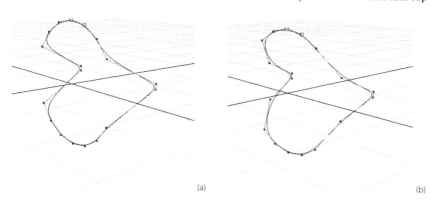

(a)　　　　　　　　　　　　(b)

Vertically flatten and pull back the points that are near to the Y-axis, so your "circle" looks like the one in the first part of Figure 5.4. Now select the points directly up and down from the ones you just moved. Pull them back some; try to make a shape that looks like the second image in the figure.

> I always work in Y up. If you're getting results that don't match mine, check to see whether you have another axis up.

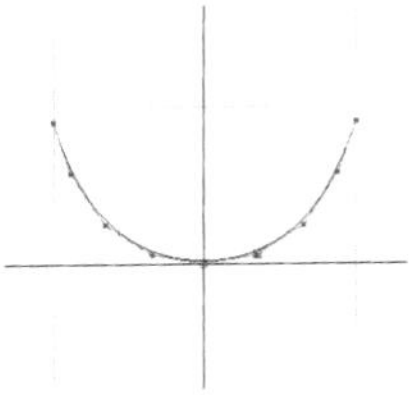

We're going to shape this line, as viewed from the *top*, into a semicircle, so pull points as needed until you get something like Figure 5.5.

Your profile has changed as a result of our work in the top view. Move points in *Y only* (vertically), so as not to disturb the shape as viewed from the top, until you get a shape like Figure 5.6(a). Then duplicate the curve, and scale it to about 0.85 uniformly in X, Y, and Z. Translate the curve back a little in Z (b).

Duplicate the outside curve, the largest one, and this time scale the duplicate larger uniformly and pull it back in Z. Create a surface out of all three curves. You should have a shape that looks like Figure 5.7.

Making the Structure Accurate

The first hurdle is already behind us—now I'll explain what it was. To look at real lips without analyzing them too heavily, they appear to be almond shaped. The lips in Figure 5.8 appear thick and plump near the center and then taper to thin edges where lips meet at the sides.

This analysis isn't wrong, it's just incomplete. If I open my mouth slightly (Figure 5.9), you see some more.

Figure 5.5
_____

Sculpt the spline into a semicircle, as viewed from the top.

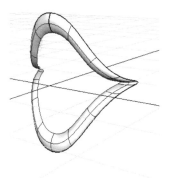

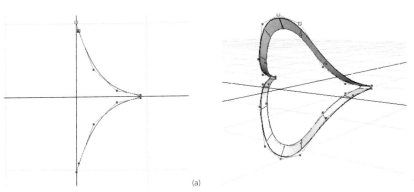

(a)

(b)

Figure 5.6
_____

Fix the profile (a), then duplicate, scale, and translate to get (b).

Figure 5.7
_____

The three curves lofted

Figure 5.8

A closed mouth

Figure 5.9

An open mouth

Figure 5.10

A view of the lips turning inward

Do you see it? That outside edge where the lips taper thinner doesn't exist! The lips don't gradually turn into a point at the sides; they actually turn *inward* into the mouth. *In, not thin.* Well, they thin a little bit, but the main reduction of the mass comes from where the lips *go*—inside. This might be clearer from Figure 5.10. The lips are part of the inside of the mouth, not a separate entity. Think of the lips like cuffs on pants.

What you see is actually the inside of the pants on the outside, not something else pasted on top. I think of the lips as facing each other, not just sitting on top of one another. If we were to build a mouth to look only like Figure 5.11, sure, we'd have a mouth, but not one capable of much—when it opened it wouldn't look natural, probably too wide and not very fleshy. Certain shapes, Narrow especially, would be very difficult to build, and not mix well with other shapes.

Artistic Side Effects of Structure

You've already created a shape that will lead to some interesting detail; I'll point out how. If you look at a person in profile, they have little areas at the very corners of their mouth that are in shadow. By building the model according to the methods outlined here, that usually happens for free, it's a side effect (Figure 5.12). This detail brings finesse to a character, and it's very often overlooked.

CREATING A SURFACE

In every program the details will be different, but creating a surface should be easy. In Maya, what you'd do to create a surface from curves is *loft* the curves using Surfaces → Loft in the modeling module. Use the command after selecting the curves in the order you want them lofted.

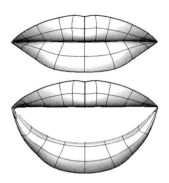

Figure 5.11

A mouth built with the points converging at the sides, closed and open

Figure 5.12

The sides of the mouth pull inward and create a shadow.

Figure 5.13

The mouth has depth; it is not flat on the "front" of the face.

Also notice that we modeled the mouth in a semicircle as viewed from the top view. One of the keys to good facial models is proper depth. There is no *front* to a face, or *sides*, it's all a single curved surface (Figure 5.13 demonstrates this). It's common practice in drawing to think of the face in planes—it makes the faking of perspective easier, and simplifies the process of creating perspective, with great-looking results. We in CG, on the other hand, get the perspective for free, so we have to supply that perspective with a pretty accurate model, and proper depth.

Defining the Lips

Let's start to give these lips some shape. Insert isoparms just left and right of the center on the upper lip and pull the topmost new points up and inward, defining the lower edge of the philtrum (the little divot under your nose). Reshape some of the outside points to create a shape like Figure 5.14a. Then manipulate the outside row of points on the lower lip to plump the center up more than the sides, as in Figure 5.14b.

Duplicate the inside row, scale it bigger uniformly, and translate it back in Z. This is now your lips' inner edge (Figure 5.15). Skin' em up!

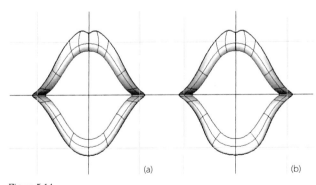

(a)

(b)

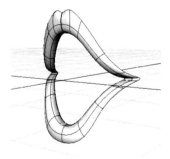

Figure 5.14

The upper lip starting to take shape (a), and the lower lip being plumped (b).

Figure 5.15

The lips with the inside row attached

Setting the Default Position

By now we've got what we need to properly shape and size the lips, but we'll need to close the mouth. To look at it simply, we just need to scale the whole object smaller vertically (Y), but if we were to do that, Figure 5.16 shows that the lips would thin quite unattractively as we went.

To start selecting points in that tighter object to repair the look would not be very fun, either. What we'll do is prepare for that thinning by fattening the lips up, scaling the inside rows first (Figure 5.17a). By pre-fattening them, we can get them closer to where we want them after they're thinned! *Now* we can grab the whole thing and shrink it down into the right proportion, something like Figure 5.17b.

We made preparations for the change, but there's still likely some prettying up to do. Spend a few minutes applying your artist's touch to the lips. Figure 5.18 is where I ended up with mine. I brought down the curviness of the profile, made them less wide across (about 40% less), and brought down the general cartooniness of the curves. I also pulled the lower lip back, since in most people the upper lip protrudes farther than the lower one. I had you build the lips into the shape I did, so they're flexible going into a variety of styles; I've just chosen to go more realistic with the visuals in the rest of my example.

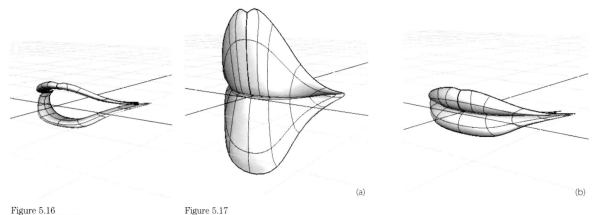

(a)   (b)

Figure 5.16

If we were to scale the shape down in Y

Figure 5.17

The bizarre-looking pre-fattened lips (a), and lips at a more attractive scale (b)

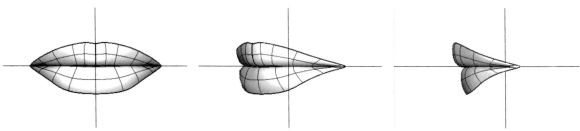

Figure 5.18

A little sculpting helps out.

This is the point where, even though I will refer to the images printed here and talk as if you're working with identical ones, you can start to diverge into your own character's face. The main thing to watch for is structure; the exact shape can be different.

Transitioning the Lips to the Face

From here, duplicate the outside line, scale it larger, and pull it back in Z, doing both slightly (Figure 5.19). This will define the edge where the lips meet the face. We're adding this line of points to create that edge. It shouldn't be uniformly distant from the previous outside row all the way around—in fact, on the sides of the mouth, near the corners, it should be quite smooth, and therefore more spaced out. All you need to do is spread the points out from each other on the sides, leaving the more central points tighter together.

Take the new outside line and duplicate it. Scale it larger in X and Y, then pull it back in Z. Soften the border to be more ovular and less like the shape of the lips. The profile of lips should really start to emerge, as in Figure 5.20.

Finishing Up the Lips

As I'm sure you're used to doing by now, duplicate the outside row, scale it up, and add it into the shape. The outside edge should be reshaped so it looks like Figure 5.21. At this point we're really working on the face more than the lips. Spend some time sculpting the face further; the outside edge should be quite ovular.

Now, one pretty invisible but important detail should be added. Duplicate and scale up the row that ends on the inside of the mouth, and loft the whole thing back together. Right now, you can't see that much into the mouth, but later, there are key shapes that will expose the "end" of your face, if you don't add another row to play with.

There you go! These lips are ready to be changed into any character's shape you want! The lips we just built aren't the end-all be-all ready-for-feature CGI Holy Grail—that's up to you, and the character you want to create—but these lips' malleability when it comes to key shapes will be flawless, and as I said earlier, that's the important thing: to build for motion.

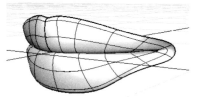

Figure 5.19

Adding the lips' edge and tweaking

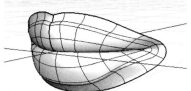

Figure 5.20

Moving beyond the lips

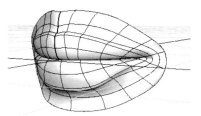

Figure 5.21

The first steps working on the face

Building the Surrounding Mouth Area

A mouth can't do a whole lot all alone, so it's best we go ahead and build further out into the face to include the area that creases, where the good stuff really happens in animation. We'll make many facial expressions possible by building the face to be able to crease, as I made such a fuss about in Chapter 3.

Picture the way a dust mask fits on someone's face, the area that it covers. From the lips we just built, we'll build out to that area of the face. You should have a good idea of what you want your character to look like before beginning this step. If that involves changing the lips, do it first, it'll be easier than doing it afterward.

Getting Started

With the lips, we built steadily from the inner lines outward, but here we'll go to the outer edge, and work back in. The first step for us here is to duplicate the outside spline, and reshape it as the border of that dust mask shape I described, including where it would go over the nose. For now, ignore details like the nostrils. The nose can be a lump—we'll add greater detail later.

If you plan on matching your model to a photograph, now is a great time to load it into your scene, as we're starting to make some real shape decisions.

I've talked a lot about creasing, and that's what this outside "dust mask" spline will be involved in: creating the outside border of the creases in the key shapes we'll make next, in Chapter 6. Go ahead and include the spline in the shape (Figure 5.22).

Add in a row/isoparm between the outside edge of the mouth and the new outside border, to define the tip of the nose, and to help alleviate some of the awkward NURBS overlapping that's happening around the *old* outside edge (Figure 5.23a). Pull some points forward so that in profile you see a big ugly lump that will eventually be the nose, as in Figure 5.23b.

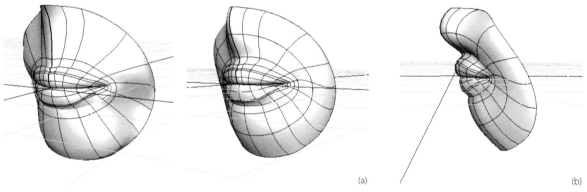

(a)   (b)

Figure 5.22

The dust mask line added into the object

Figure 5.23

The first row added after the perimeter, helping to shape a very simple start to a nose

ADDING MORE TO THE SURFACE

As I build starting from NURBS, I personally go through the somewhat tedious task of duplicating curves, deleting the old loft, and re-lofting the whole set of curves at every step. It's not for everyone, but I like having the curve-level control. Another way to follow along would be to insert isoparms on the shape and then manipulate the outside rows. But although this method is faster to create, it's more time-consuming to manipulate, and I don't recommend it.

Defining What *Will* Be the Nose

Take a look at the rows that are tighter together, that border where the mouth model ended before we started adding this surrounding area, the third "row" in (the third set of curves counted from the outside edge of the model). Take those points and start pushing them outward. As you move them, try to follow the trajectories of the lines, so your layout stays smooth and even. Later, when you build key shapes, you'll thank yourself for maintaining some order. Use the third row in to define the bottom of the nose. It already does that; we're just going to do it more attractively. Push those points up until the profile looks more nose-like at its base. As you do this, you'll likely develop a need to also adjust the second row in. My model looks like Figure 5.24 after all that.

Defining the Chin

Take a second to be sure the new row is being cooperative with your clean, even layout, all the way around. You'll probably need to do quite a bit of pushing back of points around those lines at the bottom of the mouth, as they're not really fitting in with the overall contour yet. Go ahead and start defining the chin to counteract that (Figure 5.25).

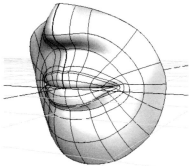

Figure 5.24

The curves rearranged to help create some definition under the nose

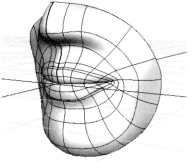

Figure 5.25

Start pulling the chin forward.

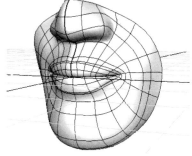

Figure 5.26

The extra rows are now providing sufficient detail to make the nose emerge more sharply from the face.

If you are working with polygons, this is a good time to stop and make sure you are following this structurally. By building this with NURBS, the proper structure of circles around the mouth and nose is automatic, and has exactly the desired effect. With polys, you could be anywhere as far as strucutre goes. Pretend you've got the restrictions of square patches.

Finishing Up the Surrounding Mouth Area

We're getting very close to finished with the important structure in this area now. The next thing to add is another row of points just inside the outside edge, and two bordering the nose. Using these new rows, sharpen the area where the nose meets the face (Figure 5.26).

This comes down to a bit of a rule I have. There must always be at least three rows coming off of the side of the nostril. Preferably there are five, but three will do under limitations. The reason for this is simple: proper creasing.

Creasing Locations

You always need at least three rows for proper creasing, and those rows need to be laid down in the right spot before they ever crease. The "right" spot depends on what you want your character to look like when creasing. You have to think about your character's smile, frown, and sneer before you go too much further.

When deciding how your character will crease, think also about the layout. The rows that will crease need to reach to certain places, if you want them to look right. Figure 5.27 shows where the lines should ideally end up in relation to the nose:

1. The bottom of where the nostril starts to come out of the face

2. The middle of the nostril's edge

3. The top of the nostril

4. and 5.   Above the nostril

Figure 5.27

The locations against the nose where crease lines end up

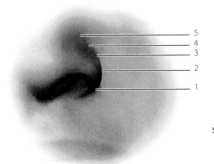

Knowing now where creases go, you'll need to know a bit more about how they behave. A proper crease has only very few possible cross-sections, all shown in Figure 5.28.

When skin mass is moved around and creates a crease, one of two things is happening: it's being pushed or being pulled. In the case of things being pulled, they're being pulled *toward* a crease. In the case of things being pushed, they're running out of places to go, so they bulge out from the crease. The crease is where both motions come together, so you get a hard edge where all the different crease effects meet up. To create this hard edge effect, and the associated proper bulge in volume for your model, you need at least three rows of points for the crease (as in the crease in Figure 5.29). Any less and it just doesn't work.

Building the Nose

Noses, unlike much of the rest of the face, aren't terribly restricted as far as construction technique goes. The mouth, the eyes, and the forehead can have very demanding motions that, with the wrong layout, can be a headache. The nose, on the other hand, is pretty easy. The bulk of the nose's motion comes from the outside edge of the nostrils moving up and down along with certain mouth keys, which is usually an easy thing to do, regardless of layout. I've built the details of the nose differently almost every time I've built a head, in search of the perfect layout, only to discover that it doesn't really matter. It would be awful of me, however, not to give you some guidance, as the nose, and specifically the nostrils, are a very difficult shape to build. The only thing you need be aware of as far as layout goes is that the anchor points, the spots where the nose meets the face, doesn't change too much from the point layout we just worked so hard to create on the face.

Poly/SubD Noses

Polygon modeling is the way I like to do things, and it's also the way I'm going to follow through with the instruction.

Converting NURBS to Polys

For our purposes, we'll need some specific settings to get this to work right. Select your face, and then go into Modify → Convert → NURBS to Polygons ❐.

1. Inside the dialog that comes up (Figure 5.30), select Quads as the type and General as the tessellation method.

2. More options pop up, and within those select both U and V type as Per Span # Of Iso Params, and set the number to 1.

3. Hit Tessellate!

Figure 5.28

"Crease-sections"

Figure 5.29

The crease in the smile, for bearings (a) and close-up (b)

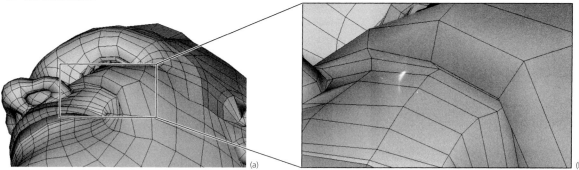

(a)   (b)

Isolating the Work Area

After converting your model to polys, you have some freedom to sculpt your nose independent of the rest of the mesh, or you can work out of the mesh already there. For ease, I tend to separate them out. To do that, duplicate your object. On the original, delete the area shown in Figure 5.31, and in the copy delete everything else. What we're left with is two pieces that fit together perfectly. So even in the version we're modeling independently, we really are working from the original mesh, just not *all* of it.

Select all the faces except the first row on the outside left and right, and subdivide them at level 1. Edit Polygons → Subdivide ❐. Select subdivisions level 1 and Quads as the mode. Figure 5.32 shows the result.

Since we're working in polys, we can work on one side and then mirror it later. Looking up at the nose, use the split polygon tool, Edit Polygons → Split Polygon Tool, to draw the outline of the nostril, as shown in Figure 5.33.

At this point, there should be enough geometry to start building a real nose out of what's there. I sculpted for a few minutes and ended up with what you see in Figure 5.34. I've left the other (character right, viewer left) side still unworked for comparison.

There is a need for more detail in the middle underside of the nose, between the nostrils. I added one point, a connecting edge across, and one row starting near the tip of the nose, going all the way down to the base. This has resulted (Figure 5.35) in added points to the outside edge, or perimeter of the shape, a change that will need to be done on the face as well, before connecting the two again.

Something that noses do, more in some people than others (me being a pretty strong example), is, in the middle area under the nose there, not just point back into the face but meet the face, and then curl upward into the inside of the nose.

Figure 5.36 has three stages of making this happen. First, I deleted the edge that was creating a triangle between the tip of the nose and the nostril, then I added the points (you can see the path they follow swooping in), and finally I shaped the points. How strange, I'm leading a guided tour into my nose.

To help define this shape, I'm going to pull the points along the very bottom forward, altering the perimeter, something we'll have to also do on the face to match. This really starts to show the curl inward, but also shows that it needs work. From there, just add points and edges as needed to organize the area. Figure 5.37 shows a good shape to aim for.

Figure 5.30

The options box for converting NURBS to polys

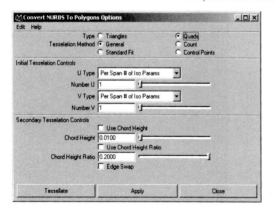

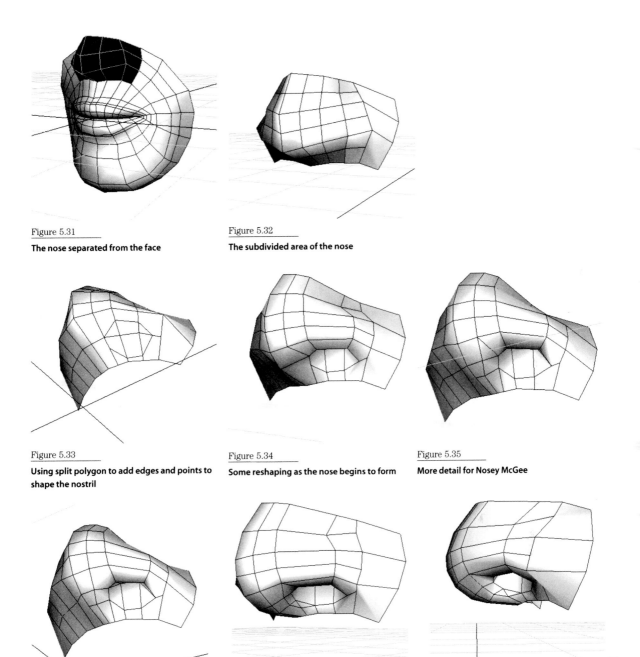

Figure 5.31

The nose separated from the face

Figure 5.32

The subdivided area of the nose

Figure 5.33

Using split polygon to add edges and points to shape the nostril

Figure 5.34

Some reshaping as the nose begins to form

Figure 5.35

More detail for Nosey McGee

(a)

(b)

(c)

Figure 5.36

I deleted the edge on the poly near the front of the nose, leaving a 5-point poly (a). I added a row of points that follows both the line around the nose (b) and the one coming down from on top of the nose and then moves inside the nostril (c).

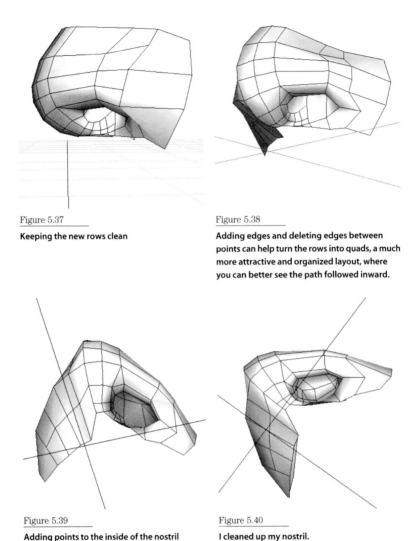

Figure 5.37

Keeping the new rows clean

Figure 5.38

Adding edges and deleting edges between points can help turn the rows into quads, a much more attractive and organized layout, where you can better see the path followed inward.

Figure 5.39

Adding points to the inside of the nostril

Figure 5.40

I cleaned up my nostril.

This leaves some very complicated polygons, namely the inside wall of the nostril, but to clean that up we'll first need to define the whole area better. I added a row around the outside edge of the nostril that connects up with the curl we just made, and after some tweaking ended up with what's in Figure 5.38.

This change visually makes obvious our next needed step, which will be to add more to the inner nostril. Doing so and doing some sculpting left me with Figure 5.39.

To "clean up" the inside of the nostril at this point can be done a number of ways. Just try and have all the lines cleanly go somewhere toward the inside of the nose, where they can then be much messier, as no one can see them! Have your goal be to simply get rid of any really undefined polygons—try to make everything three-, four-, or five-point polys. Figure 5.40 shows what I did with the area.

The last bit here is going to go fast. The two main things left are that we need to define the back of the nostril where it meets the face, and I'd like to more clearly define the separate masses of the nose and the nostril. To do these, we'll need more detail. Figure 5.41 shows the points and edges first added, and then sculpted.

And there you have it! Nosalicious! You can add even more detail to areas you think need it for your character, or you can jump right on to mirroring the geometry. To mirror, first delete the half of the nose you don't want. Then, simply go to Polygons → Mirror Geometry ❐. In the dialog box, select –X and check the box that says Merge With The Original. When it does that, it'll create faces that "close" the top, back, and bottom of the nose. In face mode, select those faces and delete them; the result is Figure 5.42. All done!

Merging the Nose Back into the Face

We did some tweaking and made some changes to the perimeter of our nose, so to merge it with the face again (Figure 5.43), there's a little bit of "meeting up" to be done. I'm pretty happy with the nose, so I'll make most of the adaptations on the face.

You should be using the face with the hole cut out, where the nose started from. If you've got two noses there, things could get ugly. Okay, the first thing I want to do is get our point numbers the same. Again, as this is polygonal modeling, we can make the changes on one side and then just mirror them. To the face, add extra rows as in Figure 5.44. If the points aren't lining up in exactly the same spot as those on the nose, no worries, we'll take care of that in a second.

Now using "snap-to points," drag the face points each individually toward their matching points on the nose, and they should snap right into place, as in Figure 5.45!

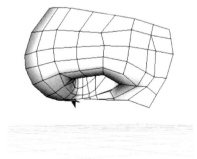

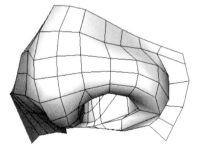

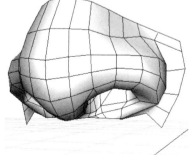

Figure 5.41

More detail added

Figure 5.42

The mirrored nose geometry

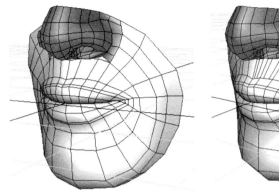

Figure 5.43

The new nose on the old face

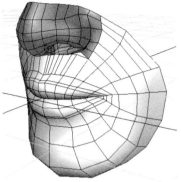

Figure 5.44

Adding points to the face in order to link up with the nose

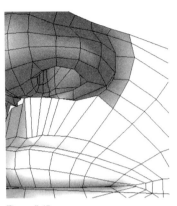

Figure 5.45

The face points snapped to those of the nose

Now, you'll need to do three things:

1. Combine the nose and face: Select both, and then hit Polygons → Combine.

2. Merge the vertices: Grab all the vertices along the border rows where the two objects joined, and then select Edit Polygons → Merge Vertices.

3. Mirror the geometry: Delete the faces on the "unfixed" side, then select Polygons → Mirror Geometry, and you should get Figure 5.46.

From here you can do as you wish for your needs. There are some edges that terminate into the middles of squares, but they usually shade just fine, and if you'd like more detail, you can follow those all the way around the bottom of the chin and into the lip to keep everything nice and squared out. It is perfectly acceptable, having taken this concentric-circles-making-quad-polygons approach this far, to have some triangles, as long as they don't interfere with what needs to crease. Figure 5.47 is the face I continue on with in later chapters.

I added some more detail into the back of the nose. I continued the lines of quads down and around the mouth. I let some of the rows that meet up at the top of the nose go to triangles, knowing the creases I wanted wouldn't be affected.

NURBS Noses

To make the nose out of NURBS is more trouble than it's worth. Basically, to create a spline nose, you should follow the imagery of the above steps, and just keep adding more and more rows as are needed to force the all-quad layout to shape well. You really won't be able to match the structure, only the shape, but in the case of the nose, that is okay. As you can tell, I do not personally enjoy the NURBS approach nor recommend it. Had this been only a year or two ago, NURBS may have been my primary instruction, but now that some variety of polygons and subD surfaces that work well are available in just about any software, there's no need to go through the pain of a spline head anymore. There was a time, oh yes, there was a time…

Building Teeth

I've done a lot of talking about references, and things being relative. With the teeth, we have the main reference point for the lips and the shapes they make. You know that someone has their upper lip raised when you can see their gums. When someone's smiling, same deal: the teeth are out there for the world to see, gums and all. Remember the pupil-and-iris-o-meter? Well, the mouth has its own version, the teeth-and-gums-o-meter (Figure 5.48).

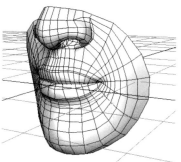

Figure 5.46

The combined, mirrored geometry

A Real-Life Lesson in Gums

I once worked on a project where the clients had it in their heads that we should never see the main character's gums. They had concluded in their own minds that as a concept, gums were unattractive. The resultant effect was that the character looked like she was wearing a mouth guard, or was never really smiling. If you can't see the top of the teeth and the gums, it's like they're not there. If there are no gums above teeth, there's no proof the character is really giving a big smile, raising their lip, because seeing those gums is how we know. There's also nothing to tell you that the character doesn't just have *really* big teeth, either.

Figure 5.47

Where I took my model after the last steps

Placement

We'll build the teeth, but that's only half of the battle. On average, it takes me as long to place the teeth in a character's head as it takes me to model them. Properly placing, scaling, and shaping teeth is something not easily done.

Figure 5.48

The teeth-and-gums-o-meter

One thing that always amazed me was that, in my experience, directors, producers, and executives—even supervising animators and modelers, everyone with an opinion that counted—never asked to see the character's teeth during the model approval process. Seeing the teeth does two things: First, if they don't closely match the shape of the area around the lips, they just look fake. Second, stylistically, there are simply right and wrong teeth for a character's look. I don't even mean something as broad as yellow-brown crooked teeth versus perfect pearly whites, either; I mean that there are infinite kinds of teeth, and not many are really interchangeable with faces. This is

one of those things that I can't handhold you through, and I can't give you a set of absolute rules—I can just make you aware of it. After I build teeth, I don't consider them finished until after I've built all of my mouth shape key set, because I will continue to reshape, scale, and move them as I build the keys, until the teeth look the best in the most situations. It can be a grueling process on certain characters.

The Types of Teeth

I emphasize maximum flexibility, addressing the particular needs of each area of the face. With the teeth, we're lucky. They help us identify issues with other facial key shapes, but they themselves—for the most part—don't move. They're just a prop. Since they don't need to move, there are no rules whatsoever for how to build them that I'll preach at you. The following are merely suggestions on how to get them built quickly and painlessly, although like I said, even after they're built; *placing* them in your character's mouth can take some serious time.

There are really only two major variations on the way to build teeth. In one case, there are the one-piece teeth, in which the gums and teeth are made of one continuous object, as in Figure 5.49. These are better for cartoony characters or human stylized characters that are supposed to look like people, just not photo-real people. And then there are the one-piece gums and individual teeth, like in Figure 5.50, better suited for more realistic characters

Polygons or subDs tend to be the better tool for more realistic teeth; if cartoony and stylized is your goal, splines will get you to your goal more quickly and easily. I build teeth out of polygons, and the instruction I'll give refers to one-piece teeth, as individual teeth are a pretty self-explanatory build process. Build a tooth, repeat.

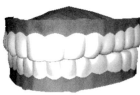

Figure 5.49

One-piece teeth

Figure 5.50

Individual teeth

Creating Teeth

Teeth are an extremely easy thing to build. I'll use polygons, but I'm going to model according to spline rules, so the lesson information can translate directly, if that's your preference. I'll leave all polys as quadrilaterals—four-sided.

> There will be no explicit tutorial on building the gums alone, for the one-piece-gums and individual teeth. For the gums portion of that, simply follow along with this one, ignoring the teeth!

My favored approach to building teeth is to start with a face, or *plane*. Create a plane that has four subdivisions along the length and only one along the height. Create it at a width and height of 1x1 and so it faces forward in the front view (flat in the side and top views, as in Figure 5.51).

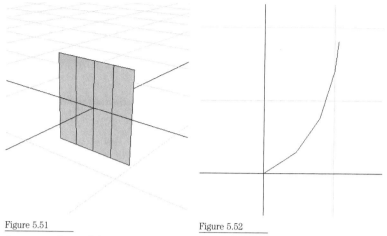

Figure 5.51

Create a 1x1 plane with divisions of 4 and 1.

Figure 5.52

A top view of the shape to make

Move the plane over to the side so that it exists only in X positive. In the top view, move the points around to create the shape in Figure 5.52. It should involve only X and Z movements, no moving of the points vertically. It's no tough guess to see we're already shaping the greater silhouette.

Grab the lower row and move it up so it's 0 in Y, flat to the axis. No need to be hyperaccurate, just close enough. Select all of the faces and subdivide them at a level of one, then round all the new points into the curve of the shape (Figure 5.53).

Subdivide all of it again, and start to define the teeth. Teeth are not perfectly straight up and down, or even in their heights, and any little detail that pushes us closer to reality is going to help. At the same time, define where the gums end and the teeth begin, as I've done in Figure 5.54.

You may notice that the very last tooth already has twice as many lines as the others. That's just the way the odd-evens worked out, starting with a plane and subdividing it—nothing to worry about. We've got most of the basic outline of what we need, so let's tweak it into a cleaner set of teeth. Add rows only vertically between the vertical rows that are already there, excluding the back tooth, as it's already got the extra level of detail for this step.

Push the new rows toward the borders of each tooth, to create more of an archway, the rounded top of where the tooth meets the gums. Figure 5.55 shows the look to go for.

From here, the teeth just need one more thing before we can start making them a little less flat. Put in one more row horizontally along the front of the teeth, so that their profiles are less angular. Whether you decide to add it above or below that middle line is irrelevant, but what is important is to space both rows back out to get the most curvature for the least cost.

Once the normals are smoothed, this is enough detail for TV and most personal projects, if you don't plan on extreme close-ups, but there still may be details you want to add or change. One thing that's nice about teeth and polys is that teeth look better when they're not perfectly smooth, and polys do that all for free. If you were to need to get closer into the mouth, you'd use *stunt* teeth (higher resolution), or you could simply do a smooth function to get rid of the visible angular silhouette edges, but for the most part, what we've done here would really be enough. Truth be told, most people don't look too much at the teeth unless you make them.

Let's make this look more like teeth and gums. First, color the gums and teeth separately. Then, make the edges over the gum-tooth divide hard, via Edit Polygons → Normals → Soften/ Harden ❑. Do the same again, between each tooth; it'll make them look less like one big object, as you can see in Figure 5.56.

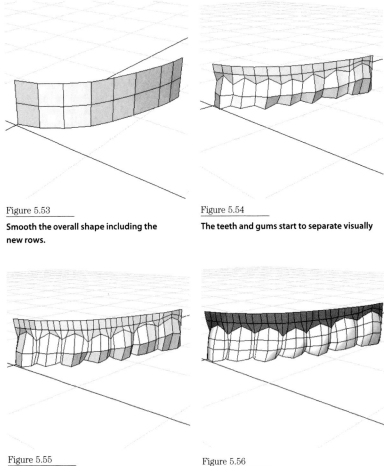

Figure 5.53

Smooth the overall shape including the new rows.

Figure 5.54

The teeth and gums start to separate visually

Figure 5.55

Using the new points, create arches at the tops of the teeth.

Figure 5.56

Now that's starting to look like teeth!

Shaping the Interior Tooth Surface

As glamorous as this topic is not, it's pretty important to what the audience sees. We'll eventually build our lower teeth out of these upper teeth, and you'll notice when someone opens their mouth, as in Figure 5.57, pretty much all that you see is the inside and topside of the bottom teeth. That directly translates to the inside and underside of what we're building now.

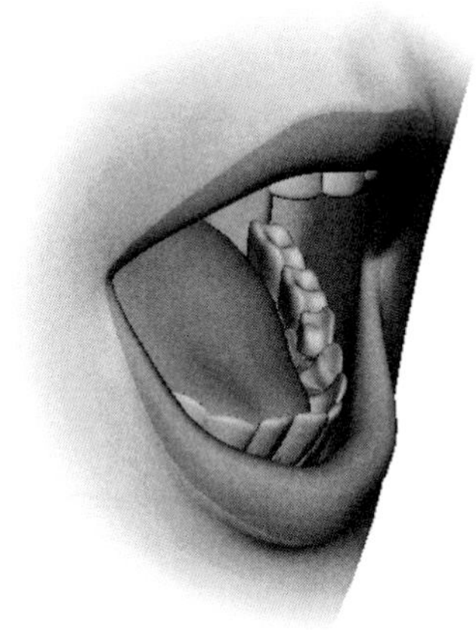

Select the teeth and duplicate them, and then scale them smaller in X, left to right, and bigger in Z, back to front. I'm not giving any magic numbers; just try to get something like Figure 5.58.

On the duplicate, select all the faces and reverse the normals. To do so, go to Edit Polygons → Normals → Reverse. If this isn't done, when these two objects are combined they won't be able to shade smoothly, due to normals going in opposite directions.

Hide the original mesh for now, and work on this new inside one. One by one, grab the points for the inside of the teeth and pull them out in the other direction. Right now their "bulges" are those of the outside of the teeth; see Figure 5.59 for how they should look. Leave two front teeth concave; that's closer to their real shape, anyway.

Next, combine the two shapes. Unhide the original and combine it and the "inside" into one object.

> For instruction on combining polygon objects, see the section "Merging the Nose Back into the Face" earlier in this chapter.

You'll need to use the Append Polygon tool to connect the two sides of the object together, the result of which is shown in Figure 5.60.

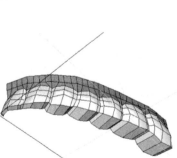

Figure 5.57

Saying AHHHH really shows off the insides of the dental work.

Figure 5.58

The new object scaled and placed, from a perspective top view

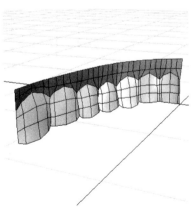

Figure 5.59

The curve on the inside of the teeth should go opposite that of the outside (we're looking at this from the inside).

Figure 5.60

The two sides connected along the bottom, from a bottom perspective view

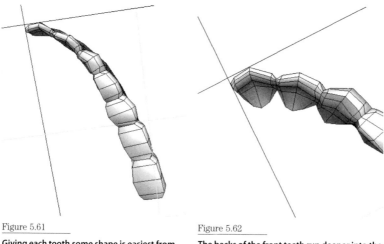

Figure 5.61

Giving each tooth some shape is easiest from the bottom.

Figure 5.62

The backs of the front teeth run deeper into the roof of the mouth.

You can see that we've worked in at least an approximation of the proper width of teeth by scaling the inside edge differently, but looking at Figure 5.60, you'll see that some of the edges don't line up. Simply go through and rearrange the shape so that the teeth line up more attractively. Try to leave the front of the teeth and do most of your modifications to the inside, which can afford to be less accurate.

The Underside of the Teeth

Looking at the bottom, pull points together at the joins between teeth, as in Figure 5.61. This helps define the proper widths for the teeth and aids the illusion that each tooth is separate.

From here, add one row down the center of the bottom. For the front teeth this will reduce the boxiness of the tooth; for the back teeth it will help us include more molar detail. Select the new row and pull it down a little bit. This softens the front, but also makes the back teeth look like marshmallows—so for the last four teeth, select the new row and pull it upward, sharpening the edges of those back teeth.

The teeth are almost done being shaped. The last few details have to do with the back of the front teeth and the roof of the mouth. The front teeth anchor to the gums in a very unique way, and to mimic that, select the base of the front few teeth, the three points at the top of each arch on the backside, and pull them back, as in Figure 5.62.

Sculpting the Gums

It's now up to you to further sculpt, smooth, and tweak the teeth themselves. The next step here is to pull the gums into more of a "roof" of the mouth. Select the points on the inside top edge, and scale them horizontally in X until they are flat against the X-axis. Snap-to-grid and the Move tool can also be good for this.

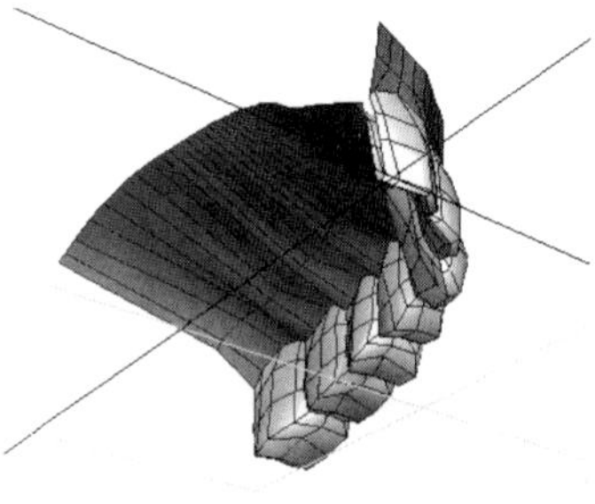

Resculpt the shape so that the new row has an arch in it, as in Figure 5.63. You'll need to pull some of the points near the front toward the back a little to get the right shape.

From here there's the small matter of mirroring what we have (Figure 5.64), so as to create a whole set of teeth. Again, the way to do that is covered earlier in this chapter under "Merging the Nose Back into the Face."

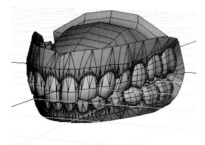

Figure 5.63

Creating something to fill the mouth

Making the Lower Teeth from the Upper Teeth

Taking the teeth we just built and turning them upside down isn't *quite* enough to qualify as lower teeth. I'm not a dentist, and I would be lying if I said I looked deep into medical or dental information to properly justify this process. I'm basing the following teeth on a mirror, a few pictures, and my own observations of what lower teeth look like.

Visually, the main difference between lower teeth and upper teeth is that the frontmost four lower teeth seem to be thinner. The four front teeth on the bottom don't take up as much room as the top front four teeth.

For humans, even though those front bottom teeth are smaller, there are the same number of bottom teeth as top ones. (Trust me; I counted.) So we can use a duplicate of our upper teeth; we just need to reshape them. I duplicated the upper teeth, rotated them 180 degrees in Z, and scaled them uniformly down a little. After moving them around, I got what looks like Figure 5.65.

If you're not fussy, that's ready to rock. If you *do*, however, want to differentiate between the upper and lower teeth, there is only one tool I recommend using to do so: a lattice. By creating a lattice around the lower teeth, you can make big changes with little effort. I created a lattice with divisions of 5, 3, and 5 in X, Y, and Z, respectively. Figure 5.66 gives a good idea of how to redistribute the shape to look different from the upper teeth—simply thin the teeth up front, and redistribute the rest accordingly.

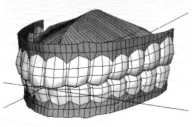

Figure 5.64

The same teeth model with more elbow grease thrown at it

Figure 5.65

A whole set of choppers

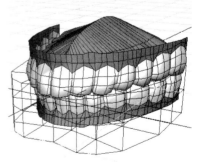

Figure 5.66

Using a lattice is the fastest way to reshape the bottom teeth.

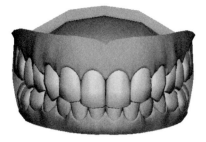
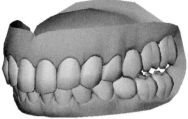
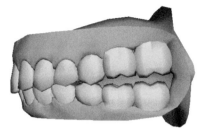

Figure 5.67

3 angles on some teeth I took to the next level of detail

Solidify the lattice's control by duplicating the geometry and deleting the original, and there you are! The tongue will be covered separately, but can definitely be made to join into this model for more realism. As far as tweaking it goes, in Figure 5.67 are some images from a model I continued on with. The main things to do, if you'd like to continue refining your teeth, is to add more points in the join areas, both between the teeth and gums line and between each of the teeth. If you'd really like to add some nice depth to the model, connect the upper and lower teeth together at the back. If you open your mouth really wide, you'll see there's a tendon back there. The model I built here shows all these additions and changes. The process mostly involved smoothing the object, tweaking it, and smoothing it some more.

Building the Tongue

I tend to preach against the tongue at every turn. You can lip-sync convincingly without it, it's extremely difficult to animate it well, and it's usually more of a distraction from the performance than a help. In a lot of my characters, I never even build it to sit at the bottom of the mouth. Unless you, as a viewer, set out to *look at* the tongue, you usually won't notice it's not there.

All that being said, you may want it. The simplest tongue to build is most definitely a squashed sphere. If the proper care is taken, though, this can be made into a very convincing and realistic tongue. If your look is cartoony, simpler is better. The next kind of tongue is built into the bottom of the mouth, just like real life. Since the tongue does have movements it has to accomplish, I do have some suggestions on construction.

Shaping a Basic Tongue

Figure 5.68

A happy little NURBS sphere

Create a NURBS sphere native to the Z-axis with 10 sections and 8 spans. You'll need to rotate it 90 degrees in Z so that there are central rows going up and down, as in Figure 5.68.

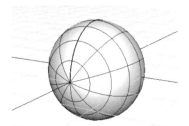

Freeze all transformations and then scale the sphere down to 0.6 in X, 0.2 in Y, and 0.8 in Z. If you'd like to build this in the same scene with your lower teeth, pull the tongue back about −1.1 units in Z—that should be in the ballpark of where your teeth are.

Select the first isoparm you can at the back of the tongue and separate the surfaces out, so it looks like Figure 5.69. You can delete the "cap" if you'd like. Now select the last two rows on the newly opened side, and manipulate the points out as in Figure 5.70.

As viewed from the bottom, pull the points so that they look like Figure 5.71. What we're creating here is where the tongue anchors. If you roll your tongue around your mouth, you'll notice that it's quite connected on the underside.

We recreate this because without the detail on the underside of the tongue, the position of the tongue, when it's raised, wouldn't be as apparent.

Following along with the teeth model can be handy because you can start to form this tongue model to the underside of the mouth, which will need to happen anyway.

From the side view, try to condense the profile (center) line to the front to more directly connect to the base. Resculpt the surrounding rows to match more closely. After that, select the rows outside of those, and do the same.

Select some of the points on the underside and scale them together in X, to thin them, as in Figure 5.72. This will help form something like the membrane located at the center bottom of your tongue.

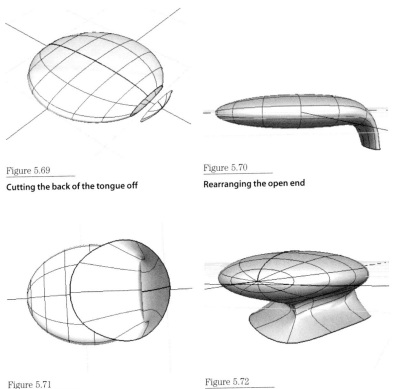

Figure 5.69

Cutting the back of the tongue off

Figure 5.70

Rearranging the open end

Figure 5.71

Forming the base of the tongue at the bottom of the mouth

Figure 5.72

Create the look of the membrane under the tongue.

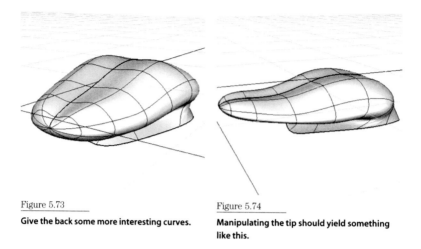

Figure 5.73

Give the back some more interesting curves.

Figure 5.74

Manipulating the tip should yield something like this.

On the topside, grab the points at the back, not including the center row, and pull them back and up slightly (shown in Figure 5.73). This will put some more shape on the silhouette when people can see into your character's mouth. Going in to the top view, pull the last row so that it's a little bit rounder. This will very seldom be seen, but it makes the overall back edge look more organic, and less like a cliff that just drops off.

From the side view, grab some rows and pull them down vertically to create more of a wave shape, as in Figure 5.74. You may want to extend the tip to make the whole shape a little bit longer.

If your character is a more stylized one, you may already be done. For a more realistic tongue, read on.

A More Refined Tongue

To make this tongue look more realistic, you will mostly rely on your own eye for what you want, but there are a few more things that you can do structurally to help you along. To go further, convert the tongue into polys. Set your options so that it turns out not too heavy. The exact settings are of little consequence; we can add that detail later. Right after the conversion, delete the faces on the very tip (Figure 5.75). When modeling in splines, you have to deal with the sphincter on the tips of your objects; in polys, no need.

Now close the tip back up, appending more polys to the open space. From here, add another row horizontally, and that should give you enough detail to round out the tip, both from the top and side views; see Figure 5.76.

The last thing we'll do to get the tongue into the mouth convincingly is actually attach it to the lower teeth model we have built. Translate the tongue up, or the teeth down—doesn't matter which—so that you can have space to work between them. Delete the inside bottom of the lower teeth, combine the two, and start to attach the tongue, at its anchor, to the teeth model, as in Figure 5.77.

After that, go ahead and sink that puppy into the bottom of the mouth. What I tend to do is fatten the tongue out most of the way to the teeth. This makes it look like the tongue is actually in the mouth instead of another separate object floating there (Figure 5.78).

From here it's just tweaking it into what you want to see. The only major thing now would be to pull the back of the tongue back farther toward where the throat would be, as that's where your tongue really sits. Other than that, happy modeling!

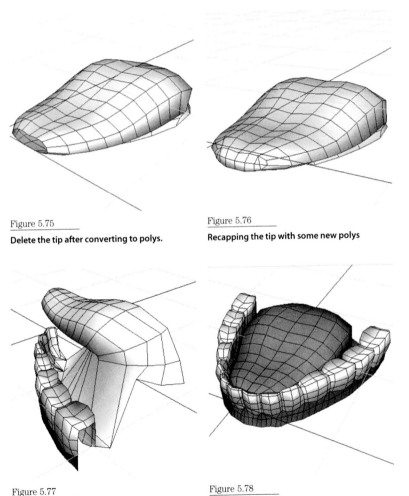

Figure 5.75

Delete the tip after converting to polys.

Figure 5.76

Recapping the tip with some new polys

Figure 5.77

Connecting the tongue to the teeth

Figure 5.78

The tongue sitting in the mouth

The Mouth Wall

That's right, it just keeps going! I can say to you, though, that this is the end of the pieces of the mouth. To keep us from seeing the inside back of the head, the characters will need what I've heard referred to as a mouth sock, a mouth wall, or even a mouth bag. All this does is give all our teeth and gums a little home to live in.

You can continue on from the lips, making more rows, and just pull the extra geometry into the mouth. In most cases, though, it's just not necessary to have that kind of detail. Usually, you can get away with an incredibly low-res object. It's so simple, in fact, that I'm not even going to guide you through it. All your mouth wall needs is enough points around the front so that when your facial key shapes start to move around, it can move around too. That usually means at least 8 points at the front, at clock positions 12, 2, 3, 4, 6, 8, 9, and 10.

I usually build my mouth walls out of a cube on which I've softened the shading, using Edit Polygons → Normals → Soften/Harden. It does the trick of being unobtrusive so well that I had to duplicate it and color it differently to show you what it looks like! The low resolution rarely shows itself unless there's too much texturing going on in the inside, which there really shouldn't be if you're going with this style of mouth wall. I've worked on several TV series that we shipped using this low level of detail in the mouth—it just works. Figure 5.79 shows several views of the mouth wall object completed.

For the times when you really do want some added realism, indeed follow and construct the lips into the inside, and then start snapping points to the gums, so it's a nice tight seal all the way around; this method is shown in Figure 5.80. The structure of this is only dependent on its ability to open and close with the jaw and to follow the mouth shapes. Other than that, it doesn't matter.

Figure 5.79

The simple mouth wall

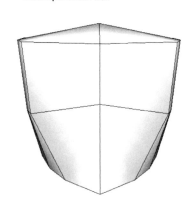
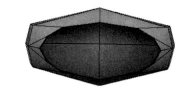
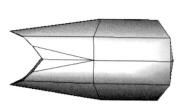

Okay, boys and girl, this is it. This was the left ventricle of the heart of the book, and there's still more heart to come. To switch metaphors, you've got the blank slate on which to create amazing sync and stunning acting; the groundwork is already laid. Next we give that slate some chalk—we build the shapes.

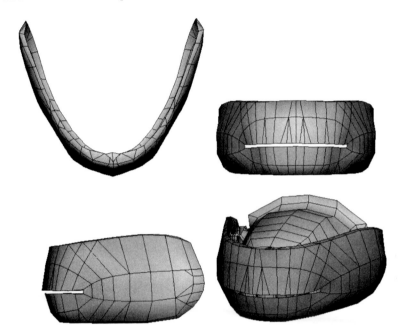

Figure 5.80

The more realistic mouth wall hugs the teeth.

CHAPTER 6

Mouth Keys

We've got a mouth we can set keys on, so let's start creating those keys. Something you have to know right here and right now is that this section is work. The fastest I've ever completed a key set *from scratch* for a model was two eight-hour days—and the bar was set pretty low on that particular project and I had already been setting up facial key sets for over two years almost exclusively as my full-time job. Expect this to take longer. The more setups you do, the faster it will go, but don't get discouraged when you hit hour 4 and you're still on your first shape. That's okay; you're on track. The first couple of shapes take forever, but the shapes that follow are much faster and easier to build. So the time cost is very front-heavy, but the crest of the hill actually comes early Smile, Frown, and OO are the only very demanding shapes, and the rest are really easy. I'll give you time estimates and guidelines so you'll know how you're doing. In most cases, I'll describe the time I spent to create the visuals.

- **How to approach the key set**

- **The default shape**

- **Basic and advanced sync keys**

- **Emotion keys**

- **Asymmetry**

Preparing to Build a Key Set

The mouth model you've built is not what your character looks like. In a scene where your character is asleep, or maybe in a scene where they are drugged or pretending to be a mannequin, yes, the face you built is what your character looks like, but in all other cases, the key set you build is how your audience will see your character.

The life some animators can put into characters is amazing. Whenever I see CGI model turnarounds on DVD special features, I think, "That's not what so-and-so looks like, that's so… dead!" It's so great to see the same model be nothing, be lifeless, just not be the character. The breath of life that appears somewhere in between the modeling and the finished film is remarkable. Life is something brought in by all sorts of movement, great acting, and most of all, good writing.

In regard to the acting, a lot of that creation of character is done in close-ups—it's done with the face. One thing I realize when looking at turnarounds is that you almost never see that base/default shape of the face in the movie or TV show; the face is always expressing somehow. The point is: the model you're starting with isn't your character, these shapes you're about to build are. Treat every shape like the only shape anyone will ever see, because combinations of the shapes you build here really *are* all anyone will ever see.

Key Set Construction via Modeling

The approach I have is simple. I build what I want to see. I grab the points, just as I did when I built the head in the first place, and I move them, and I move them, and I move them some more. Personally, I don't use clusters, I only use one joint to help me create the jaw shapes, but other than that, it's all point-pulling. There's no rabbit in the hat.

This may come as a shock, if you were expecting some method for shape building that relied on some crazy rigging and clusters and kooky gadgets. That stuff, while it can sometimes be fast to work with, usually looks awful, and in the long run causes more grief than ease, as you have to toil with several different control mechanisms for a single result. You can do anything you want to get a shape built, but for it to work in my rigs later on, you'll have to "bake" it down to a shape that, for the reasons I just described, is going to make your life easiest. Usually, to clean up (or, as I say, "bake") a shape, you can just duplicate the face mesh and delete the history, and that'll give you a clean shape.

FINISH YOUR HEAD FIRST!

One caveat here is that you really should finish your model off before working through the shapes. If you build them on the model of just the mouth, you will have to do it all again, or wrestle with seaming. This book is organized to keep all things mouth in one section, all things eyes & brows in another, etc. If your goal is just to learn, go ahead and read. If your goal is to build a model for use in a project, I recommend strongly that you move forward and finish your whole head model, and then come back to this chapter.

By making all the inputs into the facial rig almost exclusively, *blend shapes,* you can simplify your life tremendously. For each shape you want to see, you have just one blend shape value to control to get that face shape, even if initially it was a combination of clusters, sculpt deformers, joints, and point-pulling. When we start setting up four shapes on one slider, our savings in time and effort will multiply without losing us any of the complexity.

Basically, I ask, would you use heavy amounts of riggery in constructing your face? Of course not! You'd model it! I see the key set building process the same way. I model it.

Binding Sufficiently for Building

Although we're not yet setting our face up for animation, the process of key shape–building can be greatly aided by setting up a simple jaw bone. Since we've built our model to deform into many different shapes nicely, we've left ourselves some tight work in the corners of the mouth. By adding a jaw bone, we can open the mouth up to work on it; we can get into the tight spots by simply loosening them up. Instead of me guiding you through the same process twice, I'll refer you ahead to Chapter 11, "Skeletal Setup, Weighting, and Rigging," to see how the jaw binding is done. At this stage of the game, the binding can be really simplistic. You don't even need to worry about the rest of the joint hierarchy; you're only, as the heading states, binding for building.

While not at all physically accurate, best results come from the jaw joint being placed at the back corner of the jaw, but flat to the X-axis, where you'd probably put it if you were guessing. The weighting should approximately match Figure 6.1.

> Be sure to pay special attention to where the mouth corners end up. The points in that area should remain fairly close together so that when the mouth opens and closes, the opening is somewhere between circular and almond-shaped.

Deciding Inclusion

Something I recommend when creating these key shapes is looking in a mirror. I'll make you aware of the entire area affected by each shape, but the trick is going to be building certain shapes so that they *don't* include all of the effects you see in the mirror. There will be times when we need to break up a shape into two or more shapes, so that we can use the shapes independently as well as together.

A Smile, the first shape we will build, is a perfect example. When you smile, your eyes squint; this is part of what makes a smile very genuine. When we build the Smile shape, though, we are going to be using it for more than just smiling. It represents the Wide shape (Wide/Narrow) of the mouth for lip sync and it also represents, obviously, a smile. If we include the squint in the Smile shape itself, then we lose the ability to use the mouth portion, the Wide shape, *without* the smiling eyes aspect. This is no good. The squint portion all on its own is useful in any number of other expressions, as well as simply by itself. The Squint will be its own shape.

TERMINOLOGY TIME-OUT

I will use certain terms you may or may not be familiar with, so I'd best describe them all.

Blend shape, morph target, key shape, shape key These are all different ways to describe a shape that is assigned to another (by a blend shape relationship).

Key set A group of blend shapes.

Skinning, binding, or weighting The process of assigning the amount each point (CV, Vertex) will follow each joint in a skeleton.

Base shape, default shape The character's shape without any expression, or influence.

Setup, rig Terms I'll use to describe a finished head, all its shapes included and connected to an interface.

In the future, to create a smile in animation, we will add the "smile" we build with the Squint shape. At first this may seem like more work than just having a separate Smile, Wide, and Squint that each does a complete job on its own, but in fact it's much, much faster and easier this way. If we were to build the squint into the Smile and have an independent Squint as well, the transition period moving into a smile would have to be squint-free, otherwise we'd end up with a double-powered squint, which—well, would likely not look too good, as Figure 6.2 illustrates.

To deal with problems like that, we'd have to un-animate certain curves, such as the Smile, as we moved through different shapes, such as the Squint. That takes *way* longer and is not a fun, creative process; it's problem solving on an ongoing basis. The way to get around this is just to separate things out, even if that means we're building shapes that can't really be achieved by a real face. I'll represent any shapes that will need to be built in this method of "knowing non-inclusion" with an image such as Figure 6.3; I'll make it look just like a weight map.

Figure 6.1

The weighting of the jaw

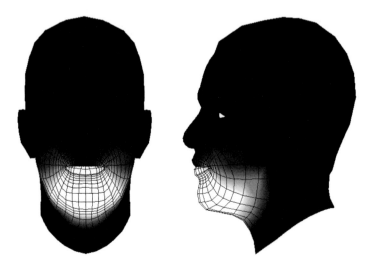

The lighter areas are the ones to build so the face will move realistically; the darker ones show the effects tapering back to the default face. So even though your goal is a realistic smile, you may have to build two unrealistic halves—the mouth portion, then the squint— that both come together to create the whole shape. The reason is that it can be difficult to stop your character's face from either being ripped to shreds from bad combinations, or difficult to get the specific expression you want. If your character's smile is too hard-wired as a whole, it's hard to customize it for just that scene and just that camera angle.

This whole thing is open-ended, but not quite as lunatic as giving you individual muscle controls—which, believe me, is not as glamorous or even as useful as it sounds; it's clunky. Some of this safeguarding against combination-breakages is done by careful choosing of the shapes we build, and some is done at the interface level, where we put certain shapes on opposite ends of the same control, so that try, try as we might we *can't* get them to break the face. All that said, you can still rip your face to pieces if you really want to; I'm just making it harder to do it accidentally.

Figure 6.2

A Smile with squint plus a Squint equals one ugly face.

What to Build?

I'll have four setups for you in Chapter 12 ("Interfaces for Your Faces"), but there are really only two different key sets to build. For the simple setup we'll build whole shapes, but for all the other setups we'll take those whole shapes and break them into half-shapes using some nifty tricks.

Something you can do to expand upon the visuals here is to load my head from the Chapter 6 folder on the companion CD, called `MouthShapes.ma`, and actually see the things I describe in motion. You can orbit around the head and look anywhere you need for more elaborate examination.

Default and Additive Shapes

The default shape is the most important shape. Everything in this whole book—all of these shapes, all of the setups—*will not work* if you do not adhere to the rules laid out here for the default shape. The reason is that we'll be using additive shape animation, the default type for most software. Additive shape animation is very powerful, and can also sometimes be very difficult to control. Take note of the list of rules for the default shape, and do your best to make sure your character follows them.

Figure 6.3

The area of effect a shape should have will be shown as if it were a weight map.

Your layout, as Figure 6.4 shows, absolutely must have:

- Circular rows all the way into the mouth
- A bored expression/expressionless mouth
- A closed mouth
- Lips that continue from the outside of the face and turn inwards to the mouth

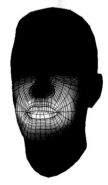

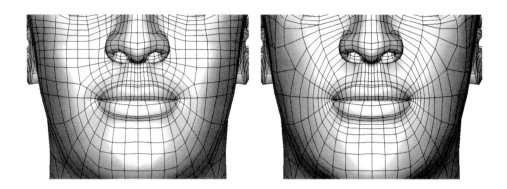

Additive Shapes Explained

With *additive shape animation*, used by most 3D software, two or more shapes do not "morph" together and meet in the middle; different shapes can actually influence the same object at the same time without compromise.

I want to state as loudly as possible and from the highest hill I can find: This concept takes a while to get used to, and if you think that it's easy and you understand it without too much effort, go back and rethink it. As backward as this may seem, additive shape animation is a concept you don't really understand until it's confusing. It's very, very deep in its details, and understanding it fully will help you fix problems you will almost surely run into, with weird things happening to your head.

Let's start at the ground floor, explain the principles of additive shape animation, and then apply the logic to a head and see what can happen.

Figure 6.5 shows four circles. The first, the regular circle, is the default, or base shape. The second and third circles, the ones with the bumps on them, are shapes that will be added to the regular circle as blend shapes. The fourth is exactly the same as the first, and that too will be used to add to the first, to help explain just how additive shapes work a little bit differently than you might guess. I will call these shapes A, B, C, and D, respectively.

Figure 6.5

Four circles to demonstrate the thinking behind additive shape animation

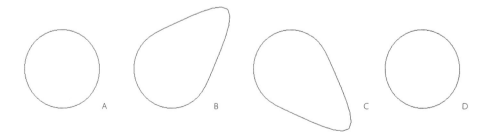

FYI, although this is not meant to be a tutorial, if you wanted to make B, C, and D blend shapes available to A, you'd select B, C, and D, and select A last. Click Deform → Create Blend Shape… and you're done!

A becomes the master shape, which gets influenced by B, C, and D. For example, once you've created your blend shapes, using B's shape slider will influence the master shape (A) to *apparently* morph toward the B shape (Figure 6.6). Increasing the C slider will influence the default shape (A) to become like the C shape.

In Maya there are two ways to affect the blend shape values. You can open the blend shape editor and use sliders, by going to Windows → Animation Editors → Blend Shape, or you can open the blend shape node under the inputs under the Channel Box and adjust the attribute values for each shape.

There Are No Shapes, Only Differences

The trick here is that this blend shape stuff is all done *additively*, with a compound effect. Using more than one slider at a time, these shapes will quite literally *add* to each other (Figure 6.7), they do not compromise and "meet in the middle," which is what a morph is.

To *add* shapes—and that's what Maya is doing; it's *adding* them, not *morphing* them— is to say that Maya looks only at their differences from the base shape and applies those differences. It's a hard thing to describe, but pretend Maya doesn't see a shape at all (it really doesn't), all it sees is what's different about a shape in relation to the base shape.

Here's where circle D comes in. Your first guess (and a very logical one) about the result of adding D into the mix is probably that it would lessen the effects of B and C, because it's more circular. That would be exactly where additive is trickier than it looks. D will not lessen the effects of B and C; it will do nothing. D won't do a thing to A, it will have no effect in any way. No matter if you crank that slider to 1000, it just won't show up, because there's nothing different. When nothing is different, it's a relatively benign concept to think about. When something *is* different, no matter how slightly, it can get very ugly.

Figure 6.8 shows first my default head, which I built all of my shapes out of, and then the same head slightly modified to make the nose thinner from left to right. Let's just say I've already got all my shapes built, but I did this thinning of the nose after the fact, so none of my key shapes have that thin nose. If I were to now make the thin-nose a base head for all of those blend shapes I had, at first everything would seem fine.

Figure 6.6

B's influence on A makes A look just like B.

Figure 6.7

B and C both influencing A

Figure 6.8

Default me (top) and a me that went for a little bit of plastic surgery (bottom)

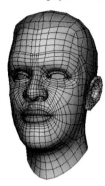

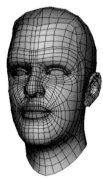

As I increase the slider for the Smile shape, however, the nose plumps back out to its width before the thinning of the nose, because the Smile shape (created before I thinned the nose) is *different* in that way. Now, as I add the Open shape, the nose actually gets even fatter than it was in the first place, *adding the difference again*. As I lower each brow, the effect compounds again. Even though I never built a nose that looks anything like the one you see at the end of Figure 6.9, I got there because, as I said, Maya (and any other program using additive shapes) doesn't care what I built or how that shape *looks*; it cares only about what changed, and if the nose moves out a little bit five, six, seven times, it's suddenly moving out pretty substantially.

This situation is simpler than most others where you'll see similar effects; this compound transformation effect can be done accidentally with surprising ease. In fact, I had most example scenes for this book done when I noticed the tongue was multi-transforming and always lifting up, which caused me to go back and fix a lot of work!

Shapes, schmapes. You always have to be careful with every single point you move and how you move it because the *differences*, not the shapes, are *added*, not mixed. If your character's head turns into a mushroom when you start using your blend shapes, this could very well be your problem—and there's no easy way to fix this after it's busted, either! It just means you're in for some elbow grease and head scratching.

The Default Shape is Bored. Period.

All this additive talk is why it is incredibly important to make the default shape of your character bored. I hate to say it, but in this book titled *Stop Staring!*, these poor characters all need to start off staring, bored, and expressionless. Pictured on the following page are the base shapes for the models you've seen and will continue to see.

The face you start with, your default, is the one you're stuck with as your base for all these mixes. This isn't to say that you couldn't put a different *facial expression* on there as the character's standard/default expression—that can be done afterward. It's to say that everything refers to your base shape on a functional level, so leave the canvas open. The complete lack of muscle influence is, in my experience, always the best base, for that very

Figure 6.9

Three stages of the nose, and its compound transformation

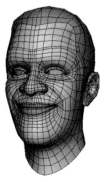 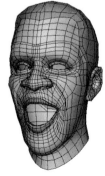 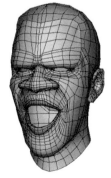

reason: there's no muscle influence. Nowhere to run *from*; every shape is going *to* its destination. If your default shape is smiling, then building a Narrow, a Frown, and a Lips Up, etc., and mixing those all together—every one of them is likely to have an element of "un-Smile" (not a Frown, just less Smile) whether intentional or not. Like we just saw with "plate nose" back there, when you mix five small amounts of "un-Smile" together, the result will be a pretty sizeable un-Smile. It's also why I base the mouth as closed. It makes getting at the points a little easier.

All of this boils down to making a bored expression as your base even if you're itching to see your character do more. The other point is just being careful and thinking hard about what you're actually doing with each shape—not just the *look* of the shape, but how you got there.

Pete

Building the Shapes

With plenty of information swimming in our heads about additive shapes mixing and coexisting, it's time to actually get into the practical work of building shapes. As I said in the introduction, this may take some time, and that's okay. Since in my methods, we'll "bake" everything down to just shapes, you can create clusters, do some joint weighting, or otherwise hack and slash your way through getting the end result of the shape. Do whatever you like, as long as at the end of the shape creation, you make a duplicate of just the mesh, thereby "baking" the deformations into good-ol'-fashioned shapes:

Smile / Wide	Lower Lip Down
Narrow / OO	Lower Lip In
Upper Lip Up	Frown
Upper Lip In	Sneer

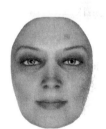

Sally Ann

Begin all shapes by duplicating the weighted default model, and renaming it as the shape you will work on. Each and every shape will benefit from you being able to open and close the mouth at will. Also, you want to work on a duplicate, so you don't lose your default!

Open

Face shape name	Jaw_Open(1 & 2)
Teeth shape name	Teeth_Open(1 & 2)
Derivative shapes	N/A

Tina

This first shape to build is so easy, I don't usually even think of it as a shape. The simplest way to do this is to take the weighted model, open the jaw joint and then duplicate the mesh and delete the history, so it's just a shape, not a shape manipulated via joints. From there, I'd go and clean up the area where the jaw meets the neck (it usually gets shoved inward in an ugly way, to look like Figure 6.10). The teeth, mouth wall, and tongue, if it's separate, need to be shaped to match.

Jason

WHEN SHAPES WON'T COOPERATE

A very talented woman I once trained in facial setups had done some great work, but at first I found myself having to explain why two shapes would or would not work together; additive thinking was making things complicated. What we decided was for her to build a whole key set using only a spline for a mouth, and then animate the mouth to see the mixes. After a very short while, she had the concepts nailed, because with only a small number of points to think about, problems mixing and where they were coming from were more obvious. Within the week she was back on production models, and within the month, I only had to look at her shapes to approve aesthetic quality, because she had the know-how to make the mixes work. If mixing your shapes together proves troublesome, try this. Bad mixes, in every situation, come down to user error, but to be fair, it's a tough thing to wrap one's head around!

Smile / Wide

Face shape name	Smile(1)
Derivative shape	LSmile(2), RSmile(2)

In the Smile (Figure 6.11), you're forced to pull some points in extreme ways, you need to create a crease, and may run into difficulties with some of these details. If this shape proves too difficult and there's no way to get it to look the way you want, then I recommend going back to the modeling phase and reordering some points around, then starting fresh on the smile. After all, you won't be losing four or five shapes; you'll just be backing up on the one (and the very easy *Open*).

I rarely get past the Smile in one try, I almost always have to go back and tweak the default shape; that's okay, it's all part of the process. After you set up a few heads, testing the default with a quickie Smile becomes just another part of building the default shape. I recommend building a quick and dirty Smile to get the testing part over with fast. For your reference, the Smile I'm using for most visual examples here took me approximately 5.5 hours to build.

Figure 6.10

The weighting, and more views of the jaw

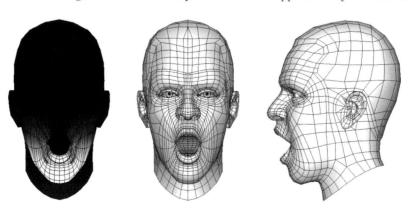

Basic Ingredients

The smile, like all other shapes we build, has important aspects that make it look right. These small descriptions are meant to help you figure out on your own, with a unique character, whether the shape will work for your setup. Each shape will have a different list of things, as each shape's important aspects are different. Go through each one first, then make a run at building your Smile, and then read through again, using this text as a checklist.

> The Smile list will be more verbose and detailed than other shapes' lists because it also doubles as the introduction to the things you should look for and why.

Inclusion The area affected by the Smile shape, as we've already discussed, should look like Figure 6.12. The mouth and the surrounding mouth area have the most effect, and as the shape moves up toward where the eyes would clearly squint, the shape we build will taper, and leave that area alone. The Smile will later mix with the Squint; this is the main reason to taper the effect in that region of the face.

Width Every character will differ, but the general rule I've come up with is that in the default shape, the mouth width comes to about the inside edge of the iris. In a Smile shape, the mouth is usually wide enough to line up with the outside edge of the iris as in Figure 6.13. It may not seem like much, but properly supported, by the right shape and creasing, it's a good guideline.

Depth The depth change from the default should be very noticeable. It is common to build a shape only from its front, but as I've stated before, the face has no front, it's a continuous curved surface. As the mouth spreads left to right, it must also move back. A good gauge of how much it should move is anywhere between half and fully the distance traveled laterally. Figure 6.14 shows this.

Height In most cases, the mouth moves up vertically, one half of the lip height. Take a look at Figure 6.15. If a character has very thin lips, this measurement reference starts to fall apart, and it should be measured by distances, from where the lips meet to the nose. Between one-fourth and one-half of that distance is a good place to move to. Someone with a long droopy face will really lift their whole face as they smile, the smile will relate to their own mouth.

Two creases on each side There are two creases on each side of the Smile, and a space between them. Commonly, it is misperceived that the mouth goes all the way up to the crease in the Smile, but that's not the case in reality (although it's a perfectly acceptable stylistic choice). The corner of the mouth pulls up and out, and generates a crease in the same area that is shadowed in the base pose. The most noticeable crease on the face, the drape-like tucking back of the cheek area, is also shown in Figure 6.16. The area between these two creases bulges slightly.

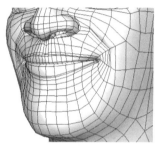

Figure 6.11

A Smile

Figure 6.12

The affected region of the face during a Smile built to work in cooperation with other shapes

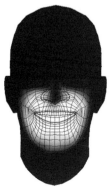

Advanced Ingredients

Beyond just the end shape, other considerations are important. We must concern ourselves with the path the points took getting to their destination and how the shape looks when opened.

Path Here's one of the places where our clean structure helps us the most—it gives us an easy map for identifying problems. When I think a shape is getting close to completion, I'll look at it in an animation. I'll set my shape up as a blend shape on a default head. On frames 0 and 20, I set keys keeping the mouth at default. On frame 10, I set a key on the shape I'm working on. Then I loop the animation, and watch the mouth go into and out of the shape. What I'm looking for is the points' paths. After staring at a shape looping long enough, you'll notice certain points that are disagreeing with the overall motion. Figure 6.17 shows a transition over a few frames.

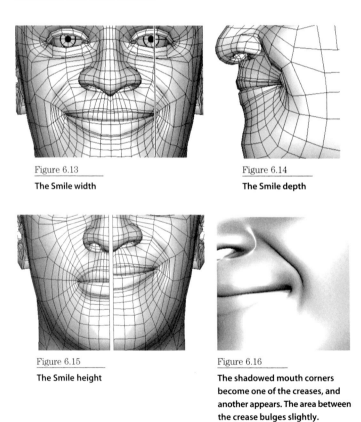

Figure 6.13
The Smile width

Figure 6.14
The Smile depth

Figure 6.15
The Smile height

Figure 6.16
The shadowed mouth corners become one of the creases, and another appears. The area between the crease bulges slightly.

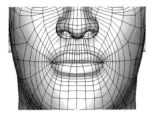 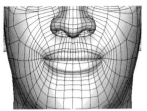 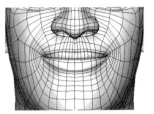 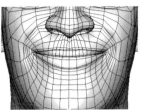

Figure 6.17

A Default-to-Smile animation to show the paths of points

If a point is not cohesive in its movements relating to other points, that point will need to be made to cooperate. Otherwise, once textured and mixed with multiple shapes, who knows what ugly stuff could happen?

Open Combining this shape with the opening of the jaw you should be able to peer to the inside edge of the mouth and make adjustments accordingly. It's easy to forget about the inside of the mouth—don't. The most likely places to freak out when combining multiple shapes are the areas hardest to see, such as the inside edge of the lips and the mouth corners. Luckily, opening the mouth gives us a better look at both. Frequently open the mouth and reshape both those areas so that they are very clean. Sometimes it may be necessary to slightly compromise the shape as it appears *closed*, so that it *opens* cleanly. This whole system relies on the mixes of these shapes cooperating; compromise of a minor detail in favor of a good mix is always the best decision. Figure 6.18 shows the combo shape.

Figure 6.18

The Smile in combination with the open shape

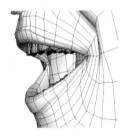

Style

In the next few paragraphs we'll talk about the dos and don'ts that are tied to working with different styles, be they realistic or cartoony.

Don't do the cartoon, unless you're doing cartoons Figure 6.19 shows you exactly not how to build a smile. This type of shape has etched itself into our minds as viable, due mostly to the way a drawn smile looks, which is too bad. It works in drawings, but not so much in 3D. The corners of your mouth can't simultaneously pull up higher than the center. This is part of why I don't like using clusters to create shapes—they make creating something ugly like this so easy to do. I will say, however, that on characters who are distinctly unhuman, this can be made to work. I recently saw a commercial for the next big CGI movie, and there's a shot of a shark pulling this off; it's not easy.

Figure 6.19

A very bad smile, and the culprit behind our impression of why we think that shape is what a smile looks like

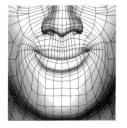

Cartoon male A smile meant for toon shading is largely the same as in regular 3D, but certain things need to be done differently. Usually, in toon shaders, there are two things that are going to evoke a line to draw: (1) A big change in the direction of normals and (2) a big difference in distance to camera. You may have to twist and contort the mesh pretty hard to satisfy one or both of those criteria. In one of my characters, Pete, the shape of the mesh to create that line looks like Figure 6.20.

This is obviously very weird in shaded mode, but rendered, it works convincingly. When working with toon characters, always take the shape way too far. Unfortunately, judging toon shapes in shaded view is almost useless; you have to render, render, and render again, because that's the actuality of what your audience will see. The last tip for cartoon smiles: Ignore the "Don't do the cartoon thing" section preceding this one!

Cartoon female Cartoon females are tough. The trick is to give them the expression without otherwise moving their face. You don't want creasing like you do on males; it becomes very unattractive. If you're working on an old hag, sure, fire up the creasers, but for cartoon females in general, it's all lips, nothing else. Figure 6.21 show's Sally Ann's smile.

Figure 6.20

A male toon Smile, shaded to show how severe the shape can get, and then rendered properly to show the final effect

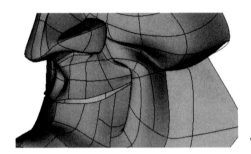

Narrow / OO

Face shape name   Narrow(1)

Derivative shape   LNarrow(2), RNarrow(2)

The second half of our Wide/Narrow pair, OO needs to be modeled into more of a pucker than an OO, as pucker plus a little bit of Open gives us that OO. As you may have guessed, the Narrow shape should be less wide than the default, and it should move forward. The lips should plump as they shift into the shape. The Narrow used for most of the visuals here took me approximately 4 hours to build. The Smile, Narrow, and Frown usually take longer to build than other shapes. Figure 6.22 shows the Narrow *beauty shot*.

Basic Ingredients

OO or Narrow shapes have a pretty easy process to them because you can scale the whole area, shape the outside rim as you want to see it, and then work out from that area, including the rest of the face in the shape and smoothing the rows of points outward.

Inclusion The Narrow has no hard and fast inclusion rules. You can choose to taper its effect quickly or have it subtly affect areas all the way to behind the eye. The more you affect, the better it will look but the more time-consuming it will be to build. See Figure 6.23.

Figure 6.21

Sally Ann's decidedly more subtle smile

Width The Narrow shape is usually a little more than half of the width of the default mouth. I accent *usually*. This shape we're building here, remember, is the furthest extreme we'll be able to take the Narrow to, so it should be pushed to an extreme. To establish the width, I usually select the points that define the lips' outside edge and everything within that, and scale. From there I'll tweak the geometry around the edges to fatten up the outside rim. This is pictured in Figure 6.24.

Height The Narrow shape can sometimes actually be a little taller than the default. In most cases, though, it should be the same height as the default. The Narrow should never ever be shorter in height than the default; that would create a look of the mouth shrinking, which is not an effect we would usually want to achieve.

Depth The Narrow shape should move forward. How much can be based on the character, but it should always move forward. Because the width is being reduced so drastically, the mass has to go somewhere. Figure 6.25 shows this.

The inside moves out In a good Narrow shape, the rows that are inside the mouth have to move toward the outside. This shape is the main reason I have you build your mouths past the point where you can see them on the inside. There's a row in the default shape that your lips meet at. In the Narrow shape, that row gets moved forward. The row inside of that row is now also a meeting point. You may need to take a close look at Figure 6.26 to see this.

Don't do the keyhole! I'm borrowing the name from a friend I used to work with; he called it "the keyhole." Don't do it. It's bad. The keyhole is another—in fact, a more common— approach to building an OO-type shape. I instruct you to narrow the mouth, but another way to make an OO shape is to tighten the sides of the mouth vertically, and pull the middle vertically apart, as in the first image of Figure 6.27. It does, kind of, portray the look of an OO, but besides not being a very natural-looking shape (It's pretty much impossible to do with your own living mouth!), it has technical limitations, too; it doesn't play nice with the other shapes.

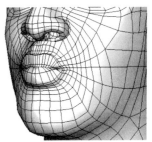

Figure 6.22

A Narrow

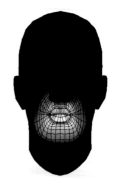

Figure 6.23

The affected region of the face during a Narrow built to work in cooperation with other shapes

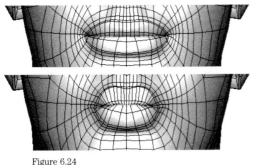

Figure 6.24

The Narrow width

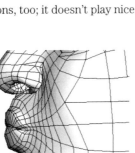

Figure 6.25

The Narrow depth

The second image of Figure 6.27 shows a keyhole-style Narrow with the open shape mixed in. Awful, just awful. You can't get AHs, OHs, any of those kinds of shapes, and you get that weird, well, "keyhole" shape. If you can avoid it, don't ever build an OO/Narrow shape that looks like Figure 6.27; I'll be very disappointed, and I'll send you to bed without any dinner.

Advanced Ingredients

Path If you've followed the structure the way I've laid it out, there's almost a built-in road map to track this. When you've first gotten your lips looking good, you can then turn your attention to the skin leading up to them. The easiest way, after the lips are done, is to (from the front view) pull points along the *track* they're already on. Figure 6.28 is a series of images showing you the path.

If, from the front view, you keep a point roughly on it's own "line's" trajectory, you're in a good position to get the shape done quickly. With the Narrow shape, you just have to keep the points lined up and spread the stretch out. When you've got the front done, move into the side view and move the points in Z only; that will finish it up.

Open Combining the Narrow with the opening of the jaw, you'll likely get a very strange shape if you open the mouth wide and up. Figure 6.29 shows this odd, but still correct version of the shape.

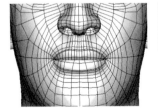

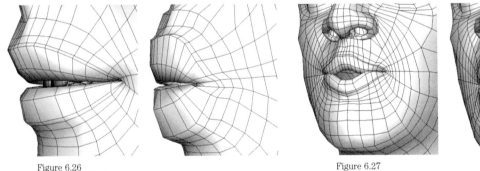

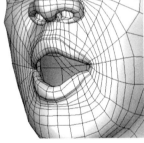

Figure 6.26

These two frames show that the rows of points actually roll out and forward in a Narrow, they don't just push.

Figure 6.27

The dreaded keyhole style OO. Don't be a statistic!

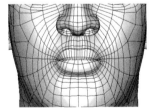

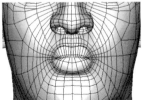

Figure 6.28

A Default-to-Narrow animation to show the paths of points

Creasing For all the talk of creasing I've done thus far, the Narrow, one-half of the most important cycle of animation, is in fact crease-free. If your character has, as a default, creases in their face along the smile lines, this shape should reduce or remove them. Generally, this is one of the smoothest shapes of them all. In most cases, the Narrow should suck the sides in slightly, so the areas usually creasing are pulled taut.

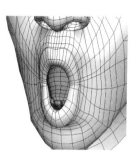

Figure 6.29

An Open Narrow

Cartoon Style

Both male and female cartoon characters have the same considerations with this shape. The Narrow doesn't need to include as much of the face as a realistic character's Narrow, because it's likely we won't see that shape anyway, after it's all tooned-out. We merely want to be sure that the shape dissipates over the face in a ramped manner, so that mixes can work out. Toon Narrows can usually be done very quickly. Figure 6.30 shows Sally Ann's and Pete's Narrows.

Upper Lip Up

Face shape name   UprLip_Up(1)

Derivative shape   LUprLip_Up(2), RUprLip_Up(2)

Figure 6.30

Sally Ann's and Pete's Narrows

The Smile will need some teeth-baring to help it look like a true EE shape. To create an F, we'll need to pull the upper lip up like this, and to make the sound of a SH, we'll need the same. All of that leads us here, to the Upper Lip Up shape (Figure 6.31).

Basic Ingredients

Inclusion If you pull your upper lip up in real life, it causes a sneer. Since a sneer is something we'll have as an independent shape, we don't want that included in this shape. For the Upper Lip Up, the affected area will include only the lips, and the points above that needed to be readjusted to smoothly line up again with the face (Figure 6.32).

Width and Height The Upper Lip Up has no width change from the default; see Figure 6.33. The upper lip should form a smooth M shape with its silhouette. There are two main pulls vertically above the fangs, and the area in the middle is basically dragged along for the ride. The height should most definitely clear the top of the teeth and reveal some gums.

Figure 6.31

An Upper Lip Up

Depth The Upper Lip Up should pull its peaks back slightly, but only as much as is needed to follow the contours of the face. It should most definitely not sink into the face; see Figure 6.34. The center should not move back at all, as the teeth are in the way.

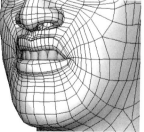

Mixing with the Smile/Wide One of the first things to check after you've roughly shaped the Upper Lip Up is its mix with the Smile. This mix is one that will occur often. The combination can take a lot of work, and very strongly affect how the Upper

Figure 6.32

The affected region of the face during an Upper Lip Up built to work in cooperation with other shapes

Lip Up looks alone. When judging the mix, cut yourself some slack. If you've got each shape individually looking good, and they mix together attractively at around 50% to 60% strength each, then you're fine. Also, this MIX isn't very attractive, but you're deciding whether it looks incorrect rather than checking to see if it's "cute." This looks like a job for Figure 6.35.

Mixing with the Narrow Don't worry about it too much. If you can get 25% to 50% of this shape mixing onto a 100% Narrow, you're doing great. You've got to lean your decision about good/bad more heavily on the Narrow shape, as it's more important. See Figure 6.36.

Advanced Ingredient: Path

Since we're not going to build the sneer into the shape, the points really are sandwiched in tightly. Pull the points sort of like a sneer but don't create the crease. Try to dissipate the shape out using as few rows as possible, but make use of the rows on the sides of the nose, and even the areas where the nose is anchored. Figure 6.37 shows a progression from default to the upper lip up shape.

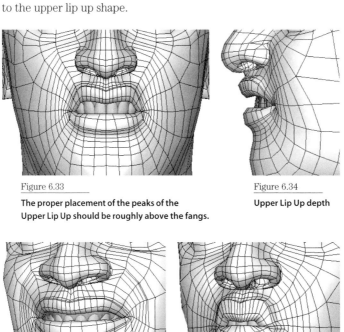

Figure 6.33

The proper placement of the peaks of the Upper Lip Up should be roughly above the fangs.

Figure 6.34

Upper Lip Up depth

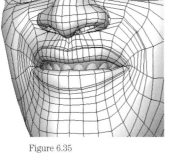

Figure 6.35

A good mix of the Upper Lip Up with a Smile

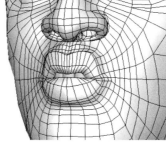

Figure 6.36

A mix of the Upper Lip Up and the Narrow

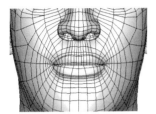
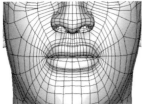
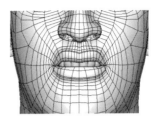
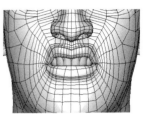

Figure 6.37

A Default-to-Upper Lip Up animation to show the paths of points

Cartoon Style

For both male and female characters in toon styling, this shape is really easy. Since you don't need to affect the whole face, it's perfect for toons, as you can't see surface detail anyway. For this style, really only focus on the silhouette created by the lips, and that's your only concern besides how it mixes with the Wide/Narrow. See Figure 6.38.

Upper Lip Down

Face shape name   UprLip_Dn(1)
Derivative shape   LUprLip_Dn(2), RUprLip_Dn(2)

There are really only two good ways to describe this shape: (1) the upper half of a good rolling-lips-in B,M,P shape or (2) "I did a bad, bad thing." For some reason there's a shame aspect to this shape that I've never quite been able to put my finger on. Take a look for yourself at Figure 6.39. The main use of this shape is as the top half of an M.

There are images in this section in which the jaw is opened for clarity. I must emphasize: *there is no jaw influence.* The jaw is open merely so you can see into places you couldn't otherwise.

Figure 6.38

Cartoon Upper Lip Up concerns are all aesthetic.

Basic Ingredients

Inclusion The inclusion of points on this shape should match exactly those on the Upper Lip Up; see Figure 6.32.

Width and Height The Upper Lip Down has no width change from the default. The height of this shape can be a strange one to wrap your head around, so peek at Figure 6.40. The actual shape can be far beyond reality, it can be a shape that stretches deep into the mouth and doesn't really look like a real thing you can do with your mouth, because it needs to work during the whole transition. Usually, to build a realistic "Upper Lip Rolled In" shape would mean that the transition would intersect the teeth. The Jaw is open only to help you see that the upper teeth are completely covered.

Depth As I mentioned above, the shape needs to cover the upper teeth, Figure 6.41 shows a cross-section. Again, *the jaw is not actually open for the shape*, just for the visual.

Figure 6.39

An Upper Lip Down

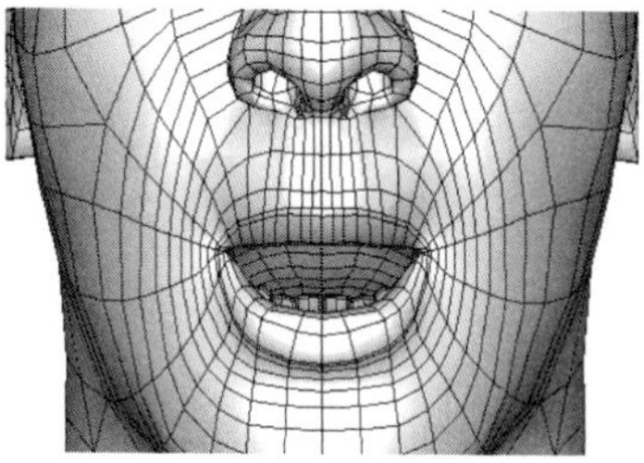

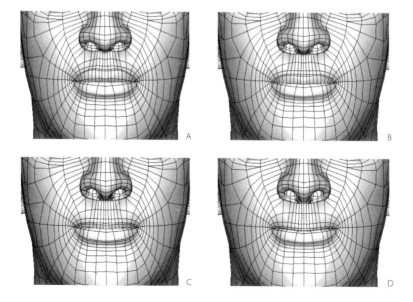

Figure 6.40

Upper Lip Down is more like a roll inward than a down movement.

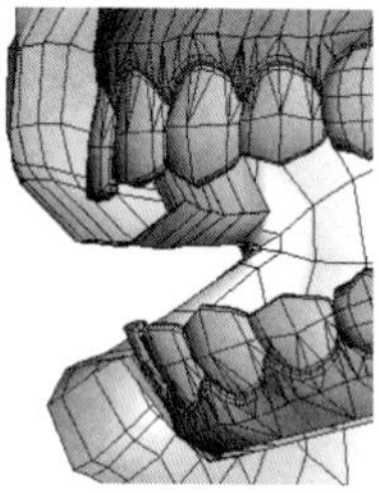

Figure 6.41

The depth goes into and behind the teeth.

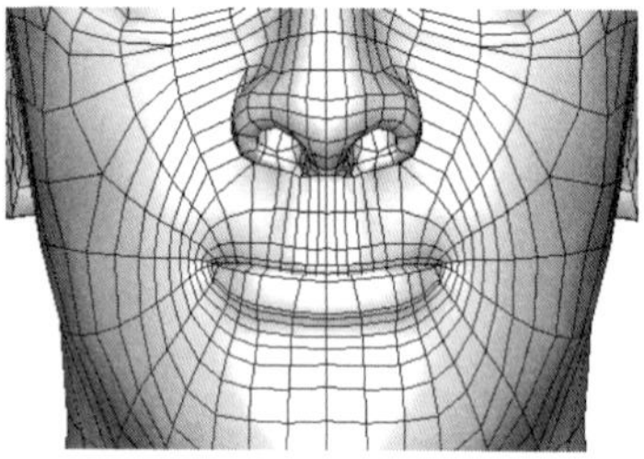

Figure 6.42

The Upper Lip rolled in

You'll also notice that I modeled some bulging on the outside of the lips, too. This helps to accentuate the overall shape of the lips leading into the mouth.

Rolling it in In my experience supervising others building key sets, this and the Lower Lip In are the shapes most commonly done wrong. Figure 6.42 shows it done right. There can be a tendency to simply flatten the lips to each other, which doesn't look nearly as good as having the lips rolling in. The contact point with the lower lip should become the area that was once above the lips, while the lip itself is inside.

Advanced Ingredients

Path Much as with the inclusion, pay special attention to this as the opposite of the Upper Lip Up. You should create and watch a cycle of animation going between Upper Lip Up and Upper Lip Down; the motion should be as smooth as possible. See Figure 6.43.

Figure 6.43

A Default-to-Upper Lip Down animation to show the paths of points

Open The mix between the Upper Lip Down and the Open is a simple one. Keep it clean. No wayward points, no problems. Figure 6.44 shows a good mix.

Style

As long as the lips disappear into the mouth, for a character of extended style, that's enough (Figure 6.45).

Lower Lip Down

Face shape name   LwrLip_Dn(1)

Derivative shape   LLwrLip_Dn(2), RLwrLip_Dn(2)

This shape is the second half of a pair with the Upper Lip Up. These two combined create a SH, or at lesser values, they create a real EE shape in conjunction with the Wide/Smile. As there's no creasing associated with this shape, and not a lot of geometry below the lips, most descriptions will be very short. This shape is very much the opposite of the Upper Lip Up shape. Most everything mentioned there can be flipped vertically and applied here. The Lower Lip Down shape pictured in most examples, including Figure 6.46, took me around 30 minutes to complete.

Basic Ingredients

Inclusion The Lower Lip Down mirrors the Upper Lip Up. The affected area is very similar, just upside down, and, well, without the nose in the way. See Figure 6.47.

Width and Height The Lower Lip Down has no particulars as far as width goes. As with the Upper Lip Up, place the main peak of the pull around the fangs of the *upper* teeth, as in Figure 6.48. The two shapes together should look very paired. Use your Upper Lip Up shape as reference for what you do here. The height, or drop in height, should match that of the upper lip up—you should be able to see gums. The upper lip up is included in the image for visual aid; it is not a part of the shape.

Figure 6.45

With toons, if it looks like teeth are covered, you're done!

Figure 6.47

The affected region of the face during a Lower Lip Down built to work in cooperation with other shapes

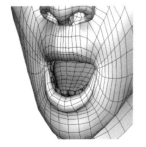

Figure 6.44

The Upper Lip Down mixed with the Open

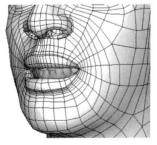

Figure 6.46

A Lower Lip Down

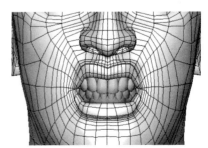

Figure 6.48

The peaks in a Lower Lip Down line up with its counterpart, the upper Lip Up.

Depth The Lower Lip Down doesn't really move forward or back as a rule, but take a look at Figure 6.49 anyway.

Mixing with the Wide/Narrow and Closed The instruction in the Upper Lip Up section applies exactly to this shape.

Advanced Ingredients and Style

All items in this area can be derived exactly from the Upper Lip Up. Toon examples of Lower Lip Down are shown in Figure 6.50.

Lower Lip Up

Face shape name   LwrLip_Up(1)

Derivative shapes   LLwrLip_Up(2), RLwrLip_Up2)

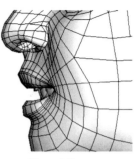

Figure 6.49

The uneventful depth of a Lower Lip Down, here just to provide you a side view

Absolutely all concepts in the Upper Lip Down apply to this shape, the only difference being that it is upside down and the lower rather than upper lip. Figure 6.51 shows views of the shape as it is completed according to the instruction in that section—of course, flipped upside down. Figure 6.52 shows toon versions of the LLU shape.

Figure 6.50

Toon Lower Lip Downs

Frown

Face shape name   Frown(1)

Derivative shapes   LFrown(2), RFrown(2)

The Frown is not something we've done too much talking about yet. The Frown is obviously the other side of the Smile/Frown pair. In the setups that I teach, the Smile and Frown are on opposite ends of the same control. For this reason, as we had to do with the Upper Lip Up vs. the Upper Lip Down (which also will share a control), we must strive to make shapes living on the same control behave like a pair. The Frown used in the visuals here required approximately 4 hours and is pictured in Figure 6.53.

Figure 6.51

The Lower Lip Up completed by mirroring the instructions for the Upper Lip Down

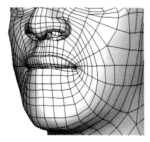

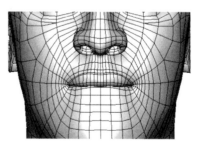

Basic Ingredients

Inclusion The Frown includes the same area of effect as the Smile does, but the emphasis is different. With the Smile we spent a lot of time in the cheeks and the creases, as they were high and obvious focal points. The area below that seemed to follow in tow. Here, the area below the mouth has the focus, and the area above is just along for the ride. Figure 6.54 shows this area.

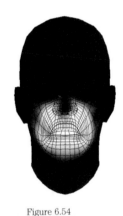

Figure 6.52

The toon version of the Lower Lip Up

Width The Frown is slightly wider than the default, but also slightly narrower. Take a look at Figure 6.55 and then let me explain: in a Frown, the mouth is pulled downward at the sides. As the muscles pull down, the upper lip is forced down into the area where the lower lip is. What it does to get around the lower lip is just that—it gets pushed around the lower lip. The Frown has a unique distinction among the shapes, wherein the mouth corners are not actually the outside edge of the mouth. The area of the lips just above the corners are the outermost areas, and the overall shape ends up slightly wider than the default. The lower lip is very slightly compressed by this action and ends up narrower across.

Height The height is different at different points in the shape. In relation to the default, the center of the lips is identical. A Frown has little effect in the center of the mouth. The corners, on the other hand, pull down to approximately the height of the lower edge of the lips—but the greater effect on the skin makes that *look* like it's quite a bit lower; see Figure 6.56.

Depth As shown in Figure 6.57, the Frown pulls back as much as it pulls vertically, sort of. The corners of the mouth shouldn't move back too far, but the area that creases shuttles back approximately as far as the corners move sideways.

Figure 6.54

The affected region of the face during a Frown built to work in cooperation with other shapes

The Bulges This same group of points from the Smile will create the crease for the Frown shape. The Frown creates a very small crease down and to the sides of the mouth. The area between the mouth corners and that crease bulges as in Figure 6.58.

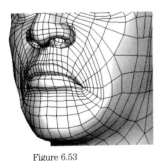

Figure 6.53

A Frown

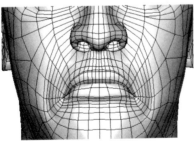

Figure 6.55

The width of Frown

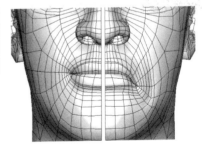

Figure 6.56

The center doesn't move; the edges pull down, quite a bit

Figure 6.57

Parts of the Frown pull back, but not the lips so much.

Figure 6.58

That familiar bulge

Figure 6.59

A Default-to-Frown animation to show the paths of points

Advanced Ingredients

Path We've all heard the expression that it takes only 4 muscles to smile but 40 to frown. This is pretty close to true, so where the Smile shape needed to look fairly cohesive in its overall point motion path, due to so few muscles, the Frown can be less organized. The complicated motion involved in a frown allows us some leverage in this regard. Figure 6.59 traces the awkward path(s) of points.

Open The Frown Open should look very much like the default Open. This is the one shape for which it's beneficial not to mess with the inside of the mouth too much. The Frown, that rainbow shape, should happen mostly on the outside of the mouth, and involve the surface mass, not the inside. Figure 6.60 looks inside.

Cartoon Style

Take a look at Figure 6.61. In this shape the need to create the creases on the sides of the mouth is unnecessary—in toon shading, there's no point in making a partial crease since it'll just show up as spotty anyway. Ignore the bulges and the creasing, and also the points regarding the seam not taking over the rest of the shape. In toon shading, this is all perfectly okay—again, assuming that the mixes involving the basics, the Wide, and the Open work well.

Sneer

Face shape name	Sneer(1)
Derivative shapes	LSneer(2), RSneer(2)

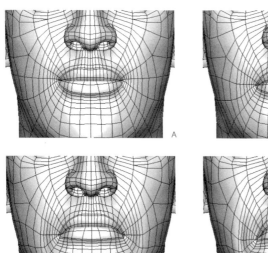
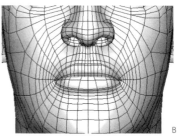
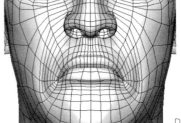

The Sneer is just that. Scrunch your nose, or lift your upper lip, and you'll have a good idea of what the shape should look like; either that or look at Figure 6.62. By creating the shape all alone, we can add it to a Frown to create a Scowl, have a Sniff shape, or add it into the Upper Lip Up shape for more reality. The shape used heavily here was about 2.5 hours of work.

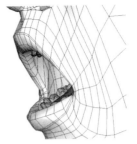
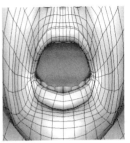

Figure 6.60

The mix between the Frown and the Open should be very compatible, and the inside edge of the mouth should look quite similar to the Open all by itself.

Basic Ingredients

Inclusion The Sneer's main area of influence is along the base and sides of the nose, as in Figure 6.63. If you intend to use this shape to create the Scowl at animation time, it's not required but it's a nice touch to include the area up on top of the nose. In a Sneer, the muscle that flexes pulls vertically. As the nose and cheek are pulled up, that same muscle pulls the middle of the forehead down, and some of the skin on top of the nose down. You can end up with a bit of a scrunched nose, and that's a fantastic detail to add.

Width and Height The Sneer does not affect the width of the mouth or the nose. The Sneer moves the base of the nose up. My advice is to start by moving it too far up; you can always pull it back down. During a Sneer, the nostrils anchor with the rest of the face, angling up. See Figure 6.64.

Depth There is no characteristic depth change associated with this shape; see Figure 6.65.

Figure 6.61

I often understate the cartoon style Frown, as sadness comes better from the eyes and brows than the mouth, and to go too far makes for an ugly face.

The crease The crease created in this shape should be on the same set of rows that lead out to the crease on the Smile. To have them occur on different rows will cause an unattractive rollover of the points, and the model stops looking like skin. Figure 6.66 shows it done right.

Figure 6.62

A Sneer

Advanced Ingredient: Path

Much like the more complicated movement of the Frown, not all points are going to move uniformly in the Sneer. See Figure 6.67. Of special note are the points on the cheek, just outside the main area of creasing. They move up, and also curl in (as viewed from the front) toward the bridge of the nose.

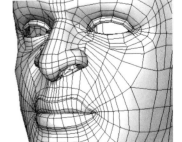

Cartoon Style

Male As with the Smile, to get this line to draw may take some odd work. I have found that I have to pull the points that in a regular model would usually crease *wayyy* up into the face on toon models. Whatever it takes to draw the line is what it gets! Figure 6.68 shows a successful attempt.

Female Also as with the Smile, Sneer lines on toon females is almost never a good idea. The best thing to do is get the silhouette of the nostrils to look angry. The shape doesn't end up looking like much if it's not combined with other things like the brows and lids; take a peek at Figure 6.69.

Joint-Built Shapes

Well, the bulk of the shapes are done, there are just a few more that are much simpler. The following shapes are achieved much like the Jaw Open was—by weighting, manipulating joints, and then duplicating the mesh.

Mouth Move Left/Right

Face shape name   Not used in simple setup
Derivative shapes   LMouth(2), RMouth(2)

This is actually two shapes, left and right, but I'll just talk through the left. For asymmetrical shapes, the way they get split in two from the symmetrical shape leaves something to be desired, as it effectively paralyzes one side. By having this left-to-right motion available, combined with our asymmetrical shapes, a sideways Smile does not have to remain static on the face, it can actually move the whole mouth over to the side. Figure 6.70 shows the LMouth shape.

Figure 6.63

The affected region of the face during a Sneer built to work in cooperation with other shapes

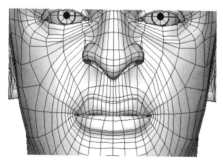

Figure 6.64

The Sneer width and height

Figure 6.65

A side view of the Sneer

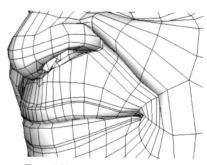

Figure 6.66

The crease in the Sneer needs to be a continuation of the crease in the Smile.

This, besides the Jaw, is all that I'll usually create using joints, since it's just so easy to do it that way. I'll usually place a joint back around where the jaw is, and weight it to include the mouth and some of the nose, and taper off from there. Remember, this is not a joint I leave in; it is added and weighted merely to create this shape, which is then duplicated. Figure 6.71 shows the area of effect.

From here, simply rotate the joint to get a shape such as in Figure 6.72. Duplicate it and you're done!

Figure 6.68

In toon males, try to evoke a line draw behind the nose.

Figure 6.69

In toon females, the effect should be minimal; the shape works best mixed with others to create emotions.

Jaw Left/Right Forward/Back

Face shape name   Not used in simple setup
Teeth shape names Teeth_Fwd(2), LTeeth(2), RTeeth(2)
Derivative shapes Jaw_Fwd(2), LJaw(2), RJaw(2)

Another set of simple ones that can all be created by simply manipulating the jaw joint. When you're done with these, as with all key shapes, you should duplicate the mesh. When building the Jaw_Fwd, be sure to only translate the jaw joint, no rotations. By doing so, you can use the opposite of the shape as a jaw *in/back*. Also make sure you do the same with the teeth mesh, since they'll need to pair with these movements. A little intersecting/poke-through is okay, too; these, like all other shapes, are meant to be mixed, and that can be fixed at animation time, it's not a big deal. See Figure 6.73 for both the forward and left shapes.

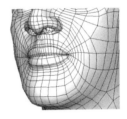

Figure 6.70

The LMouth shape

Figure 6.67

A Default-to-Sneer animation to show the paths of points

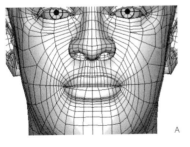
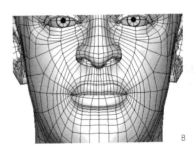
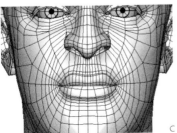
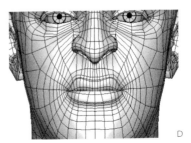

A

B

C

D

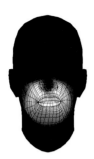

Figure 6.71

The affected region of the face during Mouth Moves built to work in cooperation with other shapes

The Tongue

Face shape name	No face shapes
Teeth shape names	Tongue_Out(1), Tongue_Up(1), Tongue_Tip_Up(2), LTongue(2), RTongue(2)
Derivative shape	N/A

The tongue will get very little in the way of shape keys, and achieving those is very easy, so they will all be put together in one section. The easiest way to make these is to weight a Tongue quickly and manipulate bones to shape it. Duplicate the shapes to "bake" them when you're done. All of the images have the mouth open so you can see the tongue, but there should be no degree of mouth Open in the shapes themselves. (You build the shapes with the mouth closed—shapes that will never actually be seen by themselves—because otherwise, you'd have your Open mouth shape and as you add in a Tongue shape that is *also* open, the mouth would "double Open"—that is, break or dislocate. You'd have to counter-animate your Open shape closed to use your Tongue shapes—and this is not acceptable.)

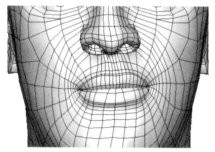

Figure 6.72

A front view of LMouth

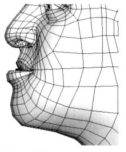

Figure 6.73

Pushing the jaw forward can help in sync with sounds like OO, and it can also do a lot for emotion—more than you might realize.

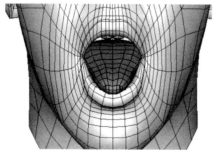

Figure 6.74

Tongue Out

THE MOUTH WALL

For the mouth wall object; you'll need to build accompanying shapes for all for the mouth shapes. This is another reason I quite like the low-resolution one I showed you in Chapter 5 ("Constructing a Mouth"). For anything that you have as an "extra" to the regular head object, you'll have to connect its blend shapes to those of the head using expressions, so that everything moves together. This will be the case if you have separate brows, as well. I'll discuss this aspect further in Chapter 11.

Out By pulling most of the points in the Tongue forward and up, you should be able to create the shape needed for *TH* shapes. See Figure 6.74.

Up Figure 6.75 shows the Tongue Up. The second half of the only necessary shapes for a simple Tongue is the Tongue rolling up. This shape will help us create Ls and Ns. Make sure the points all evenly curl up to the top; you'll need to build this bigger than reality, because it will need to reach the roof of the mouth with the mouth both open and closed.

Tip Up By turning just the tip up, not the whole Tongue, you can get some extra flair into some of your sync, using this in some places you would otherwise use the whole Tongue Up. See Figure 6.76.

Left/Right By turning the Tongue from side to side, you can get some extra character into the Tongue, even though, this isn't at all a necessary shape. Figure 6.77 shows some left/right action.

Creating Asymmetry

To create asymmetry out of the shapes we've built, we'll simply weight the effect of our blend shapes across the surface of the face, first left to right, then right to left, giving us two shapes for each shape we've built—that can then combine to give us the original whole shape, if we want that, too! Creating shapes asymmetrically by hand, and expecting a mirror of the same to mix well, is a very complex and involved task.

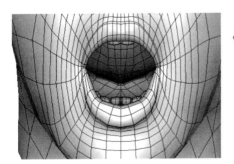 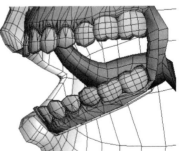

Figure 6.75

Tongue Up

The process can be made simple, really, but you need the tools to do it. Maya includes the ability to paint a texture on an object, paint the skin weights, paint cluster weights...

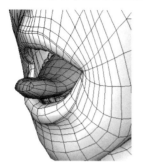

Figure 6.76

Tongue Tip Up

but to paint the effects of deformations, no dice. You can go into the Component Editor and change weights of many things—but again, to split out the information in a blend shape, no way. The only thing even vaguely like what we need is the Paint Set Membership tool, which is far too harsh, as it only allows on/off weighting. I don't know why this is or how long it'll stay that way, but it leaves us with a need for the ability to somehow adjust the weighting of our blend shapes across the surface.

On the accompanying CD is a plug-in that does just such a thing. Copy `xyWeightedBlend.mll` to your plug-ins folder.

Now, the Wgt Blend (weighted blend) button, which is already on your Stop Staring shelf, should work.

> The `xyWeightedBlend.mll` plug-in is for Maya 4.0. A similar script for later versions of Maya is available at `http://jasonosipa.com/SS_Downloads.htm`.

Using the Plug-in

To use the plug-in, simply follow these steps.

1. Make all the shapes you've built blend shapes to be owned by a duplicate of your default head called LeftShapes.

2. After the blend shape relationship is established, with LeftShapes selected, press the Wgt Blend button.

3. Open Window → General Editors → Component Editor and go to the Weighted Deformers tab.

Now when you select vertices on the face, you can weight them by their value in the Weighted Deformers column. 1 is 100%, 0 is 0%. It's not as elegant as painting the values,

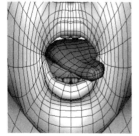

Figure 6.77

Tongue Left/Right

but that feature is just not available yet—although if some plug-in-savvy person reading this wants to make it paintable, go for it and send it to me, and I'll post it on the book's site! Even though this is equivalent to point-weighting (not the most fun aspect of 3D), it ensures that mixes will work together, which is much easier and faster than building the two half-shapes separately; trust me!

MAKE A MOUTH GRAPH

When you're all finished building your shapes, something you should do is put all of your heads together in one scene. I like to call this scene my mouth graph. Organize your head in some pattern that makes sense, because when you get 30 or 40 in a scene together, it can be easy to lose track!

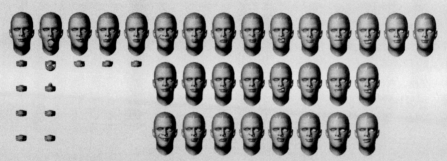

I organize the heads and teeth at even intervals, with the symmetrical shapes in a row on top, the left-side derivatives below that underneath their source shape, and the right-side derivatives on the bottom. All the teeth shapes that relate to face shapes should also be near their counterparts for easy reference. It's a good idea to keep the various weighted heads and teeth around, too. I keep this around because it leaves me my workshop. If you need to fix a shape, you know where it is, you know where they *all* are: right here.

Using the Weighted Values

As I have done with the area of effect for shapes, I'll show you how the area of effect looks for this weighting. Figure 6.78 shows the halved weighting on my model.

- A vertex on one side of the mouth must line up as exactly complementary weighting of the vertex on the other side, meaning that if the mouth corner is weighted 90% on one side, the mouth corner should be exactly 10% on the other.

- The center row must be weighted exactly 50%, or 0.5

This is so the two half-shapes you built will pair perfectly back into the original shape you're breaking in two.

Once you've got your weighting done, you should be easily able to pose your head, using the blend shape slider, into each of the shapes you've built, which will show only the tapered half shape. When it's posed, duplicate the mesh and rename the shape with an L or R in front of the name (so UprLip_Up would become LUprLip_Up). There you are! Half-shapes, perfect for characterful asymmetry!

Figure 6.78

The asymmetrical envelope weighting

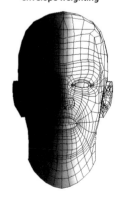

Mirroring the Weights

When you're done with one side, save your scene as left_shapes or something to that effect. Now take the head object LeftShapes, select it, and hit the Mir Wgt button, also on the Stop Staring shelf; this will mirror (technically, inverse) your xyWeightedBlend weights. Rename your object RightShapes and go ahead through the duplication process again, "baking" the right-side shapes.

> As you duplicate heads remember to do it with construction history off, or to delete history on the duplicates. It's best for these new heads to be devoid of extraneous inputs.

When you're done, save the scene as right_shapes or something like that, and then import the left_shapes scene. There you are! You have a whole asymmetrical mouth graph to work with. Figures 6.79 and 6.80 show a few examples.

Figure 6.79

A symmetrical smile split into two smirks as described

Figure 6.80

One upper lip up can become two, creating a fantastic tool for emotion and specific dialogue delivery.

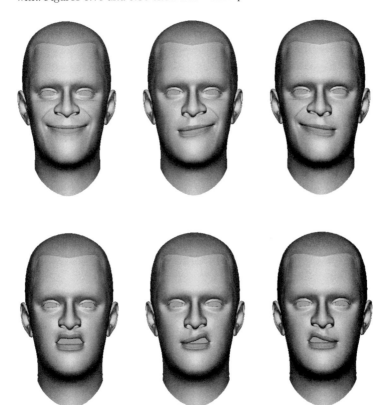

PART III

Animating and Modeling the Eyes and Brows

Well, *here we are. What Part II was to the lower half of the face, Part III is to the top half of the face. With the mouth, and mainly sync, the focus is functional—the bulk of the work is in convincing people that the character is speaking. Here, in the eyes and brows, the goals have flipped. The eyes and brows convince an audience that our character lives, and so emotion has priority over function. Our characters plot the things they do before they do them, they react—in short, they think.*

First I'll review and expand upon the concepts I talked about in Chapters 2 and 3 ("What the Eyes and Brows Tell Us" and "Facial Landmarking," respectively), and then I'll guide you through creating a tool to see some of those concepts in practice. From there, you'll learn about what I think is the most important part of facial animation, the eyes, and how to create focus and thought. At the end of Chapter 7, I'll go over how some of the different emotions are actually achieved, in contrast to how they've commonly been explained. In Chapter 8, I'll show you how to build the top half of a human face, and in Chapter 9, you'll be guided through the different key shapes and their individual goals and needs. On with the show!

CHAPTER 7

Building Emotion:
The Basics of the Eyes

The brows and the eyes tell us what we need to know about a character's thoughts. Primarily, the brows have two major movements, brows Up/Down and brows Squeeze. The brows Up/Down alone don't tell us a whole lot about emotion; they are used in conjunction with the brows Squeeze and different combinations of the lids. Generally, brows Squeeze is in every emotion; regardless of type of emotion, it denotes thought.

The upper lids tell us the alertness of a character, and the lower lids intensify emotions. The eyeballs mainly just communicate where a character is looking. The subtext of that can lead to some powerful emotion, but the eyeballs themselves don't say a whole lot; it's the entire eye area acting together that creates a feeling. That being said, the effect of the angle of the head itself can make all the difference in the world to an expression. It can change the viewer's perception of all the things listed above.

If you need a refresher introduction for any of these topics, take a peek back at Chapters 2 and 3; you should find all that you need.

- **Building an upper face for practice**
- **Rules of the eyes and brows game**
- **Example animations**

Building an Upper Face for Practice

In Chapter 1, "Learning the Basics of Lip Sync," you created a simple mouth to work with and got a taste of the mouth setup in action. We didn't do the same thing for the eyes in Chapter 2, so we'll do it here. Many of the behaviors of the eyes are better to see and do yourself than to have me explain them. It really is much better if you can play along.

Figure 7.1

What a handsome face!

Everything to do with emotion is subjective. The same choices made for scene A could be all wrong for scene B. This section is going to boil down to the choices I would make in certain situations and the reasons why.

Modeling the Pieces

The face I'll use to describe how the eyes and brows work is called Box Head, shown in Figure 7.1. You can load this scene from the Chapter 7 folder on the companion CD, `BoxHead.ma`.

> I recommend that you actually go through and construct Box Head by yourself. In Chapter 12, "Interfaces for Your Faces," I talk about expressions, and some more intricate work with expressions, but the majority of setting up your more complicated character is done with the automatic setup buttons (you'll learn about those in Chapter 12). By doing the work here yourself, you can get some good easy practice in expression writing, which, if you want to design your own interfaces, you'll need to know!

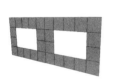

Figure 7.2

The grid with the eye holes already punched out

We're going to construct and rig an extremely simple eye area for you to see the concepts I explain. We'll build the face "backdrop," cut out eyes, make flats to represent the brows and eyelids, and make a sphere and flatten it for our eyeballs. After that, we'll load in the spline mouth from Chapter 1 and give Box Head a mouth!

The Face

Create a plane of Width 1, Height 0.4 with 10 subdivisions along the width and 4 along the height. By choosing the Z axis option, the plane will be created facing forward in the front view, where we'll do our work with this face.

> Planes can be created by selecting Create → Polygon Primitives → Plane □.

Delete the faces that are missing from Figure 7.2. Select the outside edges of the holes and scale them down in Y. Now select the points that define the top of the holes and pull them higher. These will be our eye sockets. Select all the points around the outside perimeter of the grid and scale them out—we want the "face" to have a bigger edge around it. Make the lower edge reach farther than the others, as in Figure 7.3; the mouth will have to live there eventually. Rename the plane "Face."

The Brows

Create another polygonal plane, this time of Width 0.4, Height 0.1, with subdivisions along width and height of 1. Move this shape to –0.25, 0.2, 0.2 in X, Y, and Z respectively. This is to be our right eyebrow. Create a lambert material and make it black.

> There are many ways to create a material. The fastest is to right-click over the object and select Assign New Material from the bottom of the marking menu.

Rename the plane "RBrow." Duplicate RBrow, and move it to 0.25, 0.2, 0.2. That should place it on the other side of the face. Rename it LBrow. You should start to see the beginnings of a *very* simple face (Figure 7.4).

The Upper Lids

Create yet another plane, this time of Width 1, Height 0.25, with subdivisions of only 1 in both width and height. Move the new plane to 0, 0.2, 0.01 (Figure 7.5). Rename the plane UprLids.

The Lower Lids

Duplicate the upper lid(s) and move it down to –0.225 in Y (Figure 7.6). Rename it Lwr-Lids. Make both eyelids children of Face and then freeze the transformations of the eyelids (Modify → Freeze Transformations). This is done so that later, when we apply expressions, we can be sure the lids' translations at default are 0, 0, 0.

> When freezing transformations, if it doesn't seem to work, you may need to check your settings in the option box to make sure that all boxes (scale, rotate, translate) are checked.

Figure 7.3

The grid will provide the backdrop for the face.

Figure 7.4

Now, that is some good-looking brow action.

Figure 7.5

The upper lid plane is outlined where it should be placed.

Figure 7.6

The lower lids placed just below the silhouette of the eyes

The Eyeballs

Create a polygonal sphere of Radius .8, subdivisions along axis of 20, along Height of 4, and make it native to the Z axis. Move the sphere to –0.25, 0, –.01. Scale the sphere to 0.1, 0.1, 0.01. You should have a very flat sphere sitting in the right eye socket of your face. Rename the sphere REye, and assign it the same material of the eyebrows, black.

Since we already have a material created, right-click over the object and from the Marking menu at the bottom select Assign Existing Material, then select the material you created for the brows.

Duplicate the eyeball and move it across the other side to 0.25, 0, –0.1. Rename the new object LEye. Your new practice face should look like Figure 7.7.

Save before you continue, just in case any problems arise. The one last thing to do is *import* your spline mouth from Chapter 1 (or load it from the CD). It should show up right in the middle of Box Head. If it doesn't, feel free to move it into place. Select Mouth (the spline itself), and then Face, and parent them, making Mouth the child of Face. Move Mouth to 0, –0.3, 0.1 and scale it to 0.25 uniformly. Duplicate Mouth and scale the duplicate to 0.01 uniformly— very, very small (Figure 7.8). Now, be sure you have construction history turned on, and loft Mouth and Mouth's duplicate together. Once this is done, turn construction history back off. Now, so you can see it, assign the black lambert material to the loft, and you're ready to go!

Figure 7.7

Box Head is almost born. There's just one more noisy bit to go…

Parenting Our Face Together

Now that we have the pieces we need, it's time to rig them up for use. First, let's start with the eyeballs. Create a locator and scale it to 0.1, 0.1, 0.1 so that it's very small and not too obtrusive. Duplicate the locator and name the duplicate "Eyes." Make both REye and LEye children of Eyes and then make Eyes a child of Face. We will use this locator to control our eyes' positions in the sockets.

Duplicate the original small locator and rename the duplicate Brows. Parent both eyebrows to Brows and make Brows a child of Face.

Rigging Our Face

The first thing we'll need to do is create a slider control, similar to the one we made in Chapter 1 for the mouth, so we can control the things that we need to.

Figure 7.8

Box Head looks mild-mannered, but the things that come out of that mouth…!

Creating Our Control

We'll make one slider control out of a locator and circle that we'll duplicate for the other ones we'll need. We'll make one slider control out of a locator and a circle, and duplicate it to create the other ones we'll need.

Create a locator, scale it to 0.25 uniformly, and move it away from the face. Rename the locator Ctrl_Prnt. Now create a NURBS circle of Radius 0.1 and native to the Z axis. Make the circle a child of Ctrl_Prnt and rename the circle "Ctrl." If you now type zeros into the translate channels for the circle, it should center itself on Ctrl_Prnt (Figure 7.9).

In the Attribute Editor, limit Ctrl's motion so that it can only travel between –1 and 1 in X and Y axes and cannot move in Z, a minimum-maximum limit of 0 and 0. Now, with Ctrl still selected, open the Channel Control (Window → General Editors → Channel Control). Select all but translateX and translateY from the left-side window and hit the "Move" button on the bottom-left side of the window. Now, the only attributes you'll see for Ctrl are translate X an Y. Go ahead and close the window.

> If you're having trouble locating the particular windows for applying translation limits, see the tutorial in Chapter 1.

The circle is now going to be used as a slider with which we can control aspects of the face! You can move the slider's location without affecting its output value by moving it from the Ctrl_Prnt level. Ctrl_Prnt can be anywhere you like in your scene, just as long as...values for the Ctrl itself are 0 and 0 in X and Y; or we'll use those attributes to drive our expressions.

Rigging the Face Control

Duplicate the Ctrl_Prnt hierarchy (the locator and circle, both) and rename the duplicate *circle* Ctrl_Face. (The locator's name is of no real consequence.) Select Face, and in the Channel Box click the rotateY attribute. If you then right-click, you can select Expressions from the menu that appears.

In the Expression Editor, type:

```
Face.rotateY = Ctrl_Face.translateX * 15
```

When you've typed that in, hit the Create button on the bottom-left corner of the window to create your expression. Now, click another attribute of Face's—which attribute doesn't matter. Enter the following in the expression window:

```
Face.rotateX = Ctrl_Face.translateY * -35
```

> You can enter any expression in the Expression Editor in relation to any object and attribute at any time. The only danger in doing so is overwriting another expression that you've just written. To keep that from happening, you need to clear the window; to clear the window, you just have to select an attribute that has no expression.

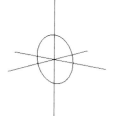

Figure 7.9

A NURBS circle is the slider of choice for most of my setups; by hiding locators, selection is easy.

Throughout this chapter, remember to select the circle, not the locator!

Figure 7.10

Box Head looking top (screen) left and then bottom (screen) right. I had to cheat and move his eyes to help the images, since with his parallel lines, both poses tended to look very similar!

As before, hit the Create button to make your expression take effect. If you close the Expression Editor, you should be able to drag the Ctrl_Face slider left, right, up, and down and see the whole face move, as in Figure 7.10. Set the slider to 0,0 and we'll continue with our setup.

Rigging the Eye Control

Duplicate the *original* Ctrl slider hierarchy again (*not* the one with Ctrl_Face), and move it away so it has its own space. Select the circle and rename it Ctrl_Eyes.

Select the locator that is parent to both eyes; it should be named Eyes. In the Expression Editor, enter and create both these expressions, one at a time:

```
Eyes.translateX = Ctrl_Eyes.translateX / 10
Eyes.translateY = Ctrl_Eyes.translateY / 10
```

As before, create both expressions and then close the window. When you move the new Ctrl_Eyes slider around, the eyes should move (Figure 7.11). Once that's working, set the Ctrl_Eyes slider to 0,0 and keep moving along.

Rigging the Upper Lids

Duplicate the original Ctrl hierarchy, move it away to its own spot, and rename the circle Ctrl_Lids. Select UprLids, and enter the following expression:

```
UprLids.translateY = (Ctrl_Lids.translateY / 5)
```

Figure 7.11

The eyes posed on opposite corners of their range

Notice the parentheses; they're there because of how we're going to change this expression in just a moment. . When you move the Ctrl_Lids slider, its up and down motion should control the upper eye lids' height. There's one problem, though. Select the *Ctrl_Eyes* slider and move *it* around. See how the eyes are moving around and the lids are not relating to them? Figure 7.12 shows that when you pull the EyesCtrl slider up, you have a sleepy-eyed character, and when you pull it down, you have an alert character. Now, maybe for some people that's good enough, but not us. Knowing what we know about lids and eyes' relationships, this expression needs work.

Having read Chapter 2, we know that the upper lids should follow the eyeballs' motion so that we aren't spontaneously changing expression like this. I was animating this effect manually myself for over a year when a friend of mine who also was doing the work of facial setups smartly decided that maybe this should be automated, as it's something you always want to happen. Taking his lead, we'll need the upper lids to consider the *eyeball* movement as well.

Since we want to mimic the eyes' motion as well as what we're doing already, the easiest thing is to simply add the eyes' expression into the lids' expression we already have. On UprLid, change the expression from this:

```
UprLids.translateY = (Ctrl_Lids.translateY / 5)
```

to this:

```
UprLids.translateY = (Ctrl_Lids.translateY / 5) + Ctrl_Eyes.translateY / 10
```

When you modify an expression instead of creating it, you must first select the object and attribute so the old one appears. When you've finished with your changes, you click the Edit button instead of the Create button to update it.

Now if you test the Ctrl_Lids up and down motion, you'll see that it does the exact same thing as before. The difference is apparent when you use the Ctrl_Eyes slider. The lids now move up and down with eyeballs, too! To reiterate, all we did to create this effect was to *add in* the same math we're doing for the eyes themselves.

> This expression leaves something to be desired, since, if the eyes look all the way up, the upper lids can't close to the bottom. For the level this face is at, that's an acceptable flaw. In the automatic setup, there's a more robust expression for the upper lids' movements. For most of the Ctrl_Lids slider's movement, it behaves like this, but for the last part of the slider's range, the expression calculates the total remaining distance between upper and lower lids, and moves to a percentage of that distance, based on the slider's value" Closed will always mean closed regardless of where the eyes are, but the lids, when opened, will follow the eyes' motion as well.

Rigging the Lower Lids

You may have noticed that in the two previous sliders, up and down have an effect as well as left to right. For our Ctrl_Lids slider, the up and down movements control the upper lids and the left to right motions control the lower lids.

Select the plane named LwrLids and type in the expression:

```
LwrLids.translateY = -Ctrl_Lids.translateX / 5
```

This merely links LwrLids to the left and right motion of that same slider used for the upper lids; don't miss the minus sign! Moving the Ctrl_Lids slider up, down, left, and right can create all sorts of combinations for the eyelids (Figure 7.13).

Rigging the Brows

As with all the other pieces, we'll need to create a control for the brows. Duplicate the original Ctrl_Prnt hierarchy again and rename the new circle Ctrl_Brows.

Figure 7.12

The ol' eyes-up-being-sleepy and eyes-down-being-excited just doesn't cut it.

Figure 7.13

Different slider positions yield interesting expressions.

Select the brows' parent object *Brows* and enter the following expression:

```
Brows.translateY = Ctrl_Brows.translateY / 15
```

That will make the eyebrows move up and down. Now, we need to fake some emotion. I've talked a lot about what is and is not right on a human face, but this is decidedly not very human. For this face, and an introduction to the interface style and practice, I'm going to go with some more classic cartoony poses. Select LBrow and add the following expression:

```
LBrow.rotateZ = Ctrl_Brows.translateX * 10
```

And to the right brow add the same, but with a minus sign in front of the expression, so that the right brow does the opposite:

```
RBrow.rotateZ = -Ctrl_Brows.translateX * 10
```

What that added, effectively, was the ability to set sad and mad poses like those in Figure 7.14.

Re-Rigging the Mouth

To fit in with our new control scheme, let's connect the mouth to a slider like the other kids. You can now use Ctrl itself, and not a duplicate, as this is the last slider we'll need for Box Head. Rename Ctrl to Ctrl_Sync, and you'll need to make one more adjustment. Open the Attribute Editor and limit Ctrl_Sync's motion in Y, so the maximum is 0. Now, select Mouth, open the MouthShapes node under the inputs (below the Channel Box), then select and right-click over WideNarrow. Once in the Expression Editor, select WideNarrow from the list on the right, and in the Expression that appears, rewrite the whole thing to read:

```
MouthShapes.WideNarrow = Ctrl_Sync.translateX
```

And then change the expression on the OpenClosed attribute to:

```
MouthShapes.OpenClosed = -Ctrl_Sync.translateY
```

You've now got yourself one rigged-up face that works very similarly to the more complicated setups later on. For ease of use (and the reason we moved the expression on Mouth over to a new slider), you can now, if you like, turn off locators' visibility (Show → Locators (Off)), and you won't select the wrong things, just your new sliders. Also, if it makes it easier for you to differentiate them, reshape the circles to be more like icons as I've done in Figure 7.15, or label them.

Figure 7.14

The brows' control in different positions can create most anything you might need on such a simple character.

Using "Box Head"

The best thing I can do for starters is take you through some examples of things like the tilt of the head, and the eyelids following the eyeballs, which you've heard about but not yet seen in action. Here I'll acquaint you with the tools, and then we'll use the face to create some expressions and emotions, so you can see in practice how things work.

The tilt of the head, in action Just do it. Just move the Ctrl_Face slider up and down to alter the tilt of the head, and watch as the eyeballs' relationship to the brows changes dramatically, due to distance relationships and perspective (Figure 7.16). This is how I recommend getting most of the brow up/down effects, by moving the head rather than the brows. Granted, the proportion in this setup is as if our character had a 4-inch forehead, but it does make the point, and gives you something very obvious to practice with.

The eyelids following the eyeballs Take the Ctrl_Lids and slide it downward so that your new character looks unimpressed or sleepy (Figure 7.17). Now move the EyesCtrl around, and watch the lids follow—no matter *where* the eyes are looking. Even on this simple face the added reality of the lids tracking is pretty neat, but when you get this on a realistic face it's creepy. I find myself playing with this part of the setup for hours, even though I've seen it a hundred times before.

Adding the lower lids Go ahead and create yourself a little angry face. Pull Ctrl_Brows down and to the right, tilt the head forward to condense the space between the Brows and Eyes further, and take a look (Figure 7.18). Now move Ctrl_Lids to the left, adding some squint into the mix. Bounce back and forth including, and not including, the squint, to see the big difference it makes. As I've said before, it intensifies this as well as any other expression.

Okay, playtime's over for now, but to keep you fresh on the uses of things, Table 7.1 is a cheat-sheet for Box Head's interface.

Rules of the Game

Our eyes move around a lot. They move around to look at different things we need to know about, or just want to observe. Our eyes also sometimes move not just *to* things, but *away* from them as well. Avoiding eye contact or shielding ourselves from things too bright are reasons our eyeballs would be doing some avoiding. I've said before, and I'll elaborate now, that the eyes themselves tell us next to nothing about emotion. It's all in the context, and it's all in the timing.

Figure 7.15

A snapshot of my own little icon creations for each slider: top is the face, next the brows, then the lip sync control After that are the lids and the eyes.

Figure 7.16

The expanded and contracted distances perceived during tilts of the head are pretty extreme.

(a) up

(b) down

CONTROL ACTION	FACE ACTION
Ctrl_Face up/down	Tilts the entire head forward and back. Condenses and expands the vertical distances between features.
Ctrl_Face left/right	Turns the head left and right, only in a limited way because this face is really only meant to be seen from the front.
Ctrl_Eyes up/down	Moves the eyes up and down within a range.
Ctrl_Eyes left/right	Moves the eyes left and right within a range.
Ctrl_Lids up/down	Moves the upper eye lids up and down. Shows alertness.
Ctrl_Lids left/right	Moves the lower lids up and down. Increases and decreases emotional intensity.
Ctrl_Brows up/down	Moves the brows up and down. Only applies contextually, has no guaranteed effect without other influences.
Ctrl_Brows left/right	Moves between the brows looking sad and mad.

When I say context, I mean in plot-related scene, immediate situation, and also in physical surroundings. The eyes looking down when the brows are up and have a sad shape to them gives a different effect than they do when the brows are down with a mad shape—and further variations are possible by changing the height of the lids. Try to erase any preconceived notions of specific eye positions meaning different things, because right now we're going to lay down new types of rules. With lip sync we had visimes, for most of the important shapes. Most of those have pretty solid definitions, but some, like R and T, had referential or relative definitions: wider than this, narrower than that. With the eyes, the level of focus or distraction is almost 100% referential and relative.

"Almost," I say, because there are a few rules.

Eye Rules: Focus and Distraction

Most everything I consider a rule for the eyes has to do with focus and distraction, both for the character and for the audience. There's the focus as tied to the motion, there's timing, and there's involuntary distraction (which can rip an audience out of your scene).

Figure 7.17

The eyelids' tracking is extremely helpful in maintaining expressions.

Focus and Motion

The eyes move around, but not randomly. In real life when people are having a discussion and a person is darting their eyes around, their eyes aren't in constant motion. They move, and they stop. After a period of time, they move again, but they stop again. It is highly unnatural behavior for our eyes to not focus on something, anything, if they can, which is what causes the moving and stopping as opposed to a constant, even scanning. The eyes are moving from one focus to another. I tell you this so that in the next sections dealing with specific instances of focus and distraction, you'll realize that eye motion, even if it's ongoing, is not constant. There are pauses and breaks. The eyes cannot scan across a room; they must bounce from focus to focus. This is the nature of the movement. Disregard it and lose your audience. The one apparent hole in this methodology is when someone's eyes are following something that is moving—which, really, is the same rule of focus; it's just that the focus isn't still.

Some of you may be thinking, as I myself did for some time, that this eye motion rule does not apply to stylized characters. Unfortunately, it does. Even the most ridiculously styled characters in CG must have eye behavior reflecting realistic human motion. The likely reason, I've come to realize, is the way that CGI looks. An eye in computer graphics, even a badly modeled and textured one, looks a lot like an eye. Maybe it's the way computers have perfected specular highlights, maybe it's the quality of renderers—who knows. All that matters is that since the eyeballs look like eyeballs, we expect them to behave that way.

Think of a green eyeball of a monster: Mr. Mike Wazowski. Even he, as odd and far from reality as he was, had realistic timing, motion, and acting in that big ol' eye.

Figure 7.18

An angry face on Box Head, with and without the squint/lower lids

Timing

A focused character, besides having a posture that illustrates this, will behave in a focused manner in the face and especially the eyes. For animators, it can be very tempting to—well, animate. Sometimes the temptation to move things can ruin an effect we're trying to create. Eyes generally move very quickly, but in creating the illusion of focus or intensity, we need to hold back. It is okay for a character to hold a stare for a while. By interrupting the stare too soon, we would dilute the intensity or sabotage the intensity we were after.

Involuntary Distraction Is the Enemy of Performance

Distraction is the enemy of performance. If the audience is distracted by anything born of our animation, they're looking at the animation, not at the character in the scene, and they're missing what's happening. With most of the things you animate, like full body shots, you won't have this problem, they're not as susceptible to this. With the face and the eyes, though, there is so much potential for fatal distraction that you might find yourself focusing on what *not* to do rather than on what you want to do.

Brow Rules

The rights and wrongs, dos and don'ts for brows are pretty sparse, but here they are.

Limit Your Range

Try, as a conscious effort, not to ever let your brows get to the extremes of their range. It will happen, and for good reason, but if you stop yourself from maxing your brows out, you'll force yourself to be a little bit more resourceful and creative with all the tools at your disposal. I'm far more willing to believe a character who is sad than one who is the saddest he's ever been in his entire life, so sad that his face must hurt from the muscle contortion. I like to give myself that range to play with, but animation on the brow almost always looks better when it lives pretty close to the default shape. Also, as with the mouth, opposites and stepping all apply as simple good general animation principles. If you have a character who's mad on his first line of dialogue, then even more angry on the second line of dialogue, what can you do? If you blew all your range on the first line of anger, you're stuck on the second. Keeping things in a range helps a lot.

Darting Motion

Your brows don't move slowly. You can try it if you like, in a mirror. Try moving your brows up slowly, you can't. On the way down, it's eas*ier*, but still not very normal. Brows tend to jump into poses, hold that pose, and then drop back out of it.

Sometimes the Best Shape Is No Shape

My favorite CGI facial acting shot ever—so far—is in *The Lord of the Rings: The Two Towers*. Gollum is a sickly looking outcast, helping the current owner of his "precious" ring. There's a scene where he is talking to himself—not just musing, but clearly of a damaged and divided mind—and the camera cuts help differentiate the two personalities. In one moment, the whole thing went from looking like some of the most beautiful computer animation and motion capture, to surpassing all of that and becoming real. In one shot, Gollum draws back in the frame and just says "What?"

What made this scene stand out for me is that, for much of the film, the character's facial expressions, while wonderfully shaped and animated, were, well, *always* expressing— going from one extreme to another. There was never a moment's rest in the face. In that one shot, the character started with an angry expression, and an intense glare, and then bang! The muscle tension released, the eyes widened slightly. That was it. The animator resisted the urge to shoot to the opposite spectrum for effect; they stopped it in the area of "nothing," no shape. It was the absence of a shape, the release of the tension, the character's real, genuine, tangible shock at the dialogue exchange that blew me away. The character had been ripped out of himself, for just a moment—a real reaction. It showed me something I might have known, somewhere deep down, but never quantified: getting out of a shape can be even more powerful than going into one. I've looked for ways to use this since, and it has been a remarkable tool in realizing certain emotions and moments. Hats off to whoever animated that scene—great work!

Order of Operations

This is the order in which I like to do things in regard to the face; there are some production issues, but I'll address those. Also, this list is not complete, as there are still mouth emotions to address, but that won't come until the last chapter; on this list they would appear right before finesse.

1. Sync
2. Head tilt (up/down)
3. Eyes
4. Eyelids
5. Brows
6. Finesse

Sync

I do my sync first, to get my timing down. This applies to *all* animation I do. If a scene is mostly pantomime, but there happens to be sound, I'll do the sync first; it helps me get into the timing and feeling before attacking big sweeping motions. I'll also sometimes create myself a dopesheet using my sync timing.

Head Tilt

I do this second, but there are a few catches to what *second* means. In a big full-body acting shot, I'll do the full-body acting after sync and this third, but in a close-up shot, I will do this second. I treat the tilt of the head as its own entity apart from the rest of the posing of the body. If I work on a floating head in a scene such as we'll do in a minute, up is up, down is down. If I'm working on a character, like the one in Figure 7.19, who is already posed, up and down is a range defined using that pose as the zero-line.

In this step in my order of operations list, I've written "up/down" only, and that's because I don't usually like to add in any other head movements until the rest of the steps for the face animation are completed. The up and down gives a good base motion, but after that, if you

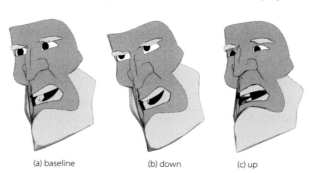

(a) baseline   (b) down   (c) up

Figure 7.19

A pose from a scene, and how to interpret up, and then down, using that pose as your new base line; it's all merely relative

Figure 7.20

With only the tilt of the head and the eyes, you can start to create expressions and thought processes.

get the whole head swooping and turning all over the place, it can be hard to keep focus as you continue your work on other things, like the eyes and brows. This potential drawback to the process, we'll actually use to our advantage later. By adding those extra head motions after we've done the rest of our work with the face, we'll make the minute details a little harder to follow, and usually that, just makes them look better; you can't sit and nitpick at a moving face! Sneaky, sneaky, sneaky.

Eyes

This is completely interchangeable in list order with the tilt of the head. In fact, I've only made them separate steps to keep the two thought processes separate for instruction. In my own animation, I do the two at the same time, but I only recommend doing that yourself after you've really learned to distinguish the individual goals. By getting the head and eyes moving early, which is all I've done in Figure 7.20, you get into the real feel of the scene before laying on the more obvious and uncreative brows.

Eyelids

This encompasses upper lids in both expression (wide, narrow) and function (blinks). This is the point where the emotion really starts to come through, as in Figure 7.21. We're looking for excitement levels, good places to blink, just getting into the thought process of the character. The lower lids come in here, too, and add in all the thought and intensity that they do.

Brows

Last but not least on the explicit steps are the brows (Figure 7.22). I got in the habit of doing these last (these and mouth emotions) when I started to *really* get into facial animation. At first, doing these last was a teaching aid I forced on myself to learn about the other things on the face. It worked so well that I realized brows had actually been hindering my animation—they're a crutch. At this point, I've just gotten used to putting them on at the end, and I recommend it. They can add a lot, but I really think of them as the last resort for creating an expression. Usually, they are the icing—at this point, after all the preceding steps, the expression is already there.

Figure 7.21

I don't trust this guy.

Finesse

Once all the pieces are in place there's inevitably something that needs to be changed. If you're doing it right, layered animation always has a little bit of do-over and repair. If you're thinking so far ahead that you're not doing things in your Eyes pass because of something you're going to do in your Brows pass, you're not giving each layer its proper, individual, unique attention—you're animating straight-ahead out-of-order! This is where I will decide that part of a scene isn't working; it's where I'll add in other motions on the head, and shift keys around to make thought happen before sound.

Example Animations

Well, since this is an eyes-and-brows chapter about acting, let's act. We'll start with a sound file and a scene from Chapter 4, "Visimes and Lip Sync Technique." To be lazy about it, if you saved the scene you worked on there, you can import that and copy the curves from the locator "MouthControl" to your new "Ctrl_Sync" slider. The animation should come over fine. To get in practice, as you should, you can also animate the scene again. Personally, that's what I recommend.

Figure 7.22

"No, no, I meant, Santa *is* real!"

I'll do quite a bit of explaining throughout this section, especially in the first example, where I've split up some of the steps to a few sub-steps to give every little thing attention. After that, I start to move faster, only explaining the things that are less obvious given the instruction thus far. These scenes could be taken further, but a lot of that last step is frame-to-frame finicking, which is not a fun thing to talk through and often comes down to "I just like it this way better!"—you can tweak these on your own.

For the rest of the chapter, you'll need to refer to the animations on the CD. I'll drop in pictures of frames from the animation here and there, but to get a feel for what I'm saying you really need to see and hear the motions.

> If your scene is not lining up with my numbers, double-check that your frame rate is at 24 fps (film) in Window → Settings/Preferences → Preferences → Settings. Also check that you're playing back in real time, under Window → Settings/Preferences → Preferences → Timeline.

"What Am I Sayin' in Here?"

To start, import the "What am I sayin' in here?" sound and/or scene you worked on before. For those of you starting fresh, you'll find the sound, `WhatAmISayinInHere.wav` and `.aif`, in the Chapter 4 folder. For this scene I blocked my frame range at 0 to 35.

Time check: This process and result took approximately 20 minutes' work.

A finished version of the scene file, `WhatAmISayin.ma`, is in the Chapter 7 folder on the companion CD. An AVI as each step is completed can also be found on the CD:

```
WhatAmI_01_Sync.avi

WhatAmI_02_Tilt.avi

WhatAmI_03_Eyes.avi

WhatAmI_04_Lids.avi

WhatAmI_05_Brows.avi

WhatAmI_06_Finesse.avi
```

I won't have notes here about the Sync step in these sample animations, as that's covered in the mouth chapters.

NODDING

When I say "nodding," it means not only dropping the head down, it means overshooting the pose, and then correcting. It gives a nice biting motion, and it's something we people do a lot of in speech—we almost throw our head forward and then catch it, like a nod cut short.

Head Tilt

Frame 12

I've talked before of animating the head to the music of the dialogue; now I'll describe actually doing that. In this delivery of "what am I sayin in here," the *what am I* sounds pretty even to me, in both tonal quality and volume. Listening to *sayin*, you can hear a pretty distinct jump in both volume and tone. For me, when the music goes up, so does the head. The sound of *sayin* is approximately from frames 12through 18, so on frame 12, I'll set a key on the Ctrl_Face to tilt Box Head up. We don't want to have this movement look like an *exact* relationship between the music and the head, so instead of dropping it again right away, I'll look to the next sound or two and see if they have a reason for me to keep the head up.

The next word, *in*, sounds about the same to me in tonal quality as *sayin*, so I'll hold the head up for that sound, too. Moving along, the next word is *here*. Here is a definite drop in tone, so on frame 25, I'm going to push the head back down, I think, even further down than level. Since *in* lasts until about frame 20, I'll set another head-up key on 20, leaving the motion between *in* and *here* to be 5 frames long. That's a pretty big motion in a pretty small space, so to keep it from looking odd, I'm going to turn that downward motion into a nod. To do that, I'll just bounce back up a little higher on frame 30, and hold that until 35, the approximate end of the scene.

When you're animating the head to sync after the rest of the body has been animated, all these motions I'm describing can be applied on top of your existing posing. Just use the existing poses as the zero, or baseline, for the motions. Moving the head as part of sync can help you hold an overall body pose longer.

Listening to and watching that, most of it looks okay, but the head creeps up slowly from frame 0 (I set a default key on all sliders on frames 0, and 35 before I started, "capping the ends"). That slow creeping motion bugs me. What I decided to do was to hold the head lower until right before the first higher key. I set a low key (not super low, just a little bit lower than default) on frame 7. After that, just because I though it would look more like a pose and less like a drift, I put another similar low key on frame 2.

Eyes

The order in which you animate the parts of the eyes and brows is less significant than with the actual lip-sync, but do try to animate some head tilts and the eyes first. With the eyes, there are a million ways to go. I'm going to pretend, for this scene, that the character is trapped in a box and is addressing no one, or a crowd—there's no specific person he's talking to. To show that, I'm going to have him look around some.

> Eyes' and lids' animations should, in almost every case, have linear function curves, during both the motions and the holds.

I'm going to pick a few locations, basically at random, for the eye darts. Most eye darting, or looking around, happens perceptibly in the left to right more than the up and down, so I tend to favor picking locations closer to level. Eyes, as I mentioned earlier, go to places quickly and stick, so I tend to key into a pose, middle-mouse drag the time slider (to advance the time, but not the state), and set the same key again. I don't want to have the eyes move in timing with the tilts of the head; that would make the motions look like a dance. I moved the eyes (character) left on frame 3 and held them there only until frame 5; then on frame 7 moved them over to the right, holding that until frame 10, and finally brought them back to center on 13 and left them there for the duration of the scene. By having the character do most of the motion early and then centering for the last half, it creates the feeling that the character himself is wondering something, and asking that question of whoever he's looking at at the end, the only sustained position.

Frame 10

Eyelids

There are two parts to this: eyelid heights for emotional effect and, of course, blinking. Let's start with heights. This line has got an elevated tone throughout, so I'll likely leave the eyes slightly more "bugged." I raised the eyelids on frame 4, and tapered them slightly (very slightly) down to frame 21. That's because the word *here*, although a tonal drop, does have a distinct volume hit. I want to make *here* have some impact, but in the same way that it's already impacting. In a little bit of an opposites approach, I lessened the incoming key, then on frame 24 jumped it back so the upper eyelids widen some more, and then hold that pose through the end.

> Sometimes (though not always) bouncing eyelids up just to hit a single key causes them, during their return motion down, to look unnatural; that's why I chose to hold the pose through the end.

Now for blinks. One basic suggestion for when to blink is during big motions of the eyes. The range over which our character is looking most definitely meets that criterion. I'm going to blink the eyes by moving the Ctrl_Lids slider down on frame 2.

I'm not, however, going to blink on the second motion of the eyes; that would turn this into the blinky-blink-blink show. Generally, stay away from groups of blinks for functional reasons. For emotional effect they're great, but groups of blinks show disbelief, shock, confusion, etc. Since this guy is asking a question, he may be a little bit concerned, but I don't think he's in shock or disbelief. Putting a blink on the second eye move would cause an emotional side effect, so I left it out. My first instinct, moving forward, is to just leave the rest of the scene alone, but there is something else to consider. In conversation, there's a subtext in blinks.

When I say something, if I continue to stare at you without blinking, you won't know when it's your turn to talk. If I instead say something and blink, it shoots you the message, albeit subconsciously, "Okay, it's your turn to talk." If there's no blink, there's no message. It's another fun little experiment to try at home: talk and then don't blink. It's likely that you'll hear no response to your statement. In any case, it makes me want to blink the eyes near the end of this line. After scanning the line a few times, I'm realizing that exactly where we have the eyes widening on *here* is where I want to blink. That's fine, I'll just change the widening into a blink instead. The word *here* still gets its eyelid animation hit—it's just a blink instead of a widening.

Frame 21

The lower eyelids—the Squint—is an emotional intensifier; it adds thought. Using that approach, I'm looking for where thought should be communicated. Listening to the sound, and watching what I've already animated, the character seems to do his thinking up front, when he's darting his eyes around. Also, it's usually smartest to change lower lid poses at the same time as upper lid poses, making blinks perfect transitions. I animated the lower lids up (Ctrl_Lids left) from frame 2 to frame 21, then back to default on frame 24. It basically appears between the two blink keys. Another thing this did was to create more punch on the word here, as it's now getting a widening of the eyes. See how it's all relative? Since the lower eyelids were tight, going back to default looks wide.

PRODUCTION NOTE

I did it in this example, but in real-world production it's almost always a bad idea to blink in the first or last 5 to 10 frames of a shot unless you're expressly asked to by your director or supervising animator. Editors will murder you. Editors need some flexibility in exactly where to come into and out of your shot. If you put blinks in that zone, and the frame they choose to cut to/from has the eyes closed, it causes a "hook-up" problem with shots around it; extra work for you, and extra grief for them.

Brows

Watching the animation, you'll notice that there already seem to be brow Up/Down motions due to the head's Up and Down. Many people animate the brows to volume. Instead, animate the tilt of the head—it's a very similar perception. The difference is that the brow Up/Down due to perspective in head tilts more accurately reflects reality, and the brows don't look manic.

Use the brows mainly to reinforce. In this situation, I like the seeming raise in the brows created by the upward tilt of the head during *sayin*. I don't, however, just want him to be "Mr. Brows in the Air," so instead of pushing the brows up, I'll push them down beforehand— this is basically using opposites, or treating it like an anticipation. I set keys for the brows Down on frames 4 and 10, and they return to default on frame 13, approximately at the right time for *sayin*.

> Do not concern yourself too much with lining up all of your keyframes for poses on the same frame quite as stringently as you might on the body. There are few enough things to keep track of in the face that the inaccuracies actually make it look better, and it's not very difficult to manage.

That's about all I want to do with the brows. As an animator, I'd like to go in and key all over the place, but I don't think it'll add anything to the performance. I don't look at it and feel a lack of brow Up/Down, so I'm not going to add any more.

On other setups, the brows will work together a little bit differently—you'll create the mads and sads out of combinations of the shapes you have available. With Box Head, though, we've got some pretty simple stuff. Sad and Mad. Sad can double for a lot of things: the right smile with a subtle Sad on the brows can be happy; it also portrays shame. Sad generally portrays the softer emotions, or even the lack of confidence, which is the way I hear this line. The character is just a little bit confused, asking a question. Asking is a lesser form of pleading; they're in the same category, one that indicates a little bit of weakness. Since the whole sentence is pretty much in the same tone, and I'd like to hit each portion a little bit harder, I'll use stepping. I went to the end of the scene, choosing the most extreme sound and pose first, which I only want at about 70% strength for the shape. Then I backtracked. I set a key on 27 so that the pose holds until the end of the animation, then between 13 and 21 *sayin in*, I set some keys back up a level, about 40% to 50%, creating a "step."

> It was no coincidence that I chose the range between 21 and 27 for an expression change. I used the blink as a device to help change expressions more believably. Blinks are good for that.

Frame 4

From there I created another step, even higher, between 3 and 10 to give *what am I* some sort of impact, and left the key I already had on 0 that goes back to default. Watching the scene through, you don't see drastic motion on the brows, you just see some acting as the brow shape shifts slightly throughout the line.

Finesse

So here's where there are really no rules, and it's up to what I or you like and don't like. I'll add in some motions on the head left to right, and see what it feels like. In this stage, you should really have something that you're reacting to on an emotional, not functional, level. If your character doesn't seem at least a little bit alive, take a look at each step again, seeing if it can steer you toward something you missed or could use more or less of.

Move the head like the eyes Not in all cases, but in some, I like to move the head along with the eyes. Making the head reach a little bit as the eyes move really takes away the feeling of the character wearing a neck brace. In this scene I'm only going to move the head left to right, as that's where the eyes are looking. I moved the head (character) left on frame 4, then (character) right on frame 9, and then back to the middle on frame 13. Leaving the head fairly still, or at least *facing forward* during the last part of the line, where I have Box Head addressing the screen/audience, gives it some focus.

Frame 35

Scene choice Next, looking at the scene, I decided I really liked the bug-eyed look for the delivery, so wherever the eyes are wide I made them wider.

Making thought happen first This scene is too short to bother trying to move the shifts in expression ahead. In short scenes, you should be more concerned with the overall expression being pretty homogenous, so that it will read in the short time an audience will see it. I'm going to leave this as it is. In longer scenes, by shifting the acting portions of your animation ahead, you can create the effect that the character *thinks* before they *do*.

Here's something really funny you can do later: By copying the animation curves from these sliders to sliders on some of the more refined looking setups, you can actually recycle this animation onto a photo-real or any kind of head if you like. It's funny to see Box Head performing the same line side-by-side with another character!

I think we can all agree that what we have here is not going to win any awards, but I think we can also agree that we got very far very fast. That is the goal at this stage of the learning, so let's keep on it!

Beautiful Perfect

"Listen up buddy, there's two kinds of people in this world: big dumb stupid heads like you, and super beautiful perfects, like me!" Woosh! That's some snarky attitude for a little girl!

Since the other two sound files from Chapter 4 are both also very short questions like the last example, I'm going to move right along to some other sound files that can provide more instruction. To proceed, import `BeautifulPerfect.wav` from the Chapter 7 folder on the CD into your Box Head scene. I put my scene range at 0 to 250. A finished version of the scene file is on the CD as well: `BeautifulPerfect.ma`.

Time check: This should take, on your own, about 30 to 45 minutes total.

> I added one little twist in this one, just for the sake of instruction. Sometimes, as with this sound, there may be too much dead space (nothing) at the head of the sound. To move the sound so it starts earlier, right-click the timeline and go to the sound option at the bottom. Select your sound from the submenu and go to the option box. In the Audio Attributes is a value labeled Offset. By changing that number, you can influence when the sound starts; a positive number pushes it back that many frames, a negative number makes it happen that many frames earlier. For this scene, I type in a –30, and am using a range of frames 0 to 250.

An AVI of each step as it's completed can be found on the CD:

Beautiful_01_Sync.avi

Beautiful_02_Tilt.avi

Beautiful_03_Eyes.avi

Beautiful_04_Lids.avi

Beautiful_05_Brows.avi

Beautiful_06_Finesse.avi

Head Tilt

I love to animate to the actress in this sound piece, because she's very musical in her delivery, and you know I like to use those musical sounds. For *Listen up,* there's an upward shift in tone during *listen* and it's sustained through *up,* so I tilted the head up and kept it there. *Buddy* provides a fantastic shift down, in both her tonal quality and in how sharp it is. The *listen up* has unwittingly become a great anticipation for *buddy.* For the next big chunk, *there's two kinds of people in this world,* there is a nice little punch on her delivery of *two,* and another on *people.* You can't hit every shift with the head, but you can stow those two sounds away for different tools, such as some of the later brow and eyelids stuff. I tilted the head higher for the time before *people,* and then shot back down again on that word. I held that height until after *world,* where there's a silence, and the actress clicks her mouth.

This is the bread and butter. This is the good stuff. You should hope to always be so lucky as to have an actress to pause and click her mouth between lines. The perfect time to shift expressions is between lines, or phrases, almost never during. When an actor makes a noise, takes a breath, does anything in between lines, you are given a playground to do with as you please. You can bounce the character into an extreme pose, for just that sound, if it's fitting. You have a perfect, infallible spot to change expression, which otherwise can sometimes be hard to find, and that's what we're going to use it for. For this stage, it'll just be moving the head up, but we'll do something at this point on every pass through.

Big and *dumb* both climb tonally, so I'm going to step the head higher into those both, and then slam it back down with a nod on *stupid*. *Heads like you* only really peaks on *like*, so I kept the head at the same level as after *stupid* and then popped it up briefly on *like*, inadvertently causing a nice nod on *you*.

For the next section, *and super beautiful perfects like me*, the character is obviously off in world of her own wonderfulness, so I'd say, posing her head toward the sky is a good idea. I stepped it down to ease in the downward movement over *perfects*, and then brought it back down in another nod on *me*.

Frame 26

Eyes

The scene implies that she's talking to someone, and since it's not important who it is or where they are, I just picked a place, somewhere off screen left, that became the eyes' home base. Now, through this performance, she seems pretty sure of what she's saying and who she's saying it to, so I held her eyes pretty much on that one focus. During the spots where she's obviously searching for the words *big dumb* and *super beautiful perfects*, I darted her eyes up and around. I picked two spots away from whoever she's talking to. I shot her eyes up and (screen) left for *big*, then up and (screen) right for *dumb*. Knowing how eyes move, they only take two frames or so to get to each location, and then hold there until they move again. I did almost the same thing for the second "search" for *super beautiful perfects*. I returned her gaze to her off-screen focus, for *me*, as the nod provided a great time to do so.

Eyelids

Frame 101

For *listen up buddy*, the upper lids, much like the head, shoot wide open for *listen up*, and are dropped lower for *buddy*. Later on, with *there's two kinds of people*, I decided to punch the dismissive, contemptuous nature of the sound, by intensifying her expression with a squint, in two steps, on *two* and *people*. From there nothing eventful happens until she looks up on *big dumb*. For that, I blinked right in line with that clicking sound she makes. I adjusted the lower lids slightly, to track upward in relation to that eye movement.

The eyes return to her primary focus on *stupid*, so to transition her back into "reality," I gave her another blink. A blink paired with a nod of the head, and a change in focus of the eyes, really starts to show a strong acting transition there, which is good. I also used the blink to drop the lower lids back down—I was starting to run out of range with them so I used the strength of the overall shift to hide a "reset" of the lower lids. Before and after the word *you*, I left the lids where they were, but punched the word *you*.

After that there's nothing too major until she looks skyward again with *super beautiful perfects*. I threw in a blink at the start of that, and shot the lower lids up higher for the duration of that part of the line. It helped her look much prouder of herself, because it created more focus on her statements of her own fantastic amazingness. I blinked on *perfects*, and here's why: a friend of mine who also knows all about this stuff (and in fact taught me a lot about it) noticed that blinking on percussive sounds gives them a great visual punch. As the mouth closes and releases, so do the eyes. It creates a great whole-face involvement with the sound. I don't do it on all percussive sounds, only on the ones it fits, like the p in *perfect*; it's almost always a trial-and-error process. From there all that's left is a blink on the return from her gaze up, to whoever she's talking to off-screen.

Frame 189

Brows

I really wanted to intensify her through *listen up buddy*. I felt that she wasn't telling her focus *what's up*, and the dialogue really *is* telling somebody "*the deal*." I dropped the brows low, but didn't give them any real expression. Starting at *there's two kinds* I gave the brows a little bit of sad shape, which, with the brows down low, and the head tilted forward, and the kind of line this is, creates an air of arrogance. Remember, I was looking for a way to hit that part of the line earlier in the process—and finally found it here! I both raised and saddened the brows for *big dumb*, using that blink and mouth click as the place to transition, which is now turning into a great little attitude moment. As she returns down, there's really two things to accent, *stupid* and *you*. To save myself range, I decided to not drop the brows on *stupid*, but instead just shift them to angry, and then drop them and lose the expression on *you*. The reason I did it that way instead of dropping them first and then adding mad on *you*, is that I liked the look of the dropped expressionless brows better, and putting them second, makes that expression more her "final" destination than a transitional pose. This last pose also looks like the expressions near the start, giving her a more consistent performance.

Frame 35

The next shift is the skyward gaze, for which I did a pose similar to the one I did for the first. It's a good idea to do that if you can; it creates almost an anime three-frame cycle, where you bounce between your established poses. Used well, going through your three-pose cycle strengthens the scene—people are more likely to remember it. Just don't do it for *everything*!

Finesse

For this one I was pretty happy with the overall feeling, so all I did was put some of the left-to-right motions of the eyes into the head movement as well. After that, since this scene is a little longer, I moved all of the animation three frames earlier, just to see what would happen, if the illusion that thought came before action would work. In the emotion, the eyes, and the head, it was great, but my sync fell out of—well, sync. I hit Undo, and then shifted only the other four sliders (excluding Ctrl_Sync) ahead, and that worked great. That few frames of difference really helps the mind behind that square.

Default Grey

So, if you were in a world filled with colorful, photo-real, perfectly textured models—with hair and shaders and soft-body dynamics and all that jazz—wouldn't you be a little grumpy to just be a grey box? Box Head is. From the companion CD, import `DefaultGrey.wav` into a scene with Box Head. I blocked the range at 0 to 550 frames. A finished version of the scene file is on the CD as well: `DefaultGrey.ma`.

"I'm default grey. Stupid grey. Boring. Doof. You'll get yours, red. Flashy, oo! Look at me, I'm red! Oh you, srr err razafraz…".

Time check: This should take almost a full hour from start to finish.

An AVI of each step as it's completed can be found on the CD:

`DefaultGrey_01_Sync.avi`

`DefaultGrey_02_Tilt.avi`

`DefaultGrey_03_Eyes.avi`

`DefaultGrey_04_Lids.avi`

`DefaultGrey_05_Brows.avi`

`DefaultGrey_06_Finesse.avi`

Head Tilt

This is the first example involving a big breath. I treat breaths just like musical sounds: an inhale is up and an exhale is down. For this opening sigh of discontentment, I crept the head up until the peak, and then dropped pretty swiftly on the exhale. The first actual phrase, *I'm default grey*, also has a great up and down to it. As with all sounds like that, I crept the head up during *I'm default* and then nodded the head down on *grey*, right where the sound levels out. It gives the word some impact, just like the vocal performance. After that, the actor makes a sheesh, or quick exhale sound, I'm going to do a motion like a nod, but upward, as if he's tossing that sound out. It visually matches the sound and its "whatever" tone. I'm going to drop the head for *stupid*, and then do another of those reverse nods for *grey*. When an actor delivers a scene consistently, you're likely to run into these repeated sorts of motions. Until *boring*, there's a hold, nothing big happens, but *boring* is tossed out pretty hard, so I decided to nod on that sound but return the head to where it was previously. I did the same on *doof*. To get more impact on *doof*, though, I actually crept the head higher after *boring*. To nod the head down to the same level as *boring* was a bigger movement from this higher start-point.

All through the *oo flashy oo look at me I'm red*, I crept the head higher and higher, but I bounced it up and down as I did. The sound was very banshee-sounding with warbling, so I mimicked that in the head's up and down motion. After that the actor breaks into a lower-level *oh you, son of errr arr* and various other noises. I just dropped the head down for that, and that was the end of my work on the head Up and Down for now.

Eyes

I dropped the eyes for the defeated-sounding sigh at the start. Now, with all these things going on, this guy's really starting to look pathetic Eyes down, as I've said before, doesn't automatically create sadness, it just works sometimes,—like now. I decided to make straight down his "reality" point, so I held it for a long time; that makes it look as if he's actually focused on something. What it is is irrelevant, but it's something. When he then moves his eyes (character) right briefly, that just looks like where his eyes settled as he was thinking, not necessarily a focus. I moved the eyes there for the *sheesh*, and then quickly moved them to the other lower corner on *stupid*, and then picked another position on (character) left as yet another sort of "thought" point for *grey*. He stays there through *boring*, and then goes back to his dejected "home" position on *doof*.

Next was a very specific timing thing. I'm not crazy about characters looking at each other too intently if it's not clear why they would. I have Box Head look at whatever "red" item is next to him, but made the shift on the word *yours* before *red*. I could have done it earlier in the line, but that might denote some real conflict between Box Head and the color red. By making it ever so slightly before the word, it creates more of a sense that he's just angry and looking for someone to blame. I thought that was a better direction. If you want to see the difference, in your scene make the eyeline change earlier; the sense of more contempt and history between Box Head and "red" is obvious.

From here, the eyes stay on their new home focus until he gets into the heavy mocking sounds, where I shot the eyes upward. Mocking often leads to eyes upward; I don't know why, it's just an established thing in both life and cartoons. As the warbling sounds continue, I moved the eyes back toward his focus, and held them there for the rest of the scene. This now does what I was talking about earlier where I chose not to shoot the eyes over too early. He's really decided to make it personal, so now that's fitting. It also was a form of stepping over several poses. By not having "red" be the object of too much intensity earlier, we can go back to that pose and make it stronger with a hold, ending on a stronger note.

Frame 142

Eyelids

I don't often blink character's lids slowly, but a big exhale is one of the times it fits. I blinked the eyes slowly so that the fully closed eye was right on the peak of the upward head motion for the sigh, making the tilt down seem even longer and more painful, drawn out. If I did it later, it would cut that time visually. Using my friend's technique of hitting percussive or closed mouth sounds with blinks, I hit the *m* in *I'm* with a blink. I also blinked again on the first *grey*, the nod seemed like a good place to throw in a blink (nods usually are, the two actions strengthen each other).

Other than that. I left the lids until the word *stupid*. On *stupid*, I brought up the lower lids, creating a slight squint, just for the one word, giving the character extra contempt for a moment, which seemed to be in the vocal performance anyway. *Boring* was the next sound I keyed on; I blinked, and on the blink return brought the lower lids up, too. The combined head nod, blink, and change now in pose is making *boring* really have some punch. I left the lids as-are except to move the lower lids out of the way as Box Head looks down, until *oo flashy.* As there's a real attitude shift from anger to mocking, I widened the eyes there, creating a sarcastic feeling. They stay there until he looks back down, where I blinked for the transition (it's always a good idea to blink on emotional transitions).

After that, and for the rest of the scene, I pulled the lower lids up and upper lids down slightly, creating more of a narrow look for the eyes, clearly an angrier appearance.

Brows

Frame 160

For the first portion of the line all the way up to but not including *stupid*, I just put the brows in a sad pose and punctuated the head movements. On grey, I dropped the brows low, and removed the sad expression, so they were level. Happening over the tightening of the lower lids; this created a great emotional shift. You can see him going from unhappy about his colorless situation to angry about it, even though I didn't go as far as to actually turn the brows to the mad side. On *you'll get yours, red*, I actually made the brows angry, dropping in a hint of the pose I'll return to at the end, and adding some strength to the statement.

For the whole mocking section, I moved the brows up and sad, creating a decidedly weaker appearance, perfect for mocking. I accented various words and sounds, but nothing major. As he finishes up his little mocking moment, I pulled the brows back down and into an angry pose. I was tempted to bounce the brows along with the various interesting sounds, but it looked stronger to leave them held in that position.

Frame 464

Finesse

This, I decided needed work, and that's a normal part of the process. I didn't *feel* the shifts in emotion as strongly as I wanted to, and I also didn't feel as if some of the emotions themselves were really as strong or as linked to the sound as they should have been. First off, the easiest thing was to begin with the head left-to-right motions. For those I started by copying the motions of the eyes. (I literally copied the FCurve and shrunk it down.) After that, there's something I like to do during disbelief, sadness, anything with which the character doesn't really agree; I shake the head. Just shaking your head like saying "no" is a great little subtlety. During *I'm default grey* I threw in some shaking. I also did the same at the end during the mumbling nonsense. The muttering paired with the shaking and the angry expression turned into feeling almost like disapproval more than anger, and I thought it fit really well.

Something else that jumped out at me was the sigh at the start. The brows seemed to hold tension by staying up, instead of releasing tension along with the sound and the head motion. I decided to leave the brows' upward climb, but then I dropped the brows. I made the drop happen after the head was down. By making the drop on the brows later, I really dragged out the defeated impression, and it also made it less a flex and more of a release. If it all happened at the same time, he'd be moving into a pose instead of falling into defeat. This also gave me an opportunity to use the brows to accentuate some of the sound in the long hold following that. By adding a brows Up motion on *I'm default*, it just accentuated all that was going on elsewhere in the face, on both the Up for that and the Down on *grey*. Dropping the brows at the same time as dropping the head, at the same time as the blink, and all of that in time with the sound works well for me.

Frame 376

After all that I just slid the emotion stuff up a few frames, so the thought happened before the sound, and I was done!

Continuing and Practicing

We'll continue this in Chapter 13, "A Shot in Production," where we take more shots through a facial animation process from start to finish. Now that you've got a feel for the type of expressions you can create using combinations of techniques, it's time for us to move into the process of building the other most important area of the face, the eyes and brows, and the keys that area needs.

If this chapter has done anything, I hope it has shown you why I leave the more obvious things like brow poses for later, and things like smiles and frowns for even later. I really hope this has shown you how much emotion you can create with very little, even with the complete absence of a smile or frown!

To continue on with practice, there are more sound files available all over the CD, mostly in Chapter 13. Another thing I frequently do for practice purposes is record sound off movies and TV to sync to. Commercials are actually my favorite, as they usually self-contain most lines. Pulling from a movie, you can run into a minute-long line that doesn't mean too much out of context, whereas in a commercial, it's all wrapped up for you in a few seconds and makes some sense. Something I don't recommend, though, is to rotoscope your acting from the actors on-screen; it can actually block your creativity, because what the person is doing fills your head with those motions instead of you being able to make up all new ones that relate to the sound.

Constructing Eyes and Brows

The eyeballs and the area around them are not too difficult to model for movement, but there are definitely some things you can do to make them move more easily for you. The main motions are a squeeze of the brows, the raising and dropping of the brows, blinking, and, of course, squinting. When things in 3D computer graphics move, they always perform best when they have a "track" to follow, a point layout already pointed along their route. In pursuit of what we know about the movements, we're going to build the eyeballs first, to have a reference for our lids; then we're going to build the lids/sockets out of a largely circular layout, to allow the squinting and blinking; then we'll connect all of that to a very grid-like layout for the forehead, for the raising, dropping, and squeezing. When all of that is done, we'll make a simple skull, and attach everything we've built.

- **Building eyeballs**
- **Building eye sockets**
- **Building the forehead**
- **Making a skull**

Building Eyeballs

In real life, eyeballs are not spheres, but building them that way makes our lives significantly easier. By having spherical eyes we can use rotations to move the eye around without worrying too much about the eyeball poking through the eyelid.

Making eyeballs is really about as easy as it gets. The best way to start is with a NURBS sphere (Create → Nurbs Primitives → Sphere ❐). In the Options dialog box, make the sphere 8 spans by 8 sections, and make it in the Z axis. When it appears, it should be flat to the Z axis, essentially pointed toward the front and back.

Right-click over the sphere, and from the marking menu select Isoparms.

In the perspective view, click and drag the first isoparm forward, to around where the iris will start. It'll be red as you move it and turn yellow as you release it. Holding Shift, do the same again, pulling the next isoparm just barely forward of the last. You should now see another yellow line.

Do the same again, hold Shift and drag; this time, release the isoparm where you think the pupil should be. What you're doing is defining where the different parts of the eyeball will be.

If you do not Shift-click as you drag new isoparms, your new isoparm selection will override your last one. By Shift-clicking you can continue to add more.

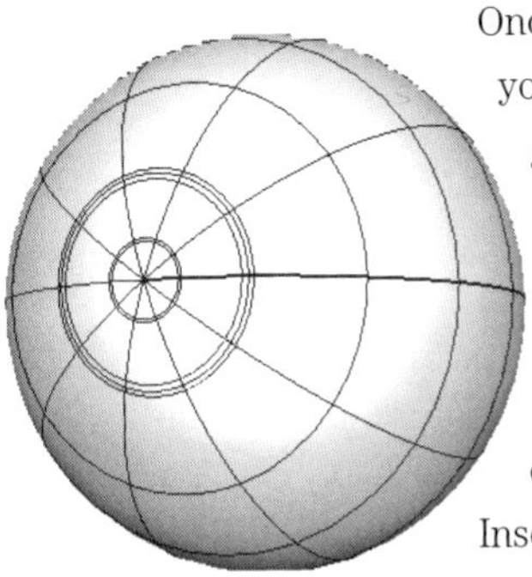

Once more, Shift-click and add one more isoparm, making it just inside of the last one you created (Figure 8.1). Once you have all four new isoparms drawn, create them by going to Edit NURBS → Insert Isoparms.

Select all the points near the front of the sphere and hit R, or click the scale manipulator in the toolbox. Press the Insert key to make the scale manipulator's pivot moveable. When the icon changes, drag the pivot so that it is lined up with the line deepest in the eye; this should be the one that was there as a part of the sphere originally, since all the lines you added should have been forward of that. Now, by hitting Insert again, you've returned to regular scale control. Scale the selected CVs inward and backward, toward the center of the eyeball. This should create a bit of a dish (Figure 8.2), making the eye look like the empire's ultimate weapon.

Figure 8.1

The sphere with the extra isoparms added

If you have strange results using Insert Isoparms, try going into the Options dialog box and using Edit → Reset Settings.

You'll notice we're not adding the cornea; that's because we'll build the cornea out of a separate sphere later. By doing so, and adding a transparent yet shiny material, we can generate the same kind of specular highlight over all the different surfaces of the eye, both the cornea and the "white" of the eye. If we were to add just a contact lens–style cornea over the eye, it might highlight differently from the rest of the eye, and as a result, the eye might not look as wet.

Two Ways to Model the Pupil

There are two ways you can proceed from here, with little or no real functional difference. You can keep what you have and sculpt the pupil forward, which has its own advantages and disadvantages, or you can cut a hole in the eye for where the pupil will be.

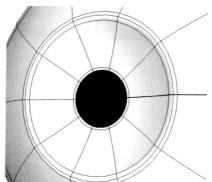

Figure 8.2

The crater in the eye will be where the iris and pupil go.

Sculpt the Pupil from the Iris

By sculpting the iris out of the existing object and applying the right materials and textures, you can actually generate an extra specular highlight on the pupil. This may seem undesirable or strange, as that area is actually supposed to be an opening into the inside of the eyeball, but as luck would have it, the extra highlight actually helps the eyeball look more real. Eyes, as you know if you've ever tried to build them, can be tricky. They're easy to make, hard to make well. Part of what's difficult is the feeling of them being wet. The extra highlight helps to make the overall look more wet.

To do this is quite simple: Select the smallest rows—the ones closest to the tip—and pull them forward, as in Figure 8.3. That little bump, textured, will work just fine as a pupil.

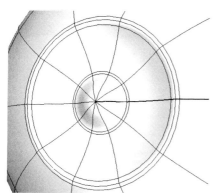

Figure 8.3

Shaded properly, this bump can make a very nice pupil.

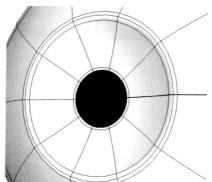

Figure 8.4

Chopping geometry out and making a hole for the pupil

Cut a Hole

The other way you can go, instead of pulling the points out, is to actually detach the surfaces where the pupil starts and put another object behind the opening. To do that, go into isoparm select mode, and select the isoparm where you want to open the hole. Separate the two objects along that isoparm by going to either Edit Curves → Detach Curves or Edit NURBS → Detach Surfaces; either will work fine.

Now take the piece that was cut, shape it, and place it behind the pupil opening as in Figure 8.4. If you wish to make the pupil dilate, you should make this back piece extend quite far, so the pupil can have a wide range to open and close.

Building the Cornea

Just as with the eyeball itself, start with a NURBS sphere of 8 × 8 in both spans and sections, and make it in the Z axis. This time, from the side, select the frontmost points, and simply pull them forward. Now, scale the whole thing up slightly, making this another surface running all the way around it. Did you blink? You're done! Take a look at Figure 8.5. You'll have to apply materials and textures to the cornea to be able to see through it, but there you go! Parent the cornea to the eyeball, and you've got yourself an eye!

In more stylized characters with bigger eyes, you may want to skip adding the cornea bump. A regular sphere should work fine and cause you less hassle. Sometimes, even on humans, I'll use a regular sphere; the specular highlight travels the surface a little better, even though it's less accurate. It all depends on what you want your model to look like!

> If you'd like to create more varied shading in the transition from the main sphere to the cornea, you can add another isoparm before pulling points forward.

Figure 8.5

The cornea object wrapped around the eyeball will actually provide nice shading all the way around the eye.

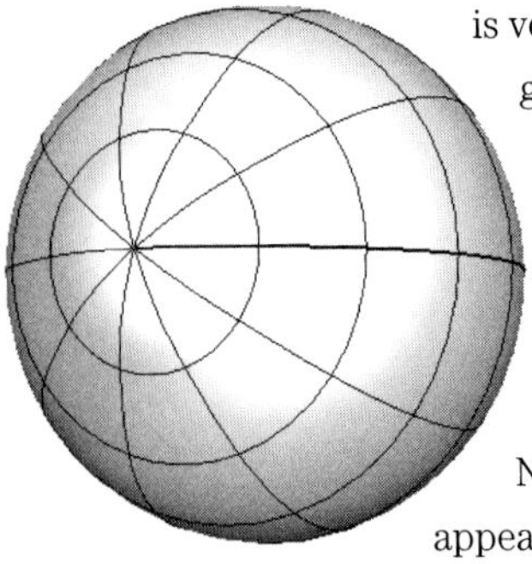

Building Eye Sockets

Now that we've got a happy little eyeball, let's give it a home. As you build the eye socket, it is very helpful to build around the eyeball. Eventually these two will cohabitate so it's good to get them ready for each other—they'll end up fitting together better. To start, load the scene with your eyeball.

First, rotate your eyeball anywhere from 5 to 15 degrees in Y. In most cases spherical eyeballs need to diverge in the head, 5 to 15 degrees each, outward. The eyeball that I'm working with, and that you'll see in the pictures, I rotated out 9 degrees, making it the character's left. We're going to be creating and manipulating NURBS curves in the front view, but if we were to start doing that right now, they'd appear in the same space as the eyeball. To avoid this, move the eyeball to –1 in Z. Now, a circle we'll create in the front view will be visible.

As I did with the mouth, I'll start you with a NURBS model that we'll convert to polys to finish off. Create a 14-point NURBS circle in the Z axis. Reshape the circle, only in the front view, so that it looks like the shape you'd usually associate with an eye, like Figure 8.6. Be sure to keep your points in roughly the same orientation as mine—it becomes important later where your points are. Also be sure to include the tear duct, which is sometimes easy to forget.

Now duplicate the eye shaped-curve and scale it up (the exact amount isn't important). Leaving your new duplicate for now, grab the original smaller curve. In the side view, move the CVs only in Z, until they are close to the cornea (Figure 8.7). Do not make this *too* tight with the cornea; other curves we'll add later go inside the eyelid, and the lofted surface will take care of the contact between the lid and the eye.

Now, reshape that second curve that you duplicated; it will form part of the shape of the outside barrier of the eyelid. Take that and duplicate it and start to form where the bags under the eyes are, and also the lower border of the brows. Loft the curves together to get a surface. You'll have to re-loft every time you add more rows. Figure 8.8 illustrates.

Duplicate the outside NURBS circle again, this time going much further out into the face. Notice in Figure 8.9, the depths; how the early rows were deeper in the middle (at the side of the eye with the tear duct); now these latest rows are farther forward in that center area (where the nose will be but farther back on the outside, by the temples) This is part of the correct shape for the eye area.

Take and duplicate the outside row. Using that, start to sculpt up and over the brow ridge, and back toward the temples (Figure 8.10).

As far as the eye socket goes, there's only a little bit left. You may need to hide the eyeball and cornea for this, to get a better view, like in Figure 8.11. Duplicate the smallest circle of the socket—the one close to the cornea—twice, and move it in toward the eye. Scale the deeper one larger slightly, loft the whole bunch together again, and you've got yourself an eye socket!

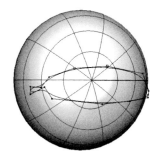

Figure 8.6

A front view of the eyelid's first line.

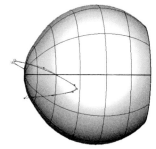

Figure 8.7

The spline should be made to fit the contour of the cornea, but not quite touch it.

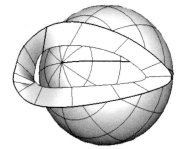

Figure 8.8

The first look at a surface around the eye.

Figure 8.9

Front and side views of
the eyelid beginning to
take shape. Notice the
depth on the side with
the tear duct; it's not
visible when viewed
from the side.

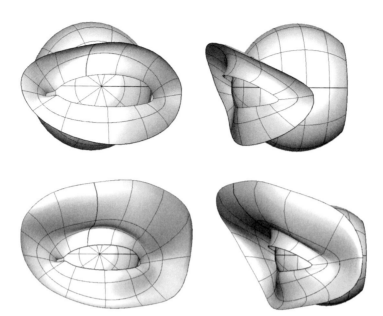

Figure 8.9

Front and side views of
the eyelid beginning to
take shape. Notice the
depth on the side with
the tear duct; it's not
visible when viewed
from the side.

Figure 8.10

Another row starts to
form the brow ridge.

Mirroring and Adding the Nose

You don't actually *need* to mirror the head until you're done with everything on one side, but at this stage, I personally like to. It helps to get a feel for what the whole shape is looking like. We're about to get into building the profile of the nose, and making our one socket into two helps to see that shape better. After I mirror the shape, I will work sometimes on both sides, sometimes on just one, depending on whether or not I need that immediate visual feedback. Eventually we'll mirror one completed side over, but to work on both simultaneously sometimes offers artistic insight you wouldn't get until you thought you were done, then mirrored it and realized you have tons more work to do!

> One way to look at a mirror of your shape and interactively see changes is to make an instance of your object and scale it to –1 in X.

Convert your NURBS eye socket to polygons (Modify → Convert → Nurbs To Polygons ❑). In Options, select Type Quads, Tessellation Method General, and then in the Initial Tessellation Controls make the U and V type both Per Span # of Iso Params, and Number U and V both 1. Take your new poly eye socket, together with the eyeball, and move it so it's almost next to the X axis but a little bit farther out to the side. (This is done so we can get a proper geometry mirror.) A little more or less in relation to my image in Figure 8.12 won't make too much difference.

In the status line there are several options for snapping. Turn on snap-to-grids.

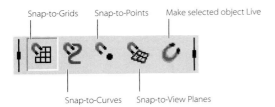

Snap-to-Grids   Snap-to-Points   Make selected object Live

Snap-to-Curves   Snap-to-View Planes

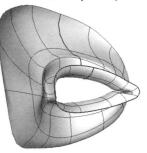

Figure 8.11

Looking at the socket from the back, and with the eye hidden, you can see the extra rows and how they are shaped.

In the front view, select the point closest to the X axis. Move the point, and it should snap to flat in the X axis, as in Figure 8.13. Now you can turn off snap-to-grid.

Select your eye socket, and in the modeling module select Polygons → Mirror Geometry ❐. Your settings should be –X and with Merge With The Original checked.

Another eye socket should have flipped over and connected itself to the original across the X axis. There will be extraneous faces across the back and between the lids. Select and delete the faces, but, counting from the cross (the X in the object), keep two faces on top and three on bottom. Figure 8.14 shows the faces left behind.

> To get a mirror of the eyeball, I usually just duplicate it and put negative values in the channel box in front of the Rotate Y and Translate X values.

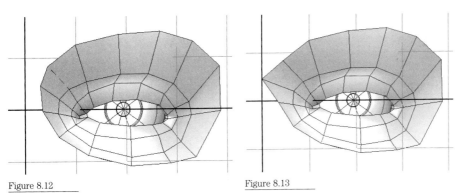

Figure 8.12

Moving the left eye and socket into position, at approximately 1.8 units in X (in my case)

Figure 8.13

Using Snap-To-Grid, the point is drawn to 0 in X.

Figure 8.14

After deleting the extra
faces, you should be
left with two on top
and three on bottom,
counting from the X
marked here.

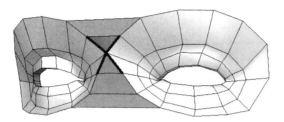

If you don't have the exact number of faces shown, then approximate visually, keeping in mind the look of the layout we're getting. There's also a version of this step in the Chapter 8 folder on the CD called MirroredSocket.ma, for you to continue on with if you'd like.

To start creating the bridge of the nose, and the profile, use the Split Polygon Tool to divide in two the faces running down the center.

The Split Polygon Tool will actually help you find the exact center of an edge because it does a little bit of snapping at the 50% mark. As you slide your new point along an edge, notice that it tends to hang up near the halfway point; that spot is 50% exactly.

Select your new points and start to sculpt a profile for the nose of your character, as in Figure 8.15.

There are a few places where the layout of these points looks like it could use some work. Using the Split Polygon Tool again, draw lines like those shown in Figure 8.16, to create straight lines running parallel to the central nose line.

After that is done, using edge select mode, select the edges that cut across diagonals, and delete them, leaving you with quads around the front of the nose as shown in Figure 8.16.

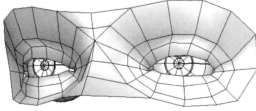

Figure 8.15

Give the bridge of the nose a good curve using the new
point running down the center.

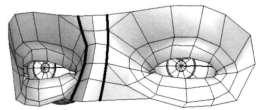

Figure 8.16

I've marked here the new edges you should be left with after
creating them and deleting some of the old ones.

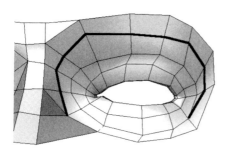

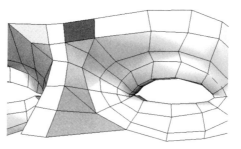

Figure 8.17

Adding another row around the eye and bringing it into the layout by rearranging some edges near the top of the nose

The next step will be to add some more detail to sculpt with. Create another line all the way around the eye socket. Start at the triangular point just off of the side of the nose and go all the way around until the lower half, and then merge back into the lines already there. This is a little hard to describe in words, so look closely at Figure 8.17. It shows the new addition darkened. After that, just add an edge and delete the existing one in the face along the top center.

Now, add one more nose row where indicated in Figure 8.18. We're getting into the work of criss-crossing cooperative points—this branches off from the ring around the eye and also runs parallel to the nose.

Detailing the Inside of the Lid

Once you're happy with the overall shape you have, it's time to add a nice detail in the upper eyelid, an overlap. Eyelids aren't simply an opening on the face, the way we have them now. The upper lid actually overlaps the lower lid. As a result of the upper lid being over, the lower lid of course needs to go under, and actually tuck into the eye socket. Figure 8.19 shows how the area will look after this step, and smoothed to show more detailed topology. I show it to you before we start because having the final shape in mind helps this particular process quite a bit.

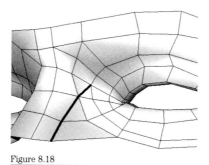

Figure 8.18

Marked is where the new line should go.

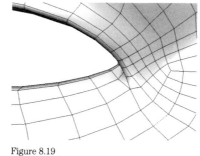

Figure 8.19

This is how the shape of the area will end up after the next few steps.

Figure 8.20

Looking closely from the front (left) and from the back/inside (right), the faces to delete are darkened.

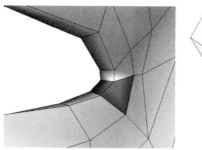

If you'd like to start from the model used in the examples, load `StartEyeDetail.ma` from the Chapter 8 folder on the accompanying CD.

To start this, select the faces shown in Figure 8.20. You should select the last face to the side, on the lower half of the eyelid, and all the faces inward in that same row. Once you're looking at your face model from the inside, also select one face above. Delete the selected faces. Look closely at the figure; these faces are a hard thing to describe, and you want to be sure to get the right ones.

Now, using the Append Polygon Tool (Polygons → Append To Polygon Tool), create a polygon from the front edge of the lower lid to the inside back edge of the upper lid. It should be four sided. Figure 8.21 shows this connection; it's very stretchy and twists awkwardly.

Next, use the Append To Polygon Tool again, to create a triangular poly on either side, using the sides of the new poly (Figure 8.22).

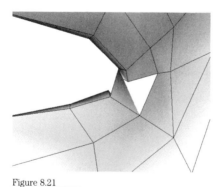

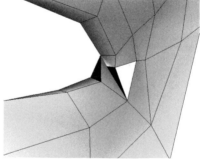

Figure 8.21

Looking from the front, the new quad face reaches from front all the way to the back.

Figure 8.22

Shown darkened are the new triangular faces, closing the gap between the lids.

One more time, using the Append To Polygon Tool, attach a poly to the open space, closing it up.

> If you want, you could definitely pay some extra attention to the pieces left open at the meeting of upper and lower lid, around on the inside. I won't discuss it here, because it's too detail-centric and complicated, and what we have to work with will animate and shade properly. Fixing this detail is for the true layout-fiend.

Now that the basics of the overlapping eyelids are completed, we're going to add another row of points using the Split Polygon Tool. Draw a row over the edge of the upper eyelid, and follow it down to the outside perimeter of the object. From the side, you can then see where the edges that lead to the newly-created overlapping upper eyelid need to be sculpted to have a smoother, more continuous line. I also added parallel lines coming out of the lower lid, reaching to the perimeter. These are going to help with "crow's feet" wrinkles. Figure 8.23 shows the new verts and edges.

Creating the Tear Duct

If you'd like, at this point you can start from a scene file on the CD: `CreateTearDuct.ma`.

Now we'll turn our attention to the other side of the eyelid. The tear duct can be an odd shape to create if you overthink it. First, look at the lid from the inside out (Figure 8.24) and select the five faces bordering the inside, and delete them.

With the new opened area, create a polygon using the Append Polygon Tool to bridge the upper and lower lid (Figure 8.25). This is going to give you some "meat" in the tear duct area.

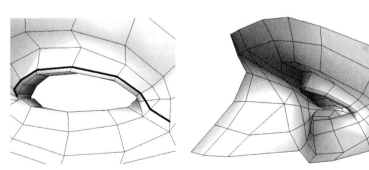

Figure 8.23

By adding another row around the upper lid, and taking those edges to the side, you can see the shape the new area takes.

Use the Split Polygon Tool to cut that new poly in half laterally and to add new polys that bridge up and down to the upper and lower lids, as in Figure 8.26. That gives you enough detail to work with for sculpting.

More Detail for the Lids

We started by getting our big masses where they needed to be, then zoned in on structural details. Now, we're working our way back out. Add a line using the Split Polygon Tool, all the way around the lids near the opening, as highlighted in Figure 8.27. Have it start where the lower lid tucks under the upper lid and have it terminate along the crow's feet wrinkle lines.

Add a second line on the upper lid, and have it terminate just on either side of the top (Figure 8.28). This will provide the new border, or front edge for the eyelid.

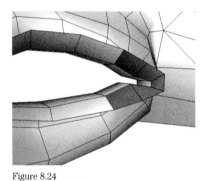

Figure 8.24

Looking from the inside, the faces to be deleted (surrounding the tear duct) are marked.

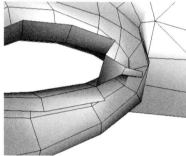

Figure 8.25

The new poly bridges across from top to bottom

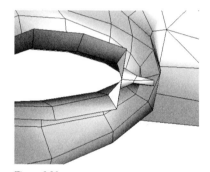

Figure 8.26

With the addition of another edge, the tear duct can now have some curve to its shape.

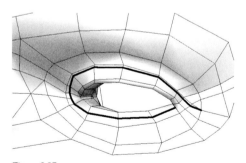

Figure 8.27

Another lap around the eye

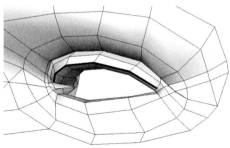

Figure 8.28

This new edge will help harden that curve where the eyelid skin transitions from outside to inside.

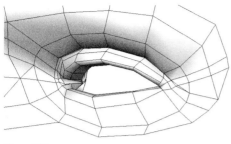

Figure 8.29

A pretty complete eyelid

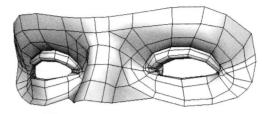

Figure 8.30

Holy Sidekick, Face Man!

After a little bit of sculpting you should have something like Figure 8.29. Try to use the points available to really tuck that upper lid into the meeting between it and the brow. I won't force it on you, but sometimes it can be smart to add just one more row around the upper lid. It's totally unnecessary now, but later when the eyelid needs to blink, it may become very important. That little dip in between the eyelid and the brow would still be there during a blink, and that means needing more detail.

> For older characters with baggier eyes, many of the rows going around need to terminate closer to the corners of the eyes, and usually more geometry would be needed.

If you choose, at this point, you can delete the unfinished side of your face and mirror the other over. It is not necessary, as I'll continue to work mostly on the character's left side, but it never hurts to see your work whole! You should have a nice-looking sidekick mask, like the one in Figure 8.30.

Building the Forehead

As with other parts in the chapter, you can start if you choose from a scene file on the CD—
BuildForehead.ma.

Even if you plan on building your character's eyebrows straight into the head's mesh, start here before moving on to that.

Creating the forehead is quite easy, once you've gotten the eye area done. Simply select the upper edges of the eye area and go to Edit Polygons → Extrude Edge. Create seven levels of extruded edges, and pull them upward approximately the way shown in Figure 8.31. Notice I kept two rows close together around the top of the mass of the brow muscles. This is going to create that extra little bit of detail and finite control with which we'll properly manipulate the brow shapes in the next chapter.

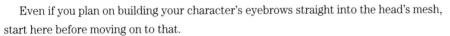

After this is done, you may (or may not) notice some strange shading going on with the new polys. The reason for this is that all of the new polys and edges aren't actually connected, they're merely really really close together. There are many ways to fix this, but I like to keep my number of tools down, for the sake of not overcomplicating things. To fix this shading, in vertex select mode, select all the vertices in the forehead. Use the Merge Vertices Tool (Edit Polygons → Merge Vertices ❐). In Options, set the distance to 0.01, then hit Merge Vertex. This will take all the vertices that are merely very close and actually weld them together. When that's done, in edge select mode, select all of the forehead area and use Edit Polygons → Normals → Soften/Harden ❐ with a value of something high like 180 to soften the edges and have the surface shade smoothly. Now, in the side view create a profile for the forehead, moving all the points together in rows; Figure 8.32 shows what I did. This is a really easy step if you're working from design drawings and have a good side view image to draw on.

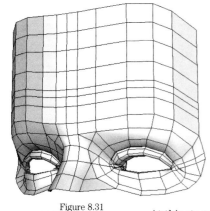

Figure 8.31

Clearly this guy is one half of a rap duo that will mercilessly take the nation by storm.

At this stage, a little bit of anatomy comes into play. I'm teaching primarily the structure of points for animation and movement, but every once in a while, some science squeezes in. In general terms, the skull of a man is slightly more sloped, or slanted, than that of a woman. The brow ridge is also farther forward. A lot is reliant on personal features, but men's foreheads *tend* to recede back farther, creating more of an angle. Women, on the other hand, tend to have more vertical profiles up the forehead, and a sharper curve back toward the rest of their head. Remember, this is a general note, not an absolute rule. Figure 8.32 is a man's head slope, and Figure 8.33 is that of a woman.

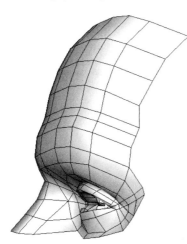

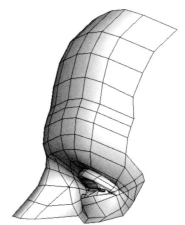

Figure 8.32

Don't try to do too much sculpting too quick; pull the points back as whole rows.

Figure 8.33

A more female skull profile

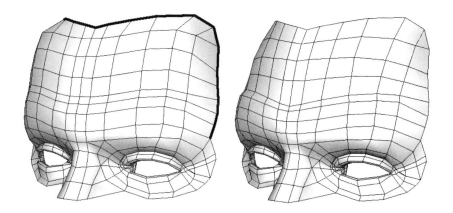

Figure 8.34

First try to decide where you want the perimeter to be, and the points between that and the brow should just fall into place.

What I like to do next is actually figure out the outside line or edge of the forehead, briefly ignoring the points left behind. Sculpt the perimeter on the sides back in Z, approximating your character's hairline. The top edge will also play a part in creating the hairline; this will merely provide the side. Once you have that, start to pull the rest of the forehead points in line. Be sure to keep the lines evenly spaced. Figure 8.34 shows the perimeter placed first and the rest of the forehead shape made to follow, a good way to create the forehead quickly.

> Because of the nature of the shape in Figure 8.34, notice that I actually chopped the top corners from quads to triangles. Framing the shapes of your face as I did here reduces the amount you'll have to texture over diagonal UVs for straight lined textures. It also makes your wireframe tell you more about the shape of your rendered model.

The Temples

A head completed up to this point can be found on the CD as StartTemples.ma.

We're going to start working our way back down and around the sides of the face, travelling downward by the temples. It's a good chunk of geometry, so instead of building out of the object, I recommend starting with a poly plane of four subdivisions along width and seven along height. Sculpt in the side view so it's a curl shape (Figure 8.35), and move it out to about where the face ends at the side.

You'll have to delete a few faces, the ones highlighted in Figure 8.35. Using snap-to-points, hook up the perimeter points of the plane, and pull the other points into relative positions. Delete the faces along the bottom (the ones you don't see in Figure 8.35), and then merge both objects back together. Depending on how divergent your model is from the images, it might require more or less edge addition or removal, but getting to a layout like the picture shouldn't take more than a few minutes. I also sculpted a little bit to keep the shape smooth and organic. Figure 8.36 highlights the new additions and changed areas.

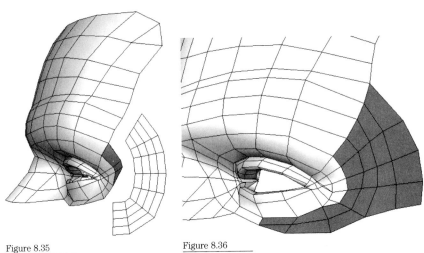

Figure 8.35

The new plane and the faces to delete

Figure 8.36

After you've combined the new objects and tweaked a bit, the shape should look something like this.

Last Nose Touch-Up

Now that the majority of the area has come together, add a few more points to the nose. This will have to marry up to the mouth we built, not exactly edge to edge—there is a gap— but the points should at least approximate the mouth area's perimeter, like in Figure 8.37.

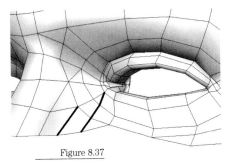

Figure 8.37

A few more rows, really as a maintenance step, to help this model and that of the mouth marry up later in Chapter 10

Brows

There are several ways to get brows on a model, and it's not a decision I'll force on you. There are options here; look at them and decide what's best for your character. For some styles, the best-looking thing is just to build eyebrows into the main structure itself, like the head in Figure 8.38. If you do that, try to keep your rows as organized as possible, so when you're building shapes you have a good layout to follow.

For Fur or PaintFX Eyebrows

Depending on your software, creating fur or any other kind of hair may involve some extra objects. For my model I used PaintFX, and with PaintFX, while you can draw strokes in mid-air, it behaves better when drawn on a NURBS surface. For either PaintFX or fur, though, you can create objects in the exact shape of your brows, and place them on or just below the surface, as in Figure 8.39. At render time, you can hide them, leaving only the hairs.

When it comes time to build your key shapes, you'll have to build accompanying shapes for these extra brow objects. If they are shaped exactly like the brows, then they are not shaped exactly like the face, and you'll have to approximate the shapes on the face with your brow shapes, with points that are not in the same place. It can be done (Figure 8.40), but it's more gruntwork than is necessary.

The smarter thing to do is to match the poly (or subD) geometry exactly point-for-point with NURBS around the brow area as shown in Figure 8.41. This is extremely easy to do, using snap-to-points. With each accompanying key shape built, you can again simply use snap-to-points, and mimic the shape perfectly. This makes the construction of shapes centralized—you just make the face shapes, and this can be forced to tag along. As before, at render time you can hide the surface, leaving only eyebrow hair.

You could, technically, use clusters and constraints on every point to glue the two objects together, but the amount of time it takes versus just snapping the points manually for the relatively few brow shapes is a close call. The clusters method will also slow interaction slightly. I don't recommend it; I prefer the "roll up your sleeves and trace a few shapes" approach.

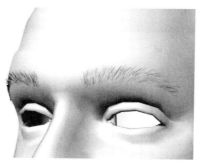

Figure 8.38

Miscy the Miscellaneous Man (a character of mine who was horribly erased in a power outage) had the "built in" brow type.

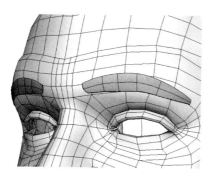

Figure 8.39

Before and after brows in the shape of brow hair

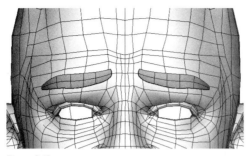

Figure 8.40

Since the objects don't line up exactly, there is interpretation and a lot of work in keeping the two moving together exactly.

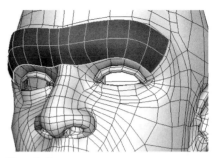

Figure 8.41

The NURBS object I use to keep the brows on my character attached. Its CVs match the underlying poly mesh.

Separate Brows: Technical Extras

I'll talk about this again in Chapter 11, "Skeletal Setup, Weighting, and Rigging," but when using separate objects for the brows, you'll need to connect all the key shapes together for the brows and the face. It'll be a simple expression tying each brow shape to the corresponding face shapes, like these:

```
BrowShapes.Brows_Up = FaceShapes.Brows_Up
BrowShapes.Brows_Squeeze = FaceShapes.Brows_Squeeze
```

If you don't do this, the face will cooperate with all the interface elements, but the brows will just lag behind.

Making a Skull

I don't like the skull too heavy in point weight, and I also don't like it arranged spherically. Usually, it looks better with even grids—or at least mostly even grids—all the way around. To try and create that as best I can, I grab the edges along the back silhouette, extrude them, snap them to grid lines, and place them so they have about the same depth behind the original edge as they are forward of it (Figure 8.42).

By pulling the points back that distance, we've gone to approximately the widest point in a skull. Take the points, and sculpt the silhouette as you'd like to see it from the front (Figure 8.43). We'll add in more detail, but we're picking on the big stuff first. If you have reference images, this is the row that should match up with any front view art or photo.

As I discussed previously, be sure to merge the new vertices, and soften the shading, to see your head properly.

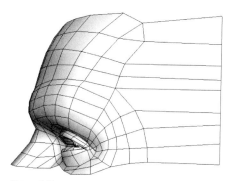

Figure 8.42

The edges extruded and scaled so that they're flat

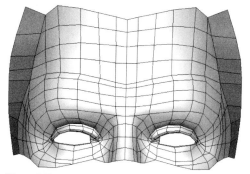

Figure 8.43

The newest rows are about as far back as the widest point in the skull.

From there, using the Append Polygon Tool, or any other you like, bridge the points across the back, and then split them down the middle. Pull the new row to create the back edge and shape of the skull, as in Figure 8.44. Something I often find handy is to use circles as reference for things like bone placement, or even as a tool to help shape objects properly. For the skull, and the area we've created, a circle creates a great trace if you make it of radius 6, native to the X axis, and move it to approximately 0, 1.7, -4.4.

Create extra vertical rows of points between each row you have now. From the top view, scale and move them to help start creating a smoother shape all the way around, as in Figure 8.45. The points and rows created if you snap to the 50% mark should provide a good general shape, too.

Figure 8.44

Two views of the newly connected and split back edge of the head

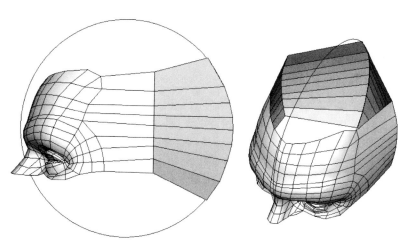

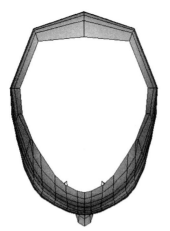

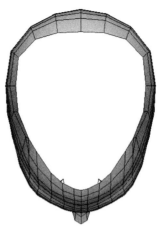

Figure 8.45

From the top down, you can see where to add the rows and what to do with them.

Figure 8.46

Adding more rows to the back half of the head helps it look a lot smoother.

Once that is done, do the same again (Figure 8.46)—split the polys vertically, but only in the back half of the head this time. The front half is almost there; it's the back that obviously needs the most detail added.

Now, if you have two halves, like I do, delete one, right down the center. Using snap-to-grids, make sure all of the points along the center dividing line are flush to the X axis, and then use the Mirror Geometry command to flip over the half you've been working on. A happy side effect of this is the faces that Maya will draw for you automatically. Go in and delete the faces that were created along the bottom, and also the ones created over the opening of the eyelids.

Split the polys on top, down the middle, and sculpt the new line to be the top part of the skull's profile (Figure 8.47).

You probably ended up, as I did, with really odd small triangular polys near the front and the back. Instead of wrestling these into a layout that is better, it's easiest to just delete them. Figure 8.48 shows what I had after I got rid of the ones I didn't like.

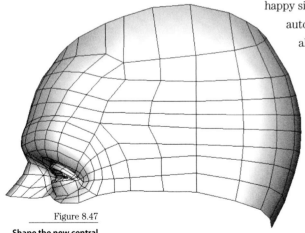

Figure 8.47

Shape the new central points the way you'd like the top of the skull to be shaped!

From there, add two rows on each side on top, running from front to back and parallel to the center line (Figure 8.49). Have the outermost line come off of a point connection with the head, and have the line closest to the center be a new edge. Use the new rows to smooth the head as it is viewed from the front and back—easiest done by just pulling the points up.

After you're happy with that, use the Append Polygon Tool to connect the open areas. You'll end up with triangles unless you add a lot more detail to the top and back of the head, but triangles never killed anybody; at least I don't think they have. After sealing up the ends, and reorienting some of the edges by creating new ones and deleting others, I ended up with what you see in Figure 8.50.

Adding a Hairline All the Way Around

If you're working on your own model, and just following structurally, you might be done following along. What I'm going to do is actually take you through building a hairline, but this can vary drastically from person to person.

Select the edges around the bottom of the back. If you're working symmetrically, that's eight edges; if you're only working on half, that's four. Extrude those down three times (Figure 8.51).

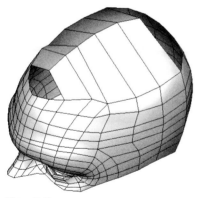

Figure 8.48

Sometimes the best way to clean points and edges up is just to get rid of them. Sorry, boys, you've been "downsized."

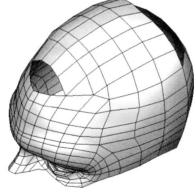

Figure 8.49

Extra rows from front to back on the head really help to create a better curve.

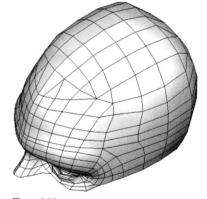

Figure 8.50

Attaching the new top to the open areas should be easy.

Using the Split Polygon Tool, draw new edges using the points already there, as shown in Figure 8.52. We're going to double up the edges along the hairline.

Delete the extra edges, making this new pair of edges quads. Add more edges, as shown in Figure 8.53, to go up to the top of the second poly up from the bottom, as shown. This is going to be where our ear will live eventually.

Delete the extra edges, again making your new lines parallel and quads, and then delete the extra faces hanging off of the bottom.

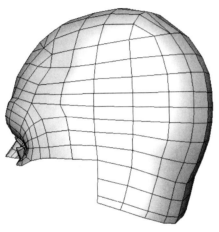

Figure 8.51

First, build a mullet. It's very important to have a mullet.

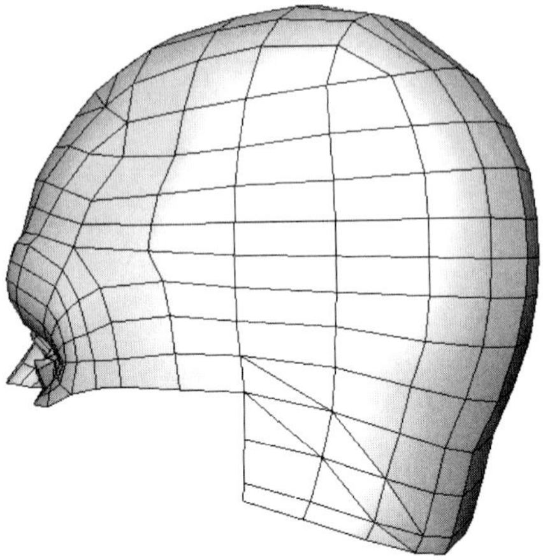

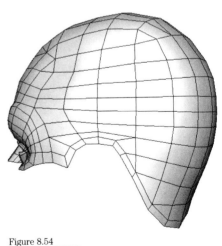

Figure 8.52

Draw the new edges using existing points for now.

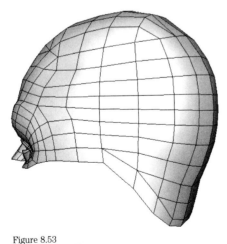

Figure 8.53

Deleting extra faces and edges makes the structure easier to see.

Figure 8.54

A bit of a jump from the last step, the rest of the work is going to be adding/deleting edges and faces where you need them for your particular model.

Add some more rows to make the shape more circular, like Figure 8.54, which will lead to a little bit of adding and deleting of edges, and then take some time to tweak the area as you see fit.

This, as I said, is a general approach to constructing the area, and almost every character will require modification. With the model I use for most of the book visuals, I actually added more to the front area, because I built in some sideburn areas of hair and just decided to continue that on. You could add more weight to the model or lighten it up. You could customize the hairline—really do anything you want.

If you've gotten this far, you have a structure that will do what you need it to. When it comes to adding and deleting more geometry, remember: with the back of the head, you can really do almost anything you want. But when you get into the eye, brow, and temple areas, try and only shape it. The structure is the way it is for a reason. Figure 8.55 shows a couple of directions you could go with the head as it is here.

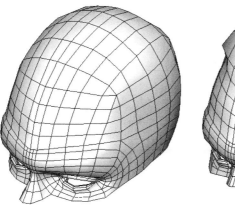 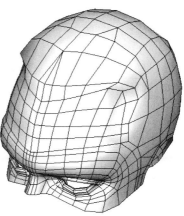

Figure 8.55

Here, there's one model I decided to rearrange to be very, very cleanly arranged, and then the model I've used in most visuals; not as clean, but very light.

Stop Staring in Color

This selection of images—some built and discussed in this book and some provided by other 3D artists—demonstrates the incredible possibilities in facial expression when you take the time to model and animate correctly. Human or animal, photo-style or toon—animated characters can look perfectly believable if you build the right shapes and move them in real-world ways.

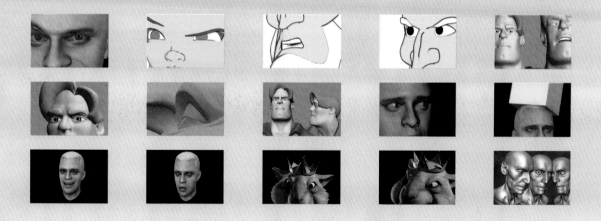

Basic Head

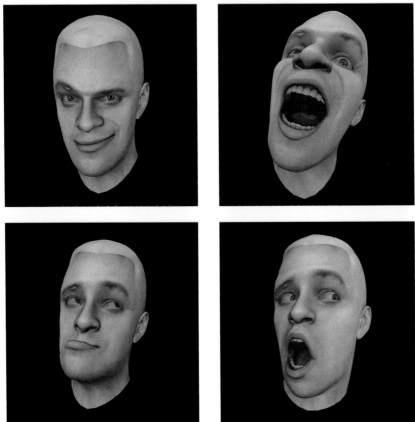

These images show the range of the basic head model developed throughout the book, in a way that would not be appropriate for most scenes—but it sure would be a shame not to flex these muscles!

Sally Ann

I usually reduce the details around the mouth in toon females—which actually allows me to make some of the mouth shapes a little wilder. Notice the complete and total difference in the shapes Sally Ann can make. If there was creasing going on around that mouth, we wouldn't be able to stretch to half of this range without her looking bizarre. Sally Ann's big brown eyes without pupils make animation a little trickier. The levels of alertness due to lid heights isn't as apparent as it might be with more eye detail. The lids have to raise a lot higher for alert and drop a lot lower for calmness/fatigue. (See Sally Ann in PinkOrBlue.mov, in the Chapter 13 folder on the CD.)

Captain Pete

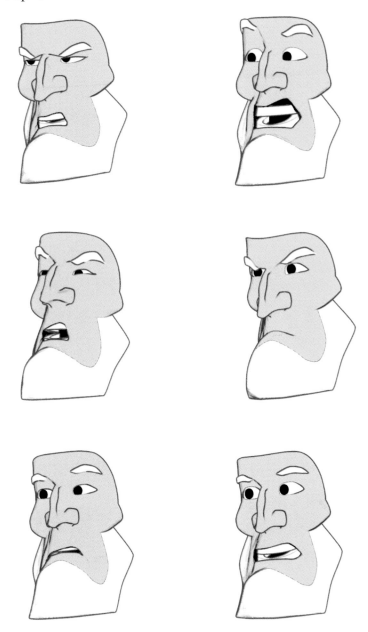

What a cranky, cranky guy. Although I'm sure Pete has a soft side, he's not going to let us see it! Notice that within the anger and focus, though, he has moments where he cracks a little—he uses that feigned softness to lure others in and lower their guard, so *wham* he can knock them down even harder. (These stills are from a movie called Captain.mov in the Chapter 13 folder on the CD.)

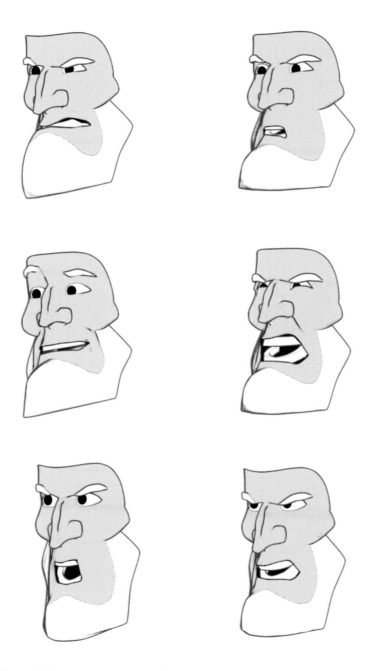

I've used this character for everything from an angry authority to a schmoozing-friendly buddy (some soundless expressing along those lines is shown in PeteNice.mov, in the CD Extras folder). The reason he works is because I can overanimate him; toons can get away with pushing their range, but only if you've set them up with natural shapes and lines in the first place.

Miscy the Miscellaneous Man

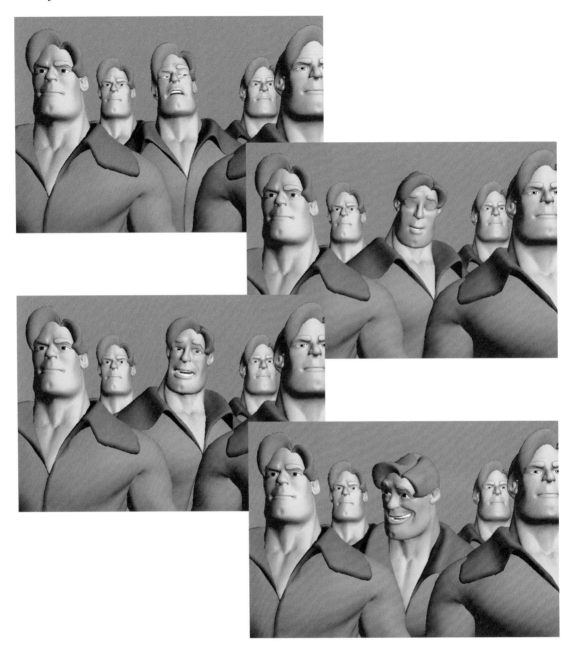

With Miscy, I gave myself a few short sound bites to test many of my own ideas on facial animation. By putting him in a crowd of immobile, staring versions of himself (GoodHardLook.mov in the Extras folder on the companion CD), you can really truly see that the default face is not the face of your character that people see. The Miscy in the middle is clearly the only one who is alive.

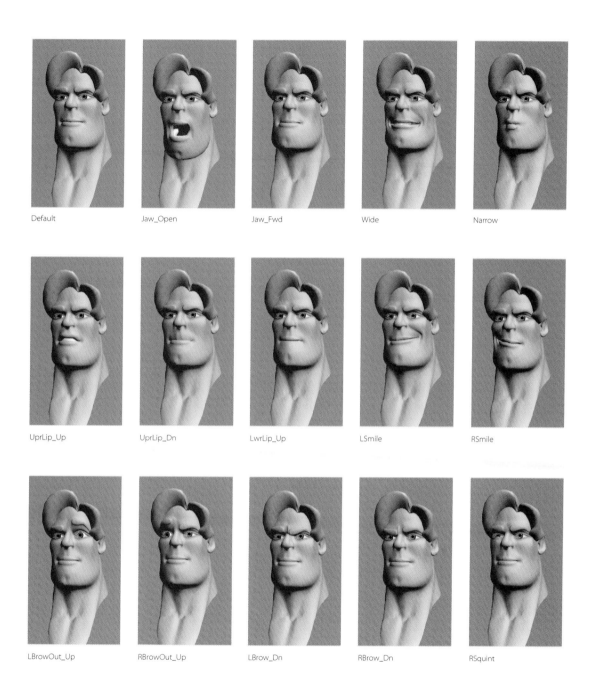

Default   Jaw_Open   Jaw_Fwd   Wide   Narrow

UprLip_Up   UprLip_Dn   LwrLip_Up   LSmile   RSmile

LBrowOut_Up   RBrowOut_Up   LBrow_Dn   RBrow_Dn   RSquint

Miscy's key set is slightly different than the ones I teach in this book; it's somewhere between the Simple and Complex setups described in Chapter 12. Of special note is that he has virtually no range with his brows, yet he still emotes quite well. His brows can only raise and drop. His mouth actually has Wide and Smile as different shapes; this can lead to an overly wide mouth when mixing, but it allows more wide range without getting too expressive, something that's occasionally beneficial. That's one of many variations you can pursue in your shape sets.

These are a few frames from another animation you can find on the CD (UAgain.mov in the Extras folder). Chris Buckley, the voice actor, decided to just make noises for a minute while we were recording. After reviewing the sound samples, that was one of the clips I chose, because it was a good, fun challenge in the character's range. And it led, of course, to some funny faces. It's always a good thing when you crack yourself up while animating.

Dog Lion

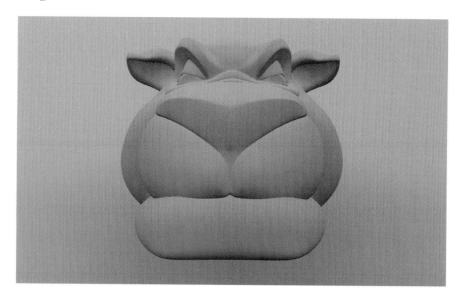

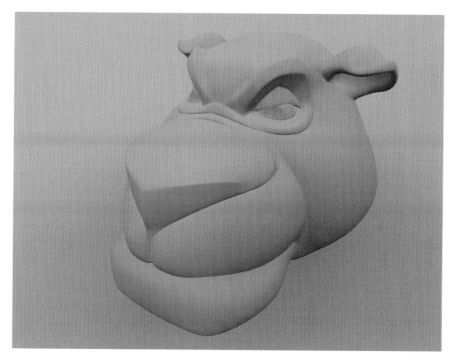

Is it a bear, or is it a lion? Maybe a dog? Whatever he is (that's part of the gag), this guy is due to be the first of some new characters featured exclusively on www.jasonosipa.com, where I'll explore and instruct on a greater number of styles. What he will do and what he will say, I can't divulge here, but I guarantee you this: he's going to be acting! Almost all rules and layout guidelines for human heads carry over to animals, even cartoony animals. Even with a character like this, you'll need circular layout around the mouth and the eyes, and the ability to create creases that look natural on the face.

Lack of Dialogue

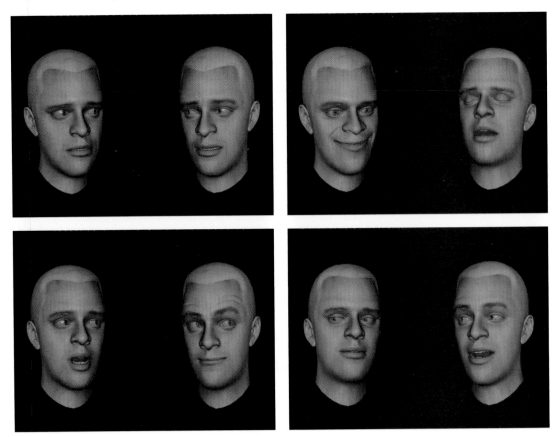

This two-character scene (Dialogue.mov from the Chapter 13 folder on the CD-ROM) is a great example of my take on eyelines. Not for one single frame of this are the eyeballs actually pointed where it seems they are, but they look correct, and that's all that matters. There's more on this concept in Chapter 2.

Dunce Cap

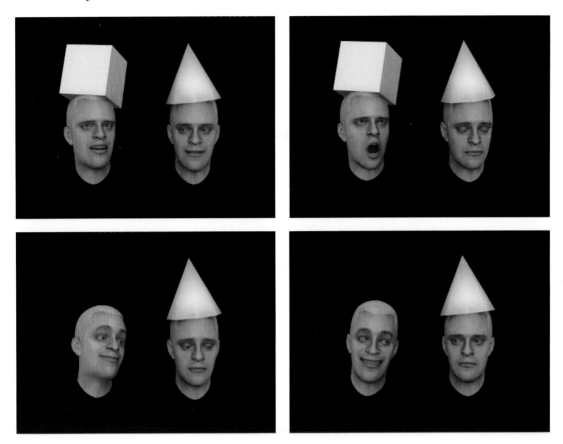

"Dunce Cap" is another two-character scene described in Chapter 13 (Dunce.mov); here, the head on our left does all the talking. Jason Hopkins animated this; he says his biggest challenge was doing dialogue without bodies: "Since there's no body, I wanted to, *had* to, gesture with the head. To really match the voice track, I had the talker gesturing to the other character and the audience." He also used subtle movements by the character on the right to keep him "alive" and get him some audience focus.

Bartender

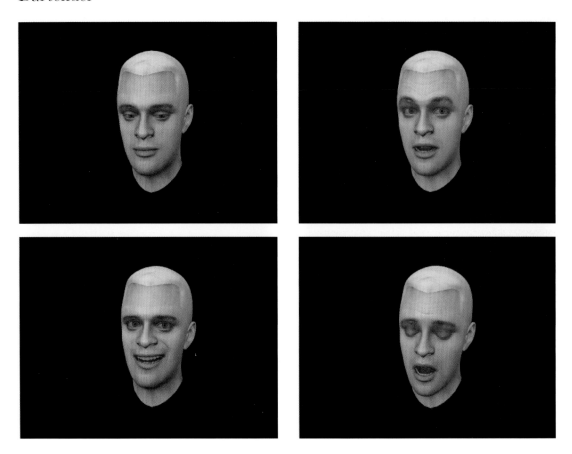

With some of these frames from an animation I talk about in Chapter 13 (Bartender.mov on the companion CD), it's easy to see how the varying combinations of smiles, squints, and brow poses can combine to create a wide range of sincerity and different subtext at any given moment.

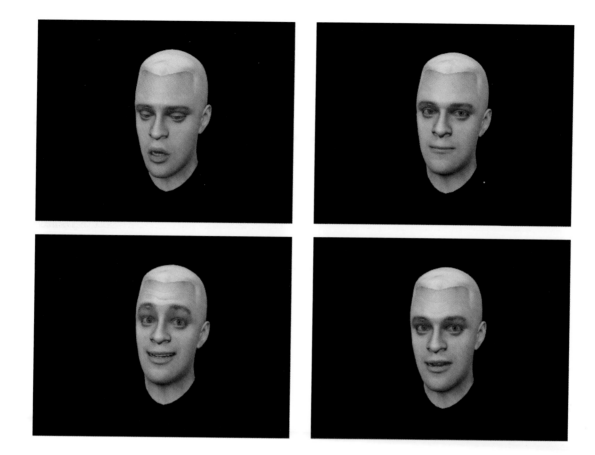

The Mouse King

MOUSE KING IMAGES OWNED BY, AND USED COURTESY OF, MATTEL, INC. © 2003 MATTEL, INC. ALL RIGHTS RESERVED.

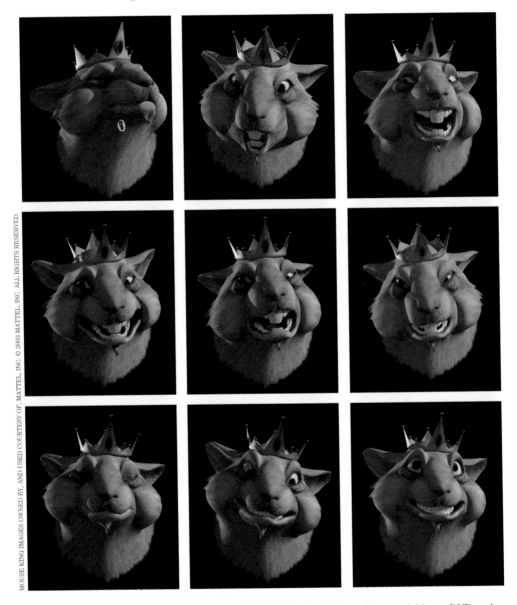

The Mouse King, from Mattel's production of *Barbie in the Nutcracker*, available on DVD and video: The Mouse King (as well as many of the characters from the second Barbie movie, *Barbie as Rapunzel*) presented a unique challenge—characters with a snout—making me re-evaluate some of my systems and key sets for animation, which until then I had based wholly on humans. The Mouse King also has a very distinctive and strong design, which forced me to come up with some creative ways to pose his face while not breaking the look of the character. In the end, after the combined efforts by voice acting, modeling, and animation, he turned out a great performance, with my facial setup being just one of the many pieces that brought him together. Pictured are frames from an animation, from the development stages of *Barbie in the Nutcracker,* where we tested the range and performance styles for the Mouse King, which is in the Extras folder on the companion CD. (Note: The voice track has been removed for legal reasons.)

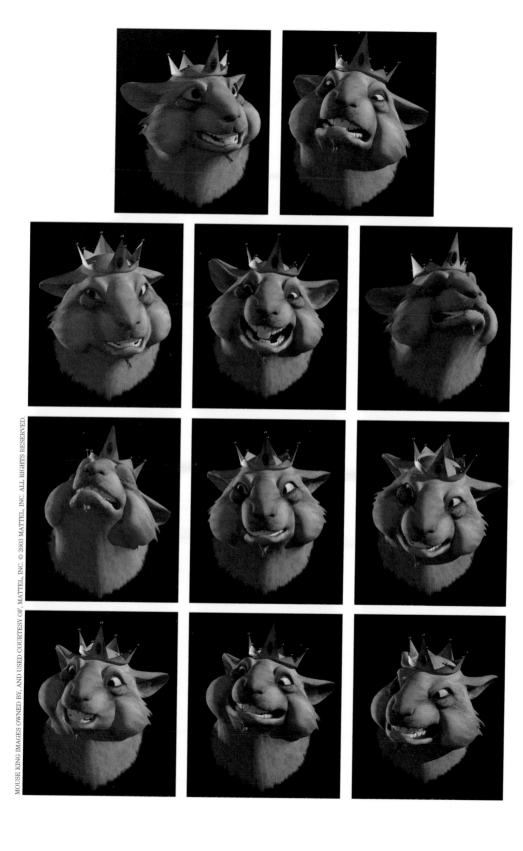

MOUSE KING IMAGES OWNED BY, AND USED COURTESY OF, MATTEL, INC. © 2003 MATTEL, INC. ALL RIGHTS RESERVED.

The Professor

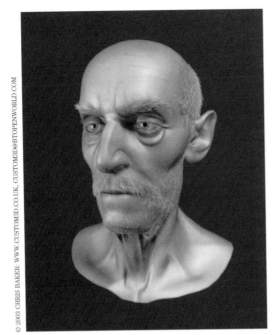

© 2003 CHRIS BAKER: WWW.CUSTOM3D.CO.UK, CUSTOM3D@BTOPENWORLD.COM

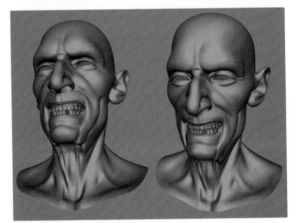

The Professor, by Chris Baker, shows great use of hard modeling in getting fantastic detail into each crease and wrinkle on the face, making him a very tangible character; he feels good and solid. The shape of the eyes and brows lend themselves very well to complex expression, opening the door to great acting. The detail in the neck and leading down towards the chest is well executed, and while realistic, still has a strong style to it. The hair was created using Maya fur on underlying NURBS patches; in the case of the jaw, lip and eye areas, these patches were then incorporated into numerous blendshapes, the eyelids included set-driven keys, and a jiggle deformer was rigged for the loose-fleshed area of the neck

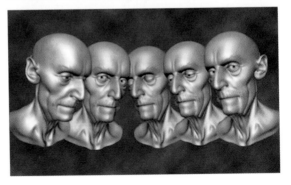

CHAPTER 9

Eye and Brow Keys

In Chapter 6, "Mouth Keys," we looked at all the keys to build for the mouth, easily the more complicated of the two areas for keys. This is the other, simpler area. With the brows, it's shorter, sweeter, has just a few more technical details, but overall is a much faster process. I can't recall the last time a brow key set took me more than one single sitting to build. As soon as you get into using textures or separate brow objects to help create a character, things can heat up as far as complexities and time go, but not so much that I can't talk you through it!

A reminder: As with the mouth shapes in Chapter 6, I recommend you have the whole head built before tackling the shapes here for the brows. I've organized the book in such a way that all things mouth are in one area, all things brows are in another, and all things rig are together as well. This makes building your first head the first time through the book a leapfrog event, but it serves as an easier way to find what you need when you're looking for "that one thing about the brows."

- Brow shapes and bump maps
- Building the shapes: standard and stylized

Brow Shapes and Bump Maps

There is a major divergence in key set styles at this point. I've talked about how you can animate all the shapes you need by making simpler shapes and combining them. This is true, but for certain more stylized characters, the easiest thing is to just build what you want to see.

With humans, we'll build Brows Squeeze, Brows Mid Up, Brows Mid Down, Brows Out Up, and Squint. With more stylized, cartoony, or anthropomorphic characters, you'll need to change that list (at least in your mind) to Brows Squeeze, Brows Sad, Brows Mad, Brows Up, and Squint. You'll name the shapes the same as the realistic head shapes, but you'll build the shapes according to a different set of criteria.

For many of the brow shapes there will be heavy creasing. With the shapes on the mouth, it's usually best to build the detail into the geometry to be able to truly do the creasing as a modeling process. With the brows, it's different; the creases, while more numerous and in some cases longer than those around the mouth, are not very deep, and they have less global effect on the overall shape of the head. For most of the creasing that goes on, I recommend texture maps and setting up expressions to link the shape to the bump map's *bump depth*. Doing this takes a couple of steps: you'll need to UV-map, and you'll need to link multiple textures' bump value into your model.

UV Mapping Information

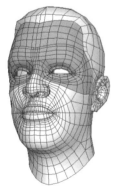

Figure 9.1

The selected faces ready to be mapped

I will not get into full texture mapping, because I really have no place preaching on a topic I am most decidedly *not* an expert on. But it is important to talk briefly on the subject, as we'll do some texturing in this chapter. We're going to use textures to create much of the creasing detail in brow shapes, and bump maps are simply the best tool for the job.

To understand texturing, you have to understand about UVs. ("UV" stands for the u,v coordinates used to locate textures, as opposed to the more common x,y coordinate system.) Models have UVs, which are a second set of points that mirror the ones used to define the geometry of your head. The UVs can be arranged over an image, and whatever imagery falls in the regions defined by the UVs then appears on the model on the corresponding poly faces. Programs provide a number of ways to go about the mapping of UVs, but for the sake of ease and simplicity, I'm going to talk only of the information *most pertinent* to what we're doing here, and of the methods specifically for Maya.

Maya's online help is extremely robust, and offers good tutorials and walkthroughs for different mapping types. I recommend reading up a bit before proceeding.

WHAT IS A BUMP MAP?

A bump map is an image where the luminance (white-to-black) value is applied to the model as a fake for depth on the surface of the model. Even if the image you use for bump mapping is in color, Maya will look only at how bright each pixel is and assign that as a depth. This is why most bump maps are black and white: it's easier to predict the effect.

If you work with mostly default settings for a bump map, 50% (0.5) gray is flat; there's no bump effect. Black will shade deepest, as if it's cutting into the surface, and white will shade tallest, as if it's bulging out. A smooth ramp from black to white would create the look of a constant-angle slope from deep to tall.

Planar Mapping

In face select mode, select the area shown in Figure 9.1, basically the frontmost area built in Chapter 8 ("Constructing Eyes and Brows"). We're going to use some polygon texture tools to map these faces flat as viewed from the front. With the poly faces selected, under the modeling module select Edit Polygons → Texture → Planar Mapping ❐.

I diverged from the base face model built in Chapter 7 ("Building Emotion: The Basics of the Eyes"), as you probably did; it was a starting point. Don't focus on the exact points and UVs I use; instead, keep track of the overall goals and affected areas in each step.

In the dialogue box that opens up (Figure 9.2), use the default settings—that is, under Smart Fit check Automatically Fit The Projection Manipulator and Fit To Bounding Box, and for the mapping direction check Z Axis and Insert Before Deformers. You should be able to leave the rest of the options as they are; in fact, all of these are the default settings. You can get by selecting Edit → Reset Settings inside the window. Click the Project button to perform the mapping.

Figure 9.2

The planar projection options

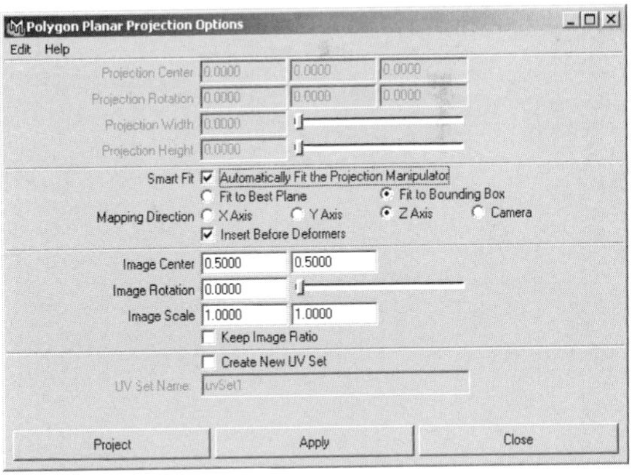

Don't lose your selection, your faces. It's important that you don't deselect as you proceed. Open up the UV Texture Editor by selecting Windows → UV Texture Editor. Inside here, you'll see the area you just planar mapped. It should look just like the forehead and eye sockets. Right click over the area where you see your forehead and change your selection type to UV. Marquee select over the area you see, and as soon as you do, the whole thing should pop and look like a jumble. When you were in face select mode, you were only seeing the faces you had selected, but as soon as you select a UV, you can see *all* the UVs on the whole model, and they all like to live in the same spot! If you selected everything you wanted in your marquee select though, you should be able to move those UVs away from the mess (Figure 9.3).

> In Maya, you move UVs the same way you do anything else—points, CVs, edges, etc.—in any other view; hot key W is translate, R is scale, and E is rotate.

So now you've got the forehead area relatively cleanly laid out and ready for textures. You can move UVs around, and if you load an image into the color attribute of the material assigned to the head, you can actually line your UVs up to a texture; when you go into the UV editor, you'll see the image in the background. This is obviously not a complete texturing tutorial, but it should give you enough information to follow along with the brow shape textures.

Multiple Bump Maps

We're going to have many separate bump maps on more realistic heads. To do this, we'll have to have maps that all line up with each other, as you can't separately position each one. I'll describe more detailed specifics along with each shape, but the way to set up multiple bump maps, technically takes a few steps:

1. Create your main color map to work from. This by itself is a very involved task, one that could take hours or days.

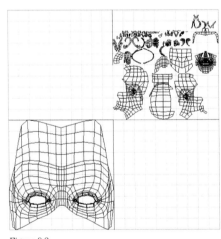

Figure 9.3

Inside the UV Texture Editor

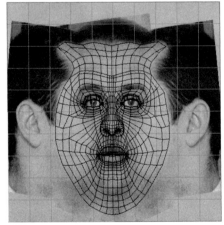

Figure 9.4

The color map I'm using

2. UV-map your head.

3. Once you have your mapping where you want it, create new 2D texture files and bump nodes in the Hypershade.

4. Connect those texture files and bump nodes in a chain that links all the way back to the base material.

That's what you'll need to do; following is how you'll do it.

First, as I said, you need to get your color map done. I'm impatient, so I usually just steam ahead at this point, get the bare minimum UV and texture work I need done, and move on. That's probably not the best thing to recommend; it's just what I do. In my model's UV set, the ears aren't even mapped and the top of the head is just recycling part of the cheek (Figure 9.4); I'm only interested in getting these bump maps on the brow, so to me, those details are left for dead on the side of the road.

For my head, which is me, I'm using photographs put together in a `.jpg` as my color map. What can I say? I'm a cooperative model!

Connecting a Color Map to Start From

To hook the texture into the color attribute of the material in Maya, select your object, open the Attribute Editor, and click the rightmost tab, which should be whatever material you've assigned to the head. In the Common Material Attributes (Figure 9.5), select the checker icon to the right of the Color slide bar.

From the next window, select File as the texture type, which opens yet *another* window; click the folder icon next to image name under File Attributes. Now you can finally go track down your texture map. When you're done, you can close all of those windows, and you should have a texture on your model (Figure 9.6). Your mapping may be wonky, and need some UV manipulation work to make it look good, but that's the basic process of how you get a color map on a model. The image you chose will now show up in the UV Texture Editor as well for you to do your UV placement.

Figure 9.5

Click the checkered icon for the color attribute and you get a window in which you select a file texture.

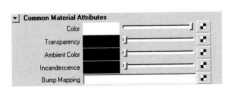

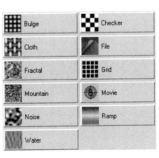

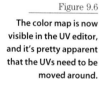

Connecting a Bump Map

Select your object, then open the Hypershade window (Window → Rendering Editors → Hypershade). When it opens, click the icon for Graph Materials On Selected Objects or, under the Graph menu, select the option of the same name.

After pressing the graph button, you should see your model's shading network (Figure 9.7). A shading network is a series of nodes connected in various ways to tell Maya *what* to do with your model, material, and textures at rendering time and *how*.

You should see a place2DTexture node, with lines and arrows connecting that to a node labeled "file*n*" (short for a node labeled "file" followed by a number) that shows your color image, which in turn is connected to whatever material your head has, and that material, finally, is connected to a shading group.

> In polygonal texturing, you don't need the 2DPlacement nodes and can delete them if you like. I will delete these for visual clarity in the examples.

To create a bump map you need two inputs: a bump node—something to tell Maya to create bump mapping—and an image to tell the bump node exactly *how* to do that bump mapping. The Hypershade is divided into two areas, the lower of which is your work area, and that's all we're going to worry about. When you graphed the network, the work area is where the network appeared. Right-click in the work area, but not over any of the nodes, and you should get a menu from which you need to choose Create → General Utilities → Bump 2D. (You can also do the same from the Create menu in the Hypershade.) Select the new bump2D node that appears and open the Attribute Editor (Figure 9.8); you can double-click the node to do so as well as using standard menus, or Ctrl+A if your hot keys are at default settings.

Figure 9.6

The color map is now visible in the UV editor, and it's pretty apparent that the UVs need to be moved around.

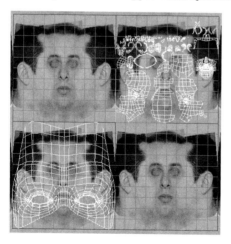

Select the checker icon next to Bump Value, click the folder icon in the following dialog, and load your color map image for now. Back in the work area, middle-mouse drag from the bump2D node to your *material* node. A small window should appear, from which you need to select Bump Map. A line should now connect your bump node to your material, as shown in Figure 9.9.

BUMP MAP VALUES DON'T "TRICKLE DOWN"

You may have a concern about a mathematical trickle-down effect on the bump maps—namely, that a 0.5 value one farther down the chain than another 0.5 value would actually be read as 0.25, assuming that Maya would calculate 0.5 × 0.5, etc. Don't be concerned. It seems that all bump nodes connected via the Out Normal: Normal Camera method are dealt with in apparent disregard of the others mathematically. A 0.5 is a 0.5 is a 0.5, no matter where in the chain of nodes it appears and regardless of the values of those before it.

If you now do a render, you'll probably see one extremely ugly bumpy head. This is because the color map isn't very well tailored to be a bump map—it's too varied—but that's not the point right now; learning to make that connection in the Hypershade is. On the CD, in the Chapter 9 folder, locate `Bumpy1.jpg`. Copy it (and all the other Bumpys) to your computer. Now go back and reset the image the bump map uses to `Bumpy1.jpg`. You won't need to recreate the connection to the material; once it's there, it stays unless you delete it. If you do a render using `Bumpy1.jpg` as the bump map, somewhere on your head you should see "UP" written using depth only (Figure 9.10). The letters U and P are written in white on the bump map, meaning they move forward/up.

The letters are blurry so that they will ramp out of the head. To see what happens without the blur, load `BumpyYuck.jpg` as your bump map file. Basically, it doesn't look good.

Figure 9.8

Click the icon to load an image to use as your bump map.

Connecting a Second Bump Map

Now to make a second bump node and include it in the network. In the Hypershade, graph your network and right-click over some empty space again. Create another bump node (Create → General Utilities → Bump 2d), and when the new node appears, double-click it to open its Attribute Editor. **BEWARE:** If you try to middle-mouse drag this bump node onto your material and choose Bump Map, you'll sever the connection with the old bump map, not

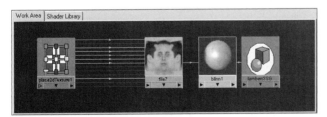

Figure 9.7

The shading network of a head with a color map

Figure 9.9

The shading network with the bump node now included

something you want to do. Since this is an additional bump map, the way to get it into the network is a little different from the first map. Middle-mouse drag from the new *second* bump node to the *first* bump node, which will open the Connection Editor (Figure 9.11).

After clicking the checker icon next to Bump Value, then choosing File from the options that appear and then opening the folder, go find `Bumpy2.jpg.` in the Hypershade.

> Be very careful to connect the *bump* nodes to each other, not the image file nodes! If you can't see Out Normal and Normal Camera as options in the Connection Editor, there's a good chance you've selected the wrong nodes. Also, make sure Show Hidden is checked in the Connection Editor filters.

On the left side of the connection editor, click Out Normal, and on the right side click Normal Camera. After that, your shading network should look like Figure 9.12. Now do another render, to take a look at your handiwork; it should resemble Figure 9.13.

Both bump maps should be on the head simultaneously, `Bumpy1.jpg` pulling the letter U and P forward, and `Bumpy2.jpg` sinking B, M, and Y deeper. To get one more practice run, because you'll need to know this well, open the Hypershade, create another bump node, stick `Bumpy3.jpg` into it, and connect the new bump node's Out Normal to the *second* bump node's Normal Camera (Figure 9.14).

You'll always connect the newest one to the previous one—sixth to fifth, fifth to fourth, fourth to third, all the way down. You can see how you can continue to connect bump maps this way infinitely! This is going to be how we connect different bump maps to different shapes to get fantastic detail in brow expressions that would otherwise require insanely detailed meshes.

Bump Depth

Figure 9.10

This guy is going up, I guess.

You may have noticed a second attribute called Bump Depth in the bump nodes. That value is how we will animate the intensity of the bump map in relation to the shapes, using expressions, in the examples throughout the rest of this chapter. Also, that's how you can scale the intensity of any bump map manually, if you need to.

Figure 9.11

Connect the Out Normal to the Normal Camera in the Connection Editor.

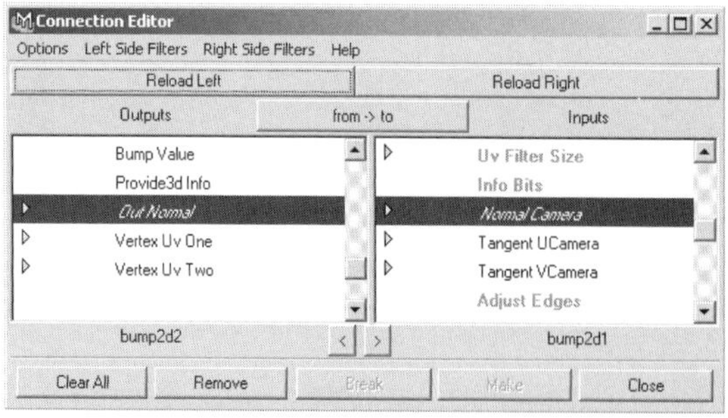

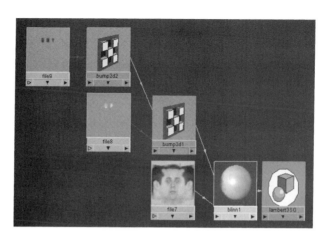

Figure 9.12

The shading network now has two bump maps.

Building Realistic Brow Shapes

Wow, with all that technical know-how, we can *finally* get down to the shape-building business. As with the mouth, I'll guide you through building symmetrical shapes and leave the splitting into halves until the end; it's just easier that way. Also, the criteria breakdown will be much simpler than that of the mouth, as there just aren't as many points or varied needs per shape. The brow keys, being significantly fewer in number and significantly easier in scope, also give me the opportunity to cover a second style.

Figure 9.13

The two bump nodes are both affecting the head simultaneously—U and P from the first and B M Y from the second.

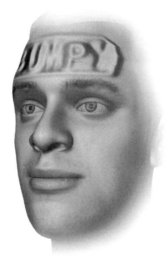

Figure 9.14

I get a book, my chance to speak to the world, and what do I do? I write "bumpy" across my own forehead.

Figure 9.15

BrowsOut_Up

In this section, I go through realistic shapes; in the following section, "Building Stylized Brow Shapes," I follow that with a "sister" set of shapes to create for cartoonier characters using my two toon models, Sally Ann and Pete. (Use one of these sets of shapes or the other, not both.)

BrowsOut_Up

Face shape: BrowsOut_Up(1)

Derivative shapes: LBrowOut_Up(2), RBrowOut_Up(2)

This is not quite as simple as raising the brows; it's raising the brows favoring the outside. The center area between the brows should not move much, if at all. To give yourself an idea of what this should look like, look in a mirror, and raise your brows, but try and keep the middle of your brows and eyelids still. You should look pretty much unimpressed. That's the shape (Figure 9.15). This is one of the shapes that is most definitely going to benefit from using bump maps to emphasize the look.

Figure 9.16

The area of effect for the BrowsOut_Up

Inclusion The area to affect (Figure 9.16) starts down by the temples and can go all the way up to the top of the hairline, although the intensity should be above the arch in the brows, and taper in effect from there. The points between the brows and the eyelids should also be moved, but they need to be moved carefully, which I'll describe in a moment. With this shape, there may be a desire to pull the eyelids wider open; you shouldn't. That's an effect best achieved at animation time.

Height The BrowsOut_Up shape for realistic motion really needs a reference. Different people can arch their brows different amounts. For my head, using myself as reference, I raised the brows approximately one eyebrow higher (Figure 9.17), so if this was on top of a default head, the brows hair would sit just above the old brow hair location. That height is focused over the arch and tapers back to the default shape toward the middle of the brow.

USE REAL REFERENCE FOR QUALITY

It doesn't matter whose face you use, your own or somebody else's. It also doesn't matter if that face looks nothing like your character. When it comes to realistic brow keys, always use reference. The main reason to use reference is going to be in getting the texture maps for creases looking real, and to create the shapes with a look that is not too simple. Everyone's face contorts in different ways, but all of those are better than what you'd come up with if you just tried to make it up on your own. I've tried to work from scratch several times with pretty decent results, but it never looks as good as when I use references; they inject fantastic character into a model, even if no one ever recognizes who those details came from.

Depth The main thing here, as with all brow shapes, is to be sure not to collapse the skull or move the eye socket. What I mean by this is that when you raise points above the eye, make sure to move them forward (Figure 9.18), so that they move into position of the points that were there before, creating the look of skin rolling over a surface instead of the appearance of a skull made of malleable mush.

Creasing As you know from earlier chapters, creasing happens at the focal point of movement and tapers away from wherever that is; the brows are no different. I put some creases pretty much following the shape of the geometry of the forehead, with the most intensity over the arches of the brows, as shown in Figure 9.19.

> With all of the creasing images for the shape descriptions in this chapter, I cranked up the effect of the bump maps to double the value at which they usually are. This is to give you clearer visual information, even though it makes the model pretty unattractive!

Texture naming and expression If you want to use a texture like the one shown in Figure 9.20 to create some nice creasing, be sure to rename the file node to BrowsOut_Up_Tex and the bump node to BrowsOut_Up_Bump. The expression you'll need to type in will be:

```
BrowsOut_Up_Bump.bumpDepth = clamp(0, 1, FaceShapes.BrowsOut_Up * 1)
```

Replace both 1s with the value that looks good for your bump map and your model, which will vary. For my model, I used 0.2.

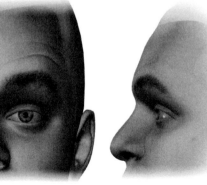

Figure 9.17

A comparison with the default brow shape and BrowsOut_Up

Figure 9.18

Always check your shapes from all angles, and remember that your character has a skull!

Figure 9.19

An extreme close-up and an overblending of the crease texture to give you an idea of what the creases should/might look like

Figure 9.20

This is a look at the important portion of the bump map image.

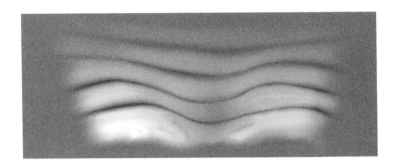

There is more discussion on expression writing in Chapter 12, "Interfaces for Your Faces." You will not *need* these expressions hooked up until you're at that stage anyway. If you're uncomfortable with expressions, come back to link these bump maps after you've read Chapter 12 and have the rest of your head hooked up to an interface.

Extra brows naming and expression As with texture maps, if you have separate brow objects to connect—or rather follow along—with the controlling object, the head, you'll need some expressions there, too. I named my extra brow object Brows, and I named its blendshape node Brow-Shapes after I finished creating all the shapes and setting up a blendshape relationship. If you do the same, naming each shape similarly as you do for the face, your expression should look like:

```
BrowShapes.BrowsOut_Up = FaceShapes.BrowsOut_Up
```

All brow expressions should look similar, where you directly equate the BrowShapes shape to the FaceShapes shape.

Figure 9.21

The Brows_Dn shape

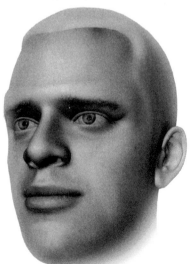

Brows_Dn

Face shape: Brows_Dn(1)

Derivative shapes: LBrow_Dn(2), RBrow_Dn(2)

This is a simple one which can be derived really easily as the opposite of BrowsOut_Up. This shape is the drop of the brows (Figure 9.21). Something deep down inside me dislikes this shape because it doesn't really exist, but we need it to make other shapes exist. The Brows_Squeeze comes up later, and its real shape involves dropping. You can't drop your brows without squeezing them, but you can squeeze them without dropping them. That means that we've got to build *squeeze* and *down* separately.

EXPRESSIONS FOR LEFT AND RIGHT DERIVATIVE SHAPES

For right and left versions, if you're building for more than the simple setup (process described in Chapter 6 and setup described in Chapter 12), be sure to substitute those left and right names in for the ones in the expressions—for instance, to connect the right and left shapes and textures, you'll first need to make two textures, one for each side. The right one's expression for the texture would read:

```
RBrowOut_Up_Bump.bumpDepth = clamp(0, 1, FaceShapes.RBrowOut_Up * 1)
```

(Here, 1 is a number that you change based on what looks best for your model and bump map, which will be a guess-and-check process.) And for the secondary brow object, you'd have:

```
BrowShapes.RBrowOut_Up = FaceShapes.RBrowOut_Up
```

You can see they both directly relate to the shape on the face. For the left side, replace RBrowOut_Up with LBrowOut_Up. Now once we hook up the model to an interface, these other pieces that bring the look of each shape together will follow along automatically with the main face model.

Inclusion Include all the same points and in the same amounts as you did for BrowsOut_Up. The area to affect is shown in Figure 9.22.

On very rare occasions, the option is not to build this shape at all! Sometimes, with really unpredictable and varying success, you can quite literally use the opposite of BrowsOut_Up. In the setup of my head I use here, that's the case, I didn't have to touch a single point. I typed in –1 for BrowsOut_Up and called it a day.

Height I usually build this shape so that its height isn't too much higher than the top of the eyelids (Figure 9.23). Something you should know, too, is that Brows_Dn can tend to look a little bit sad. This, Brows_Squeeze, and BrowsMid_Dn all push the brows down. In combination during animation, that effect is tripled. Since it pairs nicely with the Brows-Out_Up, this is the one of those three voted by me to affect the area in the center of the brows the least.

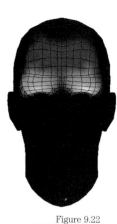

Depth As with any of the other shapes that move the brows down, try and keep the area underneath the brow ridge *plump* looking (Figure 9.24), curved outward, not collapsing inward.

Creasing There is no creasing that we'll tie to this shape directly.

Texture naming and expression There is no texture that we'll tie to this shape directly; it buddies up with two other shapes in effect, and both of those others have texturally created creasing.

Extra brow naming and expression If you have another brow object tagging along, it'll need the expression:

```
BrowsShapes.Brows_Dn = FaceShapes.Brows_Dn
```

Figure 9.22

The area of effect for the Brows_Dn is the same as that of BrowsOut_Up.

BrowsMid_Up

Face shape: BrowsMid_Up(1,2)

In the cartoonier version of this shape, I'll just refer to it as "Sad," but for more realistic characters, I want you to think of BrowsMid_Up as the middle area of the brow moving up. A sad expression made by a person will involve a brow squeeze, as well. Here (Figure 9.25), it's just the middle moving up. It's not compressing laterally or anything, just move the middle area up.

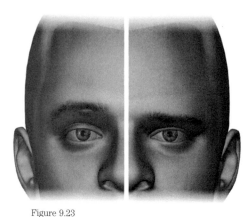

Figure 9.23

The height of the Brows_Dn is about as much *down* as BrowsOut_Up is *up*.

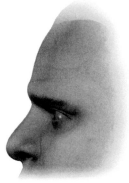

Figure 9.24

The area under the brow ridge needs to look like the skin is bunching, not hanging.

Inclusion Much as the description and name state, this is strongest in the middle of the brow, low; around brow ridge height, and the effect tapers in all directions, as in Figure 9.26. This shape's inclusion should be almost perfectly inverse with that of the BrowsOut_Up. As this takes shape, you may have the urge to push the outside of the brows down, to create a more sad shape. This will create a conflict in movements with the BrowsOut_Up shape, so just keep the motion mainly to the middle.

Height The middle brow area should move up approximately one brow height, much like the BrowsOut_Up shape, but this time (Figure 9.27) with the focus in the middle and tapering to the outside.

Depth Similar to the comment I made with the BrowsOut_Up: as you move the middle of the brows upward, carefully pull the points from below the brow ridge forward as they move up (Figure 9.28), creating the illusion that the skin is moving over bone.

Creasing The creases for the BrowsMid_Up should be the "missing link" from the BrowsOut_Up shape. With BrowsOut_Up, we terminated the creases toward the center of the forehead, and that's exactly where these are (Figure 9.29).

Figure 9.25

The BrowsMid_Up shape

Figure 9.26

The area of effect of the BrowsMid_Up

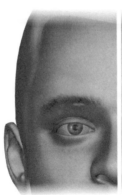

Figure 9.27

The height of the BrowsMid_Up shape as compared to the default brows

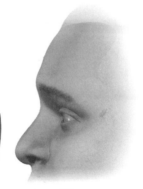

Figure 9.28

Once again, be aware you'll need to fake the look of skin moving over bone by moving the points as if they were.

Texture naming and expression To keep track of everything and to be able to copy these expressions, name the file node for the texture BrowsMid_Up_Tex, and change the bump node to BrowsMid_Up_Bump. (The texture is shown in Figure 9.30.) Connect them in series with any other bump maps as described earlier in the chapter. The expression you'll need is:

```
BrowsMid_up_Bump.bumpDepth = clamp(0,1,FaceShapes.BrowsMid_Up*1)
```

I tend to make all of my creases in one big image that has all of them, and then cover parts of that image to create the maps for each shape. By doing so, you can be assured that your creases are cooperative, so the creases created with your BrowsOut_Up shape become one with the creases from your BrowsMid_Up shape, and any other shapes, too. If you don't, the two might not merge together cleanly, and you'd have all these different lines that don't seem to relate to each other, hurting all the hard work you put into creating them!

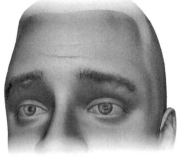

Figure 9.29

A close-up and overblending of the creases associated with BrowsMid_Up

Extra brows naming and expression If you're using an extra brow object, you'll need to connect it to the main head. Make the name for this shape BrowShapes.BrowsMid_Up. If your naming is all correct you should be able to type the expression:

```
BrowShapes.BrowsMid_Up = FaceShapes.BrowsMid_Up
```

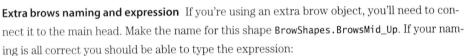

Remember that if you have an object that merely needs to shadow the face for the purposes of providing a surface for fur or PaintFX, you can use snap-to-point to copy the shape you create on your main mesh to your extra object.

Figure 9.30

The crease texture I used for my Brows-Mid_Up

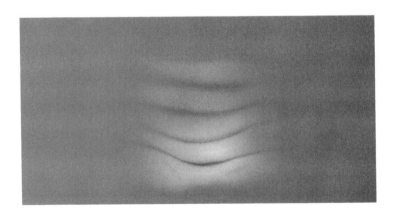

BrowsMid_Dn

Face shape: BrowsMid_Dn(2)

BrowsMid_Dn (Figure 9.31) is the exact opposite of BrowsMid_Up; where that shape basically looks like Sad, this pretty much looks like Mad. In fact, they're so conveniently opposite that you can use the same creation trick as with Brows_Dn, but this time, it's opposite BrowsMid_Up.

Inclusion The inclusion area for BrowsMid_Dn (Figure 9.32) is exactly that for BrowsMid_Up. Try not to push the outsides of the brows upward, making a Mad shape. That's not necessarily wrong; it's just that in animation you'd get that from using this in combination with BrowsOut_Up shape.

Height Compare the height of this shape to the default height, in Figure 9.33. Pushing the middle area of the brows down gets tricky because the nose is in the way. It will likely happen regardless, but try to keep an eye out for causing a ledge where the brows drop near the top of the nose. It's hard to do; you have to compromise your shape a little bit, but the result is a more natural nose/brow barrier.

Depth When you bring the brows down, and especially if you use the "negative one" trick I explained earlier, you'll want to make sure to pull down the points underneath the brows (Figure 9.34). If you don't, a real ledge can form, where it looks like the brows are melting over the area beneath them instead of moving it with main motion.

Figure 9.31

The BrowsMid_Dn shape

Figure 9.32

The region affected by the BrowsMid_Dn

Figure 9.33

A comparison with the default shape to show a reasonable height for the shape

Figure 9.34

Maintain the feel that it is skin, and the area under the brow will look good.

Figure 9.35

A close-up and extra-strength version of the creases made in a BrowsMid_Dn shape

Creasing This is going to vary based on your reference, which I will again stress you should really have. There are two main kinds of creases between the brows, as I described in Chapter 3, "Facial Landmarking." There are *vertical* creases and *bunching* creases, and of course there are combinations of those two. When I squeeze my own brows, I don't get two vertical lines; I get a messy mush of varying odd shapes. To create this in the texture, in Photoshop I rendered 3D clouds and masked them so only the area I wanted bumpy, was. My wife, on the other hand, does get those two vertical creases; it's all going to depend on who you look to for reference. For my model (Figure 9.35), I cheated and gave myself both types of creases, because it just reads better visually in black and white.

Texture naming and expression Figure 9.36 shows the crease texture. Name your file node BrowsMid_Dn_Tex and your bump node BrowsMid_Dn_Bump. Write the expression:

```
BrowsMid_Dn_Bump.bumpDepth = clamp(0, 1, FaceShapes.BrowsMid_Dn * 1)
```

I don't have to tell you what to do with the 1—you already know.

Extra brows naming and expression For your tag-along brow-buddy you'll need:

```
BrowShapes.BrowsMid_Dn = FaceShapes.BrowsMid_Dn
```

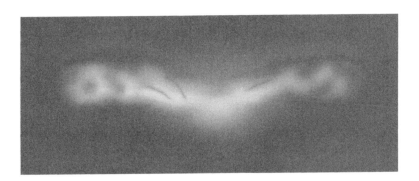

Figure 9.36

The crease texture for BrowsMid_Dn

Brows_Squeeze

Face shape: Brows_Squeeze(1)

This is the thought process embodied as a shape (Figure 9.37). Any time you need thought, this is what you use. When you build it, look at it like that. Even though your character is in a default overall pose, this should make them look like they're at least thinking a little bit about that nothing they're staring into.

Inclusion The brow's squeeze should affect approximately the same area (Figure 9.38) as the BrowsMid_Up and BrowsMid_Dn, but it's a little bit wider in its reach and not as tall. This shape is used in combination with each of those to give them their proper shape. In more complex setups, this shape can also be used on its own for portraying thought. This and BrowsMid_Dn can sometimes overlap a little bit in what they do, so try to really keep them distinct, focusing on what each one needs to do, and not giving in to the temptation to make them both almost the same!

Height This is one place to be very careful about overlap with BrowsMid_Dn. There should be some downward movement with this shape, but very, very slightly—not even a half-brow height (Figure 9.39).

Depth As was the concern with the BrowsMid_Dn, just make sure not to create too much of a ledge under the brows (Figure 9.40); keep that under-area sort of "plump."

Figure 9.37

The Brows_Squeeze

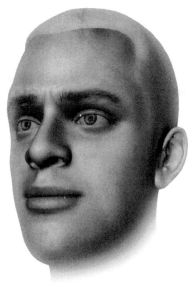

Creasing This (Figure 9.41) has almost the same bump map as BrowsMid_Dn. Usually, I make both from the same map and alter them slightly, favoring the lumpy, more turbulent look for the BrowsMid_Dn, and the vertical creases for this.

Texture naming and expression As this is probably becoming routine, here you go; texture is shown in Figure 9.42, names are Brows_Squeeze_Tex and Brows_Squeeze_Bump, and the expression is:

```
Brows_Squeeze_Bump.bumpDepth = clamp(0,1,FaceShapes.Brows_Squeeze*1)
```

Extra brows naming and expression For the extra brow objects:

```
BrowShapes.Brows_Squeeze = FaceShapes.Brows_Squeeze
```

Figure 9.38

The area of effect for the Brows_Squeeze

Figure 9.39

The height of the Brows_Squeeze is pretty uneventful.

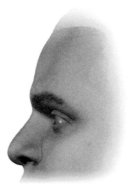

Figure 9.40

The depth of the Brows_Squeeze is also pretty uneventful.

Figure 9.41

The creasing for the Brows_Squeeze is among the most important for creating emotion. With it, you don't have to pull the brows so close together that they're touching, but you still read the expression.

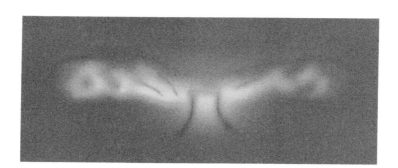

Figure 9.42

The crease texture for
the Brows_Squeeze

Squint

Face shape: Squint(1)

Derivative shapes: LSquint(2), RSquint(2)

The Squint (Figure 9.43) is the third of only three shapes that will be split in half for asymmetry in all of the brow keys (BrowsOut_Up and Brows_Dn being the others). In some cases, for the Squint, it might actually just be easier to build the one-sided keys manually, as there is absolutely no overlap in the effect of the right and left shapes.

This shape should be achieved by the combination of the lower eyelid joints' rotation and blendshapes. The actual look of the shape without the lids is pictured in all images of this section except for Figure 9.43. The reason for the combination of effects is that the lower lid gets manipulated through joint rotation, which is tied through (math) expressions to the eyeball. For this and the upper eyelid to function properly, the expressions need to know where the lower lid is at all times; as a result, the Squint, which needs the lower lids involved, must be created as a combination of influences, shape, and joint, which you will control independently.

Inclusion The Squint's area of influence (Figure 9.44) is to the outside and around the eye, with the emphasis on the outside edge where upper and lower lids meet. The effect travels all the way down, well onto the cheek and the side of the face, but must be carefully tested in combination with the smile to assure that the mix is acceptable. To a certain degree, this plus smile should create a more genuine-looking smile.

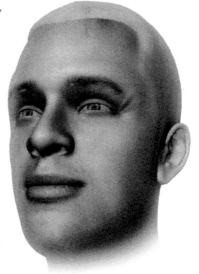

Figure 9.43

The Squint, with lower lid joint rotations added

Height The motion of the Squint pulls all areas in toward it, so the points above the eyelids should be pulled down, and the points below should be pulled up. Pictured in Figure 9.45 is the height of the shape alone; remember, you'll be able to dynamically change the height of the lower lid using the lower lid joint (once it's in there!).

Depth The area by the temples and the side of the face (Figure 9.46) should be pulled forward for this shape. As points are pulled up and down toward the Squint, make sure they all seem to travel over a surface, not just a cheek-imploding pull toward the eye.

Figure 9.44

The area of effect for the Squint

Figure 9.45

The height(s) of the Squint

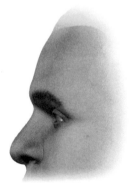

Figure 9.46

The depth of the Squint may be one of the most important factors. You should pull the corner forward as if it's being pushed by the gathering mass of skin there.

Figure 9.47

With the crease map turned up so high, virtual me looks so old!

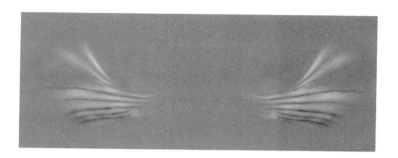

Figure 9.48

A look at the bump map texture for the Squint

Creasing This is probably the hardest crease texture to create. There should be some creasing created by the geometry out to the side where the outside of the brow meets the cheek, and the bump map should generate some crow's feet and follow along the shape that creases when you combine this with a smile, shown in Figure 9.47.

Texture naming and expression This texture (Figure 9.48) is going to be simply Squint_Tex and Squint_Bump, with an expression that reads:

```
Squint_Bump.bumpDepth = clamp(0,1,FaceShapes.Squint*1)
```

Extra brows naming and expression For an extra brow object, such as a NURBS plane that provides PaintFX a surface to live on:

```
BrowShapes.Squint = FaceShapes.Squint
```

Building Stylized Brow Shapes

I'm now going to take you through a second set of shapes that will occupy the same names and same general rules as those we've completed already, but they're a little bit looser in their interpretation. This is not a set of keys you build in addition to the previous ones; you build one set or the other None of the interfaces are designed to work with both sets of keys (nor would it make much sense if they were!).

MIXAPALOOZA

With the mouth, there were certain shapes that needed to mix well for them to be "acceptable." With the brows, every last one of these has to be able to sit mixed at 100% with any other (barring BrowsMid_Up and BrowsMid_Dn, which never occur at the same time). The best thing to do, since there are so few points to deal with, is to create a new blank head and assign all your new brow shapes to it in a blendshape relationship. As you mix them together, you'll likely see problems, some big, some small. You can then go and adjust the original target shapes and interactively see the mix update. You can work out the mix problems and see the results instantaneously!

FUN FACT: CHEATING THE SYSTEM

Let's say you don't want to build a Brows_Squeeze shape to mix with both your Mad and Sad shapes (replacing the BrowsMid_Up and BrowsMid_Dn shapes for this style). As a result, the way they get set up with an interface, they'll bounce a little bit when moving between one another, but let's say you don't care about that either. You just want a Sad and a Mad and that's it. Well, to use the setup buttons (described in Chapter 12), you'll still need a shape to sit in for the missing Brows_Squeeze shape. All you have to do is duplicate a blank head, your default, and rename it Brows_Squeeze. When it comes time to hook it up as a blendshape to your main head, include it as you would a shape that did something. The setup buttons won't know the difference either way, you'll get no errors, and the performance hit related to a head that is no different from the base head is negligible!

With the mouth, the one set of rules and images should have given you enough information to translate into various styles using your imagination. Here, with the brows, I'm taking you down one of those style paths. I'll focus on toon characters and their own fun details.

BrowsOut_Up

Face shape: BrowsOut_Up(1)

Derivative shapes: LBrowOut_Up(2), RBrowOut_Up(2)

Since this a new set of shapes, really, there's a different way to think about them. For a more stylistic approach, make your BrowsOut_Up key more of a "Brows Raise." Make the whole brow lift, center, and outside. Figure 9.49 provides a couple of examples.

Inclusion Include areas from right above the lids all the way to the top of the forehead, in tapering effect, of course, focusing on the brows themselves Include areas from right above the lids all the way to the top of the forehead—in tapering effect, of course, focusing on the brows themselves. I'll reiterate that you should include the area *between* the brows as well.

Figure 9.49

Pete and Sally Ann's BrowsOut_Up

Height This shape should pull the brows up as high as the design of your character will allow. With real humans, you want to limit the motion at *just barely beyond* extreme, to keep yourself in check as you animate. If your character isn't human, however, take this as far as you can. You'll notice on Pete, the brows shoot clean off of the forehead! (You know, I really should build a top for his head one of these days.)

Depth With realistic characters there was concern regarding maintaining the illusion of a skull; if you weren't careful, you could collapse the skull and widen the eye socket. With these more stylized characters, that isn't as much of a concern; you can get away with more when your character doesn't look real.

With this shape, you're likely to run into an issue that you might not with less range; as you pull the brows up, you also have to pull them slightly back to keep in line with the silhouette of the skull and the established profile. If you don't, it might look like the eyebrows are launching off of your character's head.

Creasing This is all up to you. Sometimes a stylized character benefits from these, sometimes they do not. In any case, if you need them, always shape them like the character's brow silhouette to make sure they look like part of the same motion and effect.

Expressions All the expressions related to the first BrowsOut_Up apply exactly the same here.

Figure 9.50

Pete and Sally Ann's Brows_Dn

Brows_Dn

Face shape: Brows_Dn(1)
Derivative shapes: LBrow_Dn(2), RBrow_Dn(2)

   This shape (Figure 9.50) can be figured out almost exactly the same as from the regular Brows_Dn described earlier in this chapter, only don't build the Sad factor into it. The horizontal crease at the top of the nose that could be generated from the mixing of all the down-moving shapes is actually somewhat desirable in non-human characters!

BrowsMid_Up (Sad)

Face shape: BrowsMid_Up(1,2)

   Where it was important to not think of this as *Sad* in the realistic shape set, this time, that is exactly what the shape is (Figure 9.51): Sad. It's Sad. Destitute, suicidal. Okay, maybe not that extreme, but the rule for this shape is that there really is no rule, except for it to look Sad.

Inclusion With this sad shape, you can include more of the brows than with the regular BrowsMid_Up. If you want to push the outside areas of the brows down, to create an even *sadder* shape, do it.

Figure 9.51

Toon sad shapes

Figure 9.52

Toon Mad shapes

Figure 9.53

I did include a squeeze shape for Pete, but not one for Sally Ann; this was simply an artistic decision. She gets a shape called Brows_Squeeze, but it has no differences from the base shape, so it has no effect.

Height You can pull the middle up as far as you need, and the outside down as far as you need. It's hard to give rules here, as the shape and style this refers to could be anything! One artistic note is to favor a curve of the brows instead of a straight line (like Box Head in Chapter 7); it tends to read better in most styles.

Depth With the portions that move up, keep them in line with the silhouette of the skull; with the pieces that move down, keep them tight to the face, otherwise it might just look like the brows are melting!

Expressions All the expressions related to the first BrowsMid_Up apply exactly the same here.

BrowsMid_Dn (Mad)

Face shape: BrowsMid_Dn(1,2)

Being a pair with BrowsMid_Dn; that was Sad, so this is… wait for it… Mad! As with most other shapes in this second set, many of the rules we followed to approximate reality are out the window; your goal in this shape is anger, hatred, all those good things that start fights, almost any way you can get them using brows only (Figure 9.52).

Inclusion This should include the same points and same amounts as those in BrowsMid_Up (Sad). Even though many rules are out the window, shapes that pair together on control sliders (which we'll set up in Chapter 12) should have reasonably paired areas of effect; it makes the transition between the shapes more believable.

Height You can pull the brows up at the brow arch if you like, as well as pulling them down in the center, a faux pas in the first style of BrowsMid_Dn. The heights here are going to be a stylistic choice for you and your character, and hard for me to describe.

Depth Comments about skull silhouette and plumpness under the brow ridge from previous shapes applies here, as well.

Expressions All the expressions related to the first BrowsMid_Dn apply exactly the same here.

Brows_Squeeze

Face shape: Brows_Squeeze(1)

It's very tricky to decide whether or not you even need this shape; Figure 9.53 shows toons with and without a squeeze shape. If you build a degree of squeeze into both the Sad and the Mad shapes, as their rules are now more lenient, then having this compound those could very well be ugly; in some instances you may not need Brows_Squeeze at all. When you do want it, the instruction in the first set will cover you just fine.

For information on adding a non-shape shape, see the sidebar at the start of this second key set called "Cheating the System."

Squint (Happy Eyes)

Face shape: Squint(1)

This is the biggest difference in shape styles from the realistic set. The guideline that you make it a combination effect between a shape and the lower eyelids' rotation still applies, but there's a lot of added shape in the lower eyelid, too (Figure 9.54). This time, the lower lid needs to appear like a rainbow shape, an upward curve, peaking in the center. By itself, this should look like a toon happy shape, but that can change based on the combinations of this and other shapes.

Inclusion This should include the same areas as did the regular Squint, but the focal point should be more underneath the lower lid than out to the side of the eye. Also, the pull on the outside of the brow should be stronger, because if you have less detail, you need to show the effect with the detail you *do* have.

Height This is a mix of up and down pulls: the outside of the brows should pull down, and the lower lids should pull up. Don't pull either too far; it can start to look odd pretty quickly. Don't let either vertically move across the pupil.

Expressions All the expressions related to the first Squint apply exactly the same here.

Tying Up Loose Ends

Well, this is the end of the key shapes that you'll need in order to do fantastic sync and acting. Here are a few more things you should know, however; some questions are answered, some extra info exposed.

If you find yourself wondering about some really extreme shapes—I mean, we're talking *loony* poses, things clearly not obtainable by combining the keys described here and in Chapter 6—yes, they exist, but we just didn't build them. Of course the situation will arise with a need beyond what we've done here, and there is a solution: specialty keys. The key shapes described here are the workhorses; they're the ones that are going to carry you through 99% of your needs; but there are going to be times when you require more. That's okay, that's normal, and that's part of the process. To build a specialty shape for a scene is not uncommon.

The key is *not* to build all of those possibilities all at once and all first, before you even start animating or could possibly know what they are. You don't need them yet. They're the icing that you apply in the extreme situations that absolutely call for them. So if you find yourself needing an extra key shape to punch that one emotion, that one scream—go for it. I'll say this: it probably won't play nice with the other shapes, so you'll need to animate them down as you animate the specialty shape in.

Figure 9.54

Toon squints can look peculiar without other emotions happening at the same time. I tend to make them much more extreme.

One more piece of advice: take the keys we've built, pose the head as close to that specialty shape as you can get, duplicate the head, and start working from there. Even in those extremes, you can use the tools you've created here to get you there faster and easier.

Asymmetry

To take the BrowsOut_Up, Brows_Dn, and Squint shapes and make their derivative left and right versions, look at Chapter 6 and its description of the process; it's the same here as it is there.

Pupil Dilation Keys

Some of you may be wondering about pupil dilation. Personally, I think it's overrated, and hard to use effectively. If you really, really want it, though, make one shape that shrinks the pupil down to nothing. You can control it through the blend shape editor and type in negative values to make the pupil bigger. Yuck. Pupil dilation: Don't fall into the trap! Don't overuse it!

The Stop Staring Expressions

I recommend that you write the expressions connecting the bump nodes and brow shapes to the main head for the sake of the learning. However, I have added a button to the Stop Staring shelf that writes all the expressions for you—of course, assuming that your objects, shapes, and nodes are all named exactly as described. If any shapes are missing or there is any misnaming, the script will bring up an error and tell you what node/name the problem is in relation to. It won't be able to exactly tell you how to fix the problem, but it will tell you where that problem is so you can zone in on it.

All the bump maps' expressions will lean on 0.2 for the blending strength. Even after using this automated approach, you may need to go in and modify the expressions manually. But replacing 0.2s with 0.3s or 0.1s isn't too much work for an ol' hand at expressions like you'll be after we're done with you!

PART IV

Bringing It Together

It's time to take all of these little pieces we've built, bring them together into one head, weight them, and rig them for use. The first thing we'll need to do is stick the pieces together. After that, we'll build an ear and neck to finish off the whole head. Next we'll set the head up for rigging, both for the shape-based rig I've used for all of the images and for a skeleton for a video-game style rig, which is bones only. If you're following along in order to create a full head, you'll need to complete this skeleton setup before doing the shape-building work in Chapter 6 ("Mouth Keys") for the mouth and Chapter 9 ("Eye and Brow Keys") for the brows.

CHAPTER 10

Connecting the Features

The eyes and brows have a structure that they need for the type of movements they do. The mouth and the area immediately surrounding the mouth, including the nose, also have their structural necessities. What we'll do now is take each piece of the head, pull all of them into a scene together, and attach them to each other, finding ways of lining up the new points that aren't destructive to the old ones.

- Bridging the top and bottom halves of the face
- The side of the face and the profile
- Building ears

Bridging the Top and Bottom Halves of the Face

Load the nose, mouth, teeth, tongue, and mouth wall that you built in Chapter 5 ("Constructing a Mouth"), and then into the same scene import the head, eyeballs, and any extra brow objects you might have from Chapter 8 ("Constructing Eyes and Brows"). For the sake of brevity, I'm going to use the head model with the whole hairline built in. If your scene looks anything at all like mine, you probably have two very differently sized objects. It's a good thing that doesn't matter. Pick either the head pieces or the mouth pieces and group them; it's your choice which. Move and scale the new group node until the parts of the head look as if they at least relate to each other. A good guide to use is the nose, since the place at which we terminated construction on both the mouth and the head is about the same place. On my model, they line up like Figure 10.1.

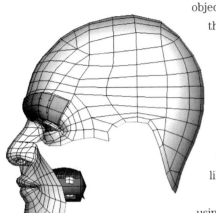

Figure 10.1

The different model chunks shown here are pulled into position and scaled so they relate well to each other proportionally.

We're going to bridge the open areas by combining the two objects and using various poly tools to fill in the blanks. The first step is to snap the points along the perimeter to each other. You may have noticed in a few of the pictures of my models that I had an extra row running down the bridge of the nose and between the brows; I knew I'd have to add those one day anyway, so I worked slightly ahead. As you match nose to nose, if there are any point number differences, you'll have to line them up. For the upper face model, I'm going to use the Split Polygon Tool to add more rows to line up with the nose from the bottom half of the face. Figure 10.2 shows the new rows with the bottom points snapped to the top of the lower half of the nose.

Once this main connection is made, select both objects and click Polygons → Combine. Select the vertices along the join of the two objects and use Edit Polygons → Merge Vertices to stick them together.

At this point, as after every supposedly successful vertex merge, I move each and every point that was involved, just to see if it really merged or not. Sometimes, as you pull a vertex, another stays behind, and the merge didn't work. You may need to re-snap the verts together or increase the tolerance in the Merge Vertices option box to ensure that the verts are really stuck together.

Maintaining Your Layout

Using the Append Polygon Tool, start to connect the top of the mouth model to the bottom of the upper face model. Something that should become apparent is that the layout we worked so hard to get doesn't seem to continue through this new area. If you're building my head, the ones in the pictures exactly, you've got a good cheat mechanism, because you can just drop points and edges in where I do and know it'll work out. In reality, though, you'll build a head that's *un*like mine far more times than you'll build this one. I purposely left a little bit of point and edge jigsaw puzzle to work through, since it's something you'll encounter in your own heads; see Figure 10.3.

What we need to do is find a way to maintain the point layouts in both main areas, the eyes and the mouth, and also create a reasonable one in this new bridge between them. This is almost always going to involve the Split Polygon Tool and deleting edges. To maneuver the layout problems like this on your own, do what I do: visualize the point and edge path from one end all the way to the other, almost like a checkers move you're planning.

> Remember to periodically select any new edges and make them shade smoothly by using Edit Polygons → Normals → Soften/Harden.

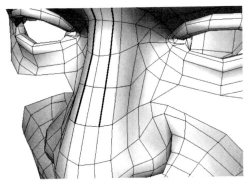

Figure 10.2

A look at the new rows added and how they connect to the lower face model

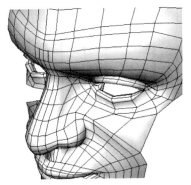

Figure 10.3

The preliminary connection between the upper and lower face

We need to maintain the proximity of the row close to the side of the nose to allow for good sneers, so we can't compromise that row too much—which means we're going to have to continue that row upward toward the eye. Figure 10.4 shows what I did, which was to add some new points and then sculpt the area to make everything happen more smoothly.

If you look at Figure 10.4, you can see I've highlighted an edge that is oriented correctly, but next to one that is forming a triangle. We're going to try to construct with quads, so what you need to do here is to delete the triangular edge and connect another in a quad with the lower half of the face (Figure 10.5a). Then grab the open edge on the upper face and continue it down towards the mouth, creating new verts and edges as you go (Figure 10.5b).

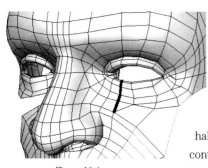

Figure 10.4

Continuing one of the mouth model rows up into the eye

The Side of the Face and the Profile

The front of the face now looks like it's taking shape, and I'm going to start adding the sides of the face. To do so, I'm actually going to create polygons that connect the front all the way to the back hairline. By doing that, and then splitting the new polys, I'll have a lot of new detail to work with, which I'd need to create later anyway. Figure 10.6 shows the new polys, which look a little like the head has got a bandage for a toothache.

These first polys don't fall in line too well with the rest of the structure, but to force them to isn't going to be too hard—we just need the polys to work with. Figure 10.7 shows what I ended up with after some Split Polygon Tool action and some patience. These areas, out by

Figure 10.5

The edge that moved over a row, and the new row added in to continue one from the upper face model

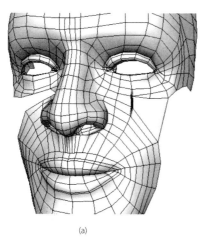

(a)

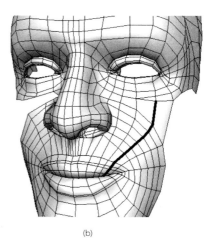

(b)

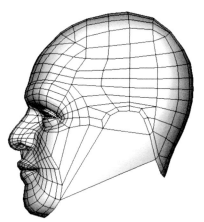

Figure 10.6

The newly appended polygons will not directly provide us anything except a place to start adding verts and edges where we need them.

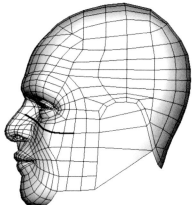

Figure 10.7

After some adding of edges and deleting of others, I ended up with this. The highlighted line found its way into the structure to provide a good transition between the top and bottom halves.

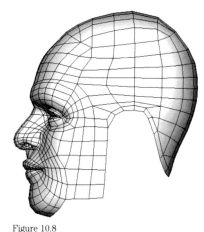

Figure 10.8

The extra faces deleted, leaving the ear area open

the chin and under the ear *can* be less structurally restrictive *because* they don't need to move as much. Take another look at Figure 10.7. In the process of creating these new polys, I had the opportunity to redirect some of the edges and points on the bridge of the nose. I led a row from the side of the face up through the middle of where the upper and lower face meet, and then up onto the nose. Finally, it seems, the front has all it needs to work as a very malleable face.

Take the really ugly stretchy polygons at the side of the head and, for now, get rid of them. We'll re-create more like them in a bit, but working cleanly is always my preference. Select the faces and delete, as in Figure 10.8.

Silhouetting the Chin

Now, let's turn our attention a little bit lower on the face. Something done far too often in CGI is pretending that the curve under the chin of a human being looks like the chin of an action figure, meaning it starts at the corner of the jaw and shoots out to the chin in a straight line, making the underside of the jaw a horizontal plane of manliness. The fact is, that just isn't the case in reality. The curve under a chin slopes pretty happily down to the neck. The look of a square jaw comes from shading near the outside corners of the jaw, not from the silhouette between the jaw and the neck. Figure 10.9 shows two images depicting the right and the wrong ways to shape the chin/neck silhouette; they are not part of this tutorial so much as informational, so I don't expect you to jump to "all finished."

My chin is significantly less square than either of the ones pictured, so for the chin I'm building, there isn't going to be a lot of that harsher chin shading. But the neck still leads to the chin the way I described, in a smooth curve; this is pictured in Figure 10.10.

Add another polygon to the bottom front, and continue that curve down and back to lengthen the neck. Add another poly on the back of the head/neck, too. With these two new polys, shown in Figure 10.11, we've finally gotten the better part of our neck silhouette done, so we can start filling in the blank areas.

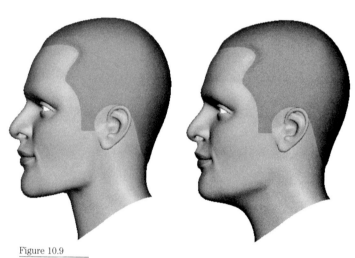

Figure 10.9

An incorrect approach to a square jaw (left) and one that's closer to the way a square jaw looks in real life (right)

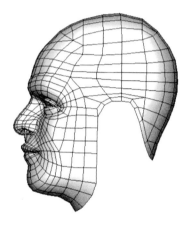

Figure 10.10

Note that the neck leads smoothly to the chin.

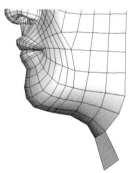

Figure 10.11

The two new polygons on the bottom give us a guideline for the shape of the neck.

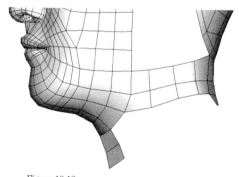

Figure 10.12

Build a ring around the collar

Building the Neck

Connect some polygons from the front to the back where they look pretty cooperative. Try to not compromise either the front or back layouts too much; let the new polys do the bending. Figure 10.12 shows what I connected.

To make the front and back play nice, it's apparent we'll need to bring some extra polys into play. I added some, creating a triangular poly where the two directions of edges come together, and leaving the open end a square, making the creation of new polys between front and back much easier. Figure 10.13 shows this.

Figure 10.14 shows the fairly self-explanatory last moves, where you connect the open polys together, and voila! You have a neck!

I left the ear area very open, because I don't like working in cramped areas if I don't have to. Before we can worry about *connecting* the ear, we're first going to have to build it!

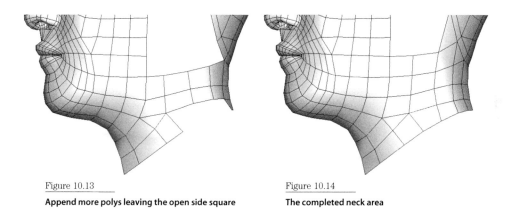

Figure 10.13

Append more polys leaving the open side square

Figure 10.14

The completed neck area

Building the Ear

I'm sure you're used to my particular modeling process now; we're going to start with NURBS to get ourselves started quickly, then convert to polys and finish the job. This time, to start, create a NURBS sphere of 10 sections by 8 spans and click on the X Axis option, as well as Cubic for Surface Degree. By right-clicking on the object, you can change your select mode to isoparm. After you do, select the middle isoparm that goes around the sphere (in the direction that doesn't pinch) and select Edit NURBS → Detach Surfaces. You can go ahead and delete one of the halves; it doesn't really matter which one. All of this should leave you with something like Figure 10.15.

Figure 10.15

A half sphere—or as we call it in fancy-land, a "hemisphere"

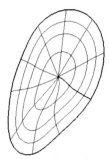

Figure 10.16

The flattened sphere shaped into the silhouette of an ear

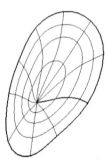

Figure 10.17

The inside of the ear being shaped to prepare for the shape it will take in a moment

Select the hemisphere you've now got and scale it to 0 in X. That should give you a flat disc. With the sphere selected, go to Modify → Freeze Transformations so that the scale is considered 1,1,1 again.

Take the outside CVs and create the silhouette of an ear. As with the brows, you should really have a reference, and it doesn't matter from whom, but ears have details best observed, not invented. I'm going to shape mine like—shocker!—my ear. Once you have the outside shaped, manipulate the rest of the interior points to follow the new silhouette. Figure 10.16 shows what I did.

The ear canal—the ear hole, you could call it—sits lower and farther forward than the center of the sphere we've got. I pulled that middle bunch of points into a more ear-canal-like position, and again, tailored points in between the center and the perimeter to follow along fairly cooperatively (Figure 10.17).

The next thing I did was rotate the ear object to make it aligned more like a real ear would be. A very common mistake is to make ears sit perfectly flat with the head, only further out. This can cause the ears to look unnatural, and in particular it can cause the joint between the ear and the head to be very unnatural, as it's thick and awkward. By rotating the ear this way, the front is closer to the side of the head, making for a more natural appearance. I rotated my ear to 5, -20, -6 in X, Y and Z, as in Figure 10.18.

Pull the third row of points (in from the outside) to create a hard rim around the outside near the top of the ear, and then have it taper back to flush down toward the ear lobe, as in Figure 10.18. Again, this is loosely based on my ear; if you have a reference, use and mimic that. You won't be able to get all the detail into this model yet, but you can get going on the big stuff, such as pulling the points for the ear canal deeper.

Before we can do too much more of that kind of work, we need to change tools. We're at that stage in the process where we wave goodbye to NURBS: goodbye, NURBS! Convert the object to polygons using the settings

- General
- Per Span # Of Iso Params, with numbers U and V of 1

Figure 10.18

The ear, first rotated to line up better with the head, and then with some depth

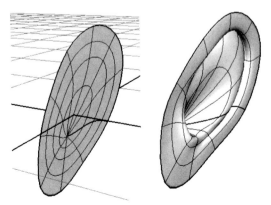

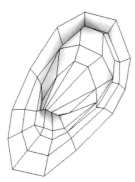

Figure 10.19

Once this ear is polygon, the process gets going fast; here there are new rows along the top half.

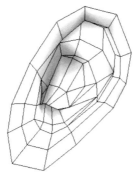

Figure 10.20

You need more detail to create sharper shapes.

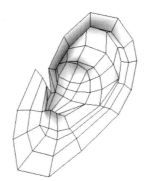

Figure 10.21

Turning the top rim of the ear in toward itself will help the look when joined with the head.

I'll say right now, this is where ears get messy, at least the way I build them. They seem to be a shape eluding an organized structure—or, more precisely, an organized structure tends to make them more detailed than is necessary. The ears have to do so little in the way of movement, I just don't pay them too much structural attention, especially not on the inside; the perimeter still needs to meet up with the rest of the face, and therefore gets *more* care. Figure 10.19 shows where I added a few more points along the top inside the ear to create some more accurate volume detail.

The next thing I added was more edges and verts just a little bit further toward the inside of the ear, to create sharper detail there before the ear recedes into the canal (Figure 10.20).

The next step, shown in Figure 10.21, is to delete some of the front of the top half ear polygons. Having the ear point to its own self where the top meets the head, and where the lobe meets the head, makes it look like a separate object from the rest of the head that just so happens to be pasted on. By breaking this layout relationship between the bottom and the top of the ear, it's more likely it will look like an organic form. The ear should only point to its own self at the top, not at both top and bottom, if that helps as a description! Figure 10.21 shows this change as well as cleaning some of the other edges and polys in relation to the change.

From there, I deleted a few more faces near the front of the ear, and added in a few more; see Figure 10.22. The polys I added were used to create the little nub at the front of the opening of the ear.

Figure 10.22

Looking from the back of the ear forward, you can see the area that was pulled out to create the dreaded "nub."

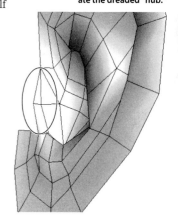

Preparing the Ear to Join with the Head

The main guts of what we need in the ear is ready to go; now we'll need to construct a back side for the thing. Select all of the perimeter edges except the very front two, and extrude them. Pull the new edges in the X axis so as to thicken the rim around the ear. Pull it much, much farther than is necessary; we'll do some modeling with the ear fattened up, and then thin it later, giving us more play room to start with. Extrude the edges three more times, creating an almost dome-like horizontal structure. This is going to be the back of the ear. Figure 10.23 shows the four new extruded rows.

Figure 10.23

We'll build the ear fat, and thin it later to give ourselves more room to work.

Figure 10.24

The extra last row gets pulled larger.

Figure 10.25

A top-down view showing the ear rim rows cutting across the others; this will help the join with the head look good.

Figure 10.26

A look at the front of the ear lobe, which is also cutting across other rows to meet more closely with the head

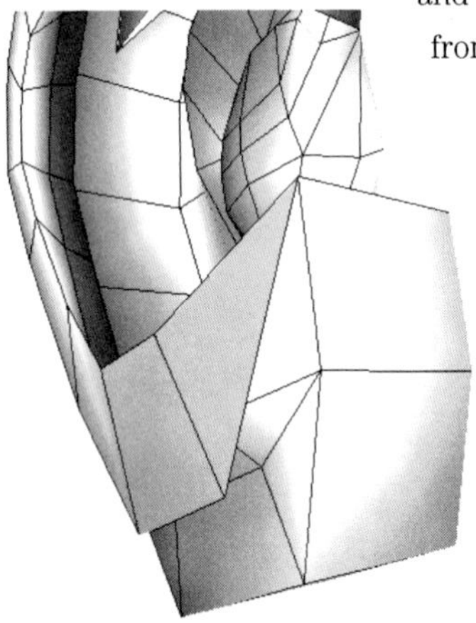

You should select all of the vertices in the new area and go to Edit Polygons → Merge Vertices, to make sure that the new edges are attached to each other. Be sure to test that the vertices merged by giving each a tug!

Figure 10.24 shows what it looks like when, next, you take the last edge, extrude it again, and this time scale it bigger. This is going to give you a good "docking" structure to start from when you later have to connect this ear you're building with the head.

One of the first things we're going to do with our flashy new ear rims is delete a bunch of them. Create new edges, delete old ones and add vertices to make it so that your outside ear edge points more directly toward the head. The way the ears are now, they will most definitely look like separate objects. We need to reduce the amount of geometry at the points where the ear rims will connect to the head. Figure 10.25 shows a top view of the ear.

You'll need to do similar work on the underside of the ear, to bring the point at which the ear lobe connects closer to the face (Figure 10.26).

We're getting very close to done with as much ear as we're going to do. Take the fat ear, and move the points on one side of it or the other to make the ear closer to the proper width (Figure 10.27). Get in there and do a little sculpting, too. The new proximity of points will undoubtedly cause you to see things you want to change. To better see what the thickness really is, smooth the polygon (of course, have an undo ready).

Ladies and gentlemen, boys and girls, we are looking at one ready-for-attaching ear.

Docking the Ear

I call this docking the ear, because that's what it feels like. You're not just smashing the head and ear together, you're intricately making connections and inching them closer together. Okay, maybe that's not what docking is either, but it sounds good.

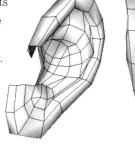

Figure 10.27

A side(ish) view and a look from the back of the ear to see what I did with my ear in pulling the two sides closer together

Normals Check

When we merge these two objects into one, we need to place them well in relation to each other, and then check to see that the normals are going to be cooperative. If they're not there already, pull the head and ear into the same scene together. Place the ear so that it sits near the hole in the side of the head where the ear should go, but leave it out to the side, giving yourself room to work while attaching the two. With both selected, go to Polygons → Combine. With your newly merged object selected, show the normals by clicking on Display → Polygon Components → Normals. If all of the lines are not pointing outward, you'll need to select the faces with the ones that aren't and reverse them by using Edit Polygons → Normals → Reverse. In my case, the ear was inverted (what it's called when the normals are backward). I had to select all the faces on the ear and reverse the normals. Figure 10.28 shows my model with the normals before I fixed them.

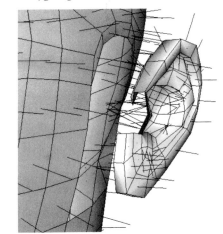

Figure 10.28

The little lines are called normals, and they point out of the side of the polygon that is considered the "front." Some of these are backward.

Connecting the Ear to the Head

Start appending polygons. Begin with all the areas along the last edge we created that fans back out behind the ear. When you get around to the front, things get a little trickier, as you'll need to create a connection between the front of the ear lobe and the area behind the rim of the top of the ear. You don't absolutely need to, but if you build it as in Figure 10.29, the way the ear sits in relation to the head will look more natural.

After patching up the remaining holes, adding edges where they are needed, and rearranging, you should have a fairly clean point layout where the ear is branching toward the head (Figure 10.30).

Grab the first row of the ear (in relation to the head), and push that toward the head. Resculpt the moved points so they match up with the skull side of things as cleanly as possible. It's a messy area, so that can be a tall order. Figure 10.31 shows where I stopped working the points.

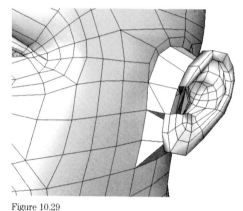

Figure 10.29

The ear's first connections to the head

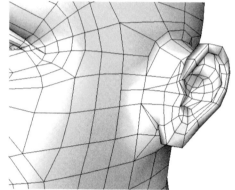

Figure 10.30

Look closely at where I've aligned the ear lobe line with those coming from on top of and behind the top of the ear.

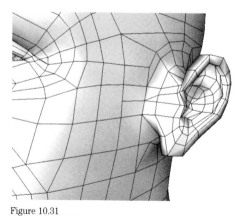

Figure 10.31

Pulling the rows in closer to the head in preparation for finishing

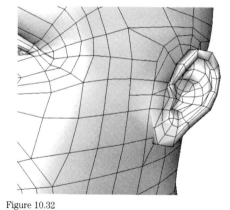

Figure 10.32

Nothing left here but some point-tickling

Now grab the bulk of the ear and pull it in toward the head. You want to do this in stages like we did, because there so much going on, in so many directions, and in such a tight space, that it's just easier to inch the ear in than to force it and fix it. Figure 10.32 shows the ear almost finished. Push the ear in just a tad past what you think you should.

Now there's nothing but some light clean-up, to make the whole area feel like it's part of the same flesh, as in Figure 10.33. You could go in and add more detail into the ear—I sure did—but at this point it's just your artist's touch and outside the realm of "why or how we build a head the way we do."

By now, you've got yourself a full head to use. If you jumped up to this from Chapters 5 and 8, racing to get yourself a finished head to work with, you can drop back and work in key shapes, or move ahead to Chapter 11 ("Skeletal Setup, Weighting, and Rigging"), to bind your head. In the lifetime of the model and in pursuit of a finished, set-up head, you'll work in both directions at different times.

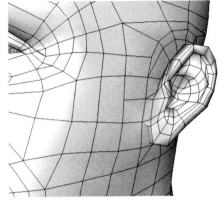

Figure 10.33
Ear-tastic!

Skeletal Setup, Weighting, and Rigging

I'll be the first to admit it. Chapter 11 is a hodgepodge. This is where many tips, tricks, and cheats have found their home, since, really, they don't belong anywhere else. Yup, you've wandered into the second-hand store on Stop Staring Street.

After a quick inventory of what you should have ready before we proceed, the focus of the chapter turns to rigging your head, which includes weighting—in and of itself not difficult. I'll guide you through the skeleton creation and point-weighting, occasionally mentioning something that is a new topic. You may or may not need information regarding each of these new topics, so I'll keep moving on with getting your head working. After that comes the last section of the chapter, which is a reference area for the concepts I bring up during the weighting process. There are small sections on how to change your character's default shape after all else is done, how to turn this character into another, how to recreate the shapes using joints for video games, and even a section on how to manipulate the way blend shapes work—to allow you to directly manipulate points on mixes of shapes, if you're up for it!

- **Final checklist for head work**
- **Weighting the head**
- **Special considerations and challenges**

Final Checklist

The work needed to reach this point is spread out over the course of the book, but if you're here you're probably close to finished. Here's a final checklist of what you need to have in place to make your head work as expected:

Build the head. Following the instruction in Chapters 5 ("Constructing a Mouth"), 8 ("Constructing Eyes and Brows"), and 10 ("Connecting the Features"), build the head you'd like to use.

Build the shapes. Choose the type of setup you want to run (that information is in Chapter 12, "Interfaces for Your Faces"), and build the shapes you'll need to make it work following the instruction in Chapters 6 ("Mouth Keys") and 9 ("Eye and Brow Keys").

Weight and rig the head. This chapter is where you see how this is done. You can actually do this before or after you build the shapes; just as long as it's done before you proceed to steps after this.

Connect your blend shapes to your head. When you have models in all of the poses described in Chapters 6 and 9, you're ready to connect your shapes to your head. Remember to do this for any and all extra objects as well.

> You can actually connect shapes to your head at any time; you'll just need to use a slightly different technique to connect any shapes after the *first* time you connect shapes to the head. To learn how to add a blend shape into an already existing relationship, look ahead in this chapter to the section called "Changing the Default Shape."

Check the names. Before you can expect any automatic setup to work, or even before steaming ahead and writing your own expressions, make sure any names that are relevant to expressions are correct—or if they are extras of your own design, make sure the names are logical. This includes object names, the names of joints, blendshape nodes, even bump texture nodes.

Connect extra objects. If you have two brow objects, a mouth wall, animating bump nodes, anything that you want to follow the interface, you'll need to connect those nodes and any pertinent attributes to the main FaceShapes attributes, to ensure that your extras will follow along with the interface.

Run the automatic setup. When everything is in place—all your shapes connected, extras connected to those, and anything else you might have cooked up is ready to rock,—save your scene, and then run the setup script for the setup you'd like to use. If you try to connect a setup that does not match the shapes you've built, you'll get errors.

Read the errors to decide if they're acceptable. The error readout you'll get may include things you are knowingly not including in your setup. Double-check to see that all you intended to include was included. If something is giving you an error that you don't expect, go and examine all parts of that aspect of the setup. It could be something simple like a misspelled or typo'd name, or it could be that you have more than one object or attribute of the same name causing conflicts.

Create your own extra controls (optional). Only after the rest of your interface is in place should you start playing with your own extra additions to the setups; if you do this before using the automatic setup buttons, you might create connections to attributes that will be overwritten by the automatic setup. You can use the Make Ctrl button on the Stop Staring shelf to create your own custom sliders for whatever you might need. You'll be prompted to name your slider, and then given a choice of what type of slider you'd like it to be. All custom sliders created this way are of group X, as opposed to 1, 2 or OF; this makes them easy to distinguish by name.

Weighting the Head

The easiest way for me to communicate all the information in this chapter regarding weighting, rigging, and related tips and tricks, while not sidetracking too much, is for me to simply describe the weighting process for the head we've been building. I will occasionally make forward references to other sections in the chapter for you to look at, when it's needed.

Placing the Joints

Before we can weight anything, we'll need to create joints to weight to. In the animation module, go to Skeleton → Joint Tool. Once you're using the Joint tool, you simply click to create a joint, and click again to create another. When you're done creating joints, you simply press the Enter or Return key, and the tool "completes."

Placing the Head and Neck Joints

Figure 11.1 shows where I put my joints. I started with a master joint, one to simply be parent over all others (it's a habit), then I clicked in the same spot to create the neck joint. I next clicked where I wanted the head to rotate from, a point approximately where the corner of the jaw is, as viewed from the side view. After that, I added a head "end" joint. This is not necessary for any technical reasons, but it makes selecting the head joint easier, as it draws a connector from the head joint to the head end joint.

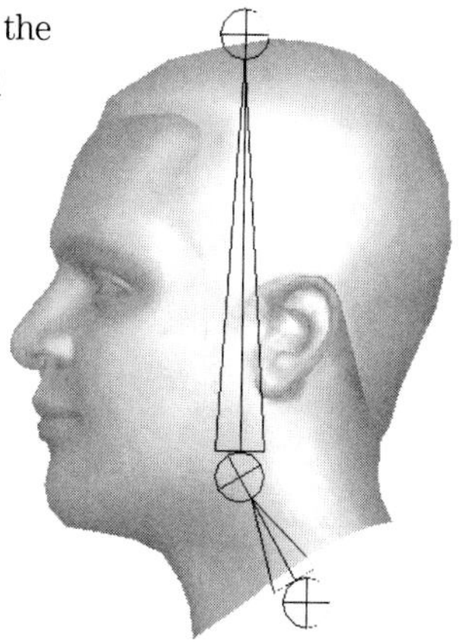

Figure 11.1

Placing the head and neck joints

Placing the Jaw

A jaw joint is shown here as an example if that's what you want to do, but the automatic setups do not support a jaw joint;

they're set up for the head to have a shape called Mouth_Open instead. You'd have to connect any jaw joint yourself manually, something like:

```
Jaw_Joint.rotateZ = - Ctrl1_Sync.ty * 25
```

But the numbers can vary based on such things as how wide you want your jaw to open.

The jaw is an easy joint to place. If you were to be ultra-realistic about it (and I've done this before with mixed results), you would put the jaw joint up where it really hinges, forward of the ears at about the same height. The motion would actually be a rotation and a translation, but we'll take the easier road, which works just as well, and place it in basically the corner of the jaw, as in Figure 11.2.

Placing the Eye Joints

The placement of the eye joints is a very particular thing. If you are even slightly off in your placement, the lids and even the eyes themselves could do some very odd things when you rotate the eye joints, like intersect, or make the eyes pop out of the socket.

> For the rest of this section on placing the eye joints, you need to have the eyeballs you created in Chapter 8 in the scene, and positioned properly in the head, where you want them to be.

Duplicate the head end joint, whatever it may be called, and rename the duplicate LEye_Joint. Constrain LEye_Joint to the left eyeball, and then, in the hypergraph, delete the constraint node that was just created; it'll be directly below LEye_Joint. Duplicate LEye_Joint and move the duplicate to flat with the X-axis—snap-to-grid is a good tool for this. Rename the newest joint to simply Eye_Joint, and then make LEye_Joint a child of Eye_Joint. Figure 11.3 shows what my skeleton looks like at this point.

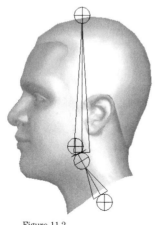

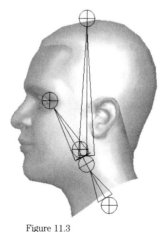

Figure 11.2

Where you'd put the jaw joint if you wanted to use one

Figure 11.3

The left eye joint placed

ROTATING THE EYE JOINTS

You've just placed the left eye joint properly; now to get it properly rotated. What we need to do is line up the rotation of this joint with the angle at which we diverged the eyes. This helps the weighted eyelids move better. I could go into why, but it's not necessary—just trust me. My eye models are diverged 9 degrees each, so that's how I'll proceed in the example; you should match the angles to your own eye models. Figure 11.4 shows a top-down of my model's eyeballs.

Select LEye_Joint and open the Attribute Editor. There's a part of the attribute editor titled Joint located below the section titled Transform Attributes. All of the boxes there should be reading zeros; if they don't, set them so that they do by typing zeros into the boxes. What we're going to do now is manipulate the values in the row labeled Joint Orient to line up the joint with the divergence of the eyeball. For my model, and my joints, I have to change the X joint orient to 9 degrees. You might have to experiment with which axis to turn and by how much based on variables stemming from your joint creation and eyeball rotation. In the top view, you should be able to see the axis line up with your eye. Figure 11.5 shows my LEye_Joint orientation, as viewed from the top. When you're satisfied, close the Attribute Editor.

> If X was not the axis that yielded the proper effect, you *will* have problems with the automatic setup buttons. You should make your joints line up so that they match mine, otherwise you'll end up with eyes that blink sideways. Try drawing the bones in the side view for an orientation like mine.

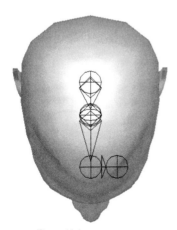

Figure 11.4

A top-view of the left eyeball joint

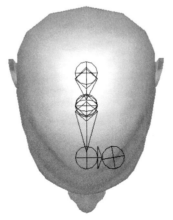

Figure 11.5

After the joint is oriented, you can see that new angle visually in the angle of the cross in the joint

Duplicate the joint twice and rename one duplicate LUprLid_Joint, and the other LLwrLid_Joint.

If after you complete this, your eyelids intersect your eyeballs—essentially making your eyeballs poke through the lids—you will need to add "fans," something you can look ahead in this chapter to read about. In such an instance, you would actually duplicate the joint we've just made one or maybe two more times. If your character has big eyes, you may want to make a few extra joints now to plan ahead.

MAKING THE RIGHT-SIDE EYE JOINTS

Do not mirror joints. Your eyes could misbehave if you do. Do this manually, as I did. Take LEye_Joint and duplicate it again. Rename the new joint REye_Joint. You can repeat the whole process you did for the left eye, but assuming your eyes are symmetrical, you can also go a little faster, as I'm about to describe. Since Eye_Joint is central, you can take REye_Joint and simply reverse the value of the one translation you have, by putting a minus sign in front of the value or taking it away (it should be in Z). Then, in the Attribute Editor, reverse the value of the joint orient—in my case I'm making it –9 in X. Duplicate REye_Joint two (or more) times, renaming the duplicates RUprLid_Joint and RLwrLid_Joint. You've got some eyelids to weight to! See Figure 11.6 for a look at the exceedingly simple skeleton.

PARENTING THE EYES

This is out of order, but it's here because the question might arise for you: After you do your binding, you should parent your eyeballs under their respective eye joints we just built. Figure 11.7 is a hypergraph snapshot of the hierarchy with the eye-related joints selected.

Diverging Skeletons

If you are setting up a head where all features are controlled by joint rotation, jump ahead to the Video Game Rig section; it describes more placement to cover more functionality via joints. If you're just rigging for a regular type of head, read on—you've already done the skeleton work!

Binding the Head

"Binding" is what they call sticking points to joints in Maya. Other programs call it "skinning" and/or "weighting." In Maya the process is, once you've got your skeleton set up and selected (*skeleton* meaning a hierarchy of joints), you select the objects you want weighted (the head, teeth, mouth wall, etc., but not the eyes), and then click Skin ➜ Bind Skin ➜ Smooth Bind. The program will try to calculate for you which points should follow which joints and how much, but since we have so many joints on top of each other, it doesn't usually guess what to do with this eye area very well.

There are two types of binding, rigid and smooth. For our purposes here, I'll only speak of smooth binding; rigid binding is not a viable option for the bones in the head.

Weighting Order

I'm not a weight-painter. I admit it. While painting weights is clearly more intuitive, it's not nearly exact enough for the precise nature of the weighting to be done on the face. Also, with the face and especially places like the corners of the mouth and the bunched up points above the eyelids, it's nearly impossible to get a good view of what you're weighting—something necessary to paint weights. I'm an old-fashioned s*elect the point and type in a number* kind of guy, and for the face in particular, that's what I recommend you do, too.

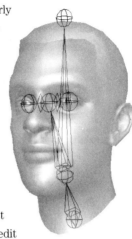

Figure 11.6

The already completed skeleton!

To adjust the skin weights, open Window → General Editors → Component Editor and click the Skin Clusters tab (Or for Maya 5.0 users, the tab is labeled "Smooth Skins") Now when you select vertices, you'll see their weighted values in the window. You can edit those values to control your weighting.

The very first thing I do when weighting is overwrite any and all of the existing weighting, by selecting all verts on the head model and then the top node of the skeleton in the Component Editor (which I've named MasterSkel) and setting all weights to 1. This assigns all weights to that joint, nullifying any other weighting. From there, I proceed to move down in the hierarchy dealing with each stage of the weighting. By going from top to bottom hierarchically (bottom to top visually) and being very broad in the weighting, you can ensure no point gets left behind—even if one does, it will be moving relative to the joint hierarchically above the one it should, meaning that its motion will be close to correct, and you won't have points hanging in space as you move your character through a scene.

Now everything is weighted to the master joint. Select all the points and add 0.5 weighting to the neck. Next, deselect the bottom row of the head, where the neck opens, and with the selection that's left, increase the weighting on the neck. to 1. With the same points selected, add about 0.25 weighting to the head joint. Deselect the new last row of selected points (making it the second bottom row on the model) and then make the weighting 0.5 on the head joint. Keep creeping upward (see Figure 11.8), deselecting points as you go and increasing the effects of the head joint.

Figure 11.7

A look at the hierarchy of the eyes in the hypergraph

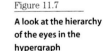

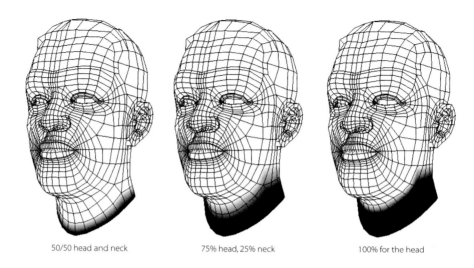

50/50 head and neck   75% head, 25% neck   100% for the head

These numbers are obviously not going to work for everyone. More important than the exact values, what I'm trying to show is how I will weight everything in the head at each stage, being sure the whole thing is weighted exactly as it should be, and then progressively narrowing down the range to work in.

Checking Poses

Instead of weighting blindly on a head in its default position, I pose my head and then tweak the weighting; by doing so, you can actually see the points move into different alignments, and it makes the tweaking of decimal numbers in the Component Editor actually mean something visual. For the head and neck, the best test is to twist the head. Figure 11.9 shows the main pose I worked on.

Figure 11.9

Two views on the main pose I used to weight the neck

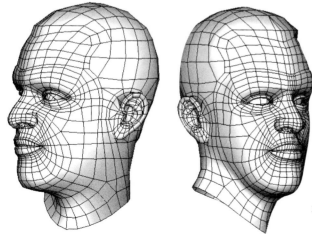

Once you do this, and get your weighting looking good through a twist, you may notice that the head probably looks okay tilting back, but not so hot tilting forward. This is, sort of, the nature of the beast. You'll lose volume slightly in most any direction of movement for a weighted model. In cases like the head tilting forward, it's particularly offensive. My favored approach for fixing that type of problem is to create a dummy blend shape that is tied to the neck's rotation, so that I can sculpt how I want the neck to look in that pose. Read ahead about dummy shapes for more information.

Weighting the Jaw

So assuming we're happy with the head and neck so far, let's move on to the jaw. I'll reiterate: following my style, there is no jaw joint—I use an open shape—but many of you may choose to have a jaw joint in your setup and could use some info. Weight points to the jaw first at values of 1, including *more* than the lower half of the mouth. Bit by bit—yes, it's tedious, but bit by bit weight the upper lip back up to the head bone. That's much easier than finicking in the tight area of the closed mouth hoping to pick all of the points precisely. After you've got a mouth opened as in Figure 11.10, weight the corners 0.5 between jaw and head, and then taper the weighting from head to jaw in such a way that the mouth looks good!

Unfortunately there isn't too much more to say than that, but by getting the corners at 50% and working around that, you're probably going to get a good-looking open jaw. Take a look at Figure 11.11 for where I called it quits on the jaw weighting.

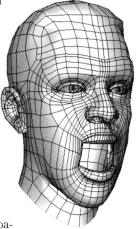

Figure 11.10

Box-mouth man has arrived! The top of the upper lip is 100% to the head, the bottom lip is 100% to the jaw, and the mouth corners are exactly 50/50. This is just the start point.

Weighting the Eyelids

I'll tell you an evil fact about this skeleton setup. Since the eyelid and eye bones are all on top of each other, there's no mirroring of weights—it doesn't work. You're going to have to weight both sides almost point-by-point. We can't move the joints anywhere else to make mirroring work, so we're stuck with the problem.

First off, so you know, weight nothing to the LEye_Joint or REye_Joint; they are there solely to rotate the eyeballs and provide the lid bones a local reference on what the eye is doing, so the lids can follow using expressions.

The best way to weight the lids is the same as the best way to weight everything else: rotate the joint into a pose, and start changing the values on mesh points until the pose looks right. I usually start with the upper lid and rotate it down about 30 to 40 degrees. Then I weight the whole leading edge of the lid 100% to the lid joint, which will create a shape like the one in Figure 11.12.

Figure 11.11

After some weighting, this is what I came up with for the jaw. I usually duplicate this and sculpt to create the Mouth Open shape.

EYELASHES

Something I don't cover in this book is eyelashes. If you do create lash objects, you'll need to weight them to the lid joints and create blend shapes for any poses in which the shape of the lids change via blend shapes on the face, the most likely being Squint or Brows_Dn.

Figure 11.12

Three stages in the weighting of the eyelid; the first rows, the refinement of those, and then the rest of the lid made to follow

Similar to the way I modeled the hairline of the forehead first, and formed the rest to follow, or got the dust mask shape and forced the rest to follow, I'm going to recommend you weight the upper lid to meet the lower lid with the leading edge and then…. Get the rest to follow. When the lid is weighted 100%, change the rotation of the lid joint to rotate back to only as far as is needed for the two lids to meet. In my case, I pulled the lid joint back to 35 degrees. Then, weight each area of points on the upper lid to follow the contour of the lower lid.

Once you've got the leading edge figured out, continue on and include more rows of the lids in tapering effect. Figure 11.12 shows the progression of the upper lid's leading edge followed by the rest of the points in the area.

> A nice touch is to weight much farther around the eye to the eyelids, but in extremely small amounts. I usually weight all the way up past the brows very slightly, so the whole area moves subtly when the eyes open and close.

After the upper lids are done, repeat the same process for the lower lids. The lower lids are usually easier, as there's no need to test them past the iris. Only rotate the lower lid joints up to about half as far as the upper lids.

The lower lids don't really move that much, and aren't really involved in blinking. I've seen in several dozen million thousand gajillion instances that animators have animated the lower lids up and the upper lids down to meet in the middle for a blink. It just doesn't work that way—it looks really weird. As I've said before, don't be a statistic. In some characters, especially those with the clamshell spherical eyeballs, it works okay, but in anything even vaguely realistic, you can't get away with it. The fact is that blinking is an upper lids thing, so the

Figure 11.13

The lower lid raised via joint rotation

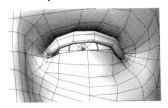

upper lids need to be weighted to travel farther than the lower lids do. The amount I pull up the lower lids to weight is shown in Figure 11.13.

If we're talking about weighting a Stop Staring–approved, ready-for-action head model, I guess we're *done* with a capital YAY! There is a version of my weighted head on the CD called `WeightedHead.ma`. That head has fan bones for the lids and a dummy shape for when the head tilts down.

Special Challenges and Considerations

The first half of the chapter talked about getting the model we've been building into a workable state. The second half ties up loose ends and offers information that I hope can be of use to you in solving any problems with your head model, or as workaround ideas for any number of varied uses in 3D.

External Eye Controls

I don't like the look of aim-constrained eyes, but I do think that eyes behave in a constrained manner. Instead of giving them a target to follow, I like to constrain the orientation of the eyes. To do so takes a little bit of setup work. Create two locators and parent them to each eye *joint*. Set all their rotate and translate values to zero, and then unparent them. What you've just done is create references for the eyes' rotations (and positions, but that's not as relevant). Create another locator, and place it approximately between the two, and then parent the two locators to the newest one. Move the trio to the side of the head, and then constrain the orientation of the eye joints to their respective locator (right to right, left to left). If you name the parent object Eyes_Cnst (eyes constraint), it'll be picked up by the automatic setups. The setup scripts will look for a node called Eyes_Cnst, and if they find it, they'll connect the eye controls on the interface to the locator; if they don't find it, they'll apply expressions directly to the eyes.

What this does is create a system where the eyes and head are on separate global controls, making the appearance of focus in the eyes practically unavoidable. It's fun to hook the eyes up like this and then just rotate the head around to watch the eyes track. It's kind of creepy, really, Figure 11.14 shows a few pictures made just by rotating the head bone around. On the CD is a scene with my head set up like this with a head control slider to see the effects quickly and easily; it's called `TrackEyes.ma`.

Figure 11.14

The tracking eyes and lids created by constraining the eyes is very cool.

Connecting Extra Nodes to the Setup: Expression Review

I've touched on this in several areas of the book, but here's one more refresher on connecting extra nodes to the blend shapes of your head, just in case your character doesn't fit the mold. Let's say you've got separate objects for the brows, or want to have textures that animate along with the main head's shapes. One other thing is a mouth wall; if you've got one, you'll need it to move along with the mouth. All of these are things that the automatic setups won't address, and you'll need to do for yourself.

First, you have to understand that since the interfaces will connect themselves to the shapes on the face, those shapes on the face are what *you* should connect *your* extra nodes to. That way, you can ensure that the interface will control your objects, as well as the main ones. In most cases, you'll be connecting blend shapes in a direct relationship:

```
Object1.ShapeA = Object2.ShapeB
```

So that's not very hard to figure out; you just have to remember that the syntax is: affected object, a dot, affected attribute, followed by an equal sign, followed by the object whose attribute you're copying, a dot, and finally the attribute you're copying. Slaving an object named Square that you wanted to have follow an object named Circle, in X translation (sideways) would be:

```
Square.translateX = Circle.translateX
```

I'm refreshing you on this because the automatic setups cover the way I set my head up: one brow object for the purpose of putting paintFX curves on it, so I had an object named Brows, with a blendshape node I named BrowShapes. All of my expressions looked like:

```
BrowShapes.BrowsOut_Up = FaceShapes.BrowsOut_Up
BrowShapes.BrowsDn = FaceShapes.Brows_Dn
```

where I simply named the shapes in both blendshape relationships the same and directly related the BrowShapes attributes to the ones in FaceShapes.

If you have two separate brow objects, you're into the world of independent expression writing. If you have RBrow and LBrow, say, and they each have blendshape nodes and shapes that match FaceShapes, you'll need to write your own expressions, which would look something like:

```
RBrowShapes.BrowsOut_Up = FaceShapes.BrowsOut_Up
LBrowShapes.Brows_Dn = FaceShapes.Brows_Dn
```

The important things to remember are the syntax, which you can reference heavily here, and the need to name your shapes well. The rest of the work shouldn't be that hard to figure out on your own; it's nothing you can't do if you've worked through most of the examples in this book.

It's also possible to connect attributes directly using the Connection Editor. Maya's online help provides very good instruction how to do that. The only drawback is that you cannot modify the relationship in any way; it's one-to-one, no math, no clamp, no flexibility.

Video Game Rigs

Most game engines want as little animation information as possible so they can run at a good frame rate. Sometimes that takes the form of highly optimized function (animation) curves, sometimes it's low poly models, and sometimes it's a small number of joints per character. Usually, it's a combination of all of these.

One other thing we can do to relieve some of the stress on a real-time engine is to limit the *kinds* of animation put into the game engine, in terms of translations, rotations, and scaling. If you can get away with using only rotations or only translations, you're obviously giving your game less to think about. In gaming reality, until full parity with blend shapes is commonplace (which, by the looks of things, could happen by the time this is in print), much of the work of facial animation needs to be done by joints. Even if face-by-joint isn't *needed*, joints are still likely cheaper than target shapes, *if* you can keep the number of joints down.

All of this leads me to a fun fact. Looking at most of the shapes we've talked about building in this book, you might think you would need to translate joints to create the effects of the shapes in this book. You might also think that you'd need dozens of joints to do so. The truth is, you only need a few; you need to place them strategically, and you don't even need to translate them. No, it's not going to look *as* good as some of the blend shapes you could build, but it's impressive considering how little there is in the way of joint cost. You can do a reasonable job with facial animation for games with four joints for the mouth, one for the jaw, one for each brow, and two for the eyes. Let me describe how you would go about doing this.

Rotating Instead of Translating

Figure 11.15 is a side view of my (high-res) model. The common way to use joints is to put them close to what you want to have them affect. In the case of moving the brows up and down, that would mean having to translate the joints. Instead, what I've done is move the joints way, way back—in some cases, even outside of the back of the head.

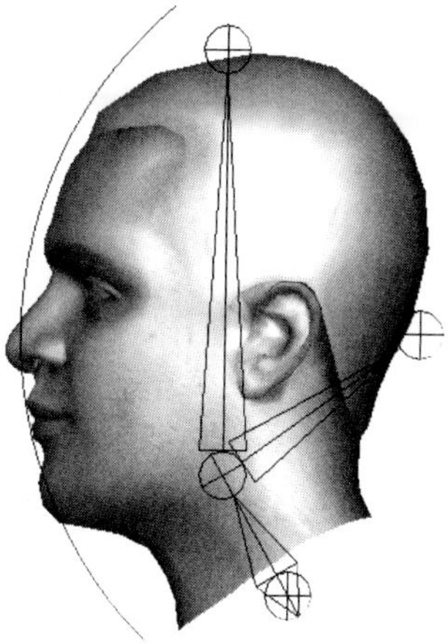

The profile of the model in Figure 11.15 also shows a circle. That circle represents the arc of the joint placed behind the head. You can see how that arc lines up with the curve of the front of the forehead. If we were to place a joint right there, and weight points on the brow to it, we'd be able to rotate the joint and have the resultant motion on the brows look more like a translation than a rotation.

You can use this idea of seemingly odd joint placement through most any part of a character you like; there are many applications. For video game characters' facial setups, I tend to put the neck, head, and jaw in the same places I usually would, but the additions are:

- Two joints for the brows, placed behind the head (children of the head joint). This is shown in Figure 11.15.

Figure 11.15

The curve in this image shows the arc around which points would travel, weighted to the brow joint—which is outside the back of the head.

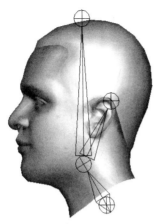

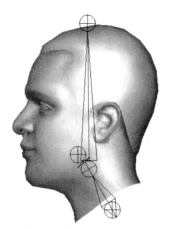

Figure 11.16

The visor-type eyes usually used in games can be controlled well by rotating a joint placed this far back in the head.

Figure 11.17

Joints in the same location as the jaw provide the necessary control needed on the mouth of a low-res character.

- Two joints approximately in the middle of the head, one to control some very low-res eyes and the other to control the upper eyelids (children of the head joint); see Figure 11.16.

- Four joints placed the same as the jaw joint, one to control the upper lip, two to control the sides of the mouth, and one to control the lower lip. All but the upper lip joint are children of the jaw joint; the upper lip joint is parented to the head bone (Figure 11.17).

Controlling a Joint Head

Although I don't recommend driven keys for blendshape faces, that's the best tool for setting up a game head. You can "trick" the automatic setup buttons into creating the interface for you, but you'll have to connect the poses you create with joint rotations to the interface via driven keys. To set driven keys:

1. Open the Set Driven Key window (Animate → Set Driven Key → Set ❏).

2. Select the *driver* object, the one to do the controlling, probably one of the interface sliders, then click the Load Driver button.

3. Select the *driven* object(s), the one(s) to be controlled, one or more of the joints. Click the Load Driven button.

4. Select the attributes you want to connect in both top and bottom windows. For these setups, you probably want one or more translations from the slider object, and one or more rotations from the joints.

5. Pose the slider and joints both where you want them for that position, and hit the key button; the two attributes are tied at those values.

6. Repeat until all of your poses and sliders are set up.

Final Video Game Setup Notes

One thing particularly good about using this technique of joints placed farther away from what they control is that, as is necessary in most game setups, you can share a common skeleton for multiple characters—tall and short, skinny and fat, big-lipped and thin-lipped. Since the joints aren't tied too directly with one set of features, you have the ability to change faces pretty drastically and maintain your rig, and in most cases transfer animations with minimal or no clean-up!

Fans, Umbrellas, or Spokes

Take your pick, call it what you like! This is a concept wherein you use multiple joints to spread out the *volume*—the space the model takes up—over a movement. I hate adding more into a model than is needed; it seems wasteful, but sometimes there is no other way to solve problems than to add extra joints. An issue I run into with many characters is making sure the eyelids *clear* the eyeball, that there is no intersection/poke-through during any stage of a blink. To do this, I use extra joints that move less than the full rotation of the *lead* joint. To give you a reason why, I need to explain a little bit about how point-weighting works.

How Point-Weighting Works

Point-weighting, or binding—the way you tell points (CVs or verts) to follow certain joints in varying percentages—really doesn't understand motion; it only understands positions. If you have one point weighted 100% (value of 1) to a joint, it will indeed move in arcs, and follow rotations; it's following the motions of the joint 100%, and since the joint is rotating, the point seems like it is rotating. As soon as you're at less than 100% weighting, it becomes apparent that the point is calculating a distance, not a motion. Let me explain further: a 50% weighted point following a joint rotating 90 degrees will not move to 50% of that joint's *motion*, it'll go to 50% of its *position*.

> **IF YOUR POSES ARE LOOKING UGLY...**
>
> The most likely unattractive shapes you'd get using this setup are clean-looking Wide and Narrows. If it proves too difficult to make this setup work, add one more joint for each lip, in the same place as the existing ones. Weight left and right sides of your lips to these new joints. This has less to do with creating asymmetry than with giving you the ability to expand and compress the lips on more than just the sides.

TO TRICK THE AUTOMATIC SETUP TO CREATE INTERFACE ELEMENTS

The Stop Staring automatic setup buttons incorporate a check to see if there is an object named Head and a blendshape node named FaceShapes. It does this as part of a pursuit to give you as much information as possible, including relevant error messages about anything going wrong with the setup. If there is nothing called Head and nothing called FaceShapes, the setup terminates. To trick the setup buttons into creating the setup, simply name one object Head and another FaceShapes. The setup will give you errors, but will create the sliders, regardless.

Doing this does not connect anything, it just creates the sliders, for you to connect for yourself.

Figure 11.18 shows several images to explain this problem and the way to work around it. Pretend you're looking at an eyeball from the side. Figure 11.18(a) shows what represents three points for an eyelid, and a joint in the center. You might expect a point weighted 50% to the lid joint to create a curve as in Figure 11.18(b), but it would in fact create a straight line between the 100% weighted point and what's left behind; see Figure 11.18(c). You can observe pretty plainly that the middle portion of the eyelid will cut into the eyeball, leaving the eye poking though the eyelid—pretty ugly stuff.

Figure 11.18

The varying numbers of fan joints provide different results on the finished model

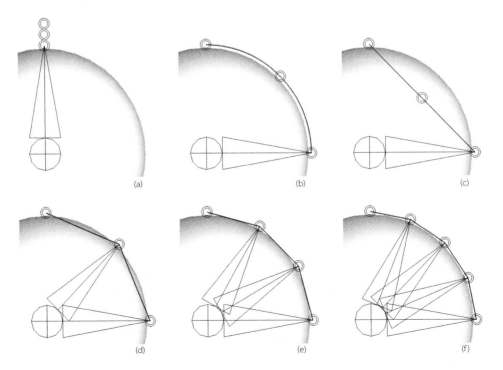

(a) (b) (c)

(d) (e) (f)

Making Weighted Points Behave the Way We Need Them To

What we need to fix this problem is indeed something that covers half of the *motion* of the eyelid. To do that, you can add another joint in the exact same place as the current eyelid, a child of the same parent as the current eyelid. Writing a simple expression saying "move half of the eyelid joint" and weighting points to the new joint, you can create an effect as in Figure 11.18(d).

> The expression would look something like `LUprLid_Joint_B.rotateZ = LUprLid_Joint.rotateZ * 0.5.`

You can see how the new joint pushes the eyelid out in the middle. Since the extra joint is following via an expression, it'll stay in the middle between 0 and whatever rotation the lid joint is at; it moves like a fan, hence the name!

Looking at Figure 11.18(d), there's still some poke-though of the eyeball. In most instances one extra joint will cover you, but there are always exceptions; usually, the bigger the eye, the more joints needed. For a character I did, I actually got up to 3 *extra* joints for each eyelid. Adding more joints is easy; you just remember to modify your expressions on each joint to account for how many joints there are total. In Figure 11.18(e) I have two *fan* joints, one following the lead 1/3 (`* 0.33`) and the second one following 2/3 (`* 0.66`). Finally, the last image of Figure 11.18, image (f), shows what it would take for this particular eye if it was on a character—a whopping three extra joints, following one quarter (`* 0.25`), one half (`* 0.5`), and three-quarters (`* 0.75`), respectively.

Adding joints that behave like this can be a great way to keep volume in most anything on a CGI character. I've added fan joints into shoulders, biceps, wrists, and butts to keep them from thinning or behaving poorly in awkward poses. Sometimes, I've used this trick in elbows and knees, as well. There is a very simple scene on the CD that illustrates this, just a few fan joints set up, and it's called `EgFans.ma`.

Dummy Shapes: The Double-Chin of Justice

I "borrowed" this idea from a standard working method of Hash: Animation Master. In the version of Hash I'm running, you're restricted to what is essentially rigid binding: a point is weighted 100% to a joint or not at all. To cover the obvious problems this would cause, there are things called "Smart Skins" that are basically blend shapes tied to joint positions; a fantastic and intuitive way to make all variety of positions for each joint look good; you pose the joint, you move the points to look good in that pose. For an example here, I'll use the problem of when your model's head tilts forward and the front of the neck collapses, which is pictured in Figure 11.19. The finished version of the weighted head involves this functionality (`WeightedHead.ma`).

Now, none of us likes to think that maybe we've got a double chin. Most of us really don't have them in most situations, but I guarantee you, if you look down, and slam your chin against your chest, there's some bulging going on. Yup. It's the truth. You may have noticed the neck weighting favoring the left to right motions of the head; that's because there's no foolproof way to weight the front of the neck to bend forward attractively without compromising other positions or at least a little bit of trickery.

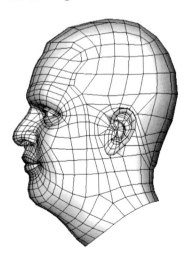

Figure 11.19

A view of the neck collapsing as the head leans forward

Let's tie this concept of smart skins to the problem with the neck weighting. We'll sculpt our way out of the ugly pose. What you'll need to do is get a duplicate of your head in the default position, and name it "FatChin" or whatever you like. Make it a blend shape to be used by the main head, the one you're weighting. If you already have a blendshape relationship, you'll have to go to Deform → Edit Blend Shape → Add. If not, you'll do the standard method of Deform → Create Blend Shape.

Building the Shape

Set the FatChin slider to a value of 1, and pose your head leaning forward, so you get the ugly neck collapse. Now, by adjusting points on the FatChin object, you can reshape the area under the chin of the main model to look better in this position. In my case, I chose to basically "fatten up" the area. Keep working until you feel good about the look of your new double chin. Figure 11.20 shows the adjustment shape posed and not posed.

Figure 11.20

The FatChin shape alone, and then as it looks with the neck posed

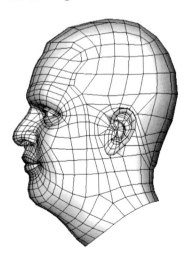
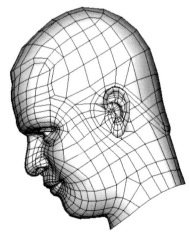

Writing Your Own Expression

Now for the technical bit: you've got to figure out an expression to control this shape, so that it automatically shows up when your head leans forward. First take note of what angle your head bone is at in the pose where you want the shape at full effect. Then what you have to do is find your zero point, the pose in which you want no effect, most likely the bind pose. You'll be looking only at the values in one axis, whichever one goes forward and back; in my case, it's Z.

Calculating the expression is going to take a little bit of effort. You need to look at two numbers—the Head_Joint rotation value at which the shape will have no effect, and the value on which the blend shape will have full effect—and equate them to a range of 0–1. Usually, that means figuring out the difference between the two, and dividing the value by that number. For example, if your start point is 0 degrees, and the head joint pose at which you want to see the shape is at –30; you'd write:

```
FaceShapes.FatChin = Head_Joint.rotateZ / -30
```

That will equate –30 degrees to 1, and 0 degrees to 0, perfect for what we want the blend shape to do. In my case, I've actually got a base pose of –30 degrees, and the place I want the FatChin shape to be 1 is at 0 degrees. My expression looks like:

```
FaceShapes.FatChin = (Head_Joint.rotateZ + 30) / 30
```

The difference between –30 and 0 is 30, so that's why I divided by 30, but I also had to add 30 because that sets the base pose to 0. – 30 + 30 = 0. I'll do a few more examples, just to make sure it all makes sense.

Since I've covered expressions already, I'll only talk of how to figure out the right expression, not the more general use of the Expression Editor.

If your base pose is –15 degrees, and the head forward pose to which you want to tie the shape is 30, you'd have:

```
FaceShapes.FatChin = (Head_Joint.rotateZ + 15) / 45
```

The 45 is the degree difference, and the 15 is how far the base pose is from 0.

One more: A base pose of 6 degrees and a Head_Joint rotation of –22 for the FatChin shape to be at full strength would be:

```
FaceShapes.FatChin = (Head_Joint.rotateZ - 6)/ -28
```

We got the –28 by finding the difference between 6 and –22.Subtracting 6 took the base pose to zero value.

Adding Clamp

The one last thing to do with this expression is to limit it. Right now, as the head tilts back, there would be the subtraction of the shape, and if the head joint leaned farther forward, the shape value would push past 1. Simply take your expression, and park it where this describes:

```
FaceShapes.FatChin = clamp(0, 1, <your expression here>)
```

And you're done! Not only will the expression calculate for the head position, it will also not give you values too big or small.

Changing the Default Shape

So there's a little problem with my model. I would love to say I planned it so I could provide this example, but I didn't; it was an honest mistake. I should know better by now, but the fact is that it provides a great example of how to fix a problem you're likely to see, too. My character's eyeballs intersect the eyelids when the eyes move around, even after adding fan joints; even though that helped tremendously. There's a good possibility yours do, too; sometimes it happens, sometimes it doesn't. So I hope I managed to make it crystal clear in Chapter 6 that you can't change the default shape—and that's still true—but there's a way around every problem. What I'll do here is explain how to adjust the base shape of your head without breaking all of the blend shapes, causing multiple transforms (remember the nose?). The way this is done is, instead of changing the base shape, which all the other shapes are based off of, you can add the changes as another blend shape.

The first thing to do, as I said in the earlier section on fans, is to try to add some fan or umbrella joints to the eyelids to make them cover the eye better. If, as in my case, that still doesn't do it, you can try the following fix.

> If your problem is specifically the eyelids, as in my case, you should use fan joints in conjunction with this fix. This fix alone will not solve the problem; in fact, it would create the same 0, 0.5, and 1 position problem described earlier.

With construction history off, duplicate your head and be very sure it's in the default pose. Rename the extra head "fix" and add it into your character's blend shape list by selecting it first, then selecting your weighted blend-shaped head and choosing Deform → Edit Blend Shape → Add.

> If you're doing this before applying all of your blend shapes, you need simply to *create* the blendshape relationship with the fix head, and you'll have to *add* the other shapes.

If you now open the blendshape editor (Window → Animation Editors → BlendShape), at the end of your sliders you should see one labeled "fix." Adjust that slider to be 100%, a value of 1, and leave it there. What this has done is let you see how the changes you make to the fix head will appear on the finished head. You can do anything you like to the fix head and it will be added into the regular head without breaking any of the other shape relationships. This is how you would turn your model into another character, with blend shapes ready to go—or in my situation, I can use it to fix the eyelid problem. On the extra head, make the adjustments that you feel you need on your base head. For me, this means I'm going to close the weighted character's eyes using the eyelid joints, and adjust the corresponding points on the fix head to puff out the eyelid areas that need to change to avoid the intersections.

There you have it! That's how you modify your character's head after the fact. You just leave this fix slider at full all the time.

> While I'll delete all of the other shapes from the scene when I've got my blendshape relationships applied, I'll usually leave the fix head somewhere in the scene; you never know what problems might crop up later that you can fix by modifying the fix shape. If you delete it, you'll need to add *another* shape to modify the base shape further.

Modeling Corrections on Compound Shapes

This is not an easy concept, and you may want to get a finished, set-up head or two behind you before trying to play with this too heavily. That's my caveat. If you experiment with this and it screws up your work, don't say I didn't warn you!

Sometimes, there are situations where you wish you could just manipulate the points on the combination of two or more shapes. For instance, if you build the tongue keys with the mouth closed, it's a big pain in the butt, because it's a tight area. Something you can do, if you're up for the potentially confusing workflow, is to start your Tongue_Up shape from the Teeth_Open shape. If you build your Tongue_Up shape off of the Teeth_Open shape, you obviously can't use that shape because applying Tongue_Up would also open your teeth further, and you'd have a doubly-opened mouth (remember back to the additive section in Chapter 6). What you can do, though, is build the shape starting with the teeth open, and then create a second blendshape relationship for the sole purpose of generating the result of your shape minus the teeth open.

The way to do this is to make a duplicate of the base teeth shape, and then assign the new Tongue_Up (with teeth open) shape and the original Teeth_Open shape as blend shapes. By setting the value for the Teeth_Open shape to –1, and the Tongue_Up shape to 1, you've "distilled" the real Tongue_Up shape you need. If you duplicate that resultant shape, you'd have a Tongue_Up without the teeth open, even though that's where you did your construction. Another way to think of it is: A + B = C. Do some modeling on C and then, C – B = A or C – A = B. For a more visual example, see Figure 11.21.

Yeah, it's a little confusing, but that's kind of the nature of the idea; feel no shame if it's warping your brain, it took me a while to figure this method out.

Figure 11.21

The combined shape, then the Teeth_Open, which was subtracted to leave the new Tongue_Up shape

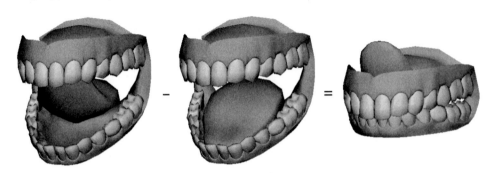

CHAPTER 12

Interfaces for Your Faces

Interface is everything, everything, everything. All the tools you need should be accessible and easy, be it for animation or for anything else in the whole world. Are you like me? Do you not read instructions? That's most people (or, at least, us guys). There's a certain satisfaction in figuring out how to use things all by yourself. If you can make that "aha" or "Eureka" moment easier for yourself and other people, the better a job you've done in designing an interface.

The setups I'll teach you have some complexities to them, but overall, they're simple. There's some math, there's some rigging, but there are only a few things to understand. I use expressions in my setups, and teach you about them in this chapter, because after learning a few tricks and rules, expressions provide both maximum flexibility *and* stability. After I've imparted these basic tools, I'll jump straight into the implementation using the StopStaring shelf buttons. I could fill chapters with just the expressions I'll use for the four main setups I'll offer up, so rather than double the size of the book, I've automated that process. I've written the scripts in such a way that you should be able to dissect them yourself with what you'll learn here.

- ▪ **Expressions**

- ▪ **Prep work for your own setup**

- ▪ **Slider designs**

- ▪ **The Stop Staring interfaces**

Using Expressions to Animate

To a lot of people, saying the word *expressions* is like saying "Boo!" All I can say is that expressions can be difficult to understand and use, but they can also be very easy if you don't let yourself get carried away. In the setups I'll describe, I make extensive use of expressions, and that isn't a scary or bad thing.

First, I have a very simple introduction to what expressions are and what they do. All the setups will have expressions for you to simply copy if you'd like, but by following the next section, you'll empower yourself to customize your setup to exactly the way you'd prefer, and be better able to troubleshoot if anything goes wrong. I'll first talk about expressions and some of the things we'll do with them, and then I'll actually take you through the process in an example before we talk about the specific slider setups.

What Is an Expression?

Expressions are just a way for you to connect two or more attributes. The connection editor does the same thing, but only does it directly. Set Driven Keys are another way to do this, but I find that for facial setups they can be a little bit too fragile. Besides added stability, an expression allows you greater flexibility. You can do things to the attributes just like you can with regular numbers in math—which on its face doesn't seem that great, but it can open up some really cool functionality.

> Confusion fighter: "setup" and "interface" are interchangeable terms.

Let's say you have a ball and a box, like the objects in Figure 12.1, and you connected the vertical (y) translation of the ball to the vertical (y) translation of the box. That expression would look like:

```
Ball.translateY = Box.translateY
```

Figure 12.1

box and a ball, ready
to be connected
through expressions

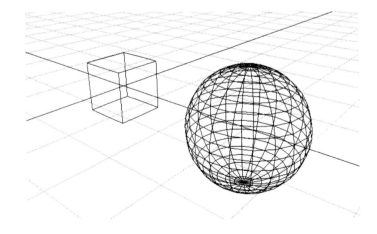

The format for reading or writing expressions is, first, the name of the object or node you want to be controlled by the expression, followed by a dot, then the attribute. After that, you'll see/write an equal sign and then another object/node and a dot and an attribute—this time, the thing that *does* the controlling. Whatever appears on the left of the equal sign is what gets affected, and whatever's on the right of the equal sign does the affecting. Reading the above expression, Box and Ball will move up and down together in Y, but only when you move Box. Ball is on the left side of the equal sign, meaning that its attribute is going to be controlled by whatever attribute is on the right side. That is always the case. If you were to try to directly move Ball up and down, it would not move, since its translation in Y is being controlled by the expression.

What Else Can Expressions Do?

Since this is an expression, we can do much more to this relationship than just have Ball do what Box does. We could make Ball move in Y twice as much as Box by multiplying it by two, just as you would if it was a number:

```
Ball.translateY = Box.translateY * 2
```

If you wanted to make `Ball.translateY` do the opposite of `Box.translateY`, you'd put a minus sign in front of Box's attribute:

```
Ball.translateY = - Box.translateY
```

And now you should be able to figure out that

```
Ball.translateY = Box.translateY /2
```

means that Ball will follow Box by half or 50%, since we're dividing that value by two.

Expressions Are Local

The numbers to and from objects and attributes in expressions are local, meaning relative to an object's parent. If an object has no parent, its values are effectively global, reacting to the world as the parent. A value of 1 in translateY is only 1 unit vertically up (globally) if an object's parent is scaled 1,1,1, is not rotated, and is sitting flat to the Y axis, just like the world. If that object's parent is scaled to 2,2,2, even though the local value in Y is 1, it is in fact at 2 units up in global space, since its "world" is twice as big. If the parent is rotated 90 degrees in X, then 1 in Y is actually out to the side, where you would expect 1 in X to be.

We are going to use this to our advantage (in fact, we already have—back in Chapter 1, "Learning the Basics of Lip Sync," when we created our first sync tool and moved it away from the mouth). Since we want to be able to move our sliders in our scenes, but not in turn be creating animation by doing so, we can move our sliders' parents. By moving, scaling, and rotating the parent objects, you are not affecting the child's local information at all. If you had a control that sent out translation values of –1 to 1 in X and Y to an expression, you could not move that slider without affecting your expression. If you had to move the slider in your scene—because, say, it's in the same spot the head is, and you'd like a clearer view of it—you would have to move its parent object so that the slider's local values are the same, even though in your scene the slider appears in a different place.

Shapes and Numbers

To understand the expressions that will be created while setting up our faces, it'll help to know what sorts of numbers mean what. In a blend shape (and in just about any other program's equivalent of a blend shape), the shape is controlled by a floating number between 0 and 1. (A floating number means that the value can be a decimal as well as a whole integer. Values like 0.2, 0.3331, or 1.0 are all allowed, and function.)

The number 0 means that the shape has no effect, and the number 1 means that it has a 100% effect. 0 is off, 1 is on, 0.5 is half. It's good to know this because most all of the expressions we write are designed to affect one or more shapes and give them a value between 0 and 1.

It is possible to use negative numbers to actually subtract a shape from the base shape, or to use numbers above 1 to force more than 100% of the shape to appear. In respect to numbers over 1, the effect is similar to a volume knob; when it gets too loud, the quality gets worse. Subtracting, using negative values, will usually yield a very weird shape.

Corralling Our Values: *clamp*

I'll get into how to actually write an expression in just a little bit, but before we can do that there's a little bit more information that you should know. I've designed the interfaces to be modular. You can, if you choose, add multiple controls for the same shape, and some of the setups will do just that. You can also mix and match your favorite aspects of each setup if you are so inclined. In fact, if you're really crazy, you can have every single different variation of control setups on the same head, so you could animate differently for every day of the week. If you're really crazy.

To take yourself into this next level of designing your own interfaces, you will need to explore the expressions and interfaces on your own. This chapter will teach you the ingredients, and the CD holds variations, but the legwork of self-design is up to you. It can be trying, but it's worth the satisfaction when you get it just the way you like it.

The sliders have built-in limitations on several levels so that if you were to use, say, three different sliders to control the smile shape, not only would the whole addition of all three be limited to numbers between 0 and 1, but each control's influence would also be limited to between 0 and 1. Since we only want values between 0 and 1 for (most) shapes, we'll use a Maya command in our expressions called `clamp`, which says to use only numbers in a certain range. Going back to Box and Ball, if we modified the expression to read:

```
Ball.translateY = clamp ( 0, 1, Box.translateY )
```

that would mean that Ball's translateY would follow Box's translateY only when it's between 0 and 1. The `clamp` keyword works by saying "Hey, I'm clamp!" and then, within parentheses, giving Maya three values to work with, separated by commas: the minimum limit, the maximum limit, and the value that determines the change. Here's another `clamp` example:

```
Ball.translateY = clamp ( -500, 723, Box.translateY )
```

This expression tells Ball's translateY value to follow Box's translateY only *if* that number is greater than –500 and less than 723. If Box's translateY is a number greater than 723, Ball will just hold at 723. Likewise, on the lower end, if `Box.translateY` is less than –500, Ball will just stay at –500.

All this comes back to the shapes. Since we want to control shapes with our controls/sliders, which work best with values between 0 and 1, we're going to be seeing `clamp` all over our expressions.

You Can Do Math Anywhere in an Expression

The `clamp` function also behaves properly when you include math functions such as those I was just talking about in the previous section. The expression

```
Ball.translateY = clamp (0,1,Box.translateY * 2)
```

says, "Ball, follow double Box's translate as long as that's more than 0 and less than 1."

Ball will only move between 0 and 1 because it is clamped between these two numbers. In addition, between 0 and 1 Ball will travel in Y at double the speed, since its translateY is multiplied by 2.

Don't be concerned if you can't picture these behaviors exactly. The purpose here is to illustrate that you can do math anywhere, even inside of the `clamp` command.

EXPRESSION NAMING SCHEMES

Expressions are picky. Expressions are very, very picky. So are all of the MEL scripts on the CD to automatically connect the setups to your heads, if you choose to go that route. You must be borderline obsessive about every last name of your shapes—before you create your blend shape relationship—making sure the names match those described in Chapter 6, "Mouth Keys." One capital, one underscore, one different text character in any way imaginable, and the expression and/or MEL scripts won't work. It's a programming thing.

Building an Example Expression and Control

By now (back in Chapter 6) you have likely built some shapes to use in this tutorial; we'll use the default Head shape, a Smile, and a Frown shape, each named accordingly; these are illustrated in Figure 12.2.

If you do not have these shapes available of your own creation, create a sphere, name it Head, and duplicate it; manipulate its shape so that it's different and name that duplicate Smile. Do the same again and name the third shape Frown. The lesson is the same, if not as visually stimulating. Move all three away from the origin to allow room for our "slider" locator. There's also a ready-for-expressions scene, in the Chapter 12 folder of the companion CD, named `ExampleExpression1.ma`; to see it finished, load `ExampleExpression2.ma`.

Creating a Control Object (Slider) for the Expression

Every expression needs input. For this example, we'll use a locator. To create a locator, select Create → Locator. When your locator appears, rename it Ctrl_Slider; we'll use this as our slider. As you've done before, limit the locator's range of motion: With the locator still selected, open the Attribute Editor by selecting Window → Attribute Editor. The locator has two parts to it, a shape node and a transform node. We need to affect the transform node, so we need to select the tab named Ctrl_Slider (not Ctrl_SliderShape; see Figure 12.3).

Under Limit Information → Translate (Figure 12.4), set the locator so it has no range in X or Z by making their maximums and minimums all 0, and make the range in Y from –1 to 1. You do this by making sure all the boxes are checked. What this has done is give us our slider for this first example. It moves up and down in Y only.

Figure 12.2

The default head, the smile, and the frown

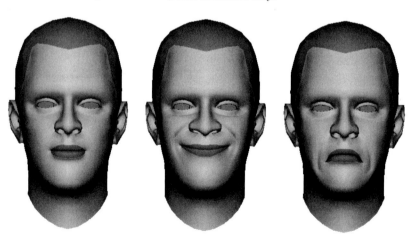

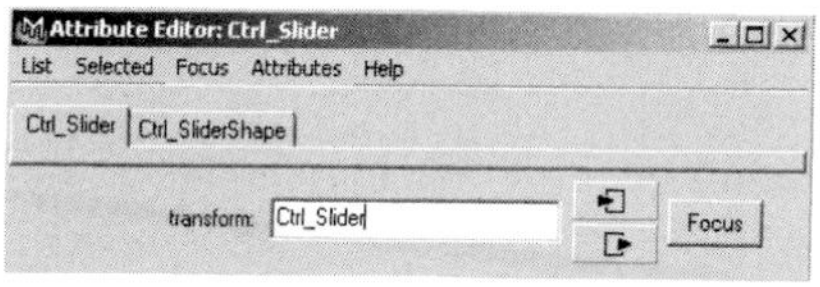

Figure 12.3

The transform and shape node tabs in the Attribute Editor

Figure 12.4

The translation limits in the Attribute Editor

Before we can control Smile and Frown as blend shapes, we need to create the blend shape relationship by selecting the Smile head and Frown head first, then shift-selecting the neutral Head, and then in the animation module choosing Deform → Create Blend Shape. Now if you select Head, you should see blendShape1 under the inputs on the right side of the screen under the Channel box (Figure 12.5).

Select blendShape1 and rename it FaceShapes. If you click FaceShapes, it should uncollapse at the bottom of the inputs to show you three channels named envelope, Smile, and Frown. If you right-click the word Smile, you can choose Expressions from the menu that appears. Now you're in the Expression Editor (Figure 12.6).

You can write any expression pertaining to any object and attribute you want at any time. However, if you select the object and attribute you want to affect now, the Expression Editor shows you the selected objects or nodes you can affect in the left-side Objects list box, and the object/node's attributes in the right-side Attributes list box. Using these windows to create the full object.attribute string is helpful in seeing the proper naming and syntax, and it's also the way you look at an expression you've previously written. By clicking one thing on each side, both objects and attributes, the Selected Obj & Attr box just below that will put the two names together for you.

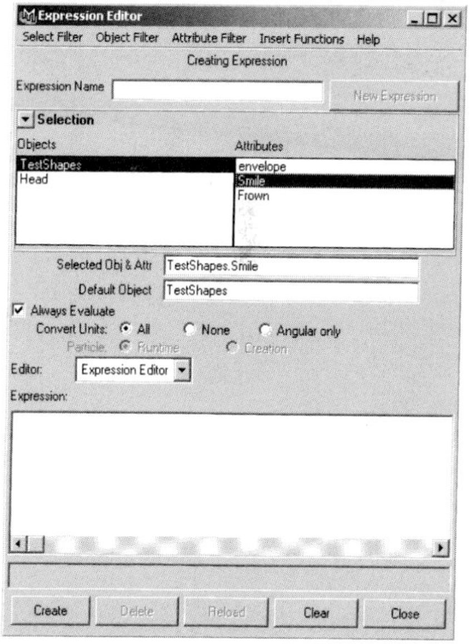

Personally, I just like to write the expressions in the Expression field—the bigger box at the bottom of the editor— myself. In that field, type in the following:

```
FaceShapes.Smile = Ctrl_Slider.translateY
```

Another way to get the object and attribute name into the expression window is to highlight the text in the Selected Obj & Attr box and middle-mouse drag it into the window to start your expression. Or you can use the standard copy and paste commands, Cmd/Ctrl+C and Cmd/Ctrl+V.

Click the Create button in the bottom-left corner, then close or minimize the Expression Editor.

As you move the slider up from 0, you'll notice that the smile shape appears. The problem, though, is that as you move down, the smile is

Figure 12.5

The newly created blendShape input

Figure 12.6

The Expression Editor

subtracted from the default shape (does the opposite) and looks mighty ugly, as you can see in Figure 12.7.

To see what is happening, keep the slider at –1 (where it's ugly), then select Head, and open FaceShapes in the inputs section (under the Channel Box). You'll notice that Smile is at –1, so it's doing exactly what we're telling it to: –1 from the slider to –1 in the shape value. But that's just not pretty, and we'll need to find a way to tell it not to do that. As would happen in a badly written movie: Who can save us now? Maybe the only other character we've been introduced to—`clamp`!

Go back into the Expression Editor and select FaceShapes and Smile so that the old expression appears in the expression window. Change the expression to add `clamp`, with a minimum of 0 and a maximum of 1, which says, "Do what you're doing, but only do it from 0 to 1." The value of `Ctrl_Slider.translateY` goes in the third slot for `clamp`. It should read as follows:

```
FaceShapes.Smile = clamp ( 0, 1, Ctrl_Slider.translateY )
```

> Your expression probably looked different when you opened it back up—where FaceShapes `.Smile` is in the example, you saw something like `FaceShapes.weight[0]` or `FaceShapes` `.weight[1]`. Maya automatically replaced the "user" name with the "Maya" name for the shape. It's not broken; that's normal. You can leave it like that, and change only what's on the right side of the equal sign. Everything will work exactly as described. If you want to retype the whole expression with `.Smile`, that will also work fine… although it will change to its Maya name again after you're done!

Hit the Edit button in the bottom-left corner where the Create button was originally, which will update your expression. Now when you move the slider it shows the smile in the top half as before, and when you pull the slider below zero, there is now no effect. We've simply limited what values we use from the slider using `clamp`.

This is how many of the sliders will work. But there's not much point to having half a slider. Right now, this slider behaves much like the standard blend shape interface. To make it better, let's put something on the other end of the same slider!

Adding More to the Slider

Now let's add Frown, a second shape, to the same slider, and reason our way through the expression, because it's just a little bit brainier. We want to put Frown on the bottom half of the same control, so we essentially need to do the opposite of what we're doing with the smile. As I discussed above, putting a negative in front of things makes them the opposite so let's try that first. Write an expression to read:

```
FaceShapes.Frown = - clamp (0, 1, Ctrl_Slider.translateY)
```

Be sure to notice that we are writing an expression for `FaceShapes.Frown`, not `FaceShapes.Smile`. If you now move the slider around, we can see that it doesn't work very well at all. At 1, we get an interesting shape that looks like Figure 12.8.

The reasoning behind this work of art is that we put the negative in the wrong spot. We're seeing 100% of Smile and –100% of Frown.

To break down the math: We told the computer to get the value of Ctrl_Slider's translateY if it's between 0 and 1 and THEN give us the opposite. What we've done is ask for values between –1 and 0! The problem is that we want the slider to be upside down, but we still need values between 0 and 1 so that the shape will work. What we need to do instead is move the negative to the front of the value coming into the expression, `Ctrl_Slider.translateY`—not in front of the whole thing—like so:

```
FaceShapes.Frown = clamp (0, 1, - Ctrl_Slider.translateY)
```

Now it says "Be the opposite value of `Ctrl_Slider.translateY` and only give me resultant values for it if they are between 0 and 1." In this instance, when you pull the slider down, it's at –1. The opposite of –1 is 1, 1 is between 0 and 1, and so you've got your frown! It's a little bit complicated, but not too bad. Just look at the effects and think about the expression and it should start to make some sense, even if this is all new to you.

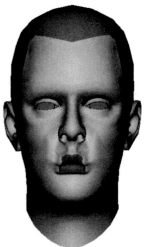

Figure 12.7

The negative effect of the smile shape is nas-ty.

The Benefits of These Expressions and Sliders

So now we have one slider controlling two shapes. I'll build on this and have some of the controls be a lot more complex, but you can see how expressions are useful—and not that hard if you don't make them too hard. The interesting thing is that what you've actually just done is solve two problems at once:

Fewer controls The more complicated the range of a face, usually the more controls you need. If you were to have 50 shapes you wanted to draw upon, that's 50 sliders you have to deal with—not fun. If you were to take all of those shapes and run them on sliders like the one we just did, you're already down to 25. 25 is still a lot of controls to be playing with, but it's better than 50!

Less un-animation This slider is a tool to reduce the amount of work in un-animating. Sometimes—and you'll know this if you've used blend shapes before—two or more shapes don't like each other. As you increase the effect of shape A, you need to reduce the influence of shape B. You find yourself in a situation where you have to un-animate as you animate. By putting two of these shapes on opposite ends of the same control, you've side-stepped the problem. By the nature of the control, one is reduced as one is increased. Certain shapes like smiles and frowns are perfect for this. It's not really conceivable that you'd want both to happen at the same time.

Figure 12.8

Another ugly mix face

I started in computer animation as an animator, and I have no explicitly mathy or programmy training beyond high school (nor "englishy" training, by the looks of it). I did not study computer science, and I am not a programmer. I hope that helps you see that expressions aren't so bad, and anyone can learn them if they want to. Using them in 3D packages is also fantastic because you have instant feedback—you can see what it is you've done. You may have no particular desire to learn expressions, but may have a desire to have cool setups and therefore *should* learn a little bit about them.

All that said, the main workflow through this chapter involves setting up your head with MEL scripts that do all the "hooking up" for you. The main reason for teaching as much about expressions as I have is to allow you the ability to customize.

The last part of this chapter describes four setups—four interfaces—that I use and that you can build. My favorite setup, as you'll see later, includes pieces of all of these controls I'm about to describe. First, I like to have the entire On Face setup available in a pinch, but it's a little too detail-oriented and slow for my tastes when it comes to trying to get work done fast. I prefer the sync slider in the Simple setup, even though, with some characters and their key shapes, there may be some hitching between the Smile/Wide and the Narrow (you'll read more about that in a minute; it has to do with using a Type C slider). I like the asymmetrical smile control from Setup2—the second of the whole interfaces you'll see—and I like the asymmetrical lips, but I might prefer a slightly different control scheme for them.

Prep Work for Your Own Setup

This is all optional material for you to cover if you'd like to know more about how the setups work. You can, if you wish, skip over to the "Setups" section. The information between here and there will, however, help you better read the names of sliders. If after working with your setup you have any questions as to what something is and how it should be working, this section may contain the answers.

NON-MAYA USERS

The rest of this is going to get pretty heavily into the Maya side of things, because if I tried to teach the various systems for expressions in all other software, we'd be here all year! If you want to create similar setups in other software, everything but the fine details is here; you might just have to cross-reference and compare the exact terms and syntax. You won't be able to exactly mimic the expressions on the eyelids with ease, but other than that, everything is pretty straightforward—that's why I do it the way I do. My main experience working this way is actually in Softimage3D; learning to do the same things in Maya was just a matter of learning the details of blend shapes and knowing where to find the Expression Editor!

Naming Conventions: Sliders

Since I'm going to be getting into expressions, I'm going to introduce you to the naming conventions in both the book and the files on the accompanying CD.

Ctrl and Ctrl_Prnt Every control slider we create and reference will have Ctrl in the name. If the control is for the upper eyelids, the name will look like Ctrl_UprLids. Since our sliders use their translation information for their control, each has a parent locator so that we can reposition it wherever we like. Each parent locator of a slider simply has Ctrl_Prnt in the name. For the upper eyelids it would look like Ctrl_Prnt_UprLids.

1, 2, and OF Since some setups require multiple controls for the same thing, and I wanted to differentiate between those, some additions in the name are necessary. Sliders with a 1 after the Ctrl in the name are native to the Simple setup, as described later in the chapter. Sliders from the Complex setup have a 2 after the word Ctrl, and sliders with OF after Ctrl are native to the On Face setup. Hence, Ctrl1_UprLids, Ctrl2_UprLids, and CtrlOF_UprLids. There is a fourth setup, My Favorite, but it comprises a combination of pieces of the others mentioned here, and therefore, sadly, doesn't get its own names. Boo.

L and R This may be obvious, but slider names that start with an L or R are shapes that apply to the left and right. Ctrl1_LUprLid refers to the left upper lid control.

Here are some examples of how I've named the sliders:

- The slider Ctrl2_RLwrLip is the control for the right lower lip from the Complex setup.
- The slider CtrlOF_LSneer is the control for the left sneer from the On Face setup.
- The slider Ctrl1_Sync is the control for lip sync in the Simple setup.

Naming Conventions: Blend Shape Nodes

When you create a blend shape relationship, as with *all* other things you create in Maya, a node is created. After you've done this, under the Inputs on the right side of the screen under the Channel box, you'll see the word blendShape as in Figure 12.5, and a number, depending on how many blend shape relationships exist in the scene, each new one being one higher. For ease, I renamed the relevant blend shape nodes in my scenes and used those names for all the examples and CD files. The blend shape node for the face/head object is named FaceShapes and the blend shape node for the teeth is named TeethShapes.

Position Limits

The expressions you write, or have created for you using the setup scripts, are going to clamp the values coming into the expressions; to limit that value again, and also to add some solidity to our control schemes, we're going to limit the actual motion of our control sliders using the Attribute Editor, as we've done a few times already. For all styles of sliders taught here, there will be no range in translate Z. To do this in the Attribute Editor, enter zeroes in both the min and max fields for Z—but, of course, you already knew that.

The Stop Staring Slider Bonanza

To see the sliders in a Maya scene, load SliderTypes.ma from the accompanying CD. Each slider in the scene is labeled accordingly; you can see the name by selecting the slider. It is easier to maneuver in the interfaces by hiding locators; in the panel View menu uncheck Show → Locators. This prevents visual clutter and also reduces the chance that you'll accidentally select the slider's parent, thereby moving it around but seeing no effect.

Type A These sliders are simple ones. Their limits are 0 and 0 for X and –1 to 1 for Y. They usually control 2 shapes. The zero, or default, position is in the center. If you pull the slider one way, you get one shape; pull it the other, you get another. There is no shape displayed in the default/center position.

Type B Slider type B functions exactly the same as type A except that the available range is from –1 to 1 in X and 0 to 0 in Y—effectively the same as type A, only on its side. Itself, like type A, this can hold two shapes, one on each end, but this slider is usually used in conjunction with others to control the asymmetry of another slider. Let's say you put a smile and frown on slider type A. If that smile was actually being created by simultaneously displaying two half smiles, left and right, you might use a type B slider as a multiplier, so that as you moved it left and right, the two half-smiles favored one side or the other.

Type C Clearly my favorite, I use them everywhere. A type C slider can function in many different ways. The effective range is from –1 to 1 in both X and Y—a box. Most commonly I'll use this to run four shapes, two asymmetrical pairs. If you pull the slider straight up, it's a 100/100 mix of the two shapes you'll see if you go to either top corner; moving to each corner, however, will show only that one shape. The same is true for along the bottom.

This slider can also be used as two perpendicular type A sliders with simultaneous control; I use this for the lips. Up and down controls the upper lip, while left and right controls the lower lip. By pulling the slider into the top-left corner, you create a strong F shape; in the bottom-left corner, you'll get a fully lips-rolled-in B, M, or P; in the top-right corner, you'll create a SH or tall shape, used in multiple visimes.

A third use is to have the left to right run two opposing shapes and the up and down run a range; I'll use this for a sync control. On one slider, you'll have the centerpiece for lip-syncing in a Wide/Narrow Open/Closed world. Up closes the Jaw up tighter than tight, left will be narrow, and right will be wide. Opening the jaw is as simple as lowering the slider.

Type D This is much like a type C slider, but with the lower half cut off; the effective range is from –1 to 1 in X and 0 to 1 in Y. This slider is useful primarily when we want to mix two shapes at 50/50 as well as be able to see each at 100%. With a type A or B slider we have two shapes on opposing sides, but they travel through the default shape to get to each other. In most cases that's good, but in some cases a 50/50 mix is an effect we want. Type D allows us to do this by treating the –1 to 1 range left to right like one big 0 to 1 slider going in one direction, simultaneously overlaid with another 0 to 1 going the other way, like two gradients going in opposite directions. The problem such a mix creates is that in the middle, you have a 50/50 mix of the two shapes involved, and that's probably not the default shape. You'd effectively always have this 50/50 shape visible—not necessarily something we would want. Type D overcomes this problem by using the vertical motion of the slider as a volume knob. At its default, 0, the slider has no effect; at 1, the top, it works as described.

Type E This one's easy. It's a box, just like C and D, but its effective range is only from 0 to 1 in both X and Y; it's like having only the top-right corner of type C. This is used when there are really only two shapes that need to interact with each other and it's faster to work with than having two sliders. The default position is in the bottom-left corner.

Type F Very similar to type A and B, this slider only moves in Y, and it only goes positive or negative. The slider sits at one end of the range or the other. This is actually the closest to Maya's blend shape controls. This is used in a few places on the On Face interface and as a volume control in other setups. It's like an uber-strength control, used to tone down the effect of all other controls when needed.

The Stop Staring Setups

Each of the facial setups comes with something like a checklist. The checklist includes the shapes you need to have built, represented as the exact names that should be used, which are also listed in Chapter 6 and Chapter 8, "Constructing Eyes and Brows," where you built them. You also have a path for the CD file with a head already rigged, so you can test-drive before you buy. There is also a scene file with an unrigged head, to show you the state your scene should be in right before using the script, and for those interested, there are also plain text files of the expressions that go into each setup. All of these files are named and their locations described for you as you go through the next few sections.

From the accompanying CD, you can install the tools you need. Go to the Chapter 12 folder and, under Setup, find `shelf_StopStaring.mel`. If you haven't already, copy this into your Maya user preference `\shelves` directory.

To use the Stop Staring Setup Scripts, simply create the blend shape relationships for both the head and the teeth, and rename those blend shape nodes FaceShapes and TeethShapes. Be sure that your skeleton is set up and named according to the guidelines, and then all you have to do is click the shelf button for the interface you want to create!

Figure 12.9

The Simple setup

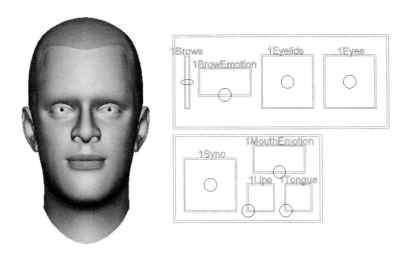

The Simple Setup

As you probably guessed from the title, this is the simplest of the setups I'll offer up; see Figure 12.9. If you want the least building of shapes, the least setup time overall, this is for you. The downfall in this setup is that it does not provide asymmetry, a mark of higher quality work, but, man, is it ever fast to work with.

To see a head with this setup, load `SetupY_Simple.ma` from the Chapter 12 folder of the CD. To see the same head in its state right before setup, load `SetupN_Simple.ma`. In the same area, you should be able to find `Simple.txt`, which has all of the expressions for this setup for your perusal; brief descriptions are included in comments.

Comments in MEL scripts are lines in the code that start with //. This just tells Maya that the line is not code to be processed. It allows scripters to leave information for others, or even to remind themselves about what the script does, and how it works.

Figure 12.10

The mouth shapes of the Simple Setup

| Jaw_Open | Smile | Narrow | Frown | Sneer | UprLip_Up | LwrLip_Dn |

Shapes to Build

To take advantage of the Simple setup, first build the following shapes:

Jaw_Open	UprLip_Up	BrowsOut_Up	Brows_Dn
Smile	LwrLip_Dn	Brows_Squeeze	
Narrow	Squint	Teeth_Open	
Frown	BrowsMid_Up	Tongue_Out	
Sneer	BrowsMid_Dn	Tongue_Up	

- Mouth shapes are demonstrated in Figure 12.10.

- Eyes and brows shapes are demonstrated in Figure 12.11.

- Teeth and tongue shapes are demonstrated in Figure 12.12.

For maximum visual communication of what a shape looks like, I used shaded only on the mouth shapes, and wireframe on shaded for the brow shapes, as many brow keys involve textures to create their whole effect, and are not as easy to see on the printed page.

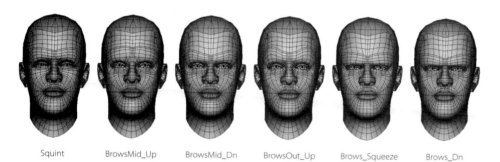

Squint   BrowsMid_Up   BrowsMid_Dn   BrowsOut_Up   Brows_Squeeze   Brows_Dn

Figure 12.11

The eyes and brows shapes of the Simple setup

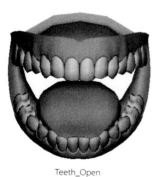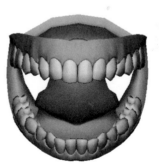

Teeth_Open   Tongue_Out   Tongue_Up

Figure 12.12

The teeth and tongue shapes of the Simple setup

_____ Figure 12.13

Typical Stop Staring slider schematics. Dragging your slider to position (a) moves the shape to the top-left corner, (b) the bottom-right corner, and (c) the top center.

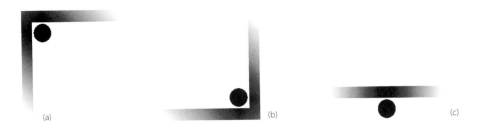

(a)   (b)   (c)

Setting Up the Sliders, Automatically

Once your head and teeth have their blend shape relationships set up, press the SS1 button on your StopStaring shelf. If you've built and named your shapes correctly, this one click creates and connects all the controls you need:

Ctrl_Sync	Ctrl_Brows
Ctrl_Lips	Ctrl_BrowEmotion
Ctrl_MouthEmotion	Ctrl_Eyelids
Ctrl_Tongue	Ctrl_Eyes

Over the next few pages, I'll show you what those sliders look like. As a reminder, there are version 1 and version 2 of most sliders. Sliders labeled type 1 are native to the Simple setup and work as described in that section, and sliders labeled type 2 are described in the Complex setup. This is useful mainly in communicating quickly how the different setups work; when you look at My Favorite, you'll see a mix of slider types 1 and 2.

To understand the graphics for the sliders, note that a dot appears corresponding to the corner or side of the slider that will create the face shape that you see. To create that shape, move the dot to that spot. Figure 12.13 shows a few examples of how this works.

Ctrl1_Sync (Figure 12.14) is a type C slider affecting the shapes Narrow, Smile, Jaw_Open, and Teeth_Open. With left and right motion, it controls the Wide and Narrow. Up and down controls the jaw's Open and Closed.

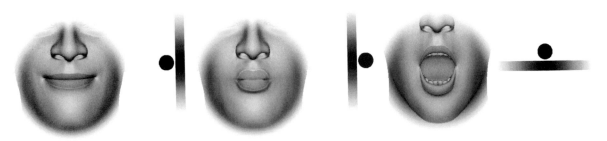

_____ Figure 12.14

The Ctrl1_Sync slider

Ctrl1_Lips (Figure 12.15) is a type E slider affecting UprLip_Up and LwrLip_Dn. The other half of sync, the Lips slider controls the lips' up and down motion. In this setup, since there are no lips-rolling-in shapes, only out, we just need the more restricted range of a type E slider. Moving the slider up opens the top lip, and moving it right opens the lower lip.

> **The Smile gets only 50% strength from this slider, not 100%; A 100% Smile would be too wide and too strong an opposite to the Narrow.**

Ctrl1_MouthEmotion (Figure 12.16) is a type D slider affecting Smile, Frown, and Sneer. The last of the mouth controls affecting the face, MouthEmotion creates a Smile when pulled to the right, a Frown when pulled left, and a Sneer when raised. It's a quick and easy way to create expressions.

Ctrl1_Tongue (Figure 12.17) is a type E slider affecting Tongue_Out and Tongue_Up. By moving the slider to the right, the tongue moves out of the mouth; by moving it up, the tongue arcs upward. It is normal for the tongue-out shape to intersect the teeth and maybe the face as you move it outward. The Tongue_Up shape should be used to overcome this.

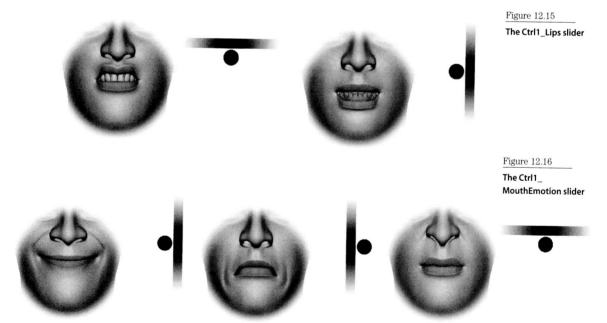

Figure 12.15

The Ctrl1_Lips slider

Figure 12.16

The Ctrl1_ MouthEmotion slider

Figure 12.17

**The Ctrl1_Tongue
slider**

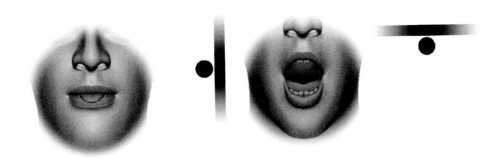

Ctrl1_Brows (Figure 12.18) is a type E slider affecting Brows_Dn and BrowsOut_Up. This slider moves much like what it controls: up and the brows go up, down and the brows go down! Easy!

Ctrl1_BrowEmotion (Figure 12.19) is a type D slider affecting BrowsMid_Up, BrowsMid_Dn, and Brows_Squeeze. Since the middle of the brows move up or down depending on the emotion, that's where this slider gets its name. Moving the slider up and to the left creates a sad look, and up and to the right creates more of a mad look.

Figure 12.18

The Ctrl1_Brows slider

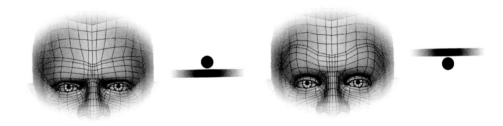

Figure 12.19

**The Ctrl1_
BrowEmotion slider**

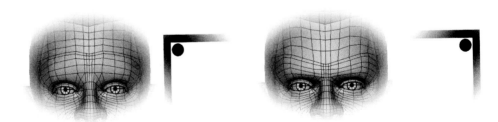

Ctrl1_Eyelids (Figure 12.20) is a type C slider affecting the following:

Shapes	Squint, LUprLid_Up, RUprLid_Up, LUprLid_Dn, RUprLid_Dn
Objects	LUprLid_Joint, RUprLid_Joint, LLwrLid_Joint, RLwrLid_Joint

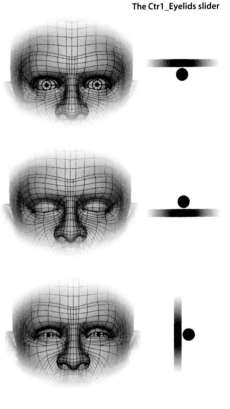

Figure 12.20

The Ctr1_Eyelids slider

This controls the eyelids' motions; up and down run the upper eyelids and left to right controls the lower lids/Squint. Of note is this slider's somewhat tricky functionality. If you dig into the expressions in the accompanying CD, you'll notice that this one is pretty intense. In regard to the upper lids, the slider goes up and down, and the eyelids will stay relative to the eyeball, a very funky thing that you'll have to see to understand. It functions this way until the slider reaches –0.25 in Y. From there on down, it's calculating the total distance from where it is now, to the lower eyelid. This is how it ensures that your eyelids will actually come to a close, even if your eyes are looking straight up.

Ctrl1_Eyes (Figure 12.21) is a type C slider affecting the objects LEye_Joint and REye_Joint. This controls the direction of the eyes; the positions in the slider correspond to where the eyes look, but it's not quite as simple as that. The information actually gets sent to a satellite hierarchy, the one we created for the eyes in the skeleton setup. This way, the eyes remain locked orientationally as the head moves around. It's significantly more solid for holding eyelines than an aim constraint, although you do have to animate it. If something like an aim constraint is more to your liking, you can set it up yourself, but you will need to free the Eye_Joints of incoming connections from the rig before doing so.

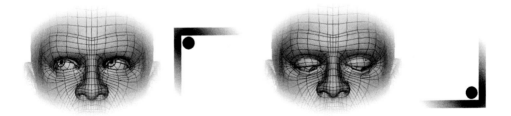

Figure 12.21

The Ctr1_Eyes slider

The Complex Setup

This setup (Figure 12.22) is for the animator who wants all the control, but not at an insane time cost. The basic work of sync and roughing in your animation does take longer with this than with the Simple setup, but it's also closer to finished after that point.

Figure 12.22

More controls can mean more work, but also … more control!

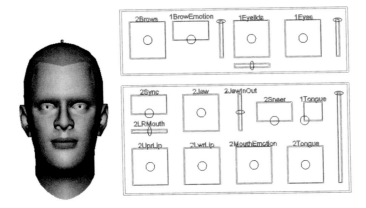

To see a head with this setup, load `SetupY_Complex.ma` from the Chapter 12 folder on the companion CD. To see the same head in its state right before setup, load `SetupN_Complex.ma`. In the same area, you should be able to find `Complex.txt`, which has all of the expressions in this setup ready for your perusal; brief descriptions are included in comments.

Shapes to Build

To take advantage of the Complex setup, first build the following shapes:

Jaw_Open	LSneer	LMouth	Brows_Squeeze
LJaw	RSneer	RMouth	Teeth_Open
RJaw	LUprLip_Up	LSquint	LTeeth
Jaw_Fwd	RUprLip_Up	RSquint	RTeeth
LSmile	LUprLip_Dn	BrowsMid_Up	Teeth_Fwd
RSmile	RUprLip_Dn	BrowsMid_Dn	Tongue_Out
LNarrow	LLwrLip_Dn	LBrowOut_Up	Tongue_Up
RNarrow	RLwrLip_Dn	RBrowOut_Up	Tongue_Tip_Up
LFrown	LLwrLip_Up	LBrow_Dn	LTongue
RFrown	RLwrLip_Up	RBrow_Dn	RTongue

- Mouth shapes are demonstrated in Figure 12.23.

- Eyes and brows shapes are demonstrated in Figure 12.24.

- Teeth and tongue shapes are demonstrated in Figure 12.25.

Please note that I'm only including images for the "right" shapes to conserve space. Everywhere you see an R shape, build the L also—for example, with LJaw build RJaw; with LBrowOut_Up build RBrowOut_Up.

Figure 12.23

The mouth shapes of the Complex setup

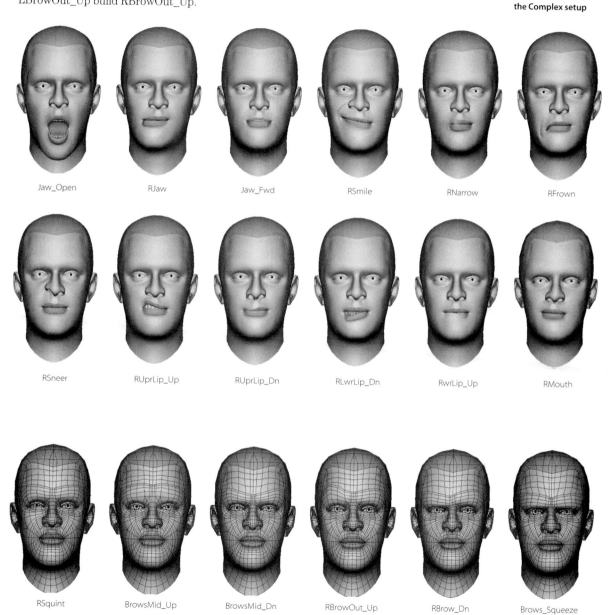

Jaw_Open	RJaw	Jaw_Fwd	RSmile	RNarrow	RFrown

RSneer	RUprLip_Up	RUprLip_Dn	RLwrLip_Dn	RwrLip_Up	RMouth

RSquint	BrowsMid_Up	BrowsMid_Dn	RBrowOut_Up	RBrow_Dn	Brows_Squeeze

Figure 12.24

The eyes and brows shapes of the Complex setup

Setting Up the Sliders, Automatically

Once your head and teeth have their blend shape relationships set up, press the SS2 button on your StopStaring shelf. As I said in the Simple setup, if you've built and named your shapes correctly, this one click creates and connects all the controls you need. What follows are descriptions of those sliders.

> Several of the sliders in the Complex and My Favorite setups are reused from earlier setups and will not be described again except where there are differences—for instance, if they now control two asymmetrical shapes in place of what was one symmetrical shape. The following sliders are explained in full in the Simple setup: Ctrl1_Tongue, Ctrl1_BrowEmotion, Ctrl1_Eyelids, and Ctrl1_Eyes.

Ctrl2_Sync (Figure 12.26) is a type D slider affecting the shapes LNarrow, RNarrow, LSmile, and RSmile. This behaves more like the Ctrl1_Brows_Emotion than the previous sync slider. It has no effect on the jaw, and allows a clean 50/50 mix of the opposing shapes. There is no sharp change in the motion between Wide and Narrow; their effects are like opposing gradients—gradually one way blending into gradually the other—instead of one ramp and then suddenly another, like the Ctrl1_Sync slider. The vertical movement is like a volume control for the shapes, all the way up for full strength, all the way down for none.

Figure 12.25

The teeth and tongue shapes of the Complex setup

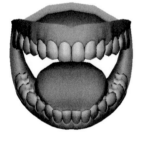
Teeth_Open

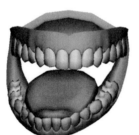
LTeeth

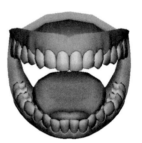
Teeth_Fwd

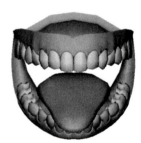
Tongue_Out

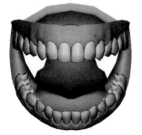
Tongue_Up

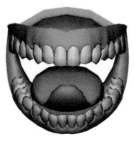
Tongue_Tip_Up

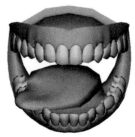
LTongue

Figure 12.26

The Ctrl2_Sync slider

Ctrl2_LRMouth (Figure 12.27) is a type B slider affecting LMouth and RMouth.

Ctrl2_Jaw (Figure 12.28) is a type C slider affecting the shapes Jaw_Open, LJaw, RJaw, Teeth_Open, LTeeth, and RTeeth. This Jaw control is very WYSIWYG. Pull the control down, the jaw opens; pull it up, it closes; pull it left, the jaw goes (screen) left, and vice versa for moving it right.

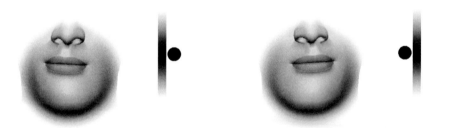

Figure 12.27

The Ctrl2_LRMouth slider

Ctrl2_JawInOut (Figure 12.29) is a type C slider affecting Jaw_Fwd and Teeth_Fwd. This really serves only one purpose, and that is to control the jaw movement forward and back. This slider is allowed to use values between –1 and 1 because the opposite of the Jaw_Fwd works well as a Jaw Back!

Figure 12.28

The Ctrl2_Jaw slider

Ctrl2_UprLip (Figure 12.30) is a type E slider affecting LUprLip_Up, RUprLip_Up, LUprLip_Dn, and RUprLip_Dn. The lips controls in the Complex setup are broken into the upper and lower lips, giving each full asymmetrical control independently. The cost is the time involved to create shapes using multiple sliders. Pull the slider up and you get the upper lip up; move it left and you'll have just that side of the lip raised; right, you'll have the other. Pull the slider down and you'll have the upper-lip-rolled-down/in, as for a B or M. The left to right functionality is the same as for moving the control up—you get each half shape.

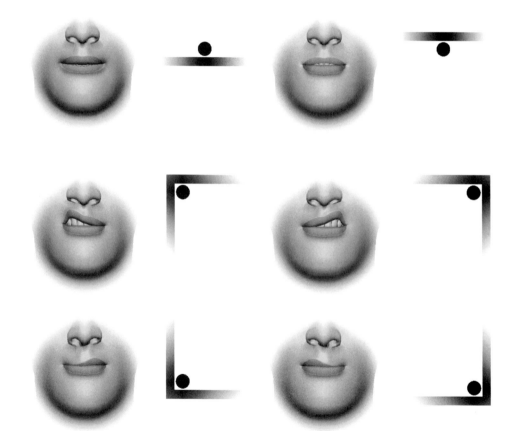

Figure 12.29

The Ctrl2_JawInOut slider

Figure 12.30

The Ctrl2_UprLip slider

Ctrl2_LwrLip (Figure 12.31) is a type E slider affecting LLwrLip_Dn, RLwrLip_Dn, LLwrLip_Up, and RLwrLip_Up. For the lower lips in the Complex setup, you've got a mirror of the functionality you had for Ctrl2_UprLip.

Ctrl2_MouthEmotion (Figure 12.32) is a type C slider affecting LSmile, RSmile, LFrown, and RFrown. The Mouth Emotion Slider in the Complex setup is pretty fun to use. Pull the slider straight up and you've got a symmetrical smile; move the slider straight down and you'll get a frown. Move the slider left or right in combination with up or down, and the side you favor with the slider becomes more dominant as the effect is subtracted from the other side. At first it might seem a little backward for a motion left to subtract a shape on the right instead of strengthening one on the left. The reason is that if you or I were to set it up that way, the symmetrical smile and frown would not be at 100% strength of the potential, since that would only be seen at each side individually. In this setup, you have the most shape available to you at all times.

Figure 12.31

The Ctrl2_LwrLip slider

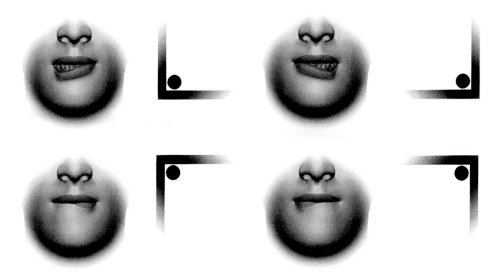

Figure 12.32

**The Ctrl2_
MouthEmotion slider**

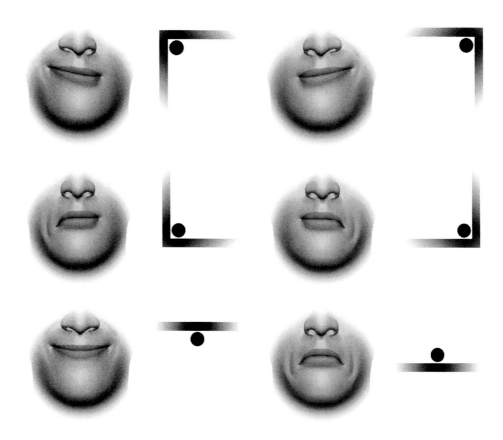

Figure 12.32

**The Ctrl2_
MouthEmotion slider**

Ctrl2_MouthEmotion (Figure 12.33) is a type D slider affecting LSneer and RSneer. Unlike most other type D sliders, you don't have a 50/50 mix in the top center, but instead a 100/100 mix like the top of a type C slider. Top left pulls the nostril up on screen left, and top right pulls the nostril up on screen right. The middle top is both.

Figure 12.33

The Ctrl2_Sneer slider

Figure 12.34

The Ctrl2_Tongue slider

Ctrl2_Tongue (Figure 12.34) is a type C slider affecting LTongue, RTongue, and Tongue_Tip_Up. Working in concert with Ctrl1_Tongue, this just adds more mobility to the tongue. The directions on the slider relate to the directions the tongue points.

Ctrl2_MouthVolume is a type F slider affecting all mouth shapes. This unlabelled slider at the far right of the mouth controls is the mouth volume control. This slider is a multiplier for all the influences from the sliders. At rest it is at the top, 100%. If you were to pull it down to 50%, all the mouth shapes would have a 50% effect. This is a quick and easy way to tone down any animation that may need to be pulled back. It is animatable, so if you are happy with most of your animation, except want a slight bit more subtlety, pull the slider down and it's done for just that area; pull it back up to resume full strength. For my own personal style, I'm usually best off to pull this down to the 60%–70% mark—I tend to over-animate!

Ctrl2_Brows (Figure 12.35) is a type C slider affecting shapes LBrow_Down, RBrow_Down, LBrowOut_Up, and RBRowOut_Up. This slider is fun. Down moves the brows down, but like the Ctrl2_MouthEmotion control, left and down makes only the left brow drop. The same asymmetry is available for up, down, left, and right.

Figure 12.35

The Ctrl2_Brows slider

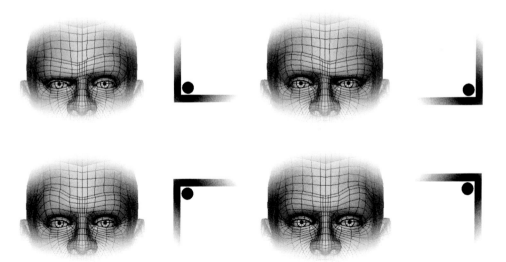

Figure 12.36

**The Ctrl2_Brows_
Squeeze slider**

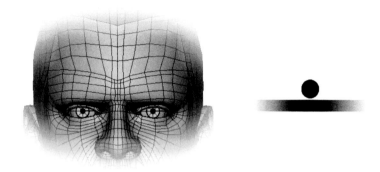

Ctrl2_Brows_Squeeze (Figure 12.36) is a type F slider affecting only Brows_Squeeze. This is the unlabelled slider between 1BrowEmotion and 1Eyelids. This slider isn't really necessary, since, as I explained in Chapter 9, "Eye and Brow Keys," brows down and brows squeeze are practically the same thing. This is here because, although I base my systems on reality, embellishment is great. The only shape affected, Brows_Squeeze, is added by pulling the slider down.

Ctrl2_Eyelids is a type B slider affecting the following:

Shapes	Squint, LUprLid_Up, RUprLid_Up, LUprLid_Dn, RUprLid_Dn
Objects	LUprLid_Joint, RUprLid_Joint, LLwrLid_Joint, RLwrLid_Joint

Figure 12.37

**A setup with the
controls directly
on the face**

This slider is merely an asymmetry control used in conjunction with the Ctrl1_Eyelids slider. Move the slider left and Ctrl1_Eyelids only affects the left side; move it right and only the right is affected; in the middle, both are affected equally.

Ctrl2_BrowVolume, the unlabelled type F slider on the far right of the eyes and brows interface elements, is a multiplier for the brows, just as Ctrl2_MouthVolume is to the mouth.

The On Face Setup

This interface is pretty light on explanation, and by looking at Figure 12.37, you can see why.

This interface is an almost direct relationship to each blend shape. It's slow because you have to deal with more manipulation to do even the most basic things. I don't recommend it for sync, but for acting, it's "crazy fun." There's a fantastic hands-on feel—you almost get the sensation of treating the face like clay, with every stroke of your thumb having just the effect you wanted. As for new and exciting shapes, this has none. This setup, and the one to follow, "My Favorite," both share the exact same key set as that of the Complex setup. I've created the sliders as ovular in shape; they travel along their length. When you see a slider that is taller than it is wide, you know it moves up and down. When you see one wider than it is tall, it moves left to right. Circular sliders move in multiple directions.

To see a head with this setup, load `SetupY_OnFace.ma` from the Chapter 12 folder on the companion CD. To see the same head in its state right before setup, load `SetupN_OnFace.ma`. In the same area, you should be able to find `OnFace.txt`, which has all of the expressions for this setup for your perusal; brief descriptions are included in comments.

Shapes to Build

As I said, the shapes to build are the same as those for the Complex setup.

Setting Up the Sliders, Automatically

Once your head and teeth have their blend shape relationships set up, press the SSOF button on your StopStaring shelf. Once again, if you've built and named your shapes correctly, this one click creates and connects all the controls you need.

In lieu of having much to describe for this setup, as it's so direct, Figure 12.38 shows some expressions created using it. I've left the controls visible.

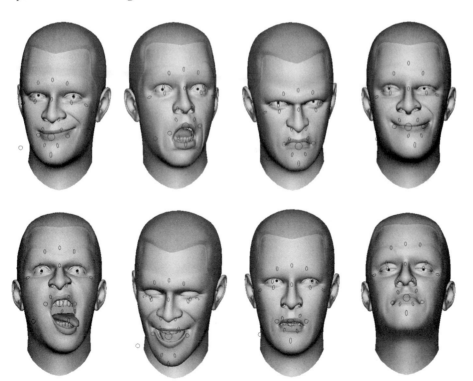

Figure 12.38

Some sample On Face positions

Of Special Note: Positioning These Sliders on Your Face

The sliders as created automatically by the SSOF shelf button will line up with my face, the one I use for examples. To adjust the sliders for your face, as you may need to, select a slider and then hit the Up arrow key. This will step you up the hierarchy one level to the slider's parent. You can move and rotate the parent into position for your own character's face.

My Favorite Setup

I can't very well call it that without good reason, now, can I? It's not going to be everyone's favorite, but it's mine and here's why: This setup (Figure 12.39) incorporates the simplicity of the Simple setup with the complexity of the Complex setup and the intuitive nature of the On Face setup.

As far as the sliders go, in almost all respects the interface looks the same as the Simple setup. The additions and changes are the swapping of Ctrl1_Brows for Ctrl2_Brows and the addition of the Ctrl2_LRMouth slider. Other than that, the major difference is the complete incorporation of the On Face interface. The way this one is meant to work is that you do 80% of your work on the Simple interface and then finish it off with the detail-centric On Face interface. Both sets of sliders work together seamlessly.

To see a head with this setup, load `SetupY_MyFavorite.ma` from the Chapter 12 folder on the companion CD. To see the same head in its state right before setup, load `SetupN_MyFavorite.ma`. In the same area, you should be able to find `MyFavorite.txt`, which has all of the expressions for this setup for your perusal; brief descriptions are included in comments.

Figure 12.39

Basically, the Simple setup moved onto the face

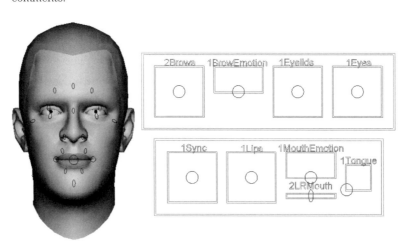

Shapes to Build

As I said, the shapes to build are exactly the same as those for the Complex setup.

Setting Up the Sliders, Automatically

Once your head and teeth have their blend shape relationships set up, press the SSMyF button on your StopStaring shelf to automatically create all the sliders you need.

Controlling the Stop Staring Interfaces

I will be creating neat doo-dads and tools for the shelf until the day this book is printed, riding the paper on the printing press with my laptop like a rodeo star. For that reason, I can, as I write this chapter, only describe one of the interface elements available to you on the Stop-Staring shelf, besides the setup scripts. I recommend highly that you explore all the buttons on the shelf.

Figure 12.40

The Stop Staring interface window

   When you press the SSUI button, it spawns a window with some buttons (Figure 12.40), all of which will pose the sliders of the interface for you.

Reset Sliders Resets all the sliders *not* on the face for your head.

Reset Face Resets all the on-face sliders.

Key All Sets a key on all the sliders in your setup so that the pose you have will stick.

Visime buttons Several visimes and, yes, phoneme buttons are also available for you to use as key poses. They do nothing more than move the sliders into positions that will create the described shape. Be aware that pushing a button may not always yield the exact same effect as the last time you pushed the button. In keeping with my supposition that there are key ingredients to each visime, and that they are not absolute, the pose buttons only affect the important aspects. If your character is smiling and you hit the F/V button, it will look different than if your character's mouth is narrow and you hit the F/V button. The reason is that since F/V has no particular width as a rule, it will not affect the width of the existing shape as you add to it.

CHAPTER 13

A Shot in Production

Here in the final chapter, I go through five animations using the techniques I've described. Whenever those techniques work particularly well, need to be ignored, or are amplified, I point it out and discuss the how and the why. This chapter is all about the doing, the art, the acting, and the performing. I am by no means God's gift to animation, but I do pretty well at making a talking head look like a living one, not just a set of gums flapping. That *life* factor is going to be most of my focus here; I'm concerned mostly with the character's *head space*, emotional outlook.

Box Head should be suitable for any and all of these scenes if you want a simpler character to get some performance practice with. The last two scenes are Pete and Sally Ann (toon) bits. They are here to show examples of another style and how the same basic techniques carry through. I have worked with all kinds of humans and animals in all kinds of ranges and styles, and I can comfortably tell you that when it comes to facial performance, it's all flavors of the same thing; it's just a matter of what the director wants.

- Scene 1: Bartender

- Scene 2: Lack of Dialogue

- Scene 3: Dunce Cap

- Scene 4: Salty Old Sea Captain

- Scene 5: Pink or Blue?

Scene 1: Bartender

So this floating head walks into a bar, and the bartender says, 'Hey, buddy! ...'
You know what? I don't have anything. This is... I really don't. If I had legs, I
would leave. (VOICE PERFORMANCE BY: JASON OSIPA)

You can load `Bartender.mov` from the Chapter 13 folder on the companion CD to see my take on the animation, and `Bartender.wav` for the audio file alone. Figure 13.1 shows a selection of frames from this piece.

With all of the scenes I talk about here, I can't stress enough that you really need to watch the animations on the CD. It's one thing to read about motion, and see snapshots of it; but we're dealing with the topic of living sounds and pictures, and for this chapter to have the most value, you've got to watch the movies.

> In my Maya scenes for these examples, I added specialty controls using the Make Control MEL script, which is in the Stop Staring shelf. I set up three controls for the head. This isn't something that's too useful in a regular scene with a body, etc, but for these heads-only shots it was good for animating with speed. Try setting a head up on your own, using the head control on Box Head as an example!

Sync Special Cases

For the vast majority of this sync, the sync is very much just following the style and techniques I've laid out already. I found the visimes, worked with the syllables, and had a talking character when I was done. There were, however, a few places where it needed some extra love. The R in the word "bar" really looked weird. Going back to the ideas in Chapter 4 ("Visimes and Lip Sync Technique") about R, I decided to add some height, although left the

Figure 13.1

A few frames from "Bartender"

Figure 13.2

Three frames of "bar"

width mostly narrow. This led me to a slightly weird shape, and I took a stab at widening the mouth a little bit, out to about default width. That worked for me; Figure 13.2 shows a short sequence of images for the word "bar."

The next spot that was tricky was the quick little "This is… I." Those sounds and shapes are all IHs and EEs, which, like any similar repeated sounds, are never too easy to sync well. This is a case where I polarized what each of the shapes is. That way, all the shapes are Wide and Tall, but they're not all at the same width and height. I emphasized the height quite strongly during IH (taller) from "this," then let the height drop and made the mouth wide for "is." At the start of the "I" (AH-EE), I let the mouth narrow much more than I would in a different context, basically using opposites to strengthen the surrounding shapes. This let me go at the third Wide/Tall shape with strength in both height *and* width. Each of the three shapes ended up different even though they would have all been the same—or much more similar—had I left it with just basic analysis of sound to Visime relationships.

I held the mouth closed in the pause after "I really don't." Pauses force you to make a decision: Do I want to lead into the following sound early, or do I want to hold the shape of the preceding sound? You can't really float slowly from one shape to the next—drifts look strange; you need to choose break points, places where the expression changes more quickly. I held his mouth closed until the breath before the last line. That also provided a strong look for the breath instead of the mouth already being open, and then just opening more (Figure 13.3).

The last place there was something interesting with sync was on the very, very last sound, the V from *leave*. This sound in the vocal performance trails off here so bad that you almost can't hear the word. I've put this in to

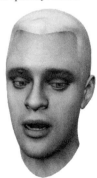

Figure 13.3

The breath will benefit from a lead-in shape that is more closed.

Figure 13.4

I animated a sound that wasn't there to clarify that it *should* have been, helping the audience to more clearly hear the line.

demonstrate a point: in real production, things like this actually happen. Actors don't give you exactly what the director or writers imagined in their heads; they emphasize different words, pause unexpectedly, enunciate inconsistently. And no matter how professional or expensive the production, there will always be some point where there's no time left to reshoot or rerecord! (Sometimes actors' interpretations work in your favor; for example, in the "Pink or Blue?" scene later in this chapter, you'll see how an unplanned pause opens up a fantastic animation possibility.)

So here, the end of the spoken line trails off. Instead of fighting that fact, I filled in the missing sound with animation. The V, although almost inaudible, is brought back to the forefront because I made it look as if it were a loud F; see Figure 13.4.

Doing this can help the audience "hear" the sound—help their brains recognize the word—even though they can't literally hear it. You can't and shouldn't do this with all sounds—you want to sync what's really there, not what's *supposed* to be there—but if it's at the end of a phrase, and it helps the line be understood, go for it.

Head Tilts

I've got more to talk about in terms of timing than anything else in this subtopic. My own voice, my cadence, is pretty weird. I've never synced to someone who says things quite like me. (Frankly, I'm not totally convinced I'm a very good voice actor; my mom says I am, but still…) With tilting the head through tonal shifts, my performance has an interesting problem. I do a lot of shifting in volume, but not as much in tone. If you strictly follow my advice, you get a string of places in a row that feel like they *should* be where you shift the tilt of the head up and down, but you're not quite sure. What I did (which is just one approach) was to use the first of those "maybe" spots to start a move and then to finish it on the last of them. For example, in the sound "and the bartender says," I say "bar" with a big shift in volume, but it's the same tone as the words before. I then give a little tonal hop upward during "TENder." This gives me two places in rapid succession that feel like either one could be the place to raise the head. I started to tilt up at the start of "bar" and stopped that move on "ten."

For "Hey buddy," I again just spoke louder, I didn't really change tone so much; so even though it felt like it might be a place to tilt the head, I only did it very, very slightly. Next, I moved the head down quickly and slightly as the character locks up, loses his train of thought. By moving him down to get into that pause, and then holding the motion very tightly, basically freezing him, it emphasizes the feeling of being "stopped in his tracks." Figure 13.5 shows that poor little deer in headlights. The rest of the scene really just followed techniques I've talked about before!

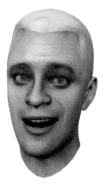

Figure 13.5

The man is all out of ideas.

Eyes

Seeing as this had only one major focus or eye-line—the audience—this wasn't too hard a step. I started the eyes down and to (screen) left just because I wanted him to catch your attention during the start of the scene. If he was already looking at you, that might not have happened. This is a case of that whole "If you don't know where it came from, you don't know where it is" thing, landmarking. Figure 13.6 shows the two eyelines.

Figure 13.6

The eyeline starts out low so it can move to land on the audience.

I darted his eyes around quickly on "and the bartender says" because I chose to create a subtext right off the bat, that this guy doesn't know where he's going with this. I started seeing more of the performance I wanted to create when I did this: he starts just talking, then he gets excited as he thinks he knows what he's going to say (the darting); he's going to focus that back on the audience; and then, when that focus breaks, he's going to keep his eyes low, or away from the audience. After his head drops, I then have his eyes point back at the audience at the start of his next line "You know what." From here until the end of the scene, I don't let him hold a stare with the audience too long.

In the next scene, where there's dialogue, I talk about how characters hand the conversation back and forth. Because I don't let this guy hold the audience in a look, he internalizes what's going on; he's not communicating as clearly or forcefully.

Lids

By the time I got to the lids, I really had a strong idea of the ups and downs in emotion I wanted to portray, so I just punctuated those. I kept his lids pretty level for the first part, and then widened them for "and the bartender says" as he gets excited—because, remember, lids, not brows, show that. After that, I just returned the lids to a comfortable level and left them there. My voice performance and the scene didn't provide much more opportunity than that for lots of lids action.

Figure 13.7

Two levels of squint

With the squint, I crept it up to create a more eyes-type smile in the first half (Figure 13.7), so when I remove that in the second half there's an extra little bit of a difference you *feel*, if not consciously register, as a difference.

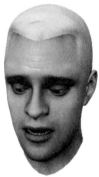

Figure 13.8

The raised and then
dropped brows, the
motion where I hid the
sad transition, so it
looked like a release
instead of a flex

Brows

This guy is trying to tell a joke, the operative word being *trying*. I'll talk more about this in the following scene, but we can often use our brows to signify a loose end, something left requiring conclusion. When the brows raise here, he's thinking and talking, but he's not sure where he's going. For a brief moment, when he feels he actually has control of the situation—the shift toward excitement during "and the bartender says"—he drops his brows. Even though he's excited, he's gained some control. To me, the control portion is the more important one; excitement is more of a reaction than an intention, and I lean toward the intentions for my acting choices. So, during the excitement, I dropped the brows to a more comfortable level, which gives the emotion in the scene some variety, too.

Later, when the character exhales (usually a smart place to relax the whole face), I actually moved the brows toward a slightly sadder shape (Figure 13.8). I did this at the same time I dropped the brows so it looked like a relaxation, but one that occurred mostly on the outsides of the brows.

Mouth Emotion

It would have been easy to start the scene smiling and keep it there until the shift in the middle, but I think that would have been boring, too homogenous. Again, just as with the eyes, unless you know where you came from, you don't know where you are. By letting the smile increase in little increments toward the portion of the scene where he feels like he's in control, you as a viewer might be coaxed into smiling yourself. Figure 13.9 shows the places I notched it up.

Just as a laugh can be contagious, so can a smile. By having it grow instead of just immediately exist, you can better lead your audience along with you through the emotions in a scene. (I often get a kick out of watching people watching my animations, contorting their faces along with what the on-screen character is doing!) Making the smile a sideways one, a real smirk, makes this a more playful thought, as opposed to, say, a happy one. When this guy hits that pause where he gets stuck, I kept the smile going. My first instinct was to pop the smile down a bit—create less of a smile in that dead space—but after doing that, and watching it that way, I wasn't sold; and I decided instead to just freeze him in his tracks.

For the rest of the scene I left the mouth just a hair toward frown, but not so much that he looked pouty. The only place I wanted to break him out of that frown was somewhere in the last line, but I hadn't decided exactly where. He's given up, he's finished. When people are in that state they smile a nervous smile. Part of what can make a smile nervous is that it's a smaller smile, and it's crooked, and it also doesn't hang around for long. I decided to smile on the word *legs*, mostly because of the fact it hangs in the air. I like to express in the dead (quiet) spots, so I just got him into a smile for that moment, and then rolled right back out of it as soon as he continued talking.

Figure 13.39

A few frames where you can see the increases in the smile

Other Tilts and Finesse

As will be the pattern in this chapter, I actually worked my overall finesse into the initial discussion, which is indicated whenever I say I tried X, then changed it to Y. The last step I want to talk about is the left-to-right twists and tilts of the head. When I say twist, I mean like shaking your head no, and when I say tilts in this last section and the final sections in the scenes to follow, I mean the left-to-right tilts like a metronome.

The first place I made a significant tilt here was in the section where he says "Hey buddy." There is another scene later on where a character talks as if she was another character ("Scene 5: Pink or Blue?"), sort of like an impression but not really; she's speaking outside of herself. In the Bartender scene, to help draw the line and differentiate that shift, I tilted his head over. Besides the voice, which obviously makes that acting difference identifiable, the tilt in the head just turns this guy askew, there's something different—for this portion of line, he *is* different. For the rest of the scene, as far as left-to-right tilts, he stays pretty central.

With the shaking of the head, here's a situation where I go with a tried and true method of my own personal style. If a character is saying something negative, they shake their head. As this guy says "I don't have anything," he gives that noggin a little shake. This isn't a universal rule or anything, just something I do that seems to work pretty well most of the time.

Scene 2: Lack of Dialogue

One: "So, you hang out here often?"

Two: "Yeah, yeah, I'm not really privy to movement."

One: "Oh, yeah, I, I can see."

Two: "Yeah, it's… you know, that's the way it is sometimes."

One: "Yeah."

Two: <cough>

One: "So, uh, what brings you to the neighborhood?"

Two: "Oo, lack of dialogue."

One: "Oh, oh, so… uh, it's going to be you and me?"

Two: "Yeah."

One: "I guess me and me?"

Two: "Yeah."

One: <laughs> "That's kind of funny."

Two: "No it's not."

(Voice performance by Jason Osipa)

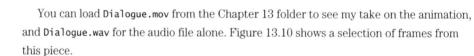

You can load `Dialogue.mov` from the Chapter 13 folder to see my take on the animation, and `Dialogue.wav` for the audio file alone. Figure 13.10 shows a selection of frames from this piece.

Figure 13.10

A few frames from "Lack of Dialogue"

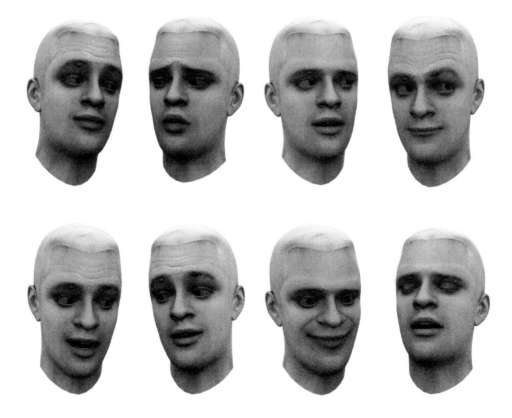

Another fine vocal performance just begging for a little animation. This one's a two-character shot, so if you're following along, I recommend doing each character separately and approximating eyelines at first. When you think you're close to done, bring the two together and tidy it all up; get your eyelines worked out, and any last final touches that only become apparent as the two characters exist together. With this scene more than any other here, I suggest you animate a version yourself first, and then come back and look at what I did, just to see where ideas ran parallel and where they were completely different.

Sync Special Cases

We'll start with Character One, the head on screen left. His first line is "Yeah, yeah, I'm not really privy…" The very first sound a character makes in a scene can often be the hardest to get right in the sync, and here's why: Once a character is talking, it's easier to continue a flow and maintain that illusion, but initiating the sense that the sound is coming out of the character's mouth can sometimes be hard. My own vocal performance makes this extra difficult, because I ease into the first sound, with some hesitation. Instead of saying "yeah," I actually say "eeeyeah," making it hard to identify a solid start point.

What I do in this type of situation is go in and key the shape where the sound *is* definite—in this case, near the EE (eey*EE*ah). This starts way too late for the sounds preceding that. What I actually did to overcome that was create another (subtle) EE shape for the very start of the word. To make that have a good effect, I then had to make sure the mouth was keyed a little bit narrower immediately preceding that first EE, so that when it widened, you would notice; keep in mind that this is all very subtle. Working out-of-order like this is perfectly normal. You may not know how you want to *lead into* a word until after you've animated it!

"That's the way it is sometimes…"

This phrase only has major width variation on the W in "way," so it gets very repetitive visually, since it consists mostly of just the jaw flapping with a wide shape. To beat this, I used the technique of opposites and made some mouth shapes narrower between the strongest wide sounds.

The Cough

I like coughs, but I hate coughs. They're great for character, but I find them hard to animate. This one, I think could still use work; Figure 13.11 shows a few frames of it.

Figure 13.11

Three frames of a cough

The problem with a cough is, there's no shape for which you can say, "That's it exactly!" so whatever one you pick usually looks weird. I find that often the best way to sell a cough is to cover the mouth with the character's hand (that is, if they have hands). As I said, I'm still not sold on this. I just went from a wide(r) shape to a narrower shape, which was decided merely by trial-and-error.

"Neighborhood"

What an ugly, ugly word and ugly, ugly delivery. It happens; not all sync is simple. "Neighborhood" has a wide-narrow-narrow sequence, making it seemingly easy, but the B gets in the middle and messes it all up by adding a need for constrasty movement in the middle of something otherwise smooth. To analyze it by visime, you'd end up with something like EH-B-OH-OO, but the B makes the word stylistically more contrasty, and so the OH-OO at the end, which to me feels like it should really be a smooth motion, needs to be made choppier to match the look of the B. If we just rolled through the OH-OO, it probably wouldn't look right. What's worse is that trying to widen the mouth on the H, to create more contrast, doesn't work either.

With this I used stepping, very carefully, and held the OH for as long as I could, and then jumped quickly into the OO. I originally had a little widening and opening to emphasize the D, but with the speed of all the speech going on, it just looked like a mistake. So instead, at the end of the word I just eased out, without being *too* floaty in my animation.

Character Two

Nothing too fancy came up with this guy, up until the end of "lack of dialogue."

I really hit the mouth clicking noise at the end of the word "dialogue"—yes, the G sound, the no-visime example sound G. The reason is that even though G isn't a visime, if I didn't do that, the word would just look like "dialoo" or "dialaw." Widening the mouth at the end would make it look like "dialoee;" so I just snapped the mouth open after the G sound, and that worked.

Other than that, Character Two's sync was simple and by the book! (By *this* book, anyway.)

Head Tilts

In regards to the forward and back movements, what can I say? I animated up and down to the tones in the recording, and then amplified and minimized the effect based on what looked good to me. There's not a whole lot of *new* teaching here, just practice on concepts from Chapter 7, "Building Emotion: The Basics of the Eyes." The main thing to notice is the nods and reverse nods. Character Two (screen right) starts off a lot of his nods upward instead of downward, animation that comes from analyzing the tones in the sound, but it also took some how-to-nod decision making.

The upward motion of a nod is the same once a character is *into* a group of nods—you go up, you go down—but the initiating motion of a nod, be it up or down, can paint what the underlying intentions and feelings are. An upward start to nodding generally looks more forced, like you're trying to show that you are in agreement instead of more naturally being in agreement, which would usually lead in with a downward motion. It's subtle, but watch the animation a few times and you should see the difference in how the character's nods *feel*. Character Two's one-word "yeah" statements at the end show this pretty clearly. This isn't by any stretch of the animation a rule, it's just something I've observed and used before. As a technique to get subtly different emotions, choosing the direction a nod starts behaves very predictably and reliably.

Eyes

This was the fun part for me. These two characters are obviously having a forced "polite" conversation. From a scene analysis perspective you can take that down to a thought level, and say these characters aren't too terribly comfortable. Not very comfortable? Move the eyes a lot, in fact; find any possible opportunity to move the eyes around. Figure 13.12 has a sampling of some of the many awkward moments.

Remember though, when animating eyes darting around, within that movement there are stops, break points, places the characters settle on, even if only for a few frames. For Character One, I had him settle on two points down and to the (screen) right. Whenever Character One stammers, or does any searching for words, I have him break eye contact, and represent that search physically with his eyes. It really emphasizes the acting in the sound by reflecting that search, or uncertainty. I also broke One's stare to Character Two whenever Two directly addresses him, also making One the shyer of the two.

Figure 13.12

The uncomfortable duo

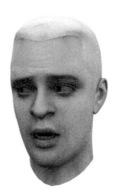

Figure 13.13

A hardened gaze gives strength to Character Two.

Figure 13.14

I'm waiting…

Character Two

This guy was really, really fun. I honestly didn't have too much a plan for this scene beyond the attitudes I wanted to portray; I wanted Character One to be lacking confidence and Character Two to be a little bit cocky, a little bit of a smart-ass. I basically wanted to amplify some of the subtleties in the sound to that effect, which actually then leads better to the sound's conclusion. To do that, I kept Character Two's stare a lot more focused (Figure 13.13).

He looks around like Character One, but he does it at times when Character One is being more forthcoming/open/vulnerable, and then, at the end, as Character One is trying to establish more of a relationship and be more comfortable. By picking those moments to break the eyeline, it makes it look like this guy is not interested in or impressed with Character One. One way he does this is by holding a stare throughout some of Character One's loss for words or polite conversation, but not nodding until prompted. This makes him look like he's expecting something. Having him look like he's waiting for "the point" definitely creates some attitude, and in turn, the social control of the scene (Figure 13.14).

Concerning amounts and timing of eye contact, it is a very fine line between polite, rude, and uncomfortable. I played this character a little more intensely with the eyelines, but don't have him do as many proper nods; that makes him a little bit snotty.

Lids

People use blinks to "hand off" a conversation. At the end of a section of speech, it's usually a good idea to blink the speaking character's eyes, to communicate that they're done and are then handing control over to the listener. I usually like to place this type of blinks *before* the absolute end of the line, which makes it look less like a conspicuous system or rule. Talk, blink, talk, blink would get pretty tiring to watch. For blinks in general, I really stuck to a generic timing of one frame longer on the return, meaning, if the blink took two frames to go down, it takes three to return; three to go down, four to return. Most blinks can hover around two or three frames for the down and look natural, but in certain situations, like where Character Two gets crankier in the second half, I slowed the blinks way down. You'll blink slowly if you're tired, or making a point to express your discontent, which is exactly what he is doing. I reserved the wider-eyed look for the times when the characters are looking around. Character Two in particular shows a real "edge" during the time when Character One coughs. Character Two looks around, but when the eyes widen during one of those gazes (Figure 13.15), it communicates a focus, or an interest, *away* from Character One.

Figure 13.15

That black pixel over there is way more interesting than the bumble-fool to my right!

At that point Character Two goes from simple avoidance to actually looking like he's *more* interested in his static surroundings than in whatever Character One might have to say. We as an audience read his emotion very well; he's not really looking at anything, but that communicates emotionally. He just does not care about Character One's babblings.

> The reason that blinking slowly looks less impressed is that it hovers longer in that *unimpressed* or *sleepy* area illustrated way back in Chapter 2 ("What the Eyes and Brows Tell Us") by the pupil-and-iris-o-meter. By spending time in that range, it becomes a pose unto itself—an "I don't care" pose, to be precise.

With the squint (lower lids) I was fairly conservative, because of the type of scene. I usually use the squint as an intensifier, but since here I'm playing the characters less intensely, leaving the squint mostly uninvolved was good for the feel. Neither of these guys really gets too intense with their delivery, so to add that into the animation would just simply be out of place.

> Don't contradict the voice track of a performance. You can always find interesting ways to act something creatively, but avoid trying to *alter* the voice performance through your animation; it can be done, but in most cases, the conflict just weakens the scene.

I chose only to use the squint to punch some big moments and create some contrast. On Character One I most noticeably did this when he's thinking through "so it's going to be you and me." The squint there helps show there's thought—he's having to think about what he's saying; he's considering something, not just talking. With Character Two I used the squint in several places, but none of them in a very strong way, nothing worth specific mention.

Figure 13.16

**Waiting and then
not waiting**

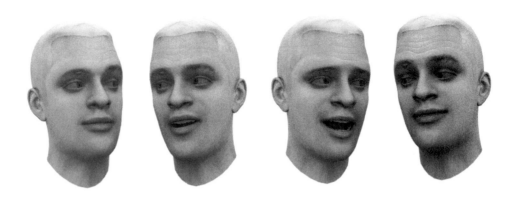

Brows

Something we do with our brows is raise them when there is something *opened up*, like a phrase or an asked question, that needs a conclusion. When I'm waiting for you to finish what you're saying, and I don't know where the sentence is going, I'll probably arch my brows, until I *do* know, which is when they'll drop again. Figure 13.16 shows one of these moments.

It's facial language for "I'm listening." On Character One, I raised the brows while Character Two initiates the conversation, and then as soon as Character One has absorbed the incoming statement, the brows drop, as he begins to respond "Yeah, yeah…". When Character Two finished the question is when his brows raise; as he's opened the conversation up, now *he's* waiting for a response. The brows stay raised until that expectation is satisfied, which, in this scene, is long *before* Character One is done talking. This also feeds into the feel I'm after of Character Two being a little unimpressed, although this only helps subtly. Character One then raises his brows again as he tosses the conversation back over to Character Two after "privy to movement." This makes him *look* like he's asking for a response, which then prompts Character Two to respond.

GENERAL BROW NOTE

Since I'm using the "My Favorite" setup from Chapter 12 ("Interfaces for Your Faces"), which uses an asymmetrical key set, I have a brows control that is able to create asymmetrical brow poses as easily as symmetrical ones. I usually pose the brows up and down first, and then use the side to side of the slider to make those original up-and-downs asymmetrical.

The next brow activity of note is on Character Two in the dead space after "lack of dialogue…". By raising the brows and looking down in silence, during a nod you can create a generally apathetic feeling (Figure 13.17).

This movement is well suited for this guy in this scene at this time, and yes, this is an extremely specific usage in a very specific circumstance; you just pile this kind of stuff up after you animate faces for a while.

With the brows, there's something I did during the cough on Character One, which I also did near the end with Character Two. If you tilt your head upward while showing stress on the forehead, (either a brows down or squeeze type shape), there's a sense of not being happy. You're being forced to do something, or think about something, you don't want to. In this case it's Character Two's patience running out with Character One's blabbing (Figure 13.18).

Figure 13.17

Apathy central.

You can see Character Two is going to be nasty before he even says anything. To catch that *consciously* might take a few viewings, but you should feel it on the first view, then his last comment, which is quite rude, doesn't feel out of place. In the sound alone, or acted differently, that line definitely could seem a little abrupt.

The last brow pose on Character Two is sad in nature. See, this is why I've condensed the set of shapes down to what it is. Even though at the end Character Two looks sad in a still frame, in context he's being rude (Figure 13.19). Sad = rude? Not likely a connection one might make out of context, but it works great if it's what you're got to work with!

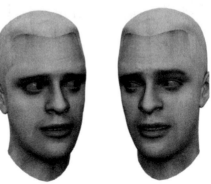

Figure 13.18

I'm so bored.

Figure 13.19

Sad brows used for jerk-ness

Mouth Emotion

This isn't the case with stylized characters, but you want to be very careful where you layer in smiles and frowns for realistic characters. You shouldn't just leave a full smile over a whole phrase or scene, just because a character is happy. One of the main characteristics of a smile is that it is wide. That's not the *only* characteristic, but it's a big one. To make the significance of that more obvious, Wide and Narrow are the main things you should focus on with your sync, so leaving a smile present over large chunks, just because a character is happy, will impact the look of your sync in a bad way; it'll all look too wide. That's why smiles don't work well when blanketed over scenes.

Frowns are better in that respect, but they also don't look good left too long; it feels like your character gets a lazy lip or something. The way to use mouth emotions best is in the pauses. You smile in the breaks, you smile during the breaths, and you smile over long syllables. If you watch real people, they do have to suppress part of their smile to properly enunciate OOs.

Figure 13.20

More apathy from our friend on screen right

In this scene, you can see very clearly how I used that information. When Character One asks "So, you hang out here often?" I have a slight amount of smile throughout, but I really turn the smile up in the second syllable of "often." Having some smile turn into more smile really feels like the smile was there the whole time; I think of it as emotional punctuation. It's at the end of the sentence, but it changes the way we perceive the whole thing! …or perhaps it changes the way we perceive the whole thing?

Moving right along, I do the same thing on Character One at the end of "privy to movement." I smiled him subtly throughout, and then made it stronger coming out of the speech. Other than that, things in mouth-emotion-land are pretty predictable up until Character Two's little tilt down after saying "lack of dialogue." I chose to smile him here to emphasize the apathetic look of "What are you gonna do?" (Figure 13.20). He already had this going, I just wanted to notch it up.

Other Tilts and Finesse

The head tilts via the "music" in the acting were easy, but here is where I went through and layered in some more animatorly touches. For the sake of instruction, I did something here a little more deliberately than I would for production animation. A little head gesture I've picked up on is that people tend to toss the conversation back and forth with their heads. Watch each character as they *finish* their lines. After "hang out here often?" Character Two tilts over to Character One (Figure 13.21). When Character One is done with his response line, he points his head back over to Character Two (Figure 13.22).

It's a very natural movement for conversation that is moving between two characters. Quickly thereafter, I added another aspect, but kept the same basic idea going. After Character One's second line about "not really privy to movement," Character Two leans away quickly. Here, he's *catching* this toss of the head, really responding, almost like an imaginary ball was passed to him (Figure 13.23), and he dribbles that ball a little bit before he tosses it back at the end of his line, " I can see."

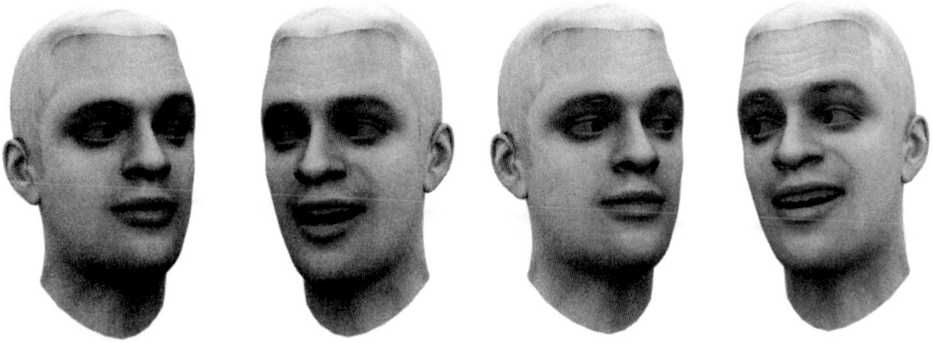

Figure 13.21

The setup and then the nod

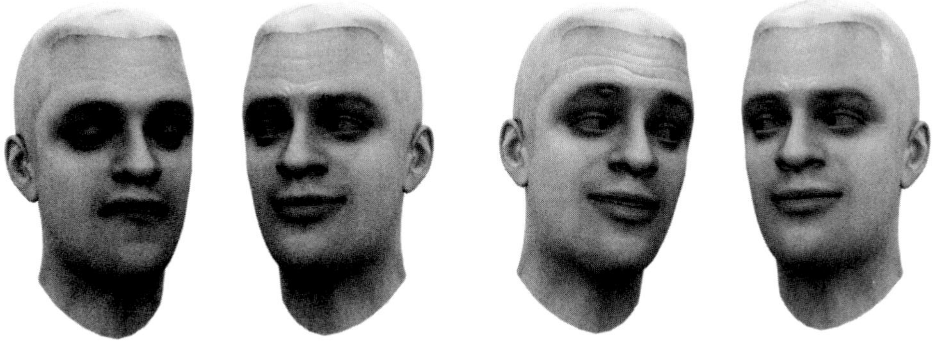

Figure 13.22

Another pass over the net, as the head tilts and tosses the conversation to Character Two

This pattern repeats throughout. Besides those motions, the only other one of this type that might be of interest is where I tilted Character One's head left to right during "That's the way it is sometimes." This paired with his look up really separates him from the state-

Figure 13.23

Head catch

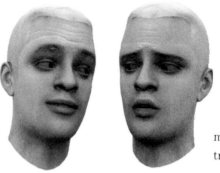

ment. It makes it feel as if he's repeating something he's heard, or just not putting too much weight into the statement. The same motion could be used for mocking, but in this context, it just sort of lightens up the phrase, and definitely makes this guy look like he's trying to be funny or entertaining. It really helps to make him the goof, and Character Two the controlling party.

As far as twisting motions, as if saying "no," I threw in very quick ones any time a character had anything negative to say (as I always do). Not negative as in mean or nasty, but negative as in *not* affirmative. When Character One says "I can't," I threw one quick one in, and then I did again during "I'm not really…". It may be very formulaic, but it does a good job of matching the vocal performance.

Scene 3: Dunce Cap

Heh, heh, heh—that guy's got a dunce cap! Ain't he stupid? Look at it, look at it, stupid head… Oh. Yeah. OK. I guess I've learned my lesson. (VOICE PERFORMANCE BY JASON OSIPA. ANIMATION BY JASON HOPKINS.)

You can load `Dunce.mov` from the Chapter 13 folder to see the animation, and `Dunce.wav` for the audio file alone.

This scene is a special little treat for me. I really wanted to get at least one section in here to talk about other animators' styles for both sync and facial acting, and this is it. Jason Hopkins is an outstanding character animator I had the pleasure to work with at Mainframe Entertainment, in Vancouver, Canada—"Hollywood North," as it's been called. Hopkins has been a Senior and Supervising Animator on a whole big bunch of great episodic television and direct-to-video CGI projects.

Instead of going through this scene like the others, I posed some questions about the things that stood out to me, and have recorded his responses. Figure 13.24 shows some of the more interesting frames from this animation.

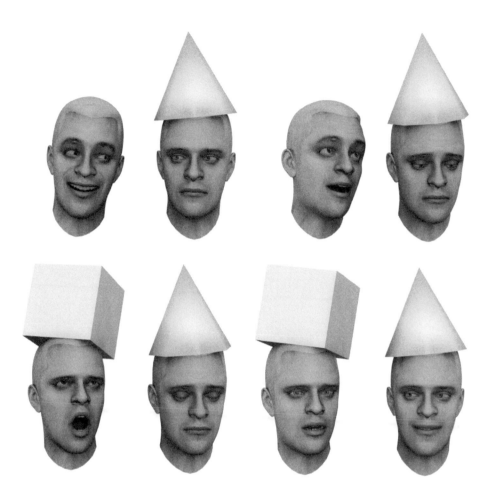

Figure 13.24

Some frames from "Dunce"

What Order to Do Things?

You've all been exposed to my approach, but Hopkins' is a little bit different. In an overall sense, what I teach and what he does are very similar but it's easy to see that there are a few swaps in the order of some steps.

Jaw first (Open/Closed) Hopkins animates the jaw first until the point where it looks like it could pass as-is—you know, everything is *readable* even if it's only the jaw.

All heights and widths (visimes) By phrase or chunks, he works in sections, not individual sounds or words. Once he's done with the whole thing he goes back and look at it as a whole.

For this one he broke it into two chunks. With long scenes, he says, you've got to work in pieces so you don't get too lost.

Brows Hopkins says that this has always been the hardest for him. They're not easy. There's so much emotion in them that it's hard to move on to other things. To get good brows, he experiments by looking for "moments" that work. Sometimes you get things you didn't expect. It always depends on what the director wants. With rare things like this, just dialogue, he doesn't see definite rules for what to do. Undirected dialogue can be turned into anything; it's just a matter of knowing which way to steer it.

Head and eyes For him, these two are intertwined. He does them at the same time because they need each other, they work together.

Tweak When he's got a working version of the rest of that stuff in, he tweaks the overall scene—adds little smirks and sneers, all the fun stuff.

Your Process with *This* Scene

After getting his thoughts on order of approach, I then asked Hopkins, "Tell me about your approach to *this* scene."

Q: What was the first thing you thought about?

Hopkins: Eyes. Much of your acting and emotion comes from the eyes, so what I did was start by basic syncing, letting my mind roam on the acting. I used that time, hearing the sound over and over, to figure out what I wanted to do with the shot. You can sync pretty well without knowing the acting so I don't worry about it too much. Going through it, I was thinking about "A little smirk here would be great" or "Here I'll cock the brow." You just sort of log that stuff away for later.

Q: Opening with a laugh is hard, it's one of my weak spots. How did you deal with that?

Hopkins: I wanted the laugh to be hearty, it felt like a real strong "Ha ha ha." I thought if I could pull that off, I would be okay. I wanted to try and get a shoulder shrug across even though there's no body there with shoulders to shrug!

Q: Were there any acting techniques you had in mind for this scene?

Hopkins: Well, since there's no body, I wanted to, *had* to, gesture with the head. To really match the voice track I had the talker gesturing to the other character and the audience.

Q: So what were the attitudes you wanted to get across?

Hopkins: The talker was a guy who's, you know, in your posse; like you're walking down the street with him, and you see this dunce cap guy. With "dunce," I wanted to draw the audience toward his character quickly, to identify with him somehow, so that when the cube shows up on the talker, you're instantly happy. I wanted to steer people toward seeing the talker as a jerk, and the little hero of the scene was the dunce.

Q: What was the hardest part of this scene?

Hopkins: There's just so much in the head. I'm always very worried about the fact that you can wreck everything by animating the head wrong.

Q: I noticed you keep the dunce cap guy pretty subdued throughout....

Hopkins: I toned down that guy's animation quite a bit because I felt like he would act embarrassed; he does have a dunce cap on his head, after all. I didn't want him completely still, but I kept his motions pretty slow. I didn't want him to *steal* your eye, I wanted him to *take* it because he was what was being talked about, and he was so calm in comparison.

Q: I really like your brow movement style; describe it for me in your words.

Hopkins: I kind of *throw* the brows with the head. I don't do it intentionally, I guess it's something that just feels like it flows. I worked on shows where the characters had no textures on the face; it was a style. If you weren't careful, it would look like the brows just crawled up and down the forehead. I got in the habit of hiding brow motions in head moves, and I guess it just stuck with me.

Q: Dunce Cap seems like the focus to me, even though he's not talking. Did you do anything to help that?

Hopkins: I hope so. I wanted you to move your eye over to him early, and play up how the talker is kind of just noise. I was trying to get a bit of "Hello, there's this guy over here, and I'm being made fun of." You can't help but notice the first guy, but I wanted the second guy to be noticed. I mean, a still head wouldn't have meant anything. I wanted to keep him alive.

Q: I didn't give too much in the way of direction for this. Did anything about that scare you?

Hopkins: Eyes. Eyes are the thing most often wrong. Little shifts, when to lead the head, when to follow the head, when to blink; all those little things mean so much; it's easy to ruin facial animation with bad eye movements.

Q: I noticed a great shift in the acting on the "talker" when the cube shows up, describe that.

Hopkins: When the cube shows up, I just felt like now he's the focus of all the negative attention he was throwing around. I thought he would start to move a lot more like the other guy, slower and more subdued.

Q: If you were to take another run at this, what would you change?

Hopkins: A lot. I look at it afterward, and that's when I learn from myself, see what I like and don't like; I just watch it like it was someone else's. I don't know, it evolves; I don't hyperanalyze like you. I will say, I kind of liked not having direction. It gave me the chance to play!

Scene 4: Salty Old Sea Captain

I've never seen a more cowardly group! If you want to make it out of this alive—see your pretty wives again—you listen and you listen good. (VOICE PERFORMANCE BY CRAIG ADAMS)

You can load `Captain.mov` from the Chapter 13 folder to see my take on the animation, and `Captain.wav` for the audio file alone (which I cut the start off of for my scene; you can do the same by changing the offset). Figure 13.25 shows a selection of frames from this piece.

Oh, my goodness, what a blast this was; I love my job. We haven't seen any anger out of characters before now, and what an angry scene to have. Pete's one cranky guy in this clip! In this scene, and this performance, the guy means business.

This scene and the next are examples of different scenarios and characters rather than tutorials, because there's a lot in the realm outside of the photo-real style I've focused on so heavily (or at least attempted!). Captain Pete here and Sally Ann in the following scene were not done in Maya; they were built in Animation:Master from Hash. I wanted to show that, indeed, the ways of doing things that I'm describing all carry over across styles and across tools.

Figure 13.25

Some frames from "Captain"

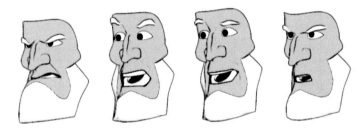

Sync Special Cases

Seeing as this is the first time we've got an angry performance—a very, *very* focused angry person—there are some new ideas to introduce. You might know the musical term *staccato*. This is how I like to animate most angry characters: I animate them quick and intense. Usually slow motions denote strength, but if a character is yelling at a good rate, speed and motion can add something scary. With the sync here, I went a step deeper than even *I* usually do; I really

Figure 13.26

These shapes from just one frame to the next are pretty different.

went frame-by-frame trying to nail every part of every word (Figure 13.26). To watch the scene over and over, it looks a little "poppy," sort of jumpy. To watch it once through, however, you just see ferocity. My sync approach here was just to over-exaggerate and over-enunciate everything in the hope that would show both rage *and* focus.

Head Tilts

These proved very tricky. It seemed, after going through this with my usual approach, that almost none of it felt right. The up and down motions felt as if they were out of place. I was almost tempted to do the tilts on gut instinct instead of making it work with the methods I've described. Instead, I started reducing the strength of the nods and completely eliminating others. There's an intensity with this sound file that lots of motion might wreck. At the start of the scene, I reversed the up and down motions. Even though, tonally, the line starts on a very sharp up, I tilted the head down. Forward/Down nods are much, much stronger than upward moves, and this guy seems pretty strong to me. I liked how that looked and found ways to slide the head up slowly so that with almost every big hit in the dialogue, I could tilt the head back down. He spends most of his time looking at you from under that brow (Figure 13.27).

Figure 13.27

By cutting into the eye silhouette, the brows get very strong.

Eyes

This was a huge challenge for me. I am an animator, first and foremost, and that means I like to animate; sometimes that can be a bad thing. I tried darting the eyes in the tiniest pauses, I tried having it look like Pete addressed a larger group, moving his eyes far left and right, almost like he was surrounded by whoever he's talking to. None of it, not one bit of it, worked. It didn't matter what I did; it all weakened the performance.

I realized that this is the exact thing I had been fighting the whole time. Pete's intense, and the more he does, the less intense he becomes. My final decision was to leave the eyes locked on one point for the whole time, and that did so much to strengthen everything else Pete did. He became like a train: he had a path he was on, and nothing was changing that.

Lids

To use this word yet again, my goal was to keep Pete intense. This is the only scene in my examples that can really make great use of the squint, so I poured it on really thick. Using mostly the same criteria I would to widen the eyes, I squinted them. Since the brow poses were so low, the upper lid was mostly invisible, so instead of trying to animate them, even though you wouldn't see them, I just left his upper lids pretty wide for the entirety of the scene, letting you as a viewer figure out how he looked under those angry brows. Especially near the end, where I may have even overdone it, you can see how the raising of the lower lids, the squint, helps strengthen his contempt for whoever he's talking to (Figure 13.28).

Figure 13.28

That's some squinting, right there.

Brows

I treated the brows very differently in this scene. I went through and picked some moments, just places where it felt like a certain pose would look right. These, I admit, were terribly unsystematic decisions; it was almost strictly instinctive—it's nice to know I still do that, too! The hardest thing was deciding that I really only wanted his brows in that lowered angry

pose, but leaving them there, along with the stillness in the eyes, almost looked unfinished. I punctuated even the slightest volume shifts (not tone shifts) with raises, but I promptly returned them to that lowered, angry pose. Everything seems to come back to me wanting to hold his focus, so as not to betray the great voice-acting intensity.

Mouth Emotion

I can't believe I made it this far without saying it, but here's where you can see why, although we *do* have a Sneer shape, we don't have other shapes that you might expect, like a Cheeks Puff. We have a Sneer because we didn't build a Mad mouth shape; while they are different, sad and mad mouths are very similar. The right amount of a sad shape combined with a sneer looks mighty angry to me. To emphasize anger further, I usually bare a little bit more upper tooth during angry times, too; in Pete's case here, it's practically *all* upper tooth *all* the time!

> To close up that *cheeks puff* thing, it just isn't necessary. It's a nice touch, but it can be easily added later as a specialty shape; you can get by without it; and everything I'm teaching here, from construction to animation, is about helping draw focus to only what's necessary.

Figure 13.29

Some frames from "alive," so you can see how the motion swoops up and around

Besides a little tiny hint of a smile during the word "wives," Pete stays pretty angry in that mouth area. Something I'll talk about briefly here is using the mouth emotion to try to emphasize figure-eight motions. It's not as easy to make work in realistic stuff, but as soon as you're into less restrictive styles, a good motion to drive for in the mouth is figure eights, circles, just something better than ups and downs. In Pete's case here, the word "alive" is the best example (Figure 13.29), but I do it to a lesser extent in several other places.

Other Tilts and Finesse

I had put so much effort into focusing Pete up until now that I felt I had my bases covered, and actually let up a little bit; I had a lot of fun with these other head motions. As always, when he says "I've never seen," which is a negative statement, I shook his head as if he were shaking his head *no*. On the word "group," I used a sideways tilt almost as another nod (Figure 13.30).

Figure 13.30

A sideways tilt to nod, but in a different way

Now he has a standard sharp biting nod followed by a new different one. They both feel similar, but not repetitive. With "If you want to make it out of this…," I wanted to have him turn slightly away from who he was talking to, almost as if he was trying to hide the rest of his statement (Figure 13.31).

He uses that opening line "If you want to make it out of this alive…" almost as a hook, and then he knows he's got them, so he opens back up on "alive." He knows they're listening now, so he can turn to them and open up a little (whoever *they* are). I'm really happy with the snappy little move on "see" from "see your pretty wives again." That little twist really *throws* the line out instead of just saying it. He's trying to appeal to his audience, but not in a warm fuzzy way. He's saying "I know what you want" subtextually, but he's doing it in a very hard way, almost like a slap. This is just a variation on handing the line over.

With the whole last line, "you listen, and you listen good," I shook his head violently back and forth. That kind of motion done quickly just communicates something negative is being said, but when you prolong it, and amplify it, it turns into something else completely. The motions at the end, to me, seemed almost like a dog tearing through a phone book, or a bull snorting and getting ready to charge. Something very animal comes through. That's a very specific style choice in a very specific scene, but, hey, it's what I was thinking!

Figure 13.31

This little turn away gives Pete some added power, since he feels as if he's holding something but not letting us see it—he's keeping his cards close.

Scene 5: Pink or Blue?

Pink or blue? Pink or blue? Oh… I just don't know! If I get the pink one, I'm all, 'Ooh, look at that little girly-girl in pink!' And if I'm blue, it's like, 'Hey, it's a boy-girl. Why don't you go do boy stuff, boy-girl?' Okay, just think it out. If I were a bow on my head, what color would I want to be? (VOICE PERFORMANCE BY ROBIN PARKS.)

You can load `PinkOrBlue.mov` from the Chapter 13 folder to see my take on the animation, and `PinkOrBlue.wav` for the audio file alone. Figure 13.32 shows a selection of frames from this piece.

For this, I used my Sally Ann model, which was made and animated in Animation:Master from Hash.

With this scene, the only real intention I had directorially was to pretend Sally Ann was talking in a mirror to herself. I wanted to really emphasize the shifts in character and present *her impression* of these groups of people she's talking about.

Figure 13.32

Frames from "Pink or Blue?"

Sync Special Cases

The first run-through, as always for me, was to do the basic sync. I've preached to you the advantages of "my favorite" interface because you can get great speed as well as great detail and intricacy by using different controls at different times. This scene is one I took to a more finished state, and part of doing that (for me) is to forgo using the simpler symmetrical sync controls designed for speed. When aiming for a higher level, and knowing I want to take a little more time, I start right at the beginning by building each and every sync shape using all the asymmetrical sliders; for the "My Favorite" interface from Chapter 12, that means the sliders directly on the face.

> This scene was actually done in Hash Animation:Master which didn't have my specialty interfaces set up. I had symmetrical versions and asymmetrical versions of all shapes, so for this scene I used only asymmetrical sliders, even when constructing mostly symmetrical facial expressions.

By forcing yourself to construct every lips-up or lips-down by pulling each side of the lips individually, you can create, almost accidentally, very character-rich mouth shapes for your scene. They'll all have little asymmetrical quirks just by the nature of how you create the shapes. So Sally Ann's sync in this scene took me a very long time (three hours), partly because of the scene length, but mostly because of the slower animation approach.

Toon Sync Differences

For toon characters or anthropomorphs (talking animals), the sync guidelines laid out in Chapter 4 get super-amplified. As a result of that style difference, these characters usually end up having a more "stepped" animation curve style, too. I find that to make sync look good for stylized characters I have to get into shapes earlier and hold them for longer, leaving the in-between times shorter.

For example, looking at the movie of this scene, notice the first three words, "Pink or blue?" Watching the animation for Wide/Narrows specifically, you'll notice that "pink" is practically one uniform width for the whole word, as is the width during "blue." More realistic characters benefit from slightly longer transitions.

Hitting the "Clicks"

Another toon sync style amplification is to punch percussive noises like the T, K, or D at the end of a word (like the end of "pink"). You'd want to do this same thing in all styles, but the farther from human, the more you *can* and should. These sounds do not have a shape (width or height), but popping the jaw open after the sound really makes the sonic *click* have a good visual representation.

Use Smiles and Frowns in Your Sync when You've Got the Time

It's always a good idea to use smiles and frowns to punctuate your sync, and create more custom per-sound shapes, but again, with toons, do it even more. I didn't wait until later on during my mouth-emotion pass to use the smile and frown controls. I did wait in reference to the *acting*, but I used those emotion shapes during the sync stage to really match the actress's performance. For instance, notice the word "pink" has a smile in the animation, and I then dropped the expression to a frown during "blue" (Figure 13.33).

Figure 13.33

A frame each of "pink" and "blue"; notice the use of smile and frown for sync, not expression

This has next to nothing to do with facial expression, and everything to do with saying the words in a mirror and paying close attention to where the *corners* of my mouth were as I said each word. The corners of my mouth raised during "pink" and dropped significantly during "blue" so I figured I'd copy that little detail onto Sally Ann. I did the same throughout the scene, usually pairing frowns with Narrows and using smiles in conjunction with Wides.

Exaggerated Closeds

With most of the B/M/P sounds in this scene, I found I had to hold the lips closed for more than a single frame for them to look good. This has a lot to do with the look and feel of a non-realistic character and how, as an audience, we've come to expect the way they will behave. Animators exaggerate holds, and most of us have watched cartoons our whole lives, so sometimes the amount you would have to close your mouth with a toon character (Figure 13.34) is much longer than you would with the same dialogue played over a realistic character—it's just what we're used to seeing.

Figure 13.34

Hold it, hold it…

Tilts

This is one of those scenes that briefly makes me reconsider my notion of animating the head musically, but I always come around in the end, and remember why I do. Robin Parks, the voice actress, performed this line in a very sing-songy fashion. Not only that, but during the line, she often slides upward tonally instead of how most people slide down in most instances. What this leads to, following my system, is a head constantly doing upward or *reverse* nods; These look strange. The whole trick to making these reverse nods work is to turn them into anticipations for downward nods, even if those don't come for a few seconds afterward (Figure 13.35). Sometimes you'll even have to swap an up-sound into a down-move, essentially reversing the rules. In any case, it's always on the big tonal shifts that the big moves should happen for them to look most in tune with the sound.

Figure 13.35

Two frames, the first an upward swing and then a downward one; these two were paired to look like one long joined motion instead of two separate ones, of course timed so as not to "float."

The opening two cases of "Pink or blue?" are great examples of this timing. Both "pink"s are upward tonal shifts, so I tilted the head up. If I were to just leave it there for eternity or raise it again on the next upward tonal shift, it would not look very good, so I slammed the head all the way back to level (and then a little further down) on each "blue." On the second "blue," there's a breath between "pink" and "blue" where I tilted the head even higher. Two upward tilts in a row is not something you'll usually want to do, but if you can get creative with how and when you *reset* the head to level, then the rare occasions they occur can be easily managed.

One place I reversed the rules and nodded the head down on an upward sound shift was at the end of "I just don't know!" Parks (playing Sally Ann) jumped up a few tones at the start of that phrase and then ended it with an even higher note. I initially had her head tilting further up at that point, but it just looked bizarre. I then changed it by using the same timing, but turned the head down instead of up. Later, when I went back and animated the brows, I raised the brows, which pretty much picked up the feeling of the sound.

> If you haven't already noticed, when something fails to work for me, my first follow-up attempt is to do the exact opposite of what I tried initially!

For the section where Sally Ann says "Ooh, look at that little girly-girl in pink!" it's all very *high* tonally. At first I was trying to find ways to fight that, and bring the head back down; with the eyes pointed forward and the head up like that, it's not attractive. Instead of fighting it, I ran with it, and decided that when I got to the eyes, I'd animate Sally Ann looking off and up into space, making that portion of the scene an aside. I did eventually have to bring her head back down later in the scene, and to do so, I jumped on the first downward tone shift I could find which happened to be "in" from "look at that little girly-girl *in* pink!" I shot the head back down quickly because the very next word, "pink," was going to be another move up. Sally Ann warbles that word, too, which for this stage of animation is something I'm going to pass on (for no other reason than the section already feels very up-and-down to me), but I'm sure I'll find some fun gesture or expression to throw in that spot later, with one of my other animation passes.

The last big thing to do with head tilts that should get some discussion is when Sally Ann talks through "If I were a bow on my head." Instead of climbing the head precisely with each tone, I found a pattern here I liked. Parks performed this line making "If I were a bow…" a tonal pair with "on my head…". When these moments happen in the sound, it's perfect for an animator to pounce. I turned the two halves of that phrase into a pair in the animation, just like they were delivered, by doing a big up and down for each half (Figure 13.36). For this forward and back

Figure 13.36

Two neat little arcs in the sound were something I copied in the motion.

"If I were a bow…"   "…on my head…"

motion, that's not so exciting, but I've timed it in such a way that later on, when I do the other rotations on the head, Sally Ann will look left then right, one direction per nod. This is a fun head movement that really punctuates a character working through a thought slowly and explicitly.

Figure 13.37

The first time through "Pink or blue?" I kept her eyes forward; I gave "pink" and "blue" each their own pose the second time.

Eyes

The eyes in this, as with most scenes, is where I really start to map out the expressions I want the character to move into and out of. With Sally Ann repeating herself at the head of this line with "Pink or blue?" twice, I didn't want to have her weigh this decision of hers completely in outer space, I wanted to start her in the here-and-now. For the first "Pink or blue?" I held her gaze dead ahead at the imaginary mirror in front of her (Figure 13.37).

For the second "Pink or blue?" I made sure she looked in two different places, as if the pink and the blue bows were in two different places (Figure 13.37). I actually had a blink in between these moves originally, but I didn't like it. What I settled on instead was to have her roll her eyes over and then down, which actually becomes a sort of anticipation to where the head drops.

With the "Oh," I went for a look as if she wasn't really focusing on anything, so I centered her eyes. On "I just don't know," she returns to her home eye position, the mirror, so that it looks like she makes the remark to herself, not just to nobody or nothing.

During "If I get the pink one, I'm all," I shot her eyes down and to screen right. This could have been up down left or right, it didn't matter; I just wanted to make that line feel more internal, more an aside, a ramp-up to the impression of a "girly-girl" she does next. Since I push her eyes up during the "girly-girl" phrase (looking at the awkward high angle of the head from earlier steps as an inspiration instead of as a hindrance; see Figure 13.38), I chose to drop her eyes previous to that, just so there would be some contrast.

Figure 13.38

What was once a weird tilt up is now a cute little "girly-girl" moment.

"And if I'm blue…" felt obvious after getting the other two previous eyelines sorted out. I went down and screen left for no fancy reason other than it mirrors nicely with the aside before "girly-girl." With "Hey, it's a boy-girl, why don't you go do," I chose to contrast the weakness in "girly-girl," the avoiding or airy-fairy nature, with a very direct eyeline, one that holds more strength and teams up nicely with Parks's delivery (where she lowers her voice a few notes) to give what Sally Ann thinks is how boys act (Figure 13.39).

The end of this section, "….boy stuff, boy-girl!" starts with a pause where it seems like Sally Ann has to search for the words. No direction from me ever got to Parks to do that on purpose; it's just how she did the voice acting. The nice part is I *love pauses!* Thanks, Robin! I just love them, that's where I play. In this pause, since it sounded to me like Sally Ann couldn't find the words, I made her show that, by darting her eyes back and forth (Figure 13.40).

Figure 13.39

And here's the tough "boy-girl."

She visually and sonically has a moment of searching; the two, I think, work very well together to show a moment of almost frustration.

Sally Ann returns to the dead-on look after she finds the words, and holds it there until she has her next internal moment. By turning her eyes away again, I broke her out of that sub-scene quickly and easily. I turn her eyes away and keep them turned away from the mir-

ror, but moving at each break in the sound. I have her do a whole lap around the frame before she returns at the end. She goes bottom-left, top-left, top-right, bottom-left, and then center. It just sort of worked out that way with the timing of the voice track and the preexisting tilts of the head. Sometimes these things just work themselves out!

Figure 13.40

I moved her eyes into similar spots as before, so as not to make her look manic and looking in every direction all the time.

Lids

You may have noticed that I made more use of the squint in this scene. On realistic characters you have to really pick your moments and wait for good intensity, whereas with a character like Sally Ann, you can throw in or take away squints all over the place (obviously, having a reason makes it look better). I actually threw a slight squint in right on the first word "pink," as an anticipation to contrast with "blue" (Figure 13.41).

Her lower lids widening while her head tilts down creates an interesting focus. I've talked about using percussive noises as timing for blinks, and this scene is no exception: I blink on almost every B, M, or P.

Something else I did with the lids early in the scene is on the "oh" near the start. Something that looks really nice is to have different parts of the face trail the overall head movement. For example, I had a blink on the "oh" anyway, but it looked strange that her head crept up slowly while her blink was fast and perky. I slowed the blink down, so that the lids didn't raise all the way again until the head was already on its way back down.

Later, I used the squint to be the lead-in to both "girly-girl" and "boy-girl" sub-scenes. (Figure 13.42)

Just before each one, I have Sally Ann squint to show the "wheels turning" before she bounces into her characterizations of what girly-girl and boy-girl are like. I also tightened up the squint on the last "boy-girl" to give that part of the line a little bit more venom. I thought Parks's performance had some nice bite there, and I didn't want to lose it in the animation by ignoring it. For lids, the rest of the scene is pretty much paint-by-numbers.

Figure 13.41

Squinty pinky

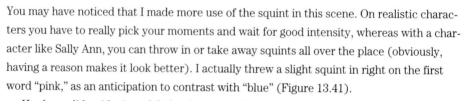

Figure 13.42

The pose before bursting into the "girly-girl" part of the line

Brows

You know how I recommend to tilt the head to get the effect you'd usually want to put on the brows? Well, in some cases—this being one—I do both, which changes my approach slightly.

I actually get the brows to complement the head and eye motions instead of the sounds, if that makes sense; it's almost as if I'm paying more attention to the brows' interaction with the rest of the face than with the sound. I end up with something very similar to mapping the volume of the voice to the brows, but it's subtly different. With "Pink or blue?" I raised her brows on the up of "pink" and dropped them, just like I did with the head, on "blue" (getting a great flat-brows shape, shown in Figure 13.43, which I personally think is *so* strong and full of character).

Figure 13.43

I find this flat brow look to be so rich in character. I make sure all my (stylized) characters are capable of it.

Figure 13.44

Raising the brow on the side a character is looking adds some nice flair to the eyeline.

On the second "Pink or blue?" I actually started a new pattern of movement. Since her eyes look in different directions for "pink" and "blue," I decided to have her brows mirror that motion instead of the head's motions. I often raise the brow on the side the character is look-ing (Figure 13.44); it makes the whole face look much more cohesive as a whole.

Raising the brow on the side of the eyeline is an inquisitive look. If you want to have a charac-ter's look to one side to be more accusatory, suspicious, or mean, don't raise it; instead *lower* the brow on the side they are looking.

The "oh" was a perfect place for an expression shift (a long drawn out sound that's *not* a word almost always is), so over the course of that sound is where I rearranged her brows to be more sad. "I just don't know" felt like I needed to drive her into an even more pathetic-looking expression (Figure 13.45), so I lowered the brows right down to below the tops of her eyes, about as sad and broken as I think she can look. I held them there until "know," where I reset both the height and the expression.

Figure 13.45

That's one frustrated little girl.

It's important to do that so that people don't forget what the character really looks like! This isn't a joke, either: If you keep the face in too extreme a position for too long, that expression could stop meaning anything.

The next place the brows really shift is during the "girly-girl" section. This is easily identi-fiable as mockery, and that—for me, anyway—means raised and saddened brows, as shown in Figure 13.46.

Between the end of "girly-girl" and the beginning of "boy-girl," I merely reset the brows and held them there. For the "boy-girl" section, I made some decisions that really didn't feel like rules or guidelines at all, but instead went purely with my own tastes. Since I went with sad brows for "girly-girl," I had sort of used it up for now (sad brows, that is). You could easily play this section with the same expression, but I thought it might be boring. I decided instead to swing her brows to the mad side of things, and also played them asymmetrically, giving her a little more attitude (Figure 13.47). Both of these sections are mocking perceptions Sally

Figure 13.46

Brows up and sad works for the "girly-girl" bit.

Figure 13.47

Angry brows for "boy-girl"

Ann has of others, but by acting them on two ends of the sad-mad spectrum, it pulls out some of the subtext of soft versus hard, prissy versus mean.

"Okay, just think it out" was another place I merely reset the brows to clean the slate for whatever comes next. I pretty much played the whole ending very simply; the only brow movements of note are how I changed the raised brow to match the side (and height) Sally Ann is looking. Instead of having the brows swapping high-and-low all over the place, I just moved one side up and down; this keeps her forehead a little more sane-looking.

Mouth Emotion

I love how far down the list this is; all the bases are already covered, and it's just a matter of prettying it all up. By using the smiles and frowns during the sync, a lot of this part of the performance has already come through, leaving mostly just the pauses and long syllables that need some attention.

The main places I made choices that might need some explanation are during the "girly-girl" and "boy-girl" sections. By now, with all the other layers of animation in there, it's clear that the character separations from one impression to the other are mainly strength and weakness. In pursuit of solidifying that, it helps to know that frowns are weak (with sad brows; a frown is strong with mad brows) and smiles are strong. It might be an obvious statement now, but I took that approach and frowned Sally Ann through the "girly-girl" stuff and smiled her through the "boy-girl" part (Figure 13.48).

Not only did that paint her as strong during the "boy-girl" section, but it actually made her a little bit evil. I like it! Don't worry, this little gal won't get too evil; that eye-dart as she's searching for her words really shows some weakness, which just leaves the evil looking more like cute than evil.

Other Tilts

The higher the quality you want to see, the more there is to this stage of the process. First, I dealt with the side-to-side movements of her head, then the twists.

With the "Pink or blue?" section, I would move her head (screen) right for "pink" and left for "blue." No reason for picking sides, I just chose a side for each and went with it. The next extra head movements were for "I just don't know!" I shook her head as if to say *no*, which I like to do on most any negative statement. I then turned her head to (screen) right for her

Figure 13.48

For the mouth, sad through "girly-girl" and smiling through "boy-girl"

look down to the right corner, which makes the head look like all parts are behaving together as one. Then, I had some fun during the "girly-girl" section, where I wiggled her head slightly left to right a few times. This movement has so many uses it's hard to describe it in simple terms. For now, I'll just say, it works really well for mocking.

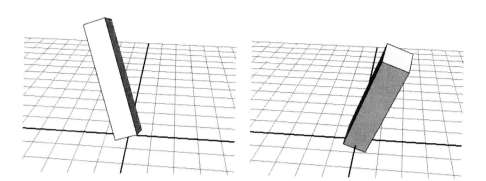

Figure 13.49

Two poses for the head to set up the trick

Then we come up to the warbly "pink" that I think is just begging for some attention. My first instinct was to simply add another side-to-side wiggle movement like the one I just did, and looking at that, I thought it looked pretty good. But I'm just not a fan of repetition. I wanted something similar, but not exactly the same. A little trick I know that works anywhere in animation, not just for the head, is to key joints—be they heads or arms—at two extremes, like Figure 13.49.

The movement you get is weird, as the joint just moves back and forth on a 45. The *trick* part of it is to take *one* of the two curves involved, and slide the keys, as a block, forward or back in time so they do the same motion, just on different frames. This creates circular or ovular motions instead of linear ones (Figure 13.50), and it animates much smoother than if you were to go in and key the head at each point in the circle.

Figure 13.50

By offsetting the curves, you can create circular motions.

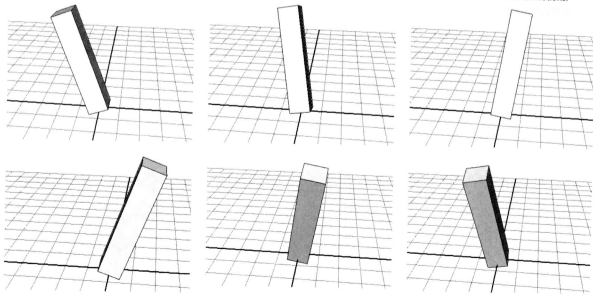

I did this with the twist left-to-right on Sally Ann's head, so now her tilting left-to-right actually became like a little fluid jiggle instead of a hard left-to-right. I liked how that matched the voice's jiggliness right there.

Next, in the aside before the "blue" section, I turned her head to (screen) left to emphasize the eyeline. I added a little twist during the word "why" because it felt as if she was *throwing* the line out. Sometimes on very stinging deliveries, you'll want to make the character look like they're *tossing* the line into the air instead of just speaking (as was the case with Captain Pete). A sharp little twist of the head works very well for that.

I gave a little tilt to the side on "boy" from the second "boy-girl." This was simply to break up the linear look of the up-and-down motions there; I had no real acting motivations.

Near the end are some motions I'm quite happy with. Sally Ann tilts her head left and

Figure 13.51

Two eyelines where the tilt actually goes opposite the direction of the look create a more contemplative look into the heavens.

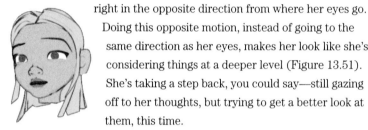

right in the opposite direction from where her eyes go. Doing this opposite motion, instead of going to the same direction as her eyes, makes her look like she's considering things at a deeper level (Figure 13.51). She's taking a step back, you could say—still gazing off to her thoughts, but trying to get a better look at them, this time.

That's All, Folks!

Well, there you have it. I wish I could just talk animation until the end of time, but unfortunately there are only so many pages and so much one guy can say in one book.

There's an infinite world of animation out there, and you'll find a few bonus examples of it on the book's companion CD. Check out the Extras folder, where I've put a few movie files not mentioned in the book for you to study (with and without sound), plus more sound files you can practice animating to. You can also find an animation, from the development stages of *Barbie in the Nutcracker,* where we tested the range and performance styles for the Mouse King shown in the color section. (Note: The voice track has been removed for legal reasons.)

I want you to realize something and pat yourself on the back. If you've come this far, and covered most or all of this material, you undoubtedly have an edge you didn't have before. Go ahead and push the camera in a little tighter. Don't be afraid to hold that close up a little longer. Get excited about adding that extra line of dialogue, or just make yourself laugh and animate a big goofy take. You've got the tools; you've got the knowledge; now go make your characters live with thought, intention, complexity, and feeling like never before… and, in the name of all that is good, please, *stop staring!*

Index

Note to the Reader: Throughout this index **boldfaced** page numbers indicate primary discussions of a topic. *Italicized* page numbers indicate illustrations.

Want to Learn More?

Alias|Wavefront publishes a variety of self-study learning materials that can help you improve your skills.

Visit

www.aliaswavefrontstore.com

and check out our books and training materials.

CAN YOU IMAGINE™

ALIAS|WAVEFRONT
EDUCATION

Alias|*wavefront*®
www.aliaswavefront.com

© 2002 Alias|Wavefront, a division of Silicon Graphics Limited. All rights reserved. The Maya logo is a trademark and Maya is a registered trademark of Silicon Graphics, Inc., exclusively used by Alias|Wavefront, a division of Silicon Graphics Limited. The Alias|Wavefront Education logo is a trademark and the Alias|Wavefront logo is a registered trademark of Alias|Wavefront, a division of Silicon Graphics Limited.

Jason Osipa has six years of professional animation industry experience, beginning in character animation and moving up to supervising animation on several television series. He quickly mastered the technical aspects of 3D, first dabbling in facial animation and modeling for production and then making these his main focus. He has been the Supervising Technical Artist at Mainframe Entertainment and a mentor in CG animation and production at the Vancouver Film School.

Jason and wife Tina are currently working on the beginning stages of an animated short film production of "Wendal, His Cat, and the Progress of Man," based on the storybook of the same title by author V. Campudoni. They now live in Northern California, and Jason works at Maxis on expansion packs for the top-selling PC game of all time, *The Sims*. His professional credits include such television series as *ReBoot!, Beast Wars, Weird-Ohs, Action Man, Max Steel,* and *Heavy Gear,* and direct-to-video projects including *Casper's Haunted Christmas, Barbie in The Nutcracker,* and *Barbie as Rapunzel.*